"Patty Randall is recognized across Canada as one of the pre-eminent experts, writer and public speakers on the topic of LTC. …Her personal story is powerful and moving, terrifying and uplifting at the same time, and always delivered with sincere passion and a healthy doze of humor and common sense."

BB, Abbotsford, British Columbia

"Not only current and highly useful—but even better by being Canadian!"

KM, Vancouver, British Columbia

"You have surely provided a wake-up call to all Canadians."

EF, North Carolina, USA

"I have referred every client I am in front of to get your book as the "bible for aging". I am one of your biggest fans!!!"

MK, Regina, Manitoba

"We learned so much … for our personal and professional lives. Your message is cutting edge for our generation and our Canadian society."

CN, Vancouver, British Columbia

"I just wanted to tell you that I think you are doing a great job with choosing our senior population to be passionate about here in Canada."

GB, Mirror, Alberta

"Thanks again for opening my eyes to the world of a caregiver."

MC in Richmond, British Columbia

"…I was completely captivated by your first hand experiences with your aging parents."

JB, White Rock, British Columbia

"I have not yet finished the book—I have read up to the end of Topic 8—but I am already convinced that your book should be mandatory reading for every adult in Canada and CERTAINLY everyone in any position in our Health System and our Federal and Provincial Governments..."

TL, Montreal, Quebec

"I am going over the resources that you provided and they are excellent."

TE, Guelph, Ontario

"You are doing great work, and from such an incredible place of personal integrity."

RK, North Vancouver, British Columbia

"Just turned 60 and realized that should I reached 90, my kids will be my age now and probably not in a position to look after their kids and me as well. It would be a terrible financial drain. Hope you make presentations to someone from Ottawa and Edmonton, so that the realities hit home to the decision makers of this country."

CC in Cochrane, Alberta

"....informative, humorous and I have to confess somewhat depressing!!! Coincidently I will be meeting with my financial planner two weeks out and I will be asking about insurance. My son has already told me that I won't be living with him. Great job and thanks."

NF, Vancouver, British Columbia

"You have put together an invaluable and comprehensive resource (website) that all Canadians can benefit from. Thank you!"

GG, Canada

"I feel enlightened and am very appreciative of you for sharing your story, your experience and your insight with me. I feel I am in a much stronger position to help my clients plan for the next stages of their lives and help them in preparing their families for the pending changes they will face."

SH, Markham, Ontario

"Let's Talk –
The Care-Years"

Taking Care Of Our Parents
Planning For Ourselves

- A Guidebook -
First-of-its-kind in Canada
Written by a Canadian
For Canadians

Based on one family's
decade long journey

Patty Randall
Daughter–Caregiver and Careguide

Printed in comfort-size
font for your reading ease

Contact Patty for a seminar @
toll-free Canada/USA 1-866-TALK-LTC (1-866-825-5582)
or via her website: www.longtermcarecanada.com

National Library of Canada Cataloguing in Publication Data

Randall, Patty
  Let's talk : the care-years : taking care of
  our parents, planning for ourselves
ISBN 0-9782-215-0-8
  1. Aging parents--Care. 2. Aged--Care. I. Title.
HQ1064.C2R36 2002   306.874   C2002-900236-2

Book sales for North America and international:
LTC Long-Term Care Planning Canada Inc.
2357 Wall Street,
Vancouver, British Columbia,
Canada
V5L 1B8

Order online at:
www.longtermcarecanada.com

This book is dedicated to Mum and Dad

*How does a daughter thank her parents for their love
and support over the years…*

*By responding during their care-years –
By showing them love, recognizing their needs,
respecting their wishes.*

*By creating opportunities for their on-going independence.
By making their days as safe and worry-free
and positive as possible.*

Family picnic

"Life is a journey and love is what makes
that journey worthwhile
– *Unknown*

Last Christmas together

Dear Reader,

"*Let's Talk - The Care-Years*" has been written as a beginner's guidebook for you to use on your caregiving-journey with one or both of your parents - a journey which each of us as a daughter or son with elderly parents will eventually make or perhaps have already embarked upon. As with any experience, we want this one to be as smooth as possible for all involved. The guidebook can also be used to assist today and tomorrow's seniors in preparation for their own care-years - to keep themselves as independent as possible with full quality of life.

I know this care issue isn't sexy or trendy, it doesn't deal with the environment, sports, fashion or the economy; it isn't about marriage, child-rearing, politics, exotic travel adventures or fulfilling one's dreams; and, it sure doesn't generate that, "Boy I can't wait to read this book" feeling - but - I guarantee, that when the time comes, this very issue will have such an astonishing and profound impact on your life that you will ask yourself what planet you've been living on - why you haven't heard any whisperings about this period of your life before now.

For those of you beginning to wonder about your parents' future as they grow older, for those of you just starting a caregiving journey with one or both of your parents, and for those of you planning for your own up-coming care-years, this guidebook offers direction; for those of you already on the journey, it offers further assistance; for everyone, it offers hope - since planning can make a difference during the care-years.

My own long-term caregiving journey with my parents, starting in the first week of January 1996, continued for

10 years until August 2005. Like me, you will find that this particular journey is unlike any other you have experienced in your life to date; why, simply because you cannot control when it will begin, how long it will go on, what you will encounter along the way, whom you will meet, what it will cost or even where it will lead you on a daily basis. Yet, even though this is a once-in-a-lifetime journey (with our parents as 'care-receivers' and ourselves as 'caregivers'), what I discovered strangely enough is that we can actually prepare to some extent for these challenging and costly years in our lives by sharing with and learning from each other.

Quite simply, planning is the main purpose of this guidebook - not only to help you manage the many demands of a caregiving journey, but also to assist you in building a good caregiving relationship with your family and a strong caregiving network in your community.

As my parents' health changed over the years, my role changed accordingly, from being a caring loving daughter to being a caregiving loving daughter. In the process, I learned that caregiving is a verb, an everyday action. I learned about my parents' needs, concerns and wishes; about continuing to listen and respect their decisions; about community care programs and support groups available to our family; about the importance of giving time; about juggling work and family and leisure commitments; about being proactive when necessary; about discussing delicate emotional, medical and financial issues with each parent, as well as with strangers who are in positions to make life-altering care-related decisions; about being an advocate for my parents' well-being during varied circumstances...and the learning never stopped.

Expo 86

Most importantly, just as my parents learned to be care-receivers, I learned to be a caregiver and to plan for when I will be a care-receiver.

So, with that introduction, here is a hands-on educational guidebook outlining common sense, easy-to-use suggestions.

Each of the practical suggestions is based exclusively on my own family's findings - I used only my family's experiences as examples and feel comfortable sharing these personal moments with you. I know that your family's situation will be vastly different from mine, but if even one of the suggestions benefits your parents or you directly or saves you some stress and worry or helps you to become a better-equipped, more organized provider of care, then great, this guidebook will have served its purpose.

The guidebook doesn't contain many statistics or detailed medical information or lists of local agencies, or gerontology theory, as you can research that information by contacting your area's community health unit, the regional hospital, a local caregivers' support group, the nearest university and your doctors. You will find that the suggestions in this guidebook are not earth-shattering ideas - if you had time you could find the needed information by using many resources. You can do your own step-by-step fact-finding by reading appropriate books or magazines, by wandering the Internet, by talking with professionals in various health fields, by writing letters or telephoning special agencies, by going to conferences and so forth; but, again, if you're like me, busy with everyday life, you probably haven't even taken much time to think about this upcoming care-years journey, never mind actually plan well for it.

As I write to you now, my journey has ended, but as the experience for the most part proved to be quite the roller-coaster ride for my entire family, it is my hope that daughters and sons and young seniors might find this guidebook helpful and as a result, be better prepared than my Mum, my Dad and I were when our journey began a few, long years ago.

I offer my very best wishes to you and your family - again, may your care-years journey be a smooth one.

Kindest Regards,

Patty

Daughter-Caregiver

2006

"Learn from the mistakes of others, you can't live long enough to make them all yourself."

– Anonymous

Table of Contents

Why was this guidebook written?

Reason # 1: *I wrote this guidebook because the care-years journey can be a damn rough one.*

When a lifestyle-altering health crisis unexpectedly occurred with my parents, I was ill prepared for the caregiver role I was to assume and I soon realized that other daughters and sons with caregiving responsibilities were in the same position – unprepared.

I often found myself referring to the care-years as "tsunami-years" since all the problems seemed of gigantic proportion, rushing at our family and sweeping over each of us with incredible speed. I wondered why we hadn't been told for planning purposes that retirement years (and at times regular working years) consist of two parts – first, the regular years which we all look forward to, save for, see advertisements about, the pre-care independent years AND second, the part we rarely talk about, plan little for, the dependent care-years – the years when 'caregiving' shapes our lifestyles.

I learned first-hand what it takes to be a caregiver and advocate for my parents as their evolving health needs prompted a greater dependency on me and on their immediate community and on our provincial health care system. I learned the value of realistic financial planning for all the retirement years as 'independence' is important.

As their ages and care needs increased, I was reminded time and time again that I was poorly prepared to meet the challenges of each situation in an effective, efficient, knowledgeable manner.

Of course, over the years, I found several superb books on various caregiving topics, I surfed the Net, I listened to experts – yet with every new mini-crisis, what I really seemed to want was a simple how-to-book, sort of a survival guide or map with suggestions I could flip to quickly on a regular basis.

Let's Define
<u>Long-Term Care</u>

Quite simply, LTC is just a time or period in our lives
(could be at any age)

When we need a combination of services
(help/assistance)

So we can live as independently as possible
(preferably in our own homes)

Long-term care does not mean 'nursing home care'!

Do you know that less than 9% of senior women in Canada and less than 5% of senior men in Canada live in nursing homes.

Long-term care can take place anywhere we are living – whether living in our own home, whether that be our own single family dwelling house or our retirement community condominium or our assisted living suite and, yes, if need be, even in our nursing home room.

But, it is important to keep in mind that LTC does not imply living in a nursing home...LTC can take place where 'you choose' for the most part—if you plan well in advance.

Reason # 2: I wrote this guidebook because knowing some 'care-years rules' can save time, tears, turmoil and money.

The basic rules include the following dozen:

1. I must remember that care-years living involves both providing and accepting quality care and that caregiving simply means "to give care": if our parent (the receiver of the care) hasn't received the

level of care required during any specific day (based on both big or little changes/needs), then, quite simply, good caregiving has not been achieved that day.

2. **I must remember that planning is possible and absolutely necessary:** we should try to anticipate 'what next' and then prepare for that.

3. **I must remember that practising patience is critical to my success as a caregiver:** when our parent's personality seems at times to be different from what we have come to know, when some of the more difficult-to-cope-with traits seem more pronounced and catch us off-guard and even when minor problems affect our schedules and routines, we need to show patience.

4. **I must remember that caregiving requires time and energy plus the constant juggling of priorities:** we must learn to reallocate our time and energies within our family, jobs and leisure in order to fit in all our caregiving responsibilities; we must learn to juggle activities in our personal life and change our priorities to match our parents' needs.

5. **I must remember that each care-situation, whether it be health, financial, emotional or organizational, will require a matching care-action:** as our parents' everyday physical and mental needs constantly change, various situations requiring quick, yet carefully thought-out responses by us, are going to pop up if not on a daily basis, on a weekly one.

6. **I must remember that our family is now entwined with community programs and support systems:** not only are we faced with understanding a complex community-care network now, one that involves doctors, experienced caregivers, pharmacists, social workers, financial planners, insurance professionals, specialists, therapists, group support leaders, health unit staff and as yet-to-be-identified strangers, but we also must accept our overall dependency on this inter-connected network (i.e. maze) with its diverse skills and special programs.

7. **I must remember that questioning is necessary for understanding:** we should ask questions often of authorities (medical, social services, legal, financial advisors…) and of our provincial, local and even our national resource agencies (e.g. CMHC); and it goes without saying,

we should ask other family members and our parents questions (often) in order to understand their requests and wishes and points-of-view.

8. **I must remember that communication is very good and procrastination is very bad:** we need to nurture 3-way communication lines between our parents, those in our caregiving network and ourselves (just to keep up-todate about what is going on); we need to know that when it comes to care-years any procrastination on our part will most likely lead to a series of crises which inevitably will create more problems sooner rather than later.

9. **I must remember that being an efficient manager is a necessary part of caregiving:** we must deal with family affairs immediately – legal and financial matters, taxes, contracts, invoices, household budgets – why wait until tomorrow to be efficient, tomorrow could easily prove to be too late.

10. **I must remember that coordination of plans between family members helps all involved:** since organizing special times of the year, family traditions, and vacation times, takes an extra effort due to the caregiving network involved with our parents, we should coordinate plans for these occasions early, with all parties involved.

11. **I must remember the importance of being a good listener especially around potential care-years problems:** the sooner we learn to listen very carefully to what we are being told by professionals AND by our parents and the sooner we look to others in similar positions and listen to what they have learned, the sooner we can apply new ideas beneficially.

12. **I must remember that my role is to make these care-years a stress-free and positive period for my whole family:** there will be good days when all is flowing smoothly, there will be upsetting days when we will wonder when the next shoe is going to fall, there will be days of fatigue when we look in the mirror and wonder how we can keep going – during all those days we should remember to take a deep breath, take one day at a time and remain focused on what we are doing – giving care.

Reason # 3: I wrote this guidebook because we can make a difference during care-years.

As a daughter plunged into a caregiver role, I came face-to-face with the magnitude of the problems involved in caring for our elderly.

During these years, I learned not to accept the 'growing older' excuse when talking about care of the elderly (these 'elderly' are my parents! my family and me in the future!), but to seek understanding, clarity and then solutions. I've started to ask questions of those working within our health system and financial planning system (how does that work, why, what do others do, what options do I have).

I've started to check for our governments' views around care-related issues; to question the reasoning behind some of the policies relating to care programs; to notice how much real attention our elected representatives pay to the issue. I have come to realize that this issue should continue to be one of our priorities long after caring for our parents is no longer required. As a daughter-caregiver, I came to understand that I might be able to, in some small way, affect change by talking with and listening to other daughter/son caregivers.

And finally I started to think and question what will be in place for my own care – remember, caregiver today, care-receiver tomorrow. I came to understand that we can make a difference – by sharing our experiences and becoming involved in the care-years time of life. I decided that it is time to talk openly, honestly and vividly about care-years.

"Accept the things to which fate binds you, and love the people with whom fate brings you together, but do so with all your heart."
– *Marcus Aurelius*

Who is your care-guide?

Whom do you want in your family (or circle of friends) to guide you with all your various care decisions when the time comes? Whom have you appointed as your 'care-guide'?

We have travel guides to help us on trips, we have executors to help guide our wishes when we have died, but what of when we are elderly and frail and need help with decisions and direction, who is going to guide us then.

We must think very carefully about the appointment of this special person as our quality of life when 'old-old' will continue to be important to us. It is then, at that time, that some decisions will be placed in the hands of someone other than ourselves – our 'care-guide'.

Have you appointed a care-guide? Have you talked to that person about that type of responsibility? If your care-guide is your spouse who is of approximately the same age as you–that is fine until 70 years of age, then, as Statistics Canada tells us, some care starts at 70, thus we may have to appoint someone other than our spouse to take on that role when age dictates. (Also remember, if appointing one of your children, that the kooky 17 year old you had may now be a kooky 38 year old later, so select wisely.)

Our care-guide is not necessarily our everyday caregiver, these may be the same person or not.

Are you going to be your parents 'care-guide'? Are you going to be your spouse's/partner's care-guide? What does being a care-guide entail? Think about and discuss your future care-years with this person, let your family and circle of friends know your wishes and thoughts and preferences. Write out your wishes.

Do appoint a 'care-guide' as part of both your present lifestyle and your retirement planning.

Reason # 4: I wrote this guidebook for those who may want to jump-start discussions on various issue-related topics with their family members and friends.

NO SURPRISES....PLEASE!-LONG-TERM CARE AND ITS IMPACT ON MY FAMILY – AND ME

My care-years journey with both my parents lasted ten years. Over that decade, as a daughter-caregiver, I would have loved easy access to information and guidance, alas, our system has no 'front-door' for such, and so we are often forced to learn as we go.

I realize that long-term care is not a sexy, glamorous or trendy issue, but since it is a relatively new and complex problem in our country and one with the ability to devastate your family both emotionally and financially, I offer this information, to boomers with aging parents, soon-to-be retirees and young seniors, as a 'kick-start' for your thinking.

So...let's begin.

As we near the end of our 'biological warranty period' and aging becomes evident, we enter a stage of our life known as the 'long-term care'. This LTC phase is a relatively new phenomenon facing Canadians, and as we are discovering, one more stage of life we must plan for well in advance...while there is still time!

What is long-term care (i.e. our care-years)?

Long-term care is that 'period of time in our lives when we need help, assistance, support services (i.e. care), in order to remain independent'.

Why is it an issue now in our country?

We are addressing this new phenomenon because four particular factors have come together at this exact period of time in our country—our increased life expectancy, our rapidly aging population, our advances in medicine, and the changes in our health delivery services away from institutional care to community care—thus creating a lengthy next stage of life (long-term care) and with that, an urgent need for each of us to plan for that particular time.

When can/does long-term care occur?

This phase of our life (i.e. need for care over a long-term) can happen at any age (think Christopher Reeves) - but - most often happens in our senior years (think your grandmother, your aging parents… yourself in later retirement). 'Measures to increase our health can only go so far then inevitably our bodies will begin to fail' and everyone of us will, sooner or later, like it or not, need some care.

What are the demographic trends in our country creating this issue? Think about each one of these points as they may impact you personally.

- Over the next 25 years, 1 in 4 Canadians will be over 60—this population movement is influencing the design of everything around us.

- By 2010, 60% of boomers over 50 years old will have a surviving parent (versus only 16% in 1960)—our 'Gucci' boomer generation will be able to make demands for quality resources and services (for their aging parents) due to their sheer size in number.

- The first round of Canada's 10 million Baby boomers will reach the age of 65 over the next decade, significantly swelling the masses of our senior population beginning in 2011—the need for care services will see a dramatic rise and will continue to increase… for the next 4 decades during this age-wave.

- In 2016, Canada will experience a 'phenomenon' never recorded before, we will have far more seniors than children (age 14 and under) in our country—the change will be visible in the economic and social fabrics of our provinces.

- 1 in 5 Canadians 45 years and older provides care to a senior at present—the care-issue will become even more 'visible' over the next 3 decades peaking in 2035 when our provinces will experience the highest demand for care as baby boomers close- in on 75.

- One seldom mentioned fact is that increasingly in our country, parents and their children will be seniors 'at the very same time'— since current research tells us that the health of those seniors providing care (whether an offspring or a spouse) is greatly at risk, the question will be where to turn for help and/or how to finance such assistance.

• Working-caregivers, who are juggling care responsibilities plus work duties, currently cost Canadian employers $16 billion per year (2003)—not only should caregiving be recognized now as an important workplace issue as 66% of informal caregivers are still in the workforce, but also it is destined to be less-silent in the near future with HR (Human Resources) departments forced to deal with its impact (watch for the term 'caregiver glass-ceiling').

• Seniors are our country's fastest growing population group with the number of persons aged 65 and over expected to double from nearly 4 million in 2000 to almost 8 million by 2026, with the most rapidly growing age group the 80 year old and older. Given that less than 10% of long-term-care in our country takes place in a nursing home, with most LTC taking place in a private home by family and friends as caregivers; given that maintaining one's independence within one's own home is ranked as a number one priority by seniors; and given that long-term-care expenses have a potentially crippling impact on a family, developing a 'care-plan' will become a priority for adult Canadians in today's environment.

What are the major challenges surrounding this issue?

• *Denial:* Do you believe you are growing older?

• *Entitlement attitude:* Do you believe that our governments will be able to provide the home and institutional programs and services you will need for your parents, your spouse/partner and your own care when required?

• *Myths:* Do you believe that your spouse and your children will help take care of you (and that they can take care of their in-laws as well, if required)? What will be the impact on their lives?

• *Procrastination:* Do you believe that you should worry about the problem...when the time comes?

- *Disconnect:* Do you simply believe that there is no need to plan now?

What are the types of questions we should be asking ourselves to kick-start our thinking on this issue?

- Have I considered caregiving as part of my current lifestyle plan?

- Should my own care (when it occurs) be part of my expectations from my daughters and sons, my daughters-in-law, my spouse, those who love me? (Do I really want my loved ones doing the basics for me, e.g. bathing me, dressing me, helping me with meals, etc?)

- Is/was caregiving of a loved one and more importantly becoming a 'care-receiver' myself part of my retirement dream?

- How well do I handle stress now and what if it is increased?

- Am I prepared to have my health or a loved one's health affected by becoming a caregiver, what are our options?

- What will be the impact of my parent needing long-term care on my job/career?

- How am I planning to handle my aging parents' care?

- How am I planning to handle my spouse's care (especially if a woman)?

- How am I planning for my own long-term care needs?

What are the 'new facts of life' for Canadians? *Yes, it is time to face these facts!*

- **Fact: There is a good probability that you will become a caregiver at some time in your life, either of a parent or a spouse**

At present, family caregivers comprise 1/3 of our total caregiver population. Caregivers are most likely to be providing care to a spouse/partner (38%) or parent (33%).

- **Fact: There is a very high possibility if you are female that you could be a caregiver two times in our lifetime, first of an elderly parent and then of a senior spouse**

77% of family caregivers are female—this gender difference is greatest among caregivers under 45 years of age, where 82% are women, many caring for a parent, compared with caregivers 65 and older, 71% are women, mainly caring for a spouse.

As would be expected, most care recipients are seniors/elderly—more than half (57%) are at least 65 years of age, with 17 percent at least 85. Parents being cared for by their children are mostly 75 and older.

- **Fact: You have to be prepared to look after a loved one with 'both' a physical and a mental disability and this situation will be of a 'long-term' nature of perhaps 3 to 10 years**

Recipients are most likely to be receiving care because of physical disabilities (61%), but close to one in five have both physical and mental difficulties requiring longer than 6 months of care—six in ten (62%) of the caregivers have already been providing such care to their family member for at least three years, and one in five (20%) have been doing so for more than 10 years.

- **Fact: You accept that caring for your loved one is your responsibility, yet you may also feel you don't have a choice as there is no one else available or there are no home care services to help out**

67% of caregivers are looking after family members because they see it as a family responsibility or because they simply choose to do so (63%). Overall, the population is divided on whether or not they had a choice, with just over half (52%) saying they did have a choice, while 44 percent felt they did not.

- **Fact: Most of your care-giving duties will be with the basics of everyday living (dressing our loved ones, bathing them, helping them move around, feeding, washing, shaving, doing hair, teeth....think about all you did from when you got up this morning and went through the day...)**

About one in four caregivers are providing daily assistance to family members in terms of basic hygiene, such as dressing, bathing, walking, feeding and assistance with toileting.

- **Fact: There is a very good chance that you may become a caregiver during your retirement years**

31% of caregivers are most likely to be retired (and that is increasing).

- **Fact: You will have to adjust personally to financial and health difficulties as a result of your care-giving role**

Caregivers also report significant or some difficulties in terms of their finances (54%) and physical health (50%).

- **Fact: Your income ability to hire someone else does not change your caregiving role**

Caregiving is not linked to overall income. Caregivers can be found in all income strata—one in three (35%) report household incomes of $45,000 or more.

- **Fact: There is a good chance that your mum and/or dad will move in with you and your family when they need care**

Just over half (55%) of parents are being cared for in their children's homes. Overall, most family care-giving is provided in the caregiver's homes (77%) when the care-receiver is a spouse/partner (97%), a child, or someone with a mental disability.

- **Fact: Your monthly expenses during LTC-years are going to increase and you must plan for this monthly budget increase**

A significant proportion (44%) of caregivers are paying out-of-pocket costs to provide care to their family member—four in ten report spending between $100 and $300 per month on such expenses, with another quarter (24%) spending in excess of $300 (Author's Note: I tracked my 'extra' out-of-pocket costs, but did not include the larger care costs, just monthly out-of pocket, in the first 3 years of our care-years journey with my parents and my 'out-of-pocket' costs were approximately $850/month).

- **Fact: No one can be a good caregiver 24-7-365 days without a break, so you will need to find ways to share care-giving or hire assistance at some times**

Caregivers are most likely to say they could use some help in allowing them to have a break from this responsibility, i.e. respite—almost seven in ten say they need a break from their care-giving duties either frequently (21%) or occasionally (47%).

- **Fact: You will not entertain the concept of institutional care for your loved one**

While many caregivers could use help in caring for family members, few (9%) believe their family member would be better cared for in an institutional setting.

- **Fact: Your provincial government provides some care programs but you need to apply and qualify to receive these and even with such your role will continue**

Less than one in four (23%) family caregivers are currently receiving any formal home care services to assist in caring for their family member (in the form of a personal care worker, nursing or homemaking assistance). If formal care is provided, it is most likely to be provided in the form of a personal care worker (40% of those who receive any form of care), nursing visits (34%), and homemaking (housekeeping, light meals) (26%).

- **Fact: You will see the LTC related-problems much clearer when immersed in the everyday activities and identify more services that you may need but you will still find yourself in the key care-giver role**

One in three (33%) caregivers identify the need for additional home care services. While formal home care services is a way to reduce or manage the amount of personal involvement in family care-giving, this does not appear to be the case- it suggests that the use of formal care is more closely associated with care recipients requiring a lot of care (both family involvement and formal services) than as a means of minimizing such involvement. Also of note is the finding that use of formal home care services is not associated with the amount that caregivers are paying in out-of-pocket costs.

- **Fact: Your stress levels are going increase significantly when you become a caregiver**

Seven in ten (70%) acknowledge that providing care has been stressful, and this is even the case among half of those who say they have been handling the responsibility very well—one in six (17%) of caregivers fit into the 'high stress group' (a rating of 4), and this group is more likely to include women—the most significant predictor (or indicator) of care-giving stress is the lack of choice in taking on this responsibility.

- **Fact: Your jobs and careers are going to be affected when you find yourself in a caregiver as well as a worker—some of you will quit, retire early or make serious changes to the pre-care-giving conditions of your jobs**

More than one in four indicate their employment situation has been affected by their care-giving responsibilities, either in terms of quitting/retiring early (9%) or having had to make other changes in their work situation (e.g. schedules, role) (18%). Among those currently employed, care-giving has been disruptive to their work, either to a significant (19%) or some (33%) degree.

More than four in ten (42%) believe it would be very helpful to receive flexible work hours (42%), while an equal proportion express similar interest in short term job and income protection through the federal government Employment Insurance (EI) program (42%). One in five (21%) feel this would not be helpful to them, while another 11 percent say it would not apply to them because of self-employment or because of other reasons. By comparison, fewer than one in five (18%) see a significant benefit in having access to a leave of absence without pay, likely because they could not manage without their employment income.

(Data Source, The National Profile of Family Caregivers in Canada - 2002: Final Report, Statistics Canada, Health Canada)

How can we begin to make a success of long-term care?

My suggested four-step 'LTC formula for success' offered to Canadian boomers with aging parents, to soon-to-be retirees and to young-seniors is:

1. Make 'care' an 'acceptable' four-letter word in your family

Develop an awareness of what is involved organizationally, emotionally and financially in long-term care as the lifestyle risks to our selves and our loved ones are great; discuss 'care-years' with your family; ask questions, talk to others who are on a care-years journey right now; understand the impact of our aging demographic on your personal living environment.

2. Make 'care' a well-thought-out component in both your current lifestyle and your future retirement plans

Understand that 'care' can happen at any age, that most care takes place in our own homes, that each of us is responsible for paying for our own care and our loved one's care needs and that the costs of that care to a family can be shocking even with our provincial governments offering some services and subsidizations; educate yourself—look ahead.

3. Make 'care' a workable process in your busy life – when it is needed

Care is not a short-term event, it must be integrated into one's life when it happens with a loved one; realize that everyday life doesn't stop when a care-journey begins, regular and new demands roll right along at the same time one is attempting to find a balance with all the various caregiving experiences—P.S. I went through divorce, career changes and remarriage while on my 10 year care- journey with my parents— I soon realized that personal responsibilities, work-responsibilities, community responsibilities, all continue at their own pace even while one is occupied with caregiving—life goes on: prepare yourself so as to minimize all the 'caregiving' surprises at least.

4. And most importantly, make a 'care-plan' for yourself – now

Recognize the importance of financial planning plus up-dated documents when it comes to this stage of our lives. We have to plan well-in-advance for our own care (can happen at any age remember) to ensure our independence, safety, and most importantly our quality of care—keep in mind, 'caregiver today, care-receiver tomorrow'.

In a nutshell, I feel that long-term care can be rewarding for both caregivers and care-receivers but it is time for millions of Canadian boomers and young-seniors to become aware of the need to address this issue and plan before care-crises create a tsunami in their personal worlds.

Bottom-Line?

Do you have a care plan in place, if not, why not?

> **Seniors are one of the fastest growing population groups in Canada.** In fact, the senior population has grown more than twice as fast as the overall population since the early 1980s. As a result, more than 1 out of every 10 Canadians is now a senior.
>
> Statistics Canada has projected that by 2021, seniors will represent 18% of our total population and by 2141, seniors will makeup 23% of the population. Of particular significance to the care-issue is the fact that the population aged 85 and over is the fastest growing segment of our overall senior population. *(Source: Prepared by Statistics Canada for the Division of Aging and Seniors)*

The age structure of Canada is being reshaped
% of seniors population

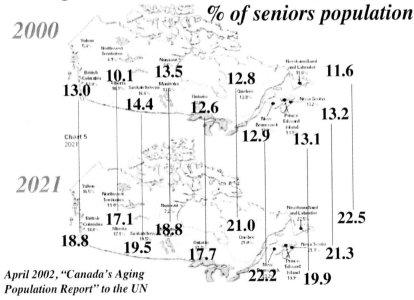

April 2002, *"Canada's Aging Population Report" to the UN*

From Canada's Aging Population Report, 2002

Population by sex and age group, by province and territory, 2006
Statistics Canada

	Population	0-19	20-64	65 and over
			(%)	
Canada	**32,623,490**	**24.0**	**62.8**	**13.2**
Newfoundland and Labrador	509,677	21.9	64.5	13.5
Prince Edward Island	138,519	24.7	60.9	14.4
Nova Scotia	934,405	22.5	62.9	14.6
New Brunswick	749,168	22.3	63.5	14.2
Quebec	7,651,531	22.4	63.5	14.1
Ontario	12,686,952	24.5	62.5	12.9
Manitoba	1,177,765	26.6	59.9	13.6
Saskatchewan	985,386	27.0	58.1	14.9
Alberta	3,375,763	26.0	63.6	10.4
British Columbia	4,310,452	22.5	63.5	14.0
Yukon Territory	31,229	25.7	66.9	7.5
Northwest Territories	41,861	32.4	62.8	4.8
Nunavut	30,782	44.2	53.0	2.9

Source: From Statistics Canada, "The Daily", October 26, 2006

Year	People aged 65 and over			As a % of the Canadian population
	Men	Women	Total	
			000s	
1921	215.0	205.3	420.2	4.8
1931	294.6	281.5	576.1	5.6
1941	390.9	376.9	767.8	6.7
1951	551.3	535.5	1086.3	7.8
1961	674.1	717.0	1391.1	7.6
1971	790.3	972.0	1762.3	8.0
1981	1017.2	1360.1	2377.3	9.6
1986	1147.6	1589.3	2737.0	10.4
1991	1349.8	1867.4	3217.2	11.4
1996	1515.3	2066.7	3582.0	12.1
1998	1588.5	2147.2	3735.7	12.3
Projections				
2016	2591.2	3302.9	5894.3	15.9
2021	3050.7	3840.6	6891.1	17.8
2026	3558.1	4438.8	7996.9	20.0
2031	3976.5	4960.1	8936.5	21.7
2036	4166.6	5261.0	9427.6	22.4
2041	4244.8	5424.6	9669.6	22.6

How is this guidebook laid out?

This book covers the basics for a daughter or son who is beginning to become involved in caregiving responsibilities of an elderly parent or a daughter or son who is already immersed in a family member's care-years.

The book, with some adaptation of the words and reading between the lines, may also serve as a guide for retirees who are addressing their own future needs and want to do some additional planning now for their up-coming care-years.

The guide has been published in an easy reading style (i.e. larger font and greater space between lines). It is meant to be *practical and grabbable*, that is to say, a book that you can carry with you, one you can actually refer to when in the midst of an important decision or dilemma.

At times, just as I did when faced with caregiving responsibilities, you may feel like you've crossed the border into a foreign country and not only must you must learn a new language right away, but also you must learn how to fit into a new culture quickly. (Who are these people? What are they saying? What does that mean for my family? What do I do now? Where do I turn for help? What is right, wrong, acceptable, unacceptable, dangerous, safe? How do we pay for all this? And on and on.) It is during these times that you may want to grab this guidebook and quickly read what one family tried.

The guidebook is *divided into topics*, instead of chapters. *Each topic attempts to respond to commonly asked care-years questions.*

Although there has been an attempt to put topics into a logical caregiving sequence, there is no priority topic. It is left up to you to decide which topic of the guidebook is important depending upon your family's situation, that is, the status of your parents' mental and physical health and your loved-ones' care-needs at any particular moment.

Of course, if you are thinking about the future or have already had a noticeable turning-point incident in a loved one's health occur – a signal that you're beginning the care-years journey – you might want to scan all the topics to familiarize yourself with the contents.

Some of the topics were selected because like mountains, they loomed large and threatening, and my family was forced to scale them while on our journey. Other topics were selected because like thorns they were prickly and irritating, such that we couldn't ignore them. And finally, some topics were selected because they kept popping up over and over again and we had no choice but to deal with them.

Of course, every important concern involved in the issue of caregiving is not raised in this guidebook; each of you can add notes based on your specific experiences and are encouraged to do so.

Each topic attempts to set a scene by offering a personal anecdote about our family's experiences when faced with that subject matter. Even though, as daughters and sons, we may ask similar questions, your personal situations will undoubtedly be different from our family's, yet the range of emotions, time, level of commitment demanded, degree of frustration, urgency to find answers and finally the degree of love will probably be exactly the same.

While involved in a family member's care, you may feel alone and completely overwhelmed, all the while trying to remind yourself that you are not the first one faced with this responsibility. It is my hope during these occasions that you will be able to zero in on and adapt the contents of each of the topics to fit your circumstances and thereby lessen your stress-load.

Each topic contains a set of suggestions. These suggestions are based on what I have come to think of as my family's trial-and-error and our try-and-try again methods for finding solutions. The suggestions given are exactly that —just suggestions — as I feel comfortable offering *only those suggestions that our family gained from our everyday personal experiences.*

Some of these suggestions are prevention-oriented, which you may want to consider putting in place sooner rather than later; others deal directly with how to handle special situations you may encounter. Some of the suggestions you may disagree with —that's okay as it's not a debate — if your methods are working for your family, then you've found solutions too. *Throughout the guidebook, it is also strongly recommended that you make time to seek information offered by legal and financial experts, health care professionals, medical specialists and support groups, as each will prove very helpful.*

Each topic discusses feelings openly. As you may often experience that nagging feeling of 'now what', even trivial suggestions are included in the guidebook as these can easily be overlooked when up to one's ears in alligators, yet these could possibly prove to be a big help in getting a day back on track. Remember, when searching for answers for your parents, you are acting from love and their best interests and you therefore will do well by them.

You may also find that it is helpful to jot down reminders as you think of them, so *space has been set aside for personal notes.*

Clippings on various care-related subjects and interesting quotations are offered sporadically throughout the guidebook as thought-provoking material.

This guidebook is part of a series of long-term care-related initiatives - by Patty – attend a seminar in your community or organize one for a group.
Call toll free 1-866-TALKLTC to arrange seminars in your community.
Browse Patty's **national educational website** *for further information and research findings and statistics on the care-years.*
www.longtermcarecanada.com

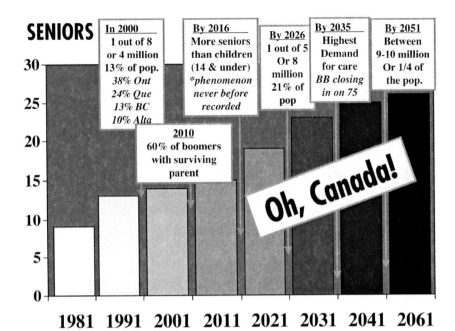

SENIORS

| In 2000 |
| 1 out of 8 |
| or 4 million |
| 13% of pop. |
| *38% Ont* |
| *24% Que* |
| *13% BC* |
| *10% Alta* |

| By 2016 |
| More seniors |
| than children |
| (14 & under) |
| *phenomenon* |
| *never before* |
| *recorded* |

| By 2026 |
| 1 out of 5 |
| Or 8 |
| million |
| 21% of |
| pop |

| By 2035 |
| Highest |
| Demand |
| for care |
| *BB closing* |
| *in on 75* |

| By 2051 |
| Between |
| 9-10 million |
| Or 1/4 of |
| the pop. |

2010
60% of boomers
with surviving
parent

Oh, Canada!

30 – 25 – 20 – 15 – 10 – 5 – 0

1981 1991 2001 2011 2021 2031 2041 2061

Graph Source: Patty's seminars based on Statistics Canada research

"Trees grow strong over the years, rivers wider. Likewise, with age, human beings gain immeasurable depth and breadth of experience and wisdom. That is why older persons should not be only respected and revered: they should be utilized as the rich resource to society that they are."

- *Kofi Annan, Secretary-General of the United Nations, 2002*

"The greatest discovery of my generation is that human beings can alter their lives by altering their attitudes of mind."
– *William James, 1842-1910*

Introductions

Since you and I are caregivers and since I have used my family's personal experiences as examples throughout this guidebook, let me introduce you to my parents – there is much to tell, but in brief, so you have a sense, a picture...

Mum and Dad, Aleta and Chuck, were married July 10, 1936; they were together 62 years through good times and challenging times, depression years, work years, war years, prosperous years, retirement years and care-years. They have one daughter, Patricia Lou (Patty), the writer of this guidebook. We three formed a close family and when Mum and Dad were in their mid-80's, we started our long-term care-years journey together.

1936 – Honeymoon

50th wedding anniversary

Holiday – Expo '86

Formal affair
– retirement years

Shared 80th surprise
birthday

Mum, Aleta Florence Caputo (nee Ivens)
Feb. 17, 1911 – August 17, 2005

Her background: A Canadian citizen of immigrant parents from Great Britain, born in Merridale, Manitoba (only daughter, three brothers), came to British Columbia at age 11. Raised in the sunny Okanagan in the fruit-growing, resort city of Kelowna, worked in the local packing house as teenager and later worked as a live-in care-giver for a large family, married age 25, and lived until retirement in the West Kootenay smelter town of Trail where she participated in family, community and school affairs, then in 1972 returned to Kelowna for retirement years – remaining there throughout her LTC-years, in her own home. She was very beautiful, with deep naturally wavy auburn hair. She was adventurous (drove a motorcycle, skied, hiked, kayaked) – always, she valued her independence, had a good sense of humour. She was a very good wife for 6+ decades, also a very good daughter caring for her own parents two months each summer and her father-in-law in his care-years. She remained a caring sister-in-law and sister (every second day, until October 2001, visited her youngest brother, 84, in an extended care center, a paraplegic due to an airplane crash) and cherished memories of her husband and her three brothers who predeceased her. She had a driving license until the age of 88 years (no accidents); enjoyed sewing and crocheting most of her life and started ceramics as a retirement hobby (one year taking first prize in the seniors category at a province-wide competition). She was interested in events in the city and loved absolutely anything associated with nature (especially birds). In her later years, she spent time shopping, lunching out, reading biographies and nature books and in the evenings watching the Discovery Channel; she always enjoyed special events (e.g. Irish Tenors concert) and news highlights (e.g. watching the space shuttle pass overhead). Mum remained busy and remained active with her family and old friends for as long as she could. Mum had always been a caring person and moved into her care-years with dignity and acceptance.

Her health history: Was healthy her whole life except for chronic indigestion. At age 72 years – open heart surgery (quadruple by-pass and valve replacement), one bout of serious depression, cataract surgery, both eyes. At age 85 years – hearing aid left ear, prone to bronchitis, serious acid reflux hiatus hernia condition requiring constant attention. At age 90+ years – problems with short-term memory, used a walker as an aid in the house and a wheelchair outside as had difficulty with walking and balance. When asked, she used to say that she was "pretty healthy" and was "so thankful" for her health.

As a Mum, she was wonderful, a best friend, a kind person, non-judgmental and always encouraging (I can honestly say she was a model mother).

How can I describe her? I remember talking to Mum about all sorts of problems and joys as I grew up; I remember the little snacks almost everyday after elementary school when we'd sit and chat, just the two of us as she listened to my tales – we talked daily almost, all during our lives together. She taught me to swim before I could walk and enrolled me in lessons year after year – later, even into my early teen years, each July and August afternoon we would spend at the beach, our time together.

Formal dinner, Mum age 78.

I remember how I learned to do regular everyday tasks ('efficiently') by doing each one step-by-step, side-by-side, we would tackle how to make the beds, how to cook and clean up as one goes along, how to set a table, how to word an invitation, how to cut a pattern, how to check the oil in the car, how to prune an apple tree…(Mum laughed when she told of my first attempts on my own at making coffee-cake, how the recipe called for 1 c. coffee which I followed carefully, then how Dad at dinner-time couldn't figure out what all the crunchy bits were in the cake.) She continued to encourage me to learn from my mistakes and well into her last year, she listened attentively and offered advice when asked, but rarely interfered.

I remember Mum's many caring ways while I was growing up – she made nutritional child-size breakfasts, a petite omelette with one homemade baking powder biscuit direct from the oven and fresh squeezed juice or fruit bowl each school morning; she put pincurls in my long hair at night;

created Hallowe'en costumes each year (for both of us). She sewed many of my school clothes and especially new skirts for Friday night teen dances (one special red velvet one I loved), she took Defensive Driving courses and taught me to drive (then argued my case when I scraped a fender), listened to boyfriend problems, laughed with me at dance recital stories, encouraged me to get an after-school job and to work hard no matter what the job was, welcomed my friends equally and motivated me to search out my maternal-roots in England (which I did years later as part of a vacation).

My well-being and happiness it seems has always been a priority for her – she participated actively in PTA all through my school years, sent care-parcels and looked after my dog while at university, wrote out quick-fix supper recipes for use during busy career times.

Later, she attended some of my presentations when I switched career paths and started consulting and speaking on large-scale social issues; she was up-beat when I telephoned while on projects in far-away India or East Africa so I wouldn't worry about her or Dad; cried with me during divorce…and even encouraged me to keep working on this guidebook.

My girlfriends and close-cousins have always commented on what a "special mother" I had – they are right. (One Mother's day, two of my cousins who lost their mothers a few years ago asked to share my mother with me – a nice compliment to her – we took Mum for lunch by the lake and then to a casino for the afternoon, where she discovered the fun of 'one-arm bandits' winning a whopping $42!)

Even at age 90+ and in her care-years, she didn't change – being an exceptionally good mother is a natural ability she always had, like a gift. I used to smile when I got surprise cards in the mail saying, "Enjoy your well-deserved holiday" or "I love you" or "Looking forward to your visit."

My mother had a heart attack in August 2005, one she couldn't survive. I stayed with her in the hospital for her last days. Her love and caring were evident as her last words to me the night before she died were, "Patty, you must be tired, I want you to get some sleep…"

I love you too Mum!

Dad, Pasqualino Charles (Chuck) Caputo
March 26, 1912 – October 18, 1998

His background: A Canadian citizen of immigrant parents from Italy, born, raised, and worked in the West Kootenay town of Trail, British Columbia; one of four children (2 brothers predeceased, always remained close to his one sister). He was tall, handsome and large-framed, with black hair and a little moustache. He worked from age 14 to 60 at Cominco Ltd (the "Smelter") except for one year off when he was asked to play baseball in an out-of-town league. He was very involved in the much-loved Italian Club of the city and held office in that Club for many years. To say he was passionate about hockey would be an understatement, as he cheered madly for the Trail Smoker Eaters (Mum tells of Dad braving a tremendous snow-storm one night just to get to the game and yelling so feverishly at the referee during another game that his top plate of false teeth flew out). Dad believed in being a good provider for his family, was a leader and fund-raiser within the community, had a dominant out-going personality, had many friends and colleagues at all times as he actively sought improvements within his city. He was proud to be the patriarch of a large extended family, enjoyed each day's routines and looked forward to local events. Upon retiring in 1972, to Kelowna, had fun tending bar part-time at a neighbourhood pub close to home and also joined the Italian Club of his retirement city; enjoyed social-grocery shopping and spending time each afternoon with his regular buddies; loved new cars and browsing the lots. Dad fell, in January 1996, breaking his hip in two places and his hand – his retirement lifestyle changed at that moment. Dad then lived one year in his own home with care and nearly two years in an intermediate caremanor where he enjoyed visits and outings with family and friends. Dad died quietly but unexpectedly October 18, 1998 in the very early morning hours.

His health history: Was healthy his whole life except for high blood pressure. By 80 years – glaucoma in one eye and cataract in other (near blindness). At 84 years – two metal pins in right hip after his fall, used a walker as a constant aide and a wheelchair when outdoors, mild dementia.

At 85 years – suffered from kidney problems and a severe congested heart condition.

As a Dad, he could always be counted on; had solid expectations for himself and his family; a very social person and a hard worker who thought nothing of holding two jobs working long hours to put me through university.

How can I describe him? I remember Dad initiating Christmas parties for us children in the neighbourhood, sponsored by the Italian Club when he was Second Vice President for many years; I remember how he loved organizing New Year's Eve and Boiler Shop Socials (the department where he worked at Cominco). As a little girl, I remember dancing often around the kitchen when he placed me on the tops of his shoes for a waltz or jived with me to his favourite Fats Domino. I remember strolling down the Gulch (our neighbourhood's nickname) with Dad for milkshakes on hot summer evenings.

Care-years, Dad age 86.

He loved spaghetti dinners, homemade bread and chocolate anything (even though he suffered terribly with hives after overindulging). I remember summer holidays in Kelowna with my grandparents (Mum's side) when Dad would rent my favourite horse and walk beside me (I was only 3-4) for hours while I rode, making sure I was in my cowgirl chaps, jeans, hat. I remember his dad, my Nono, living happily with our family for many years and how Nono and Mum would spend time during the day together and how Nono and Dad would chatter away in Italian sitting on the porch in the evenings. As a teenager, I remember that Dad successfully lobbied for school buses as so many of us lived miles from the senior high school located in another part of the city. Later, I remember Dad brushing away tears when I had left home to go to university (or on lengthy trips); encouraging me while studying Italian to write him letters home for practise, only to find out years later that he spoke the language fluently but did not read it. I also remember particular acts of kindness – how he and Mum were so very kind offering their home and attention to a young grade four student of mine who lived in an 'orphanage' and needed a summer holiday.

Dad, like Mum, encouraged me to work hard – always and wherever – even though he worried dreadfully when I travelled by air on a project, whether domestically or internationally, insisting that I call home often. (Dad only flew once in his life, he had no choice as a committee member of the Kelowna Summer Games – later his best friend and colleague teased that Dad sat in an aisle seat, made the Sign of the Cross many times and prayed the whole flight.)

Dad loved watching his retirement house being built, he enjoyed short vacations, especially ones back home to Trail. In his retirement years, Dad tended to his yard and his home's up-keep. Later in the care-years, I remember how he looked forward to our luncheon-weeks together and even though he had lost interest in most things, how he still loved Don Cherry's straight-from the-hip commentary during Hockey Night In Canada.

While writing this, I smile when I think of Dad calling me by his special nickname for me as a little girl, or holding onto my first two-wheeler bike (blue) as I struggled to keep upright, or throwing the newspaper in the air one night, murmuring "And now it begins" when I made an honest teenager mistake with two dates arriving at the same time at different doors. Dad would often shake his head at me over one thing or another or gently place a large hand over one of mine if we were sitting together. He was a loving father.

Every time Dad and I parted, saying good-bye, he would give me a hug and whisper, "I love you" – which is exactly what he did the last time I saw him.

TOPIC 1

Let's Talk: Plunging head-first into the care-years – A turning-point occurs

PART ONE

What do I do when I first find out there has been an emergency and my parent has been taken to the hospital?

Personal Anecdote:"Call as soon as you get in!"

Suggestions:

1. Gather facts efficiently and quickly
2. Don't neglect our other parent
3. Make a quick check-list and organize travel

PART TWO

What should I be paying close attention to while my parent is actually in the hospital?

Personal Anecdote:"I keep getting caught off guard!"

Suggestions:

4: Get to know the hospital
5: Leave no stone unturned
6: Prepare for a changed parent
7: Become an active team member of the hospital decision-making team
8: A pre-cautionary note – Watch for signs of dementia
9: Investigate potential assistance programs and their criteria

PART ONE

What do I do when I first find out there has been an emergency and my parent has been taken to the hospital?

Personal Anecdote:
"Call as soon as you get in!"

January 4, 1996, 9:30 AM - British Columbia interior region, city of Kelowna, a bitter cold winter morning, ice and snow everywhere. Dad, 6 foot 1 inch, 200 pounds, age 84, bundled in his boots, cap, mitts and winter working jacket, was tending to garbage day. He was moving the two trash cans (in their push-cart) from the back of his house to the front driveway on the roadside curb - a simple routine task, one done every week by him, through all seasons, for the past 24 years of retirement. But this particular morning, at he curb, he slipped and fell - and when he tried to get up, fell again.

Neighbours heard Dad calling out and quickly came to his assistance. He stated emphatically that he did not want them to call an ambulance and demanded that they just help him into the house. Rather than arguing with him at that crucial time, they attempted partly to do as he wanted and succeeded in getting him as far as the driveway. He was placed on a chair in the carport, while one neighbour ran to get his truck and another stayed with Mum. Dad was thereby taken to the hospital emergency ward and Mum was left at home. By late morning, Dad was set for emergency hip surgery and Mum was attempting to contact me, "Call as soon as you get in."

The major turning-point in Dad's health was this actual fall; the turning-point in Mum's health was also Dad's fall, as she was cast now as an elderly caregiver of her elderly spouse.

Our lifestyles changed dramatically that bleak January morn.

Suggestion 1: *Gather facts efficiently and quickly*

When we first find out that a parent has had an accident or has an urgent health problem and has been transported to the hospital, we need to make our next-step decisions based on facts, not our emotions (easy to say, tough to do).

We need to remind ourselves to be calm – maintaining a calm attitude allows us to gather the necessary facts properly and think on our feet.

It is fair to assume:

☑ That we probably have not received all the facts from the person who first contacted us with the news of the hospital emergency.

☑ That it is not going to be particularly useful to contact our parent's doctor at this time, as he/she will not have all the information yet regarding the unexpected hospitalisation.

☑ That the hospital professionals presently attending to our parent are the best sources of good information at this time.

LONG-TERM CARE DEFINED FURTHER

• **Is a catch-all phrase**

• **Refers to care lasting more than 90 days
(Statistics Canada uses ~ 6 months)**

• **Includes services for people who have lost ability to maintain
their independence**

• **Usually requires skilled care**

What should I do?

We want to remember the ol' saying, "hear it from the horse's mouth" *(translation = find out from the professionals at the hospital the exact status of the condition of our parent).*

As a first step, we should:

- ☑ Telephone the emergency ward, introducing oneself – mention if we are calling long distance, not because of the cost, but to demonstrate our immediate concern.

- ☑ Ask the name of the nurse we are speaking with at this time; write it and the time down.

- ☑ Find out the doctor who is tending to our parent, write his/her name down (have it spelled if necessary); ask if a specialist is required/being used.

- ☑ Ask where our parent is at present, that is, in what part of the hospital process (still in emergency, surgery, recovery, regular ward...); ask what the immediate next step for our parent is going to be.

Once we have that information, during the same telephone call, we should:

- ☑ Request to speak directly to the surgeon or doctor attending to our parent – only if such is possible at this moment.

- ☑ If it is not possible to speak to the attending doctor at the time of our call, establish when we can do so; in addition, leave the message that we would like the attending physician/surgeon to telephone us regarding the condition of our parent (leave our number to call collect); confirm that our request is understood.

- ☑ Find out when we can do a second follow-up call regarding the condition of our parent (how many hours, approximate time) and where our parent may be at that point (what ward).

☑ Telephone at the established follow-up time, introduce ourselves once again to re-establish our interest and concern, ask to speak to the nurse (by name if still on duty and if the same ward is still involved), find out how our parent is doing by asking specific questions (e.g. how long he/she will remain in emergency/recovery, where he/she will be transferred to after that…).

☑ If out of town, explain our situation then ask the attending doctor for his/her opinion regarding time-lines with our parent.

(For example, in Dad's case, I was told by the orthopaedic surgeon that the hip surgery took over 5 hours; that Dad would be in recovery for a long while after the surgery; that he would then be transferred to the surgical ward; that he would probably take a minimum of three days to recover from the operation and anaesthetic. The surgeon advised me that there was no urgent demand to be at the hospital within the next few days except to calm my own concerns as Dad would not be aware of my presence and there was nothing I could attend to. Armed with these facts, I was able to start making decisions regarding Mum's immediate needs.)

Thirty thousand Canadians fracture their hips each year and up to 25 per cent of those people will die within a year from complications, including pneumonia and embolisms. Canada spends nearly $300 million annually on treatment of hip fractures, which are usually caused by falls. They account for 86 per cent of hospital admissions for people over aged 65 and older, according to the Canadian Institute for Health Information. *(Source: The Vancouver Sun, July 5 2001, World Congress of the International Association of Gerontology in Vancouver.)*

When and how did the Canadian federal government get involved in medicare (Canada's system to provide health services to all people)? Health insurance for all Canadians was first proposed in 1919 by Liberal Prime Minister Mackenzie King. From then on, labour groups urged governments to enact universal health care. Devastated by the effects of the drought in the 1930's, people in Saskatchewan were the first to receive some sort of government health insurance program. In 1947, Saskatchewan began covering hospital costs using tax money. British Columbia followed in 1948. Later in 1962, Saskatchewan expanded coverage to include doctors. This was quickly copied by other provinces. In 1966, the federal government agreed to provide some money for health care. In return it required all provinces to meet the following criteria: Universality: All of the residents of the province were eligible for health services. Portability: Residents of one province needing medical care in another must be treated. Public Administration: The services had to be operated on a not-for-profit basis. In 1984, Ottawa passed the "Canada Health Act" which effectively outlawed hospitals and doctors from charging a user fee. The idea was to ensure access to health care to all Canadians irrespective of income. (Source: News Break, The Vancouver Sun, December 14, 1999.)

What do I have to keep in mind when gathering information from a hospital during an emergency?

We need to feel confident, not intimidated nor overwhelmed by our feelings of helplessness and dependency on doctors and other health team members.

We should remind ourselves when telephoning the emergency or recovery wards or individual doctors, that we are not being a nuisance – yes the doctors are busy, yes, they may even be blunt in their responses, but we are not bothering them – we are simply attempting to gather relevant information so we can make good next stage decisions about our parents' care.

(For example, I often said to a nurse/doctor at the beginning of our conversation, "I am very concerned about my Dad/Mum and I need some information from

you in order to decide if I should jump on a plane immediately or what my next step should be, can you help me?" These professionals are very cooperative and understand these types of concerns.)

We need to write down as many of the details as possible. We need to note details such as the surgeon or specialist involved with our parent—the specific doctor's name is valuable as he/she, at some later date, will be the person with whom we will want to discuss realistic expectations for the future recovery of our parent. *(For example: months later and upon my request, Dad's surgeon was able to offer a great deal more important relevant information regarding Dad's short-term progress than the family doctor.)*

And finally, when the time comes....we need 'to hear' both the words AND the tone that specialists are using when they are talking with us, giving us messages. *(For example, when Mum had her heart attack at the end of her life, and we were together in the emergency ward, her cardiologist of many years came to examine her. He gave me the 'bad news' (not unexpected, nevertheless, bad) and I was listening (but not hearing) when he said that Mum would be transferred upstairs to a bed in the hospital. I responded, "To the cardiology ward?" He responded, "No, there is no need to be there." This specialist's words and tone together gave me the complete picture.)*

Care of the elderly is not a glamorous issue. It rarely makes front-page news. It is unlikely to inspire a hit television series. However, these realities do not diminish its value for the people who need the care now, their families or for those of us who will one day need it. Long-term care must not be the sacrificial lamb by which we attempt to resolve the current health-care crisis in emergency departments. (*Source: Letter of the Day, from Dr. Elisabeth Drance, Geriatric Psychiatrist, Greater Vancouver Mental Health Service and Dr. David Harrison, Emergency Physician, Vancouver General Hospital, The Vancouver Sun, December 14, 1999.*)

Suggestion 2: Don't neglect our other parent

When a health crisis happens to one parent, we must not forget that we now actually have two parents in states of emergency – one in the hospital needing attention and medical care plus one sitting at home needing support and general care.

(This obviously does not apply if our second parent is in a carehome, although our carehome parent needs to be informed of any problems, later and gently.)

How can I ensure that my other parent is okay?

If we live in the same city, the decision is quick, we simply go to our healthy parent's home, eliminating some of the stress of the crisis and carry on with our info-gathering hospital calls from there.

If we live in a different city, a fair distance from our parents, *and if there is not a live-in caregiver* with our parents, we must:

☑ Ensure that someone (e.g. neighbour, nearby relative) goes to sit with our at-home parent, as quickly as possible, to assist him/her on a short-term basis with immediate needs and worries.

☑ As part of our planning, in advance of any crisis: We should make arrangements with one specific person (a relative, friend, or even a near-by neighbour) to be our designated short-term 'on-call caregiver', that means, if needed and called upon by us, on very short notice, she/he will move in with our at-home parent for a day/a week maximum, until we arrive.

Once such an 'on call' arrangement is firmly established as a precautionary strategy (we need, of course, to have run these plans past our parents long before an emergency occurs), we then only need to make one quick telephone call to our on-call caregiver to obtain good care for our at-home parent if a health crisis happens with our other parent (e.g. I used this method with my parents throughout their regular retirement years and always felt relieved when the on-call caregiver responded quickly).

The last thing we want to be worried about doing, when confronted with a hospital emergency with one parent, is telephoning, long-distance, various relatives/friends who live near to our parents, to find out if one of them is available to stay with our at-home parent until we can arrive perhaps a few hours or days later.

What should I do right at the time of the crisis?

At the very least, we should take these steps with our at-home parent as on-going communication will reduce worry and convey the message that we are taking control of this stressful situation.

☑ **Place a call to our parent** – The main purpose of this call is so that our at-home parent feels safe (e.g. all is under control) and we can also convey any preliminary information we have gained from the hospital. After contacting our designated on-call caregiver, we need to telephone our parent again and explain to her/him that the caregiver is on her/his way and when she/he will arrive. If we are not going to be rushing to get there ourselves, we have to explain now why not, as this parent will be seeking comfort from our immediate presence.

☑ **Up-date our parent as need be** – After we have gathered the latest facts from the hospital specialist/doctor regarding the status of our hospitalised parent, we should once again contact our at-home parent and explain calmly what we have found out.

If more than one telephone is available in the house, it is particular useful to have both our parent and the on-call caregiver on the telephones at the same time, so that each receives the same information together. It is important to speak with those in the house for communication reasons – no misunderstandings, no guessing, no need for others to telephone the hospital for the same information.

☑ **Rearrange our schedules** – As many factors are involved in our decision-making, we should take a few minutes and think about everyone affected (e.g. family, work colleagues) and any rearrangements of schedules. We must take the best course of immediate action.

An Australian research study shows hip fractures are most feared. 80% of women over the age of 75 would rather be dead than live in a nursing home after a hip fracture, researchers say. The research study found that falls and hip fractures were seen as a profound threat to quality of life. Any loss of ability to live independently in the community had a considerable detrimental effect on their quality of life, the women (interviewed) said. "About 20% of people who fracture their hips are dead within a year, and many of those who recover from hip fracture require additional assistance in daily living, Glenn Salkeld said (of Sydney University and Hornsby Kuring-gai Hospital in New South Wales, Australia). Among older women who have exceeded average life expectancy, quality of life matters, and (as well) they place a high value on their health, the study concluded. A reduction in the number of hip fractures would not only save lives but would prevent a significant reduction in their quality of life. *(Source: The Vancouver Sun, Feb 4, 2000.)*

Notes:

_____

_____

_____

_____

_____

_____

_____

_____

_____

_____

_____

_____

_____

Suggestion 3: *Make a quick check-list and organize travel plans*

If we live out-of-town and are faced with a health crisis involving our parents, we need to weigh many factors, before jumping in our car, on a bus or dashing to catch an airplane.

At crises times, during care-years, we should make only short-term decisions because circumstances change rapidly and our plans thus must be fluid:

☑ **Question the situation** – to help with decision-making, ask the attending doctor for input (e.g. Is there surgery involved? Is this the best time to be there? When later? What about my presence during recovery or rehabilitation periods? Are there any problems I should be aware of and put time aside for?)

☑ **Check on commitments** – check family commitments, job priorities and timetables; list what has to be attended to and can't wait.

What was said: "Somehow, (employers) see parents' obligations to their children as different than children's obligations to their parents." Economist Janet Fast, a co-author of "Eldercare in Canada: Context, Content and Consequences". *(Source: The Vancouver Sun, November 3, 1999.)*

☑ **Decide on a date and time to travel keeping the information gained from the doctor in mind** – check transportation schedules and conditions if winter. Reserve if necessary, and firm up departure/arrival times.

☑ **Contact our at-home parent** plus the person in attendance with that parent (e.g. on-call caregiver/live-in/shift caregivers) to outline plans.

☑ **Telephone our parents' family doctor** and schedule an appointment to discuss the status of both parents' health given the present circumstances. Also question the family doctor about the next phases of the hospital treatment and what can be expected; if he/she can't give the answers, ask who might at this time. (If at night, leave a message for the next day – to call, set an appointment to do what is required and necessary.)

☑ **Telephone the ward of the hospitalised parent** and inform the nurses as to our arrival date and time (as we will want to see our parent immediately even if for a few minutes); if it makes sense, request that our parent is advised of our pending arrival – at least that we are on the way. (When coming from out-of-town, we are usually able to visit outside of the regular hospital visiting hours, assume such is acceptable.)

☑ **If planning to travel by air,** check as to the airlines' policies regarding special fares. Question:

- Does your airline offer a special compassionate/medical fare for family members during emergency situations?

- Will you meet a competitor's fare price?

- What information (e.g. name of hospital) will you need from me now or later?

We need to be prepared with very precise information when we call to make a reservation with an airline.

- Name and telephone number of our parents' family doctor.

- Name, address and telephone number of the hospital.

If we have given all the necessary compassionate fare-related information over the telephone, when booking a flight, our ticket will be ready at the airport for instant pickup – at that point, all we have to do is sign one form indicating that the information which was given on the telephone is correct.

More importantly, if the airline is given the information at the precise time we are booking our ticket, the compassionate fare price is what we pay; if we wait to give the information at the time of picking up our ticket, we will have to pay the full fare and apply later for reimbursement at the compassionate fare price.

We need to understand that all family-related crises do not qualify under special fares categories. We must ask each time, but it seems, with most airlines, that only emergencies relating directly to the health of immediate family members qualify for special compassionate fares.

(If travelling by bus, there usually is a discount of approximately 20% on fares for family emergencies.)

About 2.1 million people over age 15 are looking after elderly relatives, spouses and friends, according to "Eldercare in Canada: Context, Content and Consequences" (the first report to tally the number of people providing unpaid care to seniors in Canada, an extensive analysis based on StatsCan's 1996 General Social Survey). The authors warn that unpaid caregivers are showing signs of strain and shouldn't be taken for granted. "There is a concern that today's caregivers are going to be tomorrow's poor seniors," said Janet Fast, a family and consumer economist at the University of Alberta and one of the report's authors. These caregivers tend to neglect their careers, which has a negative impact on their current and future income. "The less they work, the less they're contributing to Canada pension and RRSPs," she said. Employers should do more to accommodate workers who are looking after their parents. Some employers are taking steps in the right direction, Fast said, but they seem "more willing to make accommodations for child care than elder care". *(Source: The Vancouver Sun, November 3, 1999.)*

PART TWO

What should I be paying attention to while my elderly parent is actually in the hospital?

Personal Anecdote:
"I keep getting caught off guard!"

One afternoon after Dad's hip surgery, in a passing conversation in the hallway just outside his hospital room on the surgical ward, a nurse casually mentioned to me that Dad was taking "a bit longer" than he should be to get over the operation's anaesthetic. I was caught off-guard as I was not aware of any special concerns until this moment and I had no yardstick to gauge his recovery progress by, so I asked what length of time was considered appropriate for someone his age after undergoing lengthy surgery.

(That remark and all its implications taught me, from that day forward, to question health professionals immediately if I didn't fully grasp the exact meaning of their statements - I started asking, "What are you telling me, what do you mean exactly?")

In Dad's case, I discovered that the nurse (whether she realized it or not) was giving me, at that very moment, an important clue regarding Dad's ability for a total recovery as well as a glimpse into his future progress. If I could have read between the lines, she was actually conveying to me quite a significant message, she was saying, based on her experience with this type of surgery with this age group, not only was my Dad not responding as quickly as he should be, but also that his length of time to recover might be signalling other health problems.

At the end of the second week after the surgery, when the anaesthetic could no longer be a major factor, Dad was still experiencing difficulties with memory and simple walking exercises, so I requested a meeting with the ward's head nurse to discuss Dad's progress and apparent difficulties. Again, I was caught off-guard when the nurse started questioning me about Dad's drinking (alcohol) habits, while explaining that in her professional opinion, Dad's body seemed now to be adjusting to the complicated effects of alcohol withdrawal. (I found the diagnosis startling, thinking, "Okay, if you say so, since I know nothing about recovery complications and Dad was a two-beer a day man for as long as I remember - but I'd better speak with his doctor immediately.")

Given this additional complication, a meeting with my parent's family doctor was quickly arranged for the next day, when once again I was to be caught off-guard, the doctor disagreed with the nurse's analysis of the cause of Dad's slow progress.

I have since come to realize that such a debate isn't important. What really mattered was the present condition of my parent because regardless of the causes, we have to deal with the here-and-now. As a daughter, Dad's health problems seemed quite clear to me - he was recovering slowly from the surgery (walking, getting up, going to the bathroom), he was suffering apparent memory problems (names, places, time, events), his lack of coordination and poor balance were posing significant safety problems...I wanted help for him and continued to watch for positive signs of change indicating that he was improving.

By the end of the third week, I found it surprising that Dad was still in the post-surgery recovery ward (stays on that particular ward are usually for as few days as possible) and that he had yet to receive very much in the way of therapy (usually a patient is up and in physio pretty quickly after hip surgery regardless of age). Dad continued to swing between good and bad days - for short periods he seemed his old self, yet at other times, he would ask questions out of context or forget one of our names or make comments entirely inappropriate to the conversation. Physically he was weak and was still not mobile; mentally he was unmotivated and a bit frustrated. By now, Mum was confused as to how to handle Dad's fluctuating conditions - she was beginning quietly to voice little worries about their immediate future.

Yet, even then, Mum and I still continued to talk in terms of Dad "getting better" and things "returning to normal" even though the signals seemed to forebode a very different outcome. Since Dad was in a hospital, I assumed that his medical condition was being assessed and monitored and that his problems would be "treated". (I guess I also took it for granted that his problems were 'treatable'.) Because of that optimistic attitude, I did not make enquires at this point as to what services were available within the hospital or if there were any specialized professional staff available to help our family. I was wrong to assume 'Dad was going to get better.' I was wrong to assume that hospital care was 'the answer'. I was wrong not to have started my search for help for our family right then - while Dad was a patient. (In brief, I was wrong to assume that care-years health problems were the same as pre-care-years health problems - they aren't.)

One day, still trying desperately to seek some logical reasons, and more importantly, solutions for Dad's problems, I made an appointment to meet with the orthopaedic specialist who had operated on Dad's hip. He and I discussed the possibility of a head scan, thinking that Dad may have hit his head when he fell on the ice, resulting in a concussion.

The scan was done the next day - more surprises - the results caught me off-guard, once again. The scan showed that Dad had not hit his head (at least if so, not hard enough to pose a problem other than a bruise), so a concussion was not part of the problem - but the scan did discover something else. Dad's brain was showing clear signs of what the doctor termed "mild dementia a little beyond what should be for his age group". I was alarmed at first, but as Dad's doctors did not find this new piece of information problematic or shocking (or if they did, I certainly did not get that message), Mum and I, at this point, didn't remain overly concerned with the scan's findings either.

What I realize now is that I should not have taken lightly 'the commonly talked about condition called dementia,' mild or otherwise, as I really had no idea how dementia would impact Dad's immediate recovery or his future lifestyle. I didn't know what everyday adjustments Mum would have to make or how her lifestyle would be altered because of Dad's dementia. I remained unaware of significant changes forthcoming in my own life because of Dad's health conditions. Our family was being given news of Dad's health puzzle (albeit in a piecemeal fashion) and I was witnessing signs regarding my parents' future care-needs and yet, we still weren't getting a clear picture. At the time, I remember thinking, "Oh, mild dementia, that's something that comes with age, so what if Dad forgets a few details, we can handle that, it is common." By not giving my full attention to the condition called 'dementia', I was dismissing what should have been a big, big wake-up call.

Why didn't I ask questions? Was it because the medical professionals didn't seem to show any alarm? Was it because I knew so little about dementia other than what the general public seem to be aware of? Was the word 'mild' misleading? (I didn't know that the word 'mild' could not be applied as in 'mild flu' - but that mild dementia is more of a classification level for the condition.) Was it because I thought our health system would meet all our needs...?

Like many other families worried about an elderly parent/ spouse in the hospital, Mum and I were feeling bewildered and a bit overwhelmed - we were hoping Dad would "get better" (to a good degree) and we were spending long periods of time with him every day. As well, we were trying to work within a hospital system, seeking some help for specific problems. We were starting to make some plans for when he was to be released.

Then, still more surprises. A few days after the scan's results, on a regular morning visit to Dad, who was at this point still on the post-surgery ward, I casually asked a passing nurse how Dad was progressing that day. She responded, "He was given some tests this morning and he's going to be moved this afternoon."

This sequence of events was startling news, I questioned her on the type of test, the purpose of the testing program and the outcomes. I was informed, standing in this very informal setting, that, as a result of the findings of the morning's tests, Dad was being transferred immediately to another wing of the hospital, into a very specialized ward for the aged in need of advanced levels of rehabilitation - a ward known as the GMAT ward (Geriatric Medical Assessment Team). She told me that GMAT is a ward which specializes, not in diseases which is usually how specialty wards are categorized, but in the aged - a ward with services and staff trained to work with the elderly, a ward that until that moment was unknown to our family.

That afternoon, Dad was transferred to the hospital's GMAT ward. It was during this period that my awareness, as a daughter of an elderly parent, grew - my parents' future care-needs were surfacing. It was then that I started to ask questions, to seek help, to rely on my own efforts for my family.

Both of my parents had entered a new span in their retirement lives - their care-years.

Suggestion 4: **Get to know the hospital**

Where do I begin?

We want to marry up our parent's needs to the available services offered by the hospital, so, we should begin by taking a realistic look at our parent's health at this point in time **and** a good look at the hospital and all it provides for the elderly.

Step 1 – We must find out what our parent needs – while our parent is in the hospital, we should:

☑ Question the ward nurses and our family doctor carefully regarding our parent's progress – ask them to describe what they are noting (weight loss, memory lapses, slow/excellent/normal rate compared to others of similar age with similar health problems…). If anything irregular is mentioned, ask immediately what this may indicate regarding future care demands.

☑ Watch to see if our parent is being assisted with the basics (e.g. sitting up in a chair with good balance, walking to the bathroom without aids) as these therapies indicate that a basic rehabilitation program (perhaps in preparation for release) has started with our parent.

Step 2 – We must find out what the hospital provides – while our parent is in the hospital, we should become familiar with:

☑ The hospital's services (for in-and-out patients) for seniors – make a list.

☑ The hospital's wards that specialize in work with seniors – ask the hospital administrator for information and visit the relevant ward(s) – note what treatment program is offered.

Step 3 – Finally, we should 'match' our parent's needs to the hospital's services – we will thus to be able to access all that is available.

☑ Meet with our parent's family doctor to make our wishes known; meet with the hospital social worker (or equivalent, such as a community case worker) in order to begin the process of using the hospital's services upon release – attempt to discuss preliminary schedules.

☑ We must then meet our health unit's community care nurse, the key person responsible for coordination of seniors' programs in our region, and discuss how hospital-related care services link to community care programs.

What should I know specifically about specialized wards for seniors?

We need to know the basics:

- Do they exist?

- What do they do?

- How can they help my parent?

- If they don't exist, how are the needs of the elderly serviced in this hospital?

Geras, Greek for old age. Helpful definitions: Geriatrician – a medical doctor certified in geriatrics which is the medical science of the physical and mental aspects of aging. Gerontologist – a person who has researched aging from a social science perspective.

While our parent is in the hospital, we should:

☑ Locate any of the specialized wards that could be of value to our parent (there won't be too many). As specialized GMAT-type wards are very beneficial in the rehabilitation and further assessment of our parent, we need to inquire if our regional hospital has such a ward, or if not, does it have geriatricians on staff or a group of health-related professionals serving as a geriatric medical assessment team.

☑ Take a few minutes during our regular hospital visitations to drop into and observe what is done on the specialized wards.

☑ If we feel a short-term placement for our parent in a specialized ward may benefit our family, we should make a verbal request for such a placement to the our parent's family doctor and follow-up the verbal request by writing a note to that same doctor with a copy to the head nurse of the ward our parent is presently on, so she/he is also aware of our family's wishes for a transfer directly to a specialized ward when the time is appropriate.

☑ We should realize that it is not uncommon for elderly patients, like our parents, to be given a type of verbal geriatric progress test (my term) in order that hospital teams can determine which specialized ward within the hospital our parent may be moved to for further 'rehabilitation learning,' if tests indicate such is required. We can request such tests be given if unsure of our parent's progress.

If a parent is relocated to a specialized ward, we should:

☑ Schedule an appointment with our parent's family doctor in order to discuss the specialized ward's programs and evaluations. It is important during this meeting to ask about expectations (what can I expect by way of progress while my parent is on this ward).

☑ Be observant when visiting our parent – what activities and special treatments does the ward offer, what exactly is my parent participating in/learning to do.

☑ Ask questions of the ward's staff (does each patient have a case coordinator for us to contact with questions, if not, whom should I contact when I have questions regarding my parent).

☑ Attempt to understand two of the main procedures of the ward:

1. How are patients evaluated for release?

2. Does the family have any input into that release schedule?

While our parent is housed on the specialized ward, we need to realize that our visit is now more than just a friendly chat, it is an opportunity to glean new insights into our parent's daily progress plus a good way to learn some methods for working with our parent upon release.

If we become concerned in the slightest, we should question the behaviour (problem) we are noticing including what is being done/can be done to help resolve that problem.

We must remind ourselves that hospital staff members are professionals with precise reasons for all the actions taken and that they are willing to explain those actions to us if approached.

Notes:

_____

_____

_____

_____

_____

_____

_____

_____

_____

_____

_____

_____

_____

_____

Suggestion 5: *Leave no stone unturned*

How can I keep one small step ahead of the next, up-coming phase of care?

One key, to staying a small step ahead, is getting out of the starting blocks early after a health crisis – while our parent is still in the hospital.

We can't be timid at a time like this, as it is part of our immediate responsibility to ask questions and make requests on behalf of our family unit. After the first health emergency, we need to:

☑ **Question the clues** we are receiving from the hospital staff, especially during the recovery stage – Why is this action being taken, is there a problem with my parent's progress, are there other problems we should be aware of, is this behaviour usual?

☑ **Analyse what we are seeing** by repeatedly asking ourselves, "Is this a person who will be capable of returning to his/her old normal habits and ways (i.e. walking, eating, sleeping, bathing, driving, grocery shopping, going out unattended…)?" We need to be brutally honest and not be lulled into believing that life will go back to 'normal' for our elderly parent, as we will have to establish a 'new normal' as we go along (i.e. things have changed dramatically).

☑ **Envision a typical day of our parent after release** – whether the problem is physical, mental or emotional or a combination, ask ourselves: what will an ordinary week look like for my parents now in their own home; is their living environment safe; how are they are going to cope with each component in a day? Glossing over answers could cause unnecessary difficulties later and a longer adjustment time.

☑ **Use all the services available** – we have to be sure we are utilizing fully all the relevant services within our hospital and accessing the hospital's community network programs. *(Note: Good rehabilitative learning, undertaken within the hospital setting under trained supervision prior to release, can significantly reduce problems at home later.)*

☑ **Ask for brief meetings with selected medical staff and ask questions – often.**What does the rehabilitation process entail; does rehabilitation focus on meeting physical needs only; what of slowly emerging mental and emotional problems being noticed; is returning to normal a remote/good possibility; what services are available after this rehab process; what do the hospital staff suggest as a next step?

☑ **Search out and attend a caregivers support group meeting** and discuss with group attendees the long-term implications of our parent's health – what is life like for similar families. When it comes to caring for our parents, we have now much to learn and a caregivers support group could be of immense assistance in pointing us in the proper direction from the beginning.

☑ **Remind ourselves daily that changes will be constantly impacting our family for the foreseeable future** – our job is to try to predict what we need to do as a result of each change (be one step ahead). Being informed regarding care-years needs and problems truly helps (e.g. read, talk to people in associations, research on the Internet…).

☑ **Reduce problem circumstances where and whenever possible during beginning care-years until good response habits are formed** – we have to learn to carry our thinking one step further than we normally would. *(For example: Is the wheelchair with us at all times? Should we take our elderly parent to the hospital to visit an old friend knowing that a hospital is full of viruses and illnesses?…)*

☑ **Redefine what the term 'normal' means now – for each parent –** think of the new meaning of what is normal from a care perspective – a normal mealtime now, a normal day with a live-in caregiver, a normal day with one parent in a care manor, a normal respite week, even a normal bathroom routine, a normal holiday time, a normal outing…(understanding what the 'new normal' for you as 'a family on a care-years journey' is a very important recognition).

Notes:

_____

_____

_____

_____

_____

_____

_____

_____

_____

_____

_____

_____

_____

_____

_____

_____

_____

_____

_____

_____

_____

> "Beware you be not swallowed up in books! An ounce of love is worth a pound of knowledge."
>
> *– John Wesley*

Suggestion 6: *Prepare for a changed parent*

Over the years, we will have noticed changes in our parents' appearances and habits due to aging or health problems but for the most part, they have probably continued to look and act in a familiar manner. Now – after a turning-point health incident – the changes we will notice during these care-years could be significant.

What are some of the changes I can expect?

By observing the patients in a specialized geriatric ward (interacting with their families and nurses), we will gradually come to the realization that our parent is part of this group and like the others we are observing, our parent too is changing physically and mentally.

We will notice some of the more obvious physical and mental changes and hopefully also some of the methods for working with our parent. These changes may include:

☑ **Weight loss:** We may detect a noticeable weight loss causing our parent to look older than before the crisis. *(For example: Dad was large-boned and he had lost an unusual amount of weight rapidly but it was during the rehabilitation time that his frame became obvious – the hollow cheeks and strong facial bone structure, broad shoulder blades…)*

☑ **Walking style:** If our parent needs to use a walker or cane now, we may detect a slight limp when mobile. We may perceive our parent to be hunched over in appearance, especially if originally a tall, well-postured person, our parent will seem smaller when mobile.

☑ **Eating – Coordination:** We should often join our parent for lunch or dinner if on a geriatric ward and quietly observe the seniors, including our parent, coping with mealtime coordination skills.

We may need to develop a polite, acceptable and subtle method of assisting our parent with the simple task of eating. *(For example:*

Dad also broke his right hand when he fell and couldn't adjust to left-handedness easily during rehabilitation, so we requested that all his food be cut into small pieces prior to being served, thus eliminating the requirement to use two hands to cut his food – this simple adjustment eliminated some frustration and allowed greater meal time independence and dignity throughout all his care-years.)

☑ **Interests:** We should try to detect if there are any major changes in interests on the part of our parent. *(For example: Dad, had been an ardent hockey fan all his life and continued to show some interest in the sport after his fall; but at the same time, Dad was not interested in local events which he had always supported within the community – this lack of interest was a very noticeable change, even at an early date.)*

☑ **Conversations:** We may begin to notice single-focus conversations (they revolve around one concern over a lengthy period of time). During these occasions, it falls to us to learn how to interject gently and patiently steer our parent, if possible, from that one topic/worry into a new conversation.

☑ **Bathroom needs:** We may observe that the simple task of going to the bathroom is no longer easy, it now takes planning (enough time) and balance and coordination (positioning, standing, sitting, getting up, reassembling clothing, hygiene).

We can learn to be of background-assistance without being overprotective – we need to accept that accidents will happen (shrug them off and emphasize that such are of no consequence) to reduce worry and especially any embarrassment on the part of our parent.

☑ **Medication use:** We need to become aware of the importance of medications now and our parent's dependency on such. We need to know the schedules and the purposes of medications (what and when). If pill taking is a necessity, adhering to strict rules and habits becomes a must. We will probably notice a slight increase in our parent's anxiety level as the importance of being on time with the daily pills becomes part of a daily routine. *(For example, our basic rules for dealing with medications were: never be late or forgetful; never get excited or overplay or underplay the value of a particular medication; never leave the pill-taking task up to a parent.)*

☑ **Dressing, undressing:** We can watch for any problems with dressing/ undressing and how aids are used for these tasks. We can then try adapting the types of clothing to be used. *(For example, Dad found his conventional clothing of dress shirt, tie, dress pants, zipper, belt all hard to handle now due to his lack of balance and damaged hand, so we, like others have done, switched Dad to good quality sweat suits for regular daily wear and velcro shoes snaps for ease of handling).*

☑ **Hygiene:** We should organize regular bath services with the local hospital if bathing hygiene at home presents a problem. *(For example, Dad was registered for a weekly bath program at the day hospital which had all the safe pulley equipment for bathing; in addition, he had daily sponge baths from community care workers during the rest of the week at home; Dad, in the first six months, called his regular barber to visit at home to trim hair, moustache and 'shoot the bull' in Italian.)*

☑ **Ways of doing regular things:** We need to watch for changes to simple habits or methods by which our parent attends to daily personal care. *(For example: Dad adapted to using an electric shaver rather than his traditional razor blade method, to sleeping on rubber pads in the night, to using numerous dressing aids. Mum had a chair placed at the sink in the bathroom and a lowered mirror so she could sit while doing make-up.)* We can ease the transition period by carefully observing what is being taught/done in the hospital regarding new methods for routine daily tasks.

☑ **Training Exercises:** We need to watch our parent during any rehabilitation-training program *(Note: Observing a parent in a new learning environment, struggling to get things right, is very difficult as it is natural to worry about safety and want to protect and assist).*

While our parent is in a rehabilitation situation, we need to make a point of participating in the exercises with that parent, learning what the correct procedures are and how the therapists work with our parent (e.g. going up/down stairs, which foot first and why; getting up from a chair with a walker, setting brakes, sitting on the seat when tired; strengthening legs, rolling over in bed and getting out of bed correctly for balance, in general how to go about everyday activities).

As we will be directly involved in managing these methods once our parent returns home, and training any types of caregivers, it makes sense to have the hospital therapists train us too. *(Note: The methods learned may come in handy later with a second parent /relative.)*

✓ **As time goes on...A greatly changed parent...More and more care required:** When a long-term care stage has gone on for some years, (e.g. when we were in our tenth year) we may witness the deterioration of many of the body functions and a very big change in mental attitude of our parent. At times like these, we must be very aware of the rapidly changing levels of care needed from one day to the next (e.g. help in the bathroom with pulling up pants; taking the cap off of the toothpaste; combing one's hair completely; lack of interest in the newspaper...). These changes signal another new level of care-attention. We must discuss the needs with the caregivers and then adjust the duties and levels of assistance one is to provide (the caregivers must also advise us when they are noting changes). We must then discuss these levels of help with our parents as well, so that they will be accepting of the assistance when offered by the caregivers. *(For example, my mother used to say, "I don't seem to be able to do anything for myself anymore" to which I would respond, "Well, sure you do, you use your walker and get around on your own, you are able to eat your meals and enjoy company, you put on your make-up each day...").* It is important to emphasize the positive actions versus having one focus on the activities one has lost. The key is independence, which at any age is valued, I found.

During my second month of nursing school, our professor gave us a pop quiz. I was a conscientious student and had breezed through the questions, until I read the last one: "What is the first name of the woman who cleans the school?" Surely this was some kind of joke. I had seen the cleaning woman several times. She was tall, dark-haired and in her 50s, but how would I know her name? I handed in my paper, leaving the last question blank. Just before class ended, one student asked if the last question would count toward our quiz grade. "Absolutely," said the professor. "In your careers, you will meet many people. All are significant. They deserve your attention and care, even if all you do is smile and say, 'hello'". I've never forgotten that lesson. I also learned her name was Dorothy. *(One of "The Five Great Lessons" – Source from an Internet site, Sept 2000.)*

Notes

Suggestion 7: *Become an active member of the hospital decision-making team*

How can I have input into hospital decisions?

At any point in time, if our parent requires a longer-than-regular hospitalization period, we should seek to become an active member of our parents' hospital medical team as we know our parent well and can offer relevant family history. Since we have to live with the results of any hospital decisions, it is in our family's best interests to become a member of any health team working towards the best possible end results for our parents.

The purpose of our participation is three-fold:

1 – **To have input** – to ensure that hospital decision-makers have all the information they require about our family situation (i.e. our two parents) in order to make correct decisions which are going to impact future homelife.

2 – **To ask questions** – to be informed regarding the therapies, treatments being tried with our parent during this important time.

3 – **To reduce any surprises** – to be 'in-the-loop' regarding decisions which otherwise may be sprung (unintentionally) upon our family.

(Note: For more ideas, refer to Topic 2, Suggestion #18, Become An Advocate.)

What are the first steps I can take to get involved?

☑ **Within the first three days of transfer of our parent to a specialized ward** – especially if the ward is a geriatric ward or one involving special training or rehabilitation for our parent, we need to find out how that ward assesses a patient's progress and makes its patient-decisions (e.g. in committees, with/without family members' input). We can telephone the ward's head nurse or the doctor-in-charge or our family doctor and ask. (Remember, the family doctor is always a key member of any medical team for his/her patients.)

☑ **Within the first week in the ward,** we should make a request to participate/be present at the ward's next team meeting when our parent's case will be discussed (send a fax/short letter stating this request in writing).

We must establish the date, time, location, and members present. If regular meetings are not held, we need to request that a special meeting be arranged in order that we can meet with those responsible decision-makers working with our parent.

☑ **Prior to the meeting,** we need to prepare for the meetings in order to ask well-thought out questions such as:

- What is my parent expected to learn on this ward (e.g. walking, dressing, climbing, eating, speaking, getting in and out of bed, exercising...)?

- What else can I expect to find occurring with my parent's health; what should I be watching for, what is normal in case like this? What advice do you offer to families who are going through similar changes?

- Do any difficult behaviours exist at present (e.g. frustration, poor cooperation, memory) – problems that our family should be aware of? What do these problems indicate (professional opinions being sought)?

- What are the milestones to be accomplished prior to my parent's release (very important question)?

- When can I observe practise sessions with any special trainers or therapists; is any special equipment needed?

- Are there associations/support groups close by in our community that deal with these types of health problems/behaviours?

☑ **During the meetings,** we should present our perspective, give our input in order to extend the other team members' understanding of the family's general/complex situation.

We must make a point of taking notes, writing out the responses to our questions and thinking on our feet when given a new piece of information. If decisions are made during the meeting, we have to be sure we understand exactly what those decisions are before we leave each meeting (i.e. ask for clarification – "As I understand it, this is what we have decided today…").

We needn't be timid or afraid of embarrassment, we do need to present ourselves as a team player.

☑ **When regularly visiting our parent on the ward,** we need to take the initiative and gather information in an informal manner (e.g. "How is my Dad today? Have you noticed any progress or problems since last week/yesterday?") These questions can be of a probing nature and asked of the attending nurse on duty each day.

While visiting, think as a 'member of the team' by observing and participating – we do not need to resign ourselves to playing the role of visitor only.

☑ **Lastly,** we should remind ourselves that by taking an active interest in our parent's care right now, we are being cost and time-efficient within our health system (i.e. we don't want to have to return).

We need to approach our parent's present situation as we have approached other situations that have demanded our participation.

I realize that every reader understands the strong emphasis within this section on being proactive, yet perhaps we can think about it further with this analogy:

If we had a young child in elementary school one experiencing a problem or who had an identified learning disorder, would we wait for an authority in the school to schedule a meeting with us so that we could be informed regarding the nature and learning implications of our child's problems? Would we sit in the background (passively) and trust that the school's learning centre was eventually going to work cooperatively with us concerning the new skills our child is to acquire? Would we wait to be informed as to our child's progress…?

The answers are clear, of course we wouldn't. We would be actively involved from the start, asking questions of the authorities and of the education specialists, observing the learning environment, participating in meetings

– we would probably be somewhat disturbed if our input was not being sought.

Is this not then, a similar situation – a loved one who is dependent upon us is experiencing a series of problems, is attempting to learn new skills and is facing challenging times. We need to be involved, we need to be a team member from the start.

Baby boomers can be confident they'll be healthier in their senior years than their parents and grandparents, a new Statistics Canada report says. That's because those born from 1947 to 1964 are better educated, wealthier and have access to better medical treatment than previous generations. And that means chronic diseases and maladies usually associated with the senior years are being postponed or even prevented. Researchers end the report on a cautionary note, stating that even with the documented improvement in health status, "the sheer growth in the absolute number of elderly people in the coming decades will represent a major challenge for the provisions of health care." *(Source: The Vancouver Sun, May 30, 2000.)*

Notes:

_____

_____

_____

_____

_____

_____

_____

_____

_____

_____

_____

_____

_____

_____

_____

Suggestion 8: A precautionary note – watch for signs of dementia

What should I know about the condition commonly called 'dementia'?

We need to realize that the condition known as 'dementia' does not occur with the aged only, it can come on at any age, but the risk may increase as one grows older.

It is a condition that is upsetting for the individual and for the family as it incapacitates the person with it and therefore causes concerns among family members.

The disease is characterized by the gradual spread of sticky plaques and clumps of tangled fibers that disrupt the delicate organization of nerve cells in the brain. As brain cells stop communication with one another, they atrophy – causing memory and reasoning to fade. *(Source: Time magazine, Canadian edition, Article: Alzheimer's, May 14, 2001.)*

At all times, but especially after a major health crisis, we should be on the lookout for some of the dementia-related warning signs:

- Memory loss (names of family members, old friends; events).

- Some confusion accompanied by high levels of frustration.

- Obvious and subtle personality changes (aggressive manner, repetitive questions, anger).

- Carelessness (maybe as to dress, cleanliness).

- Slight depression (lack of interest in normal things).

(For example: Over a period of three years, we experienced the following with Dad: memory loss (occasions, names, how to do tasks); confusion and disorientation (location and times of day), frustration (placement of articles,

schedule changes, delays, unexpected visitors); aggressiveness (if routines were disrupted), repetitive questioning (fixations and worries), yelling and tone of voice (anger and fears) and a lack of interest in his immediate environment. At the same time as we were working with Dad's behaviours, we were visiting Mum's brother on a regular basis in an extended care home and started taking greater notice of the residents with Alzheimer's, undressing when inappropriate to do so, staying in bed in a vegetative state, restlessness, wandering and even some hallucinatory behaviours. Note: When researching 'dementia', also refer to 'Alzheimer's Disease'.)

If we are confused as to our parent's illogical behaviors, we should question if dementia could be a factor with our parent – tests can be given to help with the diagnosis. *(Note: Trauma to the head and even a brief loss of consciousness can eat away at precious brain reserve; the association between strokes and Alzheimer's is even stronger.)*

(For example: In the first care-year, we tried several methods for helping members of our household, especially Dad, cope with the dementia-related behaviours – these methods included establishing firm/almost rigid routines; providing a very structured, safe, comfortable and unchanging environment; and reassuring Dad repeatedly that things were fine. At the same time, to try to keep his mind somewhat active, we encouraged him to participate in discussions with friends and family members and to read the local newspaper. We also put him on a regular multi-vitamin regime. For my mother as time went on, her short-term memory began fading, so we added some simple techniques to assist her memory, such as: notes near her living room chair; pencils and paper near her sitting areas; a calendar for her reference. We also asked her questions on topics we thought she might want to discuss from long ago, adventures she usually enjoyed telling about.)

One of the strongest findings of the Nun Study (since 1986, University of Kentucky scientist David Snowdon has been studying 678 School Sisters – painstakingly researching their personal and medical histories, testing them for cognitive function and even dissecting their brains after death) – is the link between folic acid and mental health. Found in breads, cereals and leafy green vegetables, folic acid seems to protect the brain's central learning and reasoning regions from shrinkage. Most doctors recommend starting with at least 400 micrograms a day, the amount found in most multivitamins. (*Source: Time magazine, Canadian edition, May 14, 2001.*)

What can I do if I suspect my parent may be suffering from dementia?

While our parent is in the hospital, if we 'suspect dementia', we need to become concerned.

We should:

☑ **Request a meeting with hospital care coordinators/social workers and geriatricians** – we must not only learn about the condition but also begin thinking about the changes each member of our family will have to make because of a loved one's dementia.

If possible, we should have our other parent involved in any initial fact-finding meetings so the facts are delivered first-hand to her/him too. *(For example: Mum accompanied me to the first meeting scheduled with the community health unit nurse for our area – it was both an excellent and shocking meeting as she was able to 'set the scene' for all we were going to have to face in the near future with Dad. I can still hear her cautionary words as she tried to give us a glimpse of what to expect in the future. Mum and I came away with much to think about.)*

Doctors link B12 shortage to artery ills, dementia.... One in five seniors suffers from chronic deficiency of vitamin Bas, a dietary lacuna that can markedly increase the risk of cardiovascular disease and dementia, according to new Canadian research.

"Vitamin B12 deficiency is much more common than doctors think it is, David Spence, director of the stroke prevention and atherosclerosis research center at Robarts Research Institute in London, Ontario said in an interview. ...While most Canadians are now getting adequate levels of folate, they still are not getting enough B12. Folate and B12 are both B vitamins. When levels are inadequate, levels of homocysteine, an amino acid, increase. This, in turn, leads to a buildup of plaque in the blood vessels, which greatly increases the risk of heart attack, stroke and dementia. (Experts are divided on whether a high level of the amino acid in the blood should be considered a major risk factor for heart disease, but Dr. Spence said he has no doubt. Dr. Spence who is also a professor of clinical neurological sciences at the University of Western Ontario, said he believes that all seniors should be screened for vitamin B12 deficiency. *(Source: The Globe and Mail, Andre Picard, Public Health reporter; research published in the Canadian Medical Association Journal)*

☑ **Focus on understanding what we are being told about the condition** – as most of us are probably new to the terminology of medical professionals who deal with these types of health problems daily, we need to make sure we understand what is being said or implied during all meetings discussing dementia.

We may need to be direct in our approach with health professionals at times, mentioning that we would appreciate it if all aspects of the condition could be explained in easily understood terms.

During meetings, we should ask for clear, precise descriptions regarding the behaviours we can expect to see, both now and over time, even if it means politely interrupting to gain further understanding or taking notes for questions later.

If our other parent has accompanied us, there may be a need to paraphrase right on the spot during the meeting as we want to ensure her/his understanding of the condition; we also want to keep our parent involved as an important member of the meeting.

(For example, I made a special point of always turning to Mum during all our joint meetings with Dad's health professionals, to ask her quietly if she understood what X has just talked about (what such and such a statement meant) – if she said, "No" or "I think so", I took time right at that moment to paraphrase what was presented to us. I encouraged Mum to ask questions, even if she became teary in the process. Mum appreciated the paraphrasing as she and I tried to keep our eye on the ultimate goal of the meetings – a clear understanding by both of us of Dad's problems. We continued this successful process over the years with not only medical professionals but also legal ones. It doesn't take long for the persons present to start going to extra lengths to see that our parent understands, is really clear – but we may have to set the stage first using a paraphrasing technique.)

☑ **Observe and listen to others** – we can, in a considerate manner, observe other patients who are on the same ward as our parent or are attending adult day-hospital (when dropping off or picking up our parent or during special get-togethers).

We can watch for behaviours, listen to conversations, and try to tune into some of the causes of challenging behaviours.

We can make a point of talking with other patients' family members during visiting hours to try to gain some insights about this brain disorder and all its unwanted 'baggage'.

We can observe how trained professionals work with patients suffering from mild dementia. *(For example: While on the GMAT ward, Dad had made a habit of retiring to one particular recliner after dinner – he felt that this was his chair and his routine and that all the other patients should be aware of that. One evening, when I arrived, Dad was angry, as another patient, who also had dementia, had taken 'his chair'; Dad would accept no other recliner and had remained at his dining table. He was mumbling and periodically verbally chastising the lady who was by now not only firmly ensconced in the chair but also becoming more and more defiant by the half-hour. I really was at a loss as to how to alleviate Dad's 'pain' and placate him (he would accept nothing short of someone physically picking the lady up and as he put it "plunking her down somewhere else"). After what seemed like a lengthy period, I approached the nursing staff for guidance as Dad was very agitated. I then watched how the staff came to the rescue. Over the course of a few minutes, a staff member prepared a small tray of cookies placing it on a table near where other patients were seated, she asked the lady-inthe-chair if she would like to join the others for some of her favourites, then with agreement, helped the lady to the table to enjoy the treats – all the while looking back over her shoulder as Dad immediately got up from his dining room location, grabbed his walker and moved quickly to the now vacated recliner. The staff member created a distraction, made the distraction appropriate, and kept the environment friendly and safe in keeping with routines and behaviours of the patients...)*

☑ **Attend an association support meeting** – it is to our family's advantage to become familiar with the issue of dementia on a practical level. As dementia is a disorder which is difficult to handle, we should discuss with experts and local association chapter members (e.g. Alzheimer's Association) how the condition may impact our family and how we may be able to help our parent cope with the dementia.

(For example: I made an error when I first arranged to have Mum and me attend a support group discussion sponsored by the local health unit, in that my timing was poor. It was in the first month after Dad's fall and Mum was feeling overwhelmed with new situations, new problems, confusing emotions, in short she could not handle a discussion evening. By the end of the meeting, she was exhausted from listening to the various dilemmas people were facing as caregivers and to make matters worse, throughout the session, she had felt a need to help them. No one was successful in getting Mum to attend another group session. I should have waited until we were through the major upheavals and more comfortable with our caregiving roles.)

☑ **Research on our own** – we need to find out about the progression of dementia, since the very nature of the condition could lead to greater behaviour variations in our parent (e.g. Dad's condition did not remain constant, some aspects grew worse over the months and years).

Through our own research (whether its reading a magazine article or looking at the websites on the Internet), we will come to understand the magnitude of the condition. We should never overlook dementia's synergistic effects. We may even be able to understand our feelings of helpless as we watch our parent's mental and resulting physical capacities deteriorate (ouch, strong words).

☑ **There are many challenges in dealing with Alzheimer's. Working together with your doctor can help you get the best care possible.**

Dealing With Alzheimer's?

(Source: November 28, 2002; reviewed: November 13, 2004; Robert W. Griffith, MD Working with Your Doctor When You Suspect Memory Problems. California Council of the Alzheimer's Association. www.healthandage.com)

In May 2001 the US Alzheimer's Association commissioned a survey about doctor-caregiver communications. Only a third of the caregivers who were asked (124 out of 376, or 33%) felt they received all the information they wanted from their family physicians. But 440 of 500 physicians (88%) who answered the survey believed they were providing the proper recommendations about management. Clearly something is not right with doctor-caregiver communications.

Here are some tips to keep in mind for caregivers and family members in their efforts to educate their physicians.

Before your first visit:

— Doctors only have a limited amount of time to spend with each patient. You can help by being prepared. Make lists!

— Make a list of all medications, both over-the-counter (vitamins, aspirin) and prescription, with their dosing instructions.

— Make a list of previous and present medical problems, and any relevant problems in family members.

— Make a list of symptoms, when they began, and how often they occur. Be specific ("Last Tuesday, my husband got lost on the way home from the store. It was scary.")

– Be ready to say how well the patient can perform common daily activities, such as balancing a checkbook or taking medications.

At your first (or maybe your second) visit, your doctor should:

– Explain the diagnosis, let you know what to expect in the future, and tell you where to get more information and support.

– Tell you about possible treatments, and help you select what's best.

– Schedule your next visit and let you know how often you should come back.

If you aren't getting the information you expect, ask these specific questions:

– What does the diagnosis mean?

– Can you explain it in a way that I will understand?

– What can we expect in the near future and over time?

– Do you have any written material on this disease? If not, who does?

– Are there any organizations or community services that can help?

– Are there any treatments that don't involve medications?

– Is there anything that we can change at home to make things easier or safer?

– What medications are available for memory loss or for behavior changes?

– What are the risks and benefits of the medication?

– What are the side effects?

– How long will the patient take this medicine?

– Should we consider participating in a drug trial?

– What are the risks and benefits?

– Under what circumstances should we call your office?

– Is there anything else we should know?

– Don't worry if you get home and realize you've forgotten to ask some of your questions. Make another list and call the doctor, or take them on your next visit.

For subsequent visits, make a list of:

– Changes in symptoms (memory, mood, behavior)? When they started, frequency, time of day?

– How the prescribed treatments are working. What's improved, what's worsened?

– Side effects of medications and the problems they cause.

– The patient's general health.

– The caregiver's health.

– What additional help you need.

– If you don't understand something, ask more questions. Share your point of view with the doctor.

Gather Information - take notes during the visit or afterwards, even bring a tape recorder.

Do I have to change any of my own behaviours to help my parents cope with dementia-related problems?

Yes, we do have to adapt our responses when a parent has dementia. We can:

☑ **Try new communication techniques** – we must show empathy when communicating with our parent, try to feel the condition from our parents' points of view – what it must be like to feel lost and bewildered.

We can try to catch glimpses of our reactions to our parent's struggles with memory problems and learn to use appropriate conversation techniques at certain points to help out. *(For example: Dad's struggle to remember people's names, even some old friends, frustrated him and often during a conversation, he would say, "Oh, forget it" so we learned to change the manner in which we entered into some conversations. The aim was to continue our talks together regardless of names, thus we tried not to begin a chat with an opening like, "You remember X" – instead we would start out by giving descriptions saying, "Your old friend from city hall, X, who lives down the street, was mentioned in the paper today, he…")*

We can listen carefully and hold back on immediate responses (e.g. finishing sentences for our parents).

We can learn to ask questions to help our parent out when they are showing 'non-verbal signals' of frustration (e.g. tightly folded arms; eyes looking away, food left on the plate).

☑ **Make a silent promise to have patience with our parent** – and do so each time together (e.g. when entering a room, when getting out of the car, when chatting…). At times, having patience may mean remaining quiet (e.g. Mum started telling some of the same stories many times over). Being patient is not always easy (for some of us), but our parents will let us know sometimes when our impatience bothers them.*(For example: I have a tendency to be react too quickly, so I tried to remember to ask permission when dealing with Mum, "What can I do?" or "Would you like some help with that?" before jumping in and assuming I knew what she wanted done. Other times, when I was too fast to respond during a conversation, she reminded me that I need "to wait a minute, slow down". And further, if she had really tolerated my lack of patience long enough and had become miffed, she let me know, such as she did one day saying, "If you are going to keep this up, we might as well go home.")*

☑ **Change our instant reactions** – We can't allow our buttons to be pushed by our parent's behaviour as it may be out of his/her control now to some extent due to the effects of the condition. *(For example: When Dad was angry, it was a judgement call as to how to respond – was it dementia-related frustration causing the angry behaviour or was he being controlling.)*

At all times, we have to look past what seem to be manipulative remarks and zero in on what the real request may be.*(For example: When at home or in the caremanor, the minute Dad saw me, he would say loudly in an annoyed manner, "Where have you been, you're late!" Because Dad lived by schedules and 'watched the clock', I would try hard not to be late at any time (and would telephone a message to give to Dad if delayed unexpectedly). At first when he behaved in this manner, I would venture an explanation if a logical reason ("the plane was delayed"). If I wasn't late, I used to respond with a statement of fact, "Dad, I'm not late, I said I'd be here at eleven-thirty and it is now eleven-thirty". One day, I responded, "Dad, if you are going to keep yelling at me, I'm going to have to leave" but logic and threats didn't work. Sometimes, no matter what, we were left starting our valued time together poorly – Dad was upset and I was left feeling guilty ("I need to be here more often"). Yet at the same time I also resented being greeted in this very harsh tone (silently thinking, "I'm trying my best"). My solution – I had to change how I responded to Dad's manner when he saw me, as he wasn't able to alter his behaviour. I had to focus on the causes of this behaviour and adjust my reaction. I taught myself to overlook the regular opening comment, to overlook the tone of voice. I kept reminding myself that Dad was really looking forward to seeing me, and it was his high levels of anxiety that were causing him to behave in this manner. Thus, my response to the explosive, "Where have you been, you're late?" became, "Okay Dad, but who cares, give me a hug and let's get our day started" – it is hard to be angry with anyone who is giving a hug and not reacting. Most times all went well then.)*

☑ **Open dialogue with our family** – At all times, we need to broach the topic of dementia carefully with our other parent and family members in order to give them opportunities to express their feelings concerning the problems and the responsibilities they are experiencing. We mustn't interrupt conversations during these times, we need to listen and demonstrate our support. *(For example, Mum used to say, of Dad's dementia-related behaviours, "I just can't figure out what is wrong, why he is angry." In the same manner, she did not want to acknowledge that her brother, suffered from dementia too and often said, "Oh it's his medication today causing his memory problems." Sometimes Mum decided to discuss dementia and other times not.)*

☑ **Keep a balanced attitude** – By focussing on the positive parts of the day spent with our parent, we can somewhat diminish the negative impacts of the dementia (if not too severe) on our own morale.

Notes:

An Internet Story, received April 9, 2001 – **"The Wooden Bowl"** – A frail old man went to live with his son, daughter-in-law and four-year old grandson. The old man's hands trembled, his eyesight was blurred, and his step faltered. The family ate together at the table. But the elderly grandfather's shaky hands and failing sight made eating difficult. Peas rolled off his spoon onto the floor. When he grasped the glass, milk spilled on the tablecloth. The son and daughter-in-law became irritated with the mess. "We must do something about Grandfather," said the son. "I've had enough of his spilled milk, noisy eating, and food on the floor." So the husband and wife set a small table in the corner. There, Grandfather ate alone while the rest of the family enjoyed dinner. Since Grandfather had broken a dish or two, his food was served in a wooden bowl. When the family glanced in Grandfather's direction, sometimes he had a tear in his eye as he sat alone. Still, the only words the couple had for him were sharp admonitions when he dropped a fork or spilled food. The four-year-old watched it all in silence. One evening before supper, the father noticed his son playing with wood scraps on the floor. He asked the child sweetly, "What are you making?" Just as sweetly, the boy responded, "Oh, I am making a little bowl for you and Mama to eat your food when I grow up." The four-year-old smiled and went back to work. The words so struck the parents that they were speechless. Then tears started to stream down their cheeks. Though no word was spoken, both knew what must be done. That evening the husband took Grandfather's hand and gently led him back to the family table. For the remainder of his days he ate every meal with the family. And for some reason, neither husband nor wife seemed to care any longer when a fork was dropped, milk spilled, or the tablecloth soiled. Children are remarkably perceptive. Their eyes ever observe, their ears ever listen, and their minds ever process the messages they absorb. If they see us patiently provide a happy home atmosphere for family members, they will imitate that attitude for the rest of their lives. The wise parent realizes that every day the building blocks are being laid for the child's future. Let's be wise builders and role models. Lord, we ask not that you move the mountains, but that You give us the strength to climb. (continued...)

Life is about people connecting with people, and making a positive difference. Take care of yourself and those you love, today and everyday! On a positive note, I've learned that, no matter what happens how bad it seems today, life does go on, and it will be better tomorrow. I've learned that you can tell a lot about a person by the way he/she handles three things: a rainy day, lost luggage and tangled Christmas tree lights. I've learned that, regardless of your relationship with your parents, you'll miss them when they're gone from your life. I've learned that making a living is not the same thing as making a life. I've learned that life sometimes gives you a second chance. I've learned that you shouldn't go through life with a catcher's mitt on both hands. You need to be able to throw something back. I've learned that if you pursue happiness, it will elude you. But, if you focus on your family, your friends, the needs of others, your work and doing the very best you can, happiness will find you. I've learned that whenever I decide something with an open heart, I usually make the right decision. I've learned that even when I have pains, I don't have to be one. I've learned that every day, you should reach out and touch someone. People love that human touch – holding hands, a warm hug, or just a friendly pat. I've learned that I still have a lot to learn. I've learned that you should pass this on to everyone you care about. I just did. Sometimes they just need a little something to make them smile. People will forget what you said. People will forget what you did. But, people will never forget how you made them feel.

Notes:

> "When people talk, listen completely. Most people never listen."
> – *Ernest Hemingway 1899-1961*

Suggestion 9: *Investigate potential assistance programs and their criteria*

Note: It is important 'while our parent is in the hospital' to find out about and organize any government care service programs available so such are in place right at the hospital release date or as soon thereafter as possible.

For information on the government assistance programs and services in your province or territory, go to <u>www.longtermcarecanada.com</u> and click on the menu item titled "Provincial Government Programs/ Territorial Government Programs" Those pages list all the provinces'/ territories' government care programs and services and contacts—just click on the appropriate province.

What do I need to know about assistance programs?

When it comes to applying to any programs offering financial and services assistance to help with care of our parents, we'd be on the right track to remind ourselves of one ol' piece of advice, 'timing is everything'.

If we are unfamiliar with community assistance programs (financial and service-types) and our parent is already in the hospital, we need to take the following steps:

☑ Find out if the hospital has a health unit nurse or social worker assigned to work with seniors and their families – if so, arrange an appointment (the hospital can help organize this meeting or at least direct us to the right source).

☑ Telephone the region's health unit/community care access center/health authority (or social services access agency) – to gather the information regarding care-related government programs for the elderly (also the 'disabled').

☑ Arrange for an appointment to meet with the community health co-ordinator/worker responsible for care programs within our parents' city/region.

☑ Ask the worker to list and explain briefly the possible programs available and what each offers, especially those specific to the present-day circumstances, but check all that may apply (e.g. elderly/disabled/veteran), for future use.

☑ Become familiar with the main criteria (bare basics) for each of the programs (who gets help, under what conditions and for how long).

We can also use hospital staff to extend our learning – the hospital social worker, the rehabilitation nurse, the social services agency representative, case workers, the family doctor, the extended care nurses, community care support groups are well informed and have worked with many cases like ours. Some hospitals employ persons for this very task of assisting families in applying for and organizing care assistance programs.

What do I need to find out?

☑ **We need to find out about the various government care programs offered in our parents' area. Ask what is available for seniors, for the disabled, for veterans…**

It is worth repeating that we must be aware of which programs we should apply for – in readiness for the future.

The key is to ask questions before a parent is to be released:

- What is available?

- Offered by whom?

- What are the criteria?

- How does our family access each program?

- How can I get the needed services in place immediately for my parents?

Or more specifically, we can ask:

- Is there any way I can get help with my parent's daily care and/or daily household chores?

- Are there groups in the community who can steer me in the right direction?

- What does this hospital offer by way of weekly programs?

- What if my parent cannot come home due to poor health, what programs should I know about immediately?

It is wise to review each program's criteria each time the conditions of one of our parents' health changes, we need to refresh our memories.

(For example, Mum missed receiving increased hours of homecare assistance simply because I did not realize that I had to contact the health unit to review Mum's level of need. Remember, it is not the responsibility of the agency to take the initiative and contact us for a review, it is our responsibility to be on top of these types of matters.)

☑ **We need to find out the importance of the 'timing' of our application for assistance. (Note: Timing of an application may be a factor even though most programs are based on 'need'.)**

We must be aware that timing, that is, the 'exact date' that our request is 'received and recorded,' may be a factor regarding when our parents become eligible to begin receiving benefits from some care assistance programs.

(For example, some programs use a hospital admission date as a pivotal application point – thus, we need to be on the ball right when a turning-point event takes place; some programs may have waiting lists as so many persons apply, so the sooner a name is placed on the list for a program, the better the chances of receiving the benefits prior to another major health crisis.)

☑ **We need to find out information about our parents' financial affairs.**

As income (i.e. a means test) is a very important element considered by some types of government assistance care programs, at the time of application, we need to have an understanding of our parents' financial situation – a copy of their last year's tax return statements is often sufficient.

I doubt my parents' generation will accept anything less than the best for the management of their heart disease, diabetes, cancers and chronic illnesses. Yet my boomer generation, by sheer numbers alone, will challenge the sustainability of medicare as we age into our costliest health consuming years. (Source: Article, May 10, 2000, The Vancouver Sun: by Dr. Heidi Oetter, practicing family physician in Coquitlam B.C. and Chair of the BC Medical Association General Assembly.)

What kind of programs should I ask about?

Many levels of government print directories, brochures and booklets outlining the names of care programs region-by-region or service-by-service.

One telephone call to the 'Government Department Responsible for Seniors' (i.e. relevant provincial ministry) could save a great deal of time as staff there will be familiar with the information directories and pamphlets in print or go to the internet website. Many doctors' offices have copies of directories also. All health units will have display racks of information – visit and start there.

We should ask about the following assistance programs offered in most, if not all, communities:

- Home-care service programs

- Hospital-extension service programs

- Respite programs

- Volunteer programs

- Carehome residency programs

- Special programs to help people to remain living in their own homes (e.g. CSIL, Community Support for Independent Living/ Choices)

What do home-care service programs include?

We need to have a basic understanding of assistance programs for our parents who are still living in their own home but are in need of some help for certain activities.

Home-care service programs, whether provided by a government program or through a privately hired company, may include help with these types of needs:

- Housecleaning

- Bathing

- Meals preparation

- Medications

- Special therapies

- Transportation

- Grocery shopping…

Questions:

- Can I arrange for some help with chores at home for my parents?

- What kind of help is available for each of my parents? Are these services paid for, if not, can I cost-share? What are the costs per month?

- What do they qualify for now?

- What has to change to increase the level of services (e.g. a parent's health, income level)?

- Are the workers well-trained? Supervised? How?

What are hospital extension programs?

We need to ask about the types of hospital extension programs readily available in our community, as most hospitals offer a variety of different services to assist the elderly.

These types of services include:

- Weekly baths at hospital facilities (with proper equipment) for those who can't manage at home

- Counselling services

- Rehabilitation and therapy programs (swimming and exercise)

- Support group meetings

- Adult day-care programs once/twice per week

Questions:

- What services are available through our local hospital for use by our parents who are still living at home?

- Where are the hospital programs offered?

- How often?

- What different types are there?

- How do I arrange for each of the hospital services to be put in place for one/both of my parents?

Should I be considering respite assistance programs?

Respite programs are worth researching as soon as possible if we find that we now have a parent requiring full-time care at home. It goes without saying that we need to visit the region's care manors and select the best respite facility/carehome to meet our family's needs.

- ☑ We need to contact the community agency/health unit responsible for coordinating respite time within the local caremanors in the area and discuss selection criteria for the program.

- ☑ We should ask the health unit's program managers/directors if they know of any sponsoring organizations that may assist with some respite care or if they are aware of other means by which our parent may be able to receive help (e.g. what is available for veterans? for disabled? for First Nations?).

- ☑ We need to ask questions specifically regarding financial assistance available to families needing respite time.

- ☑ If our parent qualifies for financial assistance his/her name will be placed on a 'respite list' in order to receive X number of days of respite care per year – ask how the lists work.

- ☑ As there may be a respite care list for each facility in the area, we should be prepared to state our two facility choices to the agency responsible for the respite scheduling – our parent's name is then specifically placed on those care manor lists only; the agency handles the details.

- ☑ If financial assistance is not forthcoming from a community/ government program, even on a cost-share basis, then we need to contact the care manors in the city directly and ask about their available respite spaces, the schedules, the costs, the advanced booking, the services. (We also need to ask probing questions of caremanors so as not to overlook possibilities for special financial aid programs with which they may be familiar.)

Without any financial assistance, we must make a decision as to how badly a 'break' is needed by the caregivers – respite care is extremely valuable especially if one parent is caring for another/a spouse caring for a partner.

We should keep in mind that respite is meant to benefit the caregiver but can also greatly help the care-receiver if a helpful therapy program is offered in the respite facility selected.

If we are considering respite, we should know that:

- ☑ There are a limited number of rooms set aside for respite care in each care facility and that the demand is high, therefore, respite-weeks are reserved quickly for the year.

- ☑ Requests for the desired weeks have to be booked well in advance, preferably at the beginning of each year (unless the time desired is for the January to March months, as these early year months are reserved in the prior year).

☑ It is best to reserve a space and organize around that specific date, as we can always say when the time is close, "No, we don't want the space right now" – we needn't feel badly if we change our minds as there are families always waiting to fill vacancies.

☑ Respite rooms are extremely difficult to get even when a crisis hits. *(For example, Dad was in respite with two days left of his week when our live-in caregiver had a major health problem, yet I could not extend his stay for even one day in order to allow me time to get things organized, the respite bed-space was completely reserved.)*

Should I try to access volunteer programs?

We need to telephone various local organizations in the city that work with seniors and ask about their services – for the lonely, for shut-ins, for volunteer companions, meals…

We can ask at our local health unit/hospital geriatric ward if there is a directory or list or brochure of the volunteer organizations with interests in seniors. If all else fails, we can go to the yellow pages of the telephone book and begin telephoning agencies listed under 'seniors' – soon someone will be able to give the answers or directions we are seeking (e.g. I used this method when our care-years journey started – it worked.)

Once we have a list of possible volunteer services, we need to telephone the relevant organizations to discuss their special services and criteria and arrange for an initial screening (we are screening them and they are screening us). If our telephone conversation confirms an organization could be of help to us, then we can arrange to meet with a representative volunteer. *(For example: It was felt that Dad, because he was shut-in after a very social lifestyle, may enjoy a male friend for companionship; one organization was found offering scheduled visitors for seniors and a representative volunteer visited my parents' home. It turns out that Dad did not meet the specific criteria for a companion because he already had people with him on a daily basis even though none were male – Dad was not eligible for the service.)*

What should I know about carehome financial assistance programs?

(Note: Cross-reference to Topic 8: Organizing nursing home living.)

As a responsible, loving daughter/son, we need to be realistic regarding both the advantages and the downsides of carehome living (short-term living, longer-term special placement, permanent living). Our thinking may also change once we become the actual care-guide and/or key caregiver of our parents as we will then understand what is involved in balancing all the health complexities with the quality of care required for our parent – in the best possible manner.

Finding a nursing care center that provides a loving and stimulating atmosphere and also offers a fully trained staff that can handle a senior's specific medical needs can be an overwhelming task. *(Source: USA Today, Article – FYI: Senior Care, November 1996.)*

Perhaps we should review our personal attitude regarding carehome residency living as the question is such an emotionally charged one:

☑ What are my feelings right now about having a parent reside in a care manor? What is my attitude based on?

☑ Am I being open-minded on this topic? Have I ever looked into the facts?

☑ Am I really sure that I will never have a need to use a caremanor for one of my parents?

☑ Have I visited a manor recently or talked to other families with a parent living in a manor; have I talked to any caremanor residents?

☑ Have I read anything about caremanors, what do I really know about this type of residency living?

☑ What types of caremanors are there in the area and what does each offer? What are the options?

☑ Do I understand the health needs of my parents? Where can these needs be met?

☑ Have I ever discussed the topic with anyone in the family?

☑ Have I discussed the topic with my parents in the past?

☑ What is best for each of my parents?

We need to have a basic awareness of how publicly funded carehome residency financial assistance programs are designed:

- Who is eligible to receive such financial assistance?

- What are the criteria of the programs?

- Do we need to belong to a specific group?

- Do we qualify at present? When in the future?

Every six months, we need to review the criteria in relation to our parent's new needs and in relation to the program's criteria.

We should be aware of three factors when seeking financial assistance for caremanor living:

☑ **Factor #1 – Supply is limited and the demand is big.**

Each caremanor (within its mandate) applies for and is allocated a specified number of bed-spaces/rooms for government assistance funding use (a government formula is used: X% of the total rooms based on the need of the region).

In some cases, there are not enough designated rooms in caremanors to accommodate the assistance demand; if this occurs, we shouldn't be talked into placing our parent in a caremanor we have not selected just because it has space available – sometimes it is better to wait a bit longer for our choice of carehomes to become available – of course, family circumstances dictate the decisions we have to make at any given time.

☑ Factor #2 – Lengthy wait lists and queues may exist.

The wait-lists of families eligible to receive government financial assistance with carehome living costs are very long in some regions, thus, line-ups or queues exist for residency spaces in many caremanors. *(For example: In my parents' home city, a major retirement community in Canada, there existed a 'wait-list' to obtain residency in most quality nursing homes.)*

We all know that the concept of 'wait lists' is a touchy and controversial topic. (It is not important whether the term is acceptable or not when discussing the care of our parents.) What is important though is how we access the type of assistance and how long it will take to receive such—these are the questions we must ask. We then can ask about interim programs and services should we have to wait.

☑ Factor #3 – Sign-up dates are important.

A sign-up/on date, that is the precise date our parents have their names registered (recorded) for assistance by the responsible health unit department, is very important.

As previously emphasized, we should ask questions about 'care home/ nursing home financial assistance subsidization programs' the first time our parent enters a hospital during a health crisis because that hospital entry date could be used as the registration sign-up date to gain residential financial assistance – if our parent qualifies for financial assistance. (Check in your province as all have such.)

The key is to make the request while our parent is still in the hospital as backdating is usually not allowed after checkout.

(For example: When Dad fell we were not contemplating care manor residency for him and we certainly didn't realize the importance of taking precautionary measures regarding future carehome living, nor did we realize the costs of such a residency if absolutely needed – one might say that we just weren't looking down the road. We didn't even know then that government subsidized programs existed, so the importance of sign-up dates was not an issue. We did what I

suspect most families do, we tried to cope on our own. It was one year after Dad's fall, with our family in crisis, that I started looking for answers, seeking help. I soon was made aware of the link between government assisted carehome living and actual sign-up dates. Much to our dismay, I discovered, that we could have taken a significant step in the process one year earlier, precisely when Dad broke his hip and was in the hospital getting treatment. We realized then that we had lost one full year in the queue, that we could have been registered from the start of our caregiving journey. This lack of knowledge proved very costly indeed for our family. Since those days, programs have changed somewhat as now 'wait' is related to 'need' not 'timing'. Check your area's rules.)

It is important to note that just because we have applied for, been accepted and have been placed on a list for our parent to receive government assistance for permanent residency in a specific home, we don't need to accept that space when it comes available – we can say, "No thank you, not now" and our parents' name may still remain on the list, it may not get bumped, as the 'need' remains. (Check always – ask the nurse care coordinator of LTC for your area's health unit.)

(For example, Mum's sign-up date was mid-2000 for residency in the local long-term hospital extended care home. Much to our surprise, Mum was offered a room twice since then; we declined the offers as then she was still doing well at home. We found that a little extra consideration may be given to a candidate if there already is a relative living in that residence. Mum knew that her name was on that home's list as a precautionary measure – for the unpredictable future – and she was comfortable with that understanding.)

It is also important to view 'nursing home living' from the 'care-receiver's perspective'. *(For example in year #8, Mum was in her early 90s, she used a walker around the house, a wheelchair when out, she had a stair lift from the main level of the house to the door level; she had all the bathroom equipment and bedroom equipment and safety-bars possible; she had a chair lift recliner to assist her in standing; the house had been adapted for her use; she had a 24/7 caregivers…keeping all this in mind then, here was my mother's 'perspective'. Mum and I were having lunch at I-HOP and as we chatted she asked the following, "Do you think I will need to go into a nursing home when I get really old and need help?" Needless to say, I remained speechless for a few seconds and then thought to myself – success, Mum feels independent.)*

Notes:

_____

_____

_____

_____

_____

_____

_____

_____

_____

_____

_____

_____

_____

_____

_____

_____

_____

_____

_____

_____

_____

_____

_____

"If you have an important point to make, don't try to be subtle or clever. Use a pile driver. Hit the point once. Then come back and hit it again. Then hit it a third time – a tremendous whack."
– Sir Winston Churchill, 1874-1965

"He who asks is a fool for five minutes, but he who does not ask remains a fool forever."
– Chinese Proverb

TOPIC 2

Let's Talk: Accepting this time in our lives and growing into our new caregiver role

How do I transform myself into a caregiver?

Personal Anecdote: "It ain't easy."

Suggestions:

10: Gain new insights – stop, look, listen

11: Shift responsibilities

12: Watch for 'signals'

13: Be realistic, be organized

14: Emphasize the value of emergency services

15: Obtain neighbours' cooperation regarding emergency services

16: Keep in touch

17: Take action ASAP

18: Become an advocate

How do I begin to accept this care-years time in our lives and how do I transform myself into a caregiver?

Personal Anecdote:
"It ain't easy."

Until the morning of January 4, 1996, my parents, both in their mid-eighties, were ordinary, independent senior citizens living in a quiet suburban section of a mid-sized retirement town, each driving a car of their own, going grocery shopping, browsing at the mall, watching television in the evenings, discussing the local news and gossip, fretting over the hot weather in summer and the cold weather in winter, sitting on the deck during a pleasant evening, visiting long distance with relatives, bussing to visit me for vacations, doing home and yard chores, agreeing and disagreeing on various issues, chatting over the fence to neighbours, enjoying occasional dinners out...Until that moment, I had worried about my parents' 'health' but I hadn't given my parents' actual 'care', as they got older, a huge amount of attention - did I assume the status quo with my parents' everyday retirement lives was going to continue indefinitely.

Then, that January winter morning, that unexpected turning-point health crisis happened within our family - Dad's life, Mum's life, my life, all changed the instant Dad slipped on the icy driveway of his home. During the next year, he spent days and weeks in and out of the hospital, beginning with emergency hip surgery, then geriatric assessments, rehabilitation, medication problems, dementia and other health-related problems.

Around this same time, significant changes were also occurring with Mum - they were not signaled loudly by one major physical accident like with my Dad, but by small and frequent physical, mental and emotional instances. Mum's health changes were subtle, more difficult to detect and relate to, but as of that January moment when she, at 85, became a caregiver (with others) for her husband, aged 84, her health problems become more pronounced and eventually evolved into major concerns.

Looking back now, it seems that within one 24-hour period, my parents went from being independent senior citizens to dependent elderly parents requiring full-time care - this realization was not fully grasped by any of us right away. The first six months after Dad's fall were hectic ones; as we searched for solutions, that is, ways to handle the health problems created by the fall. Like individual pieces of a puzzle, I focused almost exclusively on each of Dad's immediate physical needs and his growing demands - our family wasn't aware of the bigger care-picture, yet. So, our journey had begun, but I had not started to think of myself as a caregiver - I was still operating in the attentive daughter role.

In hindsight, I see that what I sought during those first months were quick-fixes to my parents' everyday living problems. I was in the dark, so to speak, new to the complex world of caregiving and thus remained oblivious as to the pending problems involved in the care of my two elderly parents. Their health was changing, their needs were changing, their patterns were changing, yet as a daughter, I was working hard so our lives could get 'back to normal' - was I not listening, was I not seeing, was I ignoring the signs of change. No, I just didn't know what I was looking at, as I had not experienced 'care-years' up-close and personal before now.

Sometime after the first six months, I started to realize that 'getting back to normal' was not possible; the phrase itself was even misleading for Dad, Mum and especially me as our family situation could never be the same as it was prior to that January morn. I stopped using the term 'get-well' because illness was not the real issue. Slowly and clumsily, I began to revise my thinking addressing what a 'new normal' lifestyle for our family was going to mean, while adjusting to the role I was to assume from now on. For Dad, personality, behaviour, age-related physical problems and medications now were interconnected, thereby creating questions and concerns about everyday living. By mid-year, a vicious circle of problem-solution, problem-solution, described our week-byweek circumstances perfectly.

In desperation, I sought a "settling down" period for our family, a period when some new circumstance wasn't again going to catch us off-guard creating chaos and more changes. As the summer months passed, I continued to seek more ways to put in place satisfactory home care routines for Dad. But success wasn't to be achieved as my focus was too narrow and I had yet to acknowledge all the changes also developing with my other parent.

During the first care-year, the journey was extremely rough! We had organized a good caregiving environment but we were making no progress (one step forward, one step sideways). It seemed that we had not yet settled into any sort of regular lifestyle. Each day felt like a struggle for everyone, trying to understand each of the physical and mental and emotional changes rapidly occurring within our family unit and there were many. Each week, a new crack seemed to appear offering a small peek at another potentially explosive care problem or monthly financial concern. It truly was only a matter of time before the question of what constituted the best care for each of my parents, that is, the big caregiving picture, was going to have to be addressed head-on.

As the year drew to a close, I also found myself struggling to solve the caregiving duties and problems being heaped upon my burdened mother, little molehills growing rapidly into big mountains. There seemed to be such a range of daily tasks for her to deal with, (even though we had both government and our own caregivers) all the way from the paying the bills to coping with cancelled schedules of community caregivers. Finally as winter of our first care-year approached, I came to the startling realization that by now, Mum's physical and emotional frailties were more precarious than Dad's health conditions. Her health problems had become significant and required a great deal of immediate attention and care too.

During those beginning care-years, I found myself learning a new language relating to caregiving issues. I uncovered a maze of health care systems to which I had previously not been exposed. I gathered new information about medications and their real and potential effects. I was forced to review important documents as well as minutiae which impacted our lives, from bank accounts, legal documents, respite programs, pension programs and extended health benefits, care facilities, live-in help, to meal planning. I learned to pay attention to stressful problems as soon as they arose, not to procrastinate - questionable situations did not diminish over time, they magnified. I had to locate and communicate regularly with busy strangers who had a say in the happiness and care of my parents. I had to learn to balance my time, energies and several other aspects of my personal life. I had to learn to listen in a new manner to my parents and to respect their decisions (even if I didn't agree). I had to concentrate on remaining somewhat positive, even when tired, worried or frustrated.

As I look back, I know that our family's care-years journey started long before that January day when Dad fell, but until that precise physical accident, I guess I was in ostrich-mode, unaware of the signals indicating major health changes were occurring with my elderly parents and unaware that I should be planning for their up-coming, intensive long-term care years. I have had to learn to accept that mistake. I have since addressed a range of caregiving matters, and yes, I have also taken care of heart-wrenching funeral affairs. As one might expect, I also found that many of our care-related problems could have been lessened or dealt with sooner with good planning - but there are no practise runs for handling the care-years and no education programs to prepare us.

Not only did both of my parents' lifestyles change significantly during the first years of our journey, but also our roles and responsibilities blurred and adapted when necessary. Mum and Dad and I became a different type of family unit from what we were prior to 1996 - they had moved into their care-receiving years and I, in turn, fell into my parent caregivingyears. Dad died unexpectedly at the end of 1998 and then Mum and I went through more care changes. My transformation was complete - I categorized and started describing myself as a daughter - caregiver.

During the first six years of the journey, I came to understand that every week could present a care-related challenge, some small and easily handled, others complex and threatening, but all time consuming. I learned to appreciate each telephone chat, each shared meal and every car ride together. I was aware of times of laughter and enjoyed hearing the tidbits of news about what was happening in the day. Mum and I chatted as we always had during pre-care years.

I try to remember my parents as they were over many decades rather than only how they were during the last few years when they required constant care. On Father's and Mother's Day, on the anniversary day of each of their passings, and on their birthdays, I put aside quiet time. Like in every home, there are photos of my parents in prominent spots, so each day, I am reminded of shared times.

Why did our family's journey become a little less turbulent over the course of many care-years - I think because I finally understood the on-going, comprehensive nature of my new responsibility. I changed from being a beginner-caregiver to being a productive one when I understood and accepted that what I learned yesterday and just got nicely into place today for my parents may not be suitable in addressing tomorrow's health problems and resulting care needs.

I have come to realize that there is one stage all of us with elderly parents are probably going to go through - that is becoming a good daughter/son-caregiver during care-years. And that transition, I might add, "ain't easy".

Being a caregiver brought me closer to my parents; but thinking as a caregiver taught me much about myself. Even though I refer to those care-years as my 'tsunami-years', I also think of them a 'gift'-an oxymoron you say - perhaps, but none-the-less, I feel that I have been fortunate to have had my parents as part of my life for a long while.

Every seven seconds another Boomer hits 50. This will continue for the next 20 years. And their life expectancy extends so rapidly that for those alive now, every four years survived from today adds another year to their probable life span. This means the population of Canadians aged 65 and older will grow by 168 per cent to around 8 million people between now and 2036. And Canada's over-90 population is predicted to explode by an astonishing 500 per cent, to almost 500,000 people. (Source: The Vancouver Sun, Article - The Silent Crisis, May 10, 1997.)

"How far you go in life depends on you being tender with the young, compassionate with the aged, sympathetic with the striving, and tolerant of the weak and strong, because someday in life you will have been all of these."
– *George Washington Carver*

 **Suggestion 10:** *Gain new insights – stop, look, listen*

Do I have to change the way I think of myself?

In a word, yes – to be a good caregiver requires thinking like a caregiver would think.

If we want to meet the needs of our elderly parents during their care-years, we need to revise our image accordingly – from daughters/sons only (single focus) to daughter/son-caregivers (dual focus).

Think about it: Eldercare, a silent, yet-to-be realized problem is becoming one of the most pressing issues facing Canadian companies today

Annual costs of 'working caregiver's to our companies–$16 billion a year.

Data from a study by human resources firm Watson Wyatt Worldwide (2003) estimated the annual costs to Canadian companies are $16 billion a year (Globe and Mail article, March 17, 2004)

How do I begin doing that?

To start, we can face our family's care-years future (rather than letting events sneak up on us crisis by crisis) by going back to the basics – stopping, looking and listening to our existing surroundings.

How can we gain new insights about ourselves in this role:

☑ **Be honest** – we can question, am I already taking care of my parents in some way? (Maybe we are caregivers to some extent already and haven't yet thought of ourselves in that form.)

☑ **Take a closer look at what is going on around us** – we can look at everyday things a little differently (through a new pair of glasses, so to speak), such as families with grandparents at restaurants, wheelchair ramps into stores, icy sidewalk dangers, special foods sold, the number of seniors in various locations…

☑ **Add caregiving to our 'active vocabulary'** – we can look at caregiving in action, by becoming more aware of how our society views aging, how our community's programs, our health care system, our government departments, our media…view aging.

☑ **Browse through news articles** that we may have previously skipped – we can read the information with a new perspective – articles on geriatrics in general, hospital care, senior activities, volunteer activities, insurance policies, equipment/aids, estate planning and preservation…

☑ **Initiate discussions with others** whom we know have parents who are about the same age as our parents or whose parents are ill or in carehomes – we can ask these daughters/sons what they have found out, how they cope and balance their responsibilities, what is changing in their lives, what causes their parents joy…we can listen.

These aforementioned 'caregiving familiarization' initiatives are not arduous and can advance our thinking. To begin our change, we have 'to see' the care-years in action all around us and recognize ourselves in our new role, as caregivers.

Forever-young boomers have seen the future – and to them it's 60⁺ year-old Tina Turner, not Whistler's Mother. Boomers are going to go screaming into the night, as they say," said Gloria Gutman, a gerontologist at Simon Fraser University and the incoming president of the International Association of Gerontology. "These days gerontologists talk about anybody who dies before age 75 as being a premature death." Interest in gerontology is growing in Canada, said Gutman, because the leading edge of baby boomers will hit age 65 in 10 years. Currently, about 12 per cent of Canadians are 65 or over. In 30 years, almost one in four Canadians will be 65 or over. "Boomers don't see themselves as aging," Gutman said."The boomers want to look more like Tina Turner, whose husband made the best remark about somebody (60), which was that she's (Tina's) turning 30 for the second time." "Now as boomers are approaching old age, there is the need to think about programs and policies that will make life good for them. They will be demanding more services." Societies are aging not just in developed countries, but around the world. People are living longer and fertility rates are dropping on a global scale. Societies should regard their aging population as a sign of social progress – not as a dilemma, Gutman said. "It's only a problem if you think it's a problem. In fact, we should look at it as a great accomplishment. It's a marker, the indicator of success, that so many people have overcome diseases that used to kill them in middle age to live to be old." *(Source: The Vancouver Sun, July 3, 2001, Article - What Kind Of Rocker Do You Want To Be at 61 - Tina Turner or Whistler's Mother?)*

What is my current attitude about 'caregiving' – positive,negative, neutral, never thought about it, it concerns others not me...?

If we have been catapulted into the care-years, it is important that we assess our attitude around this caregiving issue for two reasons:

1. With the correct perspective, we stand a better chance of responding well in our new role – right from the get-go.

2. With the proper understanding, we can set our sights on achieving a smoother caregiving experience for our family rather than a bumpy, disjointed experience, fire-fighting each problem as it erupts.

We need to ask:

☑ Am I aware that my parents are growing more dependent upon each other and others in the community?

☑ Am I aware that I may have to begin getting involved in certain aspects of their lives now?

☑ Am I aware that my parents may no longer be fully independent senior citizens capable of taking care of all aspects of their own lives as they once did so capably, and that I should be listening carefully when they start to talk about their needs and wishes?

☑ Am I aware that my parents have mixed feelings about growing older? "These golden years aren't always so golden" (as my mother and aunt often said) as they have some heavy, unwanted baggage (fatigue, loss of driving privileges, dull teeth, hearing impairments, brittle bones, more pills, loss of appetite, less friends, strangers appearing to help...).

☑ Am I aware that one of my main commitments is going to be to help my parents maintain their dignity and independence in the years to come (both are extremely important to our parents' everyday happiness)?

Often our descriptions reflect our present-day attitude, check:

How do I describe my parents right now when asked – as I viewed them several years ago or as they are currently; what do they need help doing; what routines are good/worrisome/in place for them.

How do I describe myself when asked now – as, a parent, a wife, a husband, a partner, a professional with certain expertise, in terms of where I work, a community volunteer, a combination of these...?

The real question is, do we describe our parents or ourselves in any terms that hint of caregiving.

Over time, we can listen for our progress – in the future, we may hear ourselves say, "I am a working woman and I'm also the main caregiver of my parents" or "I'm a husband and parent with responsibilities for two growing school-aged children and an elderly parent" (i.e. part of the "clubhouse sandwich generation").

Employees with benefit plans, that is 71% of our Canadian workforce, identified that 32% or 1/3 are already responsible for eldercare and 17% (1 in 6) have indicated 'they will have to take more time off in the next two years for care duties'. (Data from a study by Aventis, 2002)

Can I predict how I might respond to my new responsibility?

We can go through the following questions in order to gain a better understanding about how we might respond to our new and pending caregiving responsibilities – our responses may even alert us if we need to make some changes:

☑ **Do I use my time well?** How can I get better at it? Where will I find any extra time? How will I fit more things in?

We have to accept the enormous amounts of real time required when we assume some of the responsibilities for our parents' care (time away from work; time away from our partner, children; time away from our own home; shorter vacations…).

☑ **Do I know how to be proactive?** Do I know how to go about linking my parents' needs to the services available in the community?

We have to learn how our parents' region assists seniors with specific care needs; how we can establish communication channels and work out a health network for our family; how we can accomplish tasks in cooperation with doctors, live-in caregivers, neighbours, care homes, pharmacists, social workers, lawyers…

We also have to remind ourselves that we are the only ones really responsible for solving problems and concerns on behalf of our own parents, so at times, we must take action to get action (be an advocate for our own parents).

☑ **Am I generally a patient person?** Do I jump to conclusions too quickly or do I react too slowly, waiting for solutions to happen on their own? Is it my way or the highway? Am I too bossy, too passive? Do I listen to others?

Do I know to be calm, that patience is needed (not to interfere on every decision; to get the required information before taking an action; not to make assumptions without the details from each party…)?

☑ **How do I handle conflicting emotions?**

We have to be prepared for the conflicting feelings we are going to have from time to time. (Why did I feel at wits end when my Dad was asking the same question over and over even though I knew he couldn't help it; why do I feel guilty when I am convinced this is the best action; why do I jump to conclusions and not hear what Mum is really trying to tell me; why do I get upset when I think my parents aren't appreciating my efforts…).

☑ **Do I know how to gather new information?** Quickly? Efficiently? Do I know what steps to take or do I rely on other people too often and for too long? Do I know how to seek help?

Having the facts makes tasks easier to do properly – what is it that I want to know right now? Do I need to find it out immediately? As time goes on? Where can I get help? Whom do I ask questions of? What new information should I research? What questions need to be asked (regarding equipment, medications, government assistance programs, insurance plans, income taxes, costs associated with…)?

☑ **Do I value preparation and planning?** What is my style? Do I procrastinate, put things off until later, bury my head and hope everything works out?

As caregivers, we always need back-up plans – for some people, in-depth planning is second nature, others have to force themselves to do any level of planning.

Once we have come to understand the importance of having well thought-out contingency plans, we will be more capable of handling various challenges – when, not if, they occur unexpectedly.

☑ **Am I a detail person?** Why is detail important in this role?

Since so much of caregiving involves the smaller aspects of everyday living, we have to devise ways to attend to those details during care-years (appointments, prescriptions, bills...). If one is not a detail person, then a method for managing details should be devised.

☑ **How do I react in times of crises?**

We can think of a few scenarios and ask ourselves how we would react if one or all were to occur (i.e. envision it and get a feel for own responses). We may often worry about certain problems regarding our parents but rarely do we follow through with thinking about how we would handle each of these problems. We have to be fully aware that crises of all degrees (from disagreements with caregivers to accidents requiring ambulances) will occur.

Caregiving is a career we never planned for ourselves:

Six in ten (62%) of the caregivers have already been providing such care to their family member for at least three years and one in five (20%) have been doing so for more than 10 years. (*Source: National Profile of National Profile of Family Caregivers in Canada - 2002: Final Report, Statistics Canada, Health Canada*)

What else can I do to grow in my caregiver role?

We can continue our self-imposed training regime by:

☑ **Consciously reminding ourselves, when we are feeling alone and harried, to look for the positives.** There will be times when we will have to remind ourselves of our good fortune (don't take it for granted) to still have our parents to laugh with, learn with, cry with, go to lunch with, enjoy a festive time with, give a hug to, sit quietly with, watch a TV show with…and love.

☑ **Listening to our parents' conversations with each other** about household habits; noting any chores/tasks undertaken by others for maintenance purposes; and, observing when and where each is dependent on one another/on others.

☑ **Initiating touch-base discussions** with our parents on delicate subjects – powers of attorney, insurance, wills, financial portfolios, end-of-life wishes, optional living arrangements…

☑ **Observing our parents' daily routines** – watching for any habits/scheduled activities; becoming familiar with any of our parents' support networks, as they presently exist; and, discussing with our parents what we are observing (non-judgementally, if possible).

☑ **Discussing care dilemmas and solutions** with other daughters and sons who have experienced first-hand what is involved in care-years with parents.

☑ **Challenging our feelings** – especially ones that are often in-our-face, bold and mixed (e.g. worry, acceptance of the future, guilt, frustration, laughter at a potentially embarrassing moment…).

☑ **Maintaining a positive attitude towards the responsibilities** we've already encountered (e.g. emergency calls, finances, medication changes, new training with equipment, hiring many types of caregivers, respite care…). What do we say when asked during a conversation, "How are your parents doing?" Do we respond in a positive manner, do we feel sorry for ourselves, do we roll our eyes and go on and on about our load – what are our exact words and body language – such speak volumes about our attitude and how well we are growing into our new role.

Is there some way of checking from time to time as to my progress?

Yes, there is a progress-meter and it is one question – "Are my parents' needs being met?" A major indicator of our success (any day) is whether we have met the care-needs of our parents that day.

Notes:

_____

_____

_____

_____

_____

_____

_____

_____

_____

_____

_____

_____

_____

_____

_____

_____

_____

_____

_____

_____

_____

_____

_____

Suggestion 11: Shift responsibilities

Shifting responsibilities (from a parent to their child) can be tricky within a family (who is looking after whom now) and transition times and grey areas must be treated sensitively. Some people refer to these times, depending on the severity of the dependency, as a time when the parent becomes the child. *(Note: I do not like this description as at no time do I believe this role through a parent's eye changes.)*

How can I go about gradually shifting some responsibilities over to me?

☑ **If we have time on our side, we can seize moments.**

If we are planning for the pending care-years, when our aging parents may need us to help take care of them, we can begin assuming responsibilities on a gradual basis by:

- Involving ourselves little by little in scheduled activities for/with our parents (e.g. going on doctor's appointments with them, doing the driving on Sunday drives...).

- Asking about house maintenance chores and ordinary tasks that have to be attended to on a regular basis, who does what, when, costs (e.g. grocery shopping, lawn care, weekly garbage collection...).

- Building our parents' confidence in us by undertaking 'together' some of the important annual tasks they have done on their own in past years (e.g. income taxes, vehicle renewal insurance...).

- Encouraging discussions about their legal and financial affairs (e.g. types of insurance policies they have and why that type, bank account types and portfolio management, up-dating of wills...).

☑ **If we begin noticing signs of health changes or changes in the patterns of our parents' activities, we must pick up the pace and**

actively assume some responsibilities and encourage a shift in others.

We must bravely initiate subject-related chats (hint – don't forget to tread softly). In this manner, we can gather information and our parents can grow used to some of the upcoming necessary changes within their lives.

We should consider **two factors** when initiating transfer-of-responsibility type discussions with our parents:

1. **Timing:** schedule any discussions in accordance with our parents' needs, (not ours), listen for appropriate moments to open specific conversations.

2. **Topics:** choose the specific subjects carefully. Some of the less-threatening topics to explore initially could include:

   - Home Safety – for example, removal of some furniture and accessories, the addition of new living aids in the bathrooms and bedrooms.

   - General safety – for example, use of a walking aid or special clothing item, in-house emergency communication devices.

   - Emergency measures – for example, use of ambulance services, the replacement of old telephones with new memory speed dial ones.

   - Home care and household chores – for example, hiring part-time housekeeping help, hiring a part-time live-in caregiver for weekends or when one parent is ill.

We must constantly be testing the water – is this the right day, the right time? Is this an appropriate topic? We must have patience and wait for a timely-window.

We should not try to implement too many shifts of responsibilities too quickly or we run the risk of overwhelming our parents and then they may balk. *(For example, when Mum first received some government home care services for a few hours each week, she had to adjust to new persons assigned to her home which included strangers puttering in her kitchen, since on certain days, the caregiver often did some baking. Mum's feelings about 'her kitchen' changed dramatically; first, she viewed baking as solely her responsibility (even though she disliked the chore), then she came to think of the kitchen duties as the caregiver's responsibility exclusively, and she adjusted her thinking once again and liked the fact that a caregiver had this responsibility, since it freed time for her to do other things.)*

As we assist our parents more and more with some of their regular, ordinary activities (e.g. accompanying them to the bank); as we participate more and more in discussions on ways to attend to household tasks (e.g. is it time that someone came in once a month for yard-work); and as we explore topics for future decision-making (e.g. would it be safer for you to use the handidart rather than drive in the winter), it will become obvious to our parents that some of their regular responsibilities could be transferred to us or others – to make life easier and safer for them.

It seems that maintaining some independence may be key in how well our parents allow a shift in responsibilities.

☑ **If we have no choice, we have to assume care responsibilities swiftly** – the number of the responsibilities we assume for our parents will depend on the severity of any turning-point incident (e.g. a parent's mini-stroke, vision problems, noticeable dementia, heart attack, kidney failure, cancer, pneumonia, a fall…).

At the time of a crisis, one of our first care-related responsibilities is obvious, we have to reorganize our parents' immediate environment to meet their everyday safety needs – in this way, we are undertaking a task usually done by our parents for themselves, that is re-establishing order and routine as soon as possible.

In 1960, only 16 percent of Canadians over age 50 had a surviving parent. By 2010 that will rise to 60 percent. And, while many people maintain good health into their later years, by the age of 85 a majority need at least some assistance for physical or mental impairments. (*Source: Reader's Digest, June 1998, from Original Source: Chatelaine, November 1996.*)

How do I explore my parents' feelings about allowing me to help them?

What have our parents' feelings been regarding accepting our help in the past? More recently? (Even if we have discussed certain ways of helping in the past, we can't assume we know how they feel now the time has come to accept that help.)

Gaining insight into our parents' feelings is a tough task as we want to approach the whole idea of 'receiving care' in the best way possible under the current health circumstances without entering into a debate or argument on the pros or cons.

Do we know how our parents view their health problems? Do they generally trust doctors or close friends or relatives or not? Do they ask for help or go it alone? Are they overly dependent on medications or not? Have they an ostrich-attitude waiting for problems to disappear or do they confront things right away? Equally important, how have we been involved in our parents' health care in the past – did we let them handle everything in their own way in due time, did we interfere or show interest, did we take an active approach or not? (Is the scene set to explore the whole idea of accepting help because we have been involved in their health in the past, or are we starting from scratch with this topic?)

(For example: In the past, my parents' attitude regarding their health remained consistent – they generally thought, if a health problem occurs, the doctors 'will make things okay' – translation = will put things back the way they were and then normal life will continue exactly as it was, perhaps with the addition of a new pill for a week or two. During their care-years though, Mum and Dad came to the unspoken realization that the person really responsible for 'making things okay' was no longer the medical community, but their daughter. That responsibility had shifted in their eyes from the doctor to me because their problems now were not confined to an illness or a pill as a remedy, the problems were lifestyle-based. It makes sense that our parents will see us as the 'OKmaker', as they know that we care about their quality of life plus they can trust us to take over some general responsibilities without question.)

(Note: I have since read research that indicates that 'only children' have even greater expectations of care placed on them than a family with more than one child.)

How do I start viewing us as a 'care-receiver family' at this time?

In the care-years, we will have many 'a-ha moments' regarding our family – one of those moments is when we understand that we are a 'care-receiver family' – I don't think anyone actually uses these exact words, but the meaning is clear, we need to place an emphasis on 'receiving' as our family can no longer go it alone.

As our parents' health continues to vary as they grow older, we will become comfortable asking for, receiving and accepting appropriate assistance.

Often we end up 'receiving' help from many sources – relatives, medical teams, friends, close neighbours, non-family caregivers both live-in and shift/part-time, support groups, expertise associations, government programs, service providers, clubs... *(e.g. I felt like I was on a crash course, when I began to search out what kinds of help my parents required and then were eligible 'to receive', not only the local government programs and services available and their functions and criteria but also LTC networks and companies in our region).*

It's necessary to think in terms of 'care-receiving' because many types of care services from various sources are going to be required as our parents' expanding health needs become apparent.

Sweden's oldest twins (at their 100th birthday celebration, 2005) say turnip is key to longevity...

Both walk without any assistance and do all their daily chores themselves—did their best to answer some of the questions they've almost grown tired of by now. No, they repeated time and again, they do not really have a secret formula for long life. "We like to joke and say it's because we lived only on turnip back in 1914...that's all we had to eat during the world war. The first one, that is."

They have a more normal diet now, they said, but that hasn't stopped them from keeping their health. Aside from when they gave birth—they each had one child, only one has ever been hospitalized. She broke her thigh bone two years ago, but recovered quickly she said. One is 30 minutes older than her sister, and she said she has never been seriously injured or ill. "I have a toe that aches, though".

But in a country where senior citizens have access to free home-help service, the sisters do their shopping, cleaning, cooking and laundry themselves. They have both lived in the same apartment building for more than 50 years, one on the second floor, and one on the third. (*Source: The Associated Press, Stockholm, Sweden, 2005*)

Notes

_____

_____

_____

_____

_____

_____

_____

_____

_____

_____

_____

_____

_____

_____

Suggestion 12: *Watch for 'signals'*

Signals (puzzle pieces) offer a preview of what is taking place with our parents' health, leading to the bigger and clearer care picture for our family.

As caregivers, we need to be alert for signals indicating changes occurring in both our parents' health and their daily activities. We should see those, not as individual signs, as little problems requiring individual solutions, but as part of our total parent picture (i.e. their age, living conditions, past health history, present health…).

We can reduce the number of surprises we receive during the care-years, if we learn to 'look for' and 'hear' any potential signals. They may be linked to our parents' physical health and be easy to detect (e.g. hearing loss) and obvious (e.g. broken hip, pneumonia, heart attack, disease). Other signals may be linked to their mental health or daily living routines and be less understood, perhaps even overlooked (e.g. tears, forgetfulness, observance of strict routines).

Whatever the status of our parents' conditions (whether still living on their own or in a caremanor), as caregivers, we should try to operate from a prevention mind-set (e.g. my care-years motto became "No surprises" which I explain to every care team member who worked with my parents – I wanted to be informed immediately of any 'signs' of change.)

(For example, the year prior to Dad's fall, when my parents were living on their own, receiving little care-related attention from me, but lots of contact, I should have picked up on some signals regarding one of Dad's soon-to-be major health problems. In hindsight, here were the signals – Dad always had followed a daily routine for specific activities but during that prior year he would not deviate from that routine unless absolutely necessary; he would insist upon using the exact same driving routes to and from usual places and wanting others, if he was a passenger, to do the same. Dad had also become extremely precise about time, listening for the chime clock to keep to his schedules. He initiated less and less of the conversations when visitors were around; he was taking long naps after supper, snoozing in his chair until bedtime. At times, he was even

reluctant to change his shirt and pants during the week (wanting the same ones on)…Individually some of the signs were disturbing, but for the most part, we chalked them up to his personality ("just Dad's need for routine and growing worse"). Had I viewed the signals together, the picture may have warned me to look for a very common problem in some elderly, that of increasing dementia. Had I been more aware of the need to monitor signals and had I been more aware of the common signs of mild dementia, I might have asked the correct questions at the time, as Dad then was experiencing growing dementia.)

Alzheimer's is the most common neuro-degenerative disease, affecting 10 per cent of all people over 65 and 40 per cent of all over 85. Alzheimer's patients make up half of all nursing home residents. The cause of Alzheimer's, which kills brain cells and leads to severe dementia, remains unknown. Recently, doctors in England determined that people as young as 30 are now getting Alzheimer's which had previously been thought to only afflict the elderly. Researchers there say that with young and middle-aged people now being stricken, prevalence of the disease has doubled in the last 10 years. Drugs to treat the memory-robbing disease and a vaccine to prevent it will both be available in five to ten years, says Peter Reiner, researcher and professor of neuroscience at the University of B.C. He reported that drugs and a vaccine are currently in human trials and predicted that today's middle-aged people will avoid the dreaded disease. *(Source: UBC Faculty of Medicine's Golden Jubilee conference, Vancouver, as reported in The Vancouver Province, November 5, 2000.)*

If I begin noticing signals and become concerned, how can I start to make sense of them?

In order 'to read' signals and 'get a picture', we can:

☑ **Jot down simple notes** on a calendar or in a day-timer (when certain signs have been noticed and when each occurred). It is easier to see a pattern/picture when looking at an overview. *(For example: Mum's caregiver noticed over time that Mum experienced more bouts of indigestion than usual a couple of days before I was to travel anywhere*

— a definite pattern emerged relating to her stress — thus we were able to take action.)

☑ **Control our fears regarding past health problems** and avoid jumping to possibly incorrect conclusions. *(For example: In Mum's case, the constant fear was that her arm ache symptoms were heart-related, not knowing when gas build-up from the reflux hiatus hernia condition had put pressure on a nerve causing extended pain in the arm.)*

☑ **Keep everyone in the loop** if we are concerned about a sign of change with our parents — remember to explain fully a parent's past health history and conditions to all the various caregivers who are working with a parent.

☑ **Assign part of the responsibility for 'sign-watching' to the caregivers.** Ask the caregiver(s) to track one particular aspect of a parent's health and/or ageing (when a problem is suspect) by note-taking, since it is easy to forget the number of times the signals occur (within one week, one month). Review the frequency of the signals/signs with the caregiver after a couple of weeks, check if a pattern is emerging.

☑ **Ask our parents' family doctor for assistance sooner rather than later** as it might be possible to prevent a health crisis by requesting something simple such as a complete check-up, include checking vitamins, minerals…all the basics.

(For example: For one year and more, prior to the fall, Dad constantly complained about being cold, even though the rest of us often found ourselves in a very warm house with the furnace thermostat set high (a signal). Immediately after his fall, we were told that his iron count was excessively low (could this have been why he was always cold) and that he actually required several bags of plasma to correct this condition. So, what really happened that winter morning — did Dad truly slip on the ice or did he have what is termed a "conscious collapse" from the anaemic condition he was in at the time. (I'll always wonder if I could have prevented some part of Dad's health problems and perhaps their severe consequences if I had simply read that one signal—being cold — informed

the doctor of what I was noticing repeatedly and scheduled a full check-up for Dad. As for Mum, in her last months, she was constantly tired – a signal of increasing conjested heart failure.)

☑ **Keep the caremanor staff accountable, ask for a report specifically on the matter of concern – maintain constant interest if a carehome is involved** – ask the nurses to check their records regarding when the last time occurrences/signals took place. Become part of that team, show interest and explain the concern to those who have constant contact with our parents.

☑ **Contact health agencies or local associations for specific literature** – if a problem is suspect, just search the telephone directory to find an appropriate association and place a call, describing the signals, the associations are very helpful.

How do I begin to see a larger picture?

If we are monitoring our parents for signs and trying to group those signals to make sense of what is happening, we may be able to take some action quickly. (Let's think about it for a minute as we already do this on a regular basis – for example, if we notice our elderly parent coughing, dizzy, complaining about aches and a sore throat, do we not instinctively group those signals and call the doctor regarding the flu – we just have to keep doing the same process for lesser understood signs too.)

Brain diseases will outstrip heart disease and cancer as the leading cause of death and disability among Canadians in 20 years, the head of Vancouver's Brain Research Centre predicts. An aging population, prone to more brain illnesses, such as Alzheimer's and Parkinson's, will be the main factor in the anticipated rise, said Dr. Max Cynader, director of the centre, which is operated by the University of B.C. and the Vancouver Hospital. The incidence of both diseases increases with age. Vision-related brain diseases are also on the rise, including conditions such as glaucoma and macular degeneration, said Cynader. "There's a looming epidemic of brain-related blindness," he said. One in 10 people aged over 65 will suffer glaucoma, for example. "It's demographics. Our baby boomers are getting past their prime time years, he said. Not only are they facing Parkinson's, Alzheimer's and more likelihood of strokes, there are also a host of degenerative diseases ahead." *(Source: Article: Brain diseases 'loom as next big health threat' The Vancouver Sun, March 20, 2001.)*

Should I be concerned in case of overlapping problems?

If we have noticed diverse signs of changes and have tracked them (on a calendar) for a short period, we need then to try 'to group' these signals. We must take care since it is possible to have several 'pictures', emerging at any one time (i.e. we may be working on several jig-saw puzzles involving health needs, organizational problems and environmental obstacles without knowing it, with the pieces all thrown together in one box).

(For example: By the second year, Mum's health situation became fragile. I began noting increased bouts of severe indigestion; teary times during ordinary conversations; greater susceptibility to colds; more than two long distance telephone calls per day just to talk; a greater repetition of questions and stories, longer naps – all signals that something was happening.)

We need to continue to remain alert and group on-going persistent signs even if/when one problem has already been identified.

(For example, Mum's tears, frequent telephone calls and longer naps, although coexisting with a serious identified health problem, were not related to it. The

behaviours continued, indicating the existence of a second problem – this puzzle was more difficult to piece together, as it involved her unhappiness with her living conditions at the time. Once the living conditions were addressed and changed completely, the tears lessened, naptimes became normal, telephone calls were upbeat and less frequent...)

In less obvious situations we may have to probe in a round-about-way for possible explanations using open-ended type questions with our parents.

(For example, I found it wise, if concerned about a parent's unhappiness, to check first (privately) on his/her relationships with their caregivers. Close living arrangements, especially when imposed due to health problems, can cause sadness and misunderstandings – our parents may feel this aspect of their life is out of their field of control due to their dependencies.)

What else should I keep in mind about signals?

☑ **Be forthcoming with information regarding the signals we are noticing:**

> If a parent requires hospital care, not only should the full health history be given to emergency paramedics and doctors and nurses, but also the type and frequency of the signals we have been noting should also be offered (use the recorded overview notes for accuracy) – the information may be useful.

☑ **Don't get caught in the squeaky-wheel trap:**

> As we are privy to our family's interactions and history, we must try not to focus only on the most verbal parent (i.e. squeaky wheel) or the one with the most visible or most recent health problem at the expense of our other parent who also may be revealing his/her own signals of importance.

☑ **Question the professionals:**

> Dig for answers – question health professionals on what (e.g. illnesses, diseases, medications) could be causing some of the signs we are noticing.

Become a little more informed regarding some of the more common health problems and disabilities of the elderly.

Don't accept one particular reason often alluded to when it comes to diagnosing our parent's health problems, 'old-age'.

(For example: Mum was rushed by ambulance one night to the hospital for arm pain, dizziness and stomach upset whereas the emergency ward doctor, prior to examining her, noting Mum's age, promptly took me aside to suggest that resuscitation efforts if required should not be attempted as Mum was "quite old". I stood there stunned, like a dazed deer caught in a car's headlights – but what I should have said to that doctor was, "Yes, Mum is in her late 80's, but age may not be the problem here, so let's find out what is before we jump to conclusions." The problem turned out to be an extremely bad bout of acid reflux.)

☑ Respond immediately, don't put things off until tomorrow, don't procrastinate:

It won't surprise anyone to find out that failure to take immediate action when noticing signals, unfortunately, more often than not, has negative, surprising consequences, in caregiving situations. During the care-years, we should avoid procrastinating even though we all seem to have 'valid excuses' for putting things off until tomorrow (e.g. I'm too busy; things are too hectic right now; the problem isn't that big; it can wait until this weekend when I have a spare minute...).

Yes, we know sometimes that making one decision will open Pandora's box and set off a chain of further things to do, but we must acknowledge our frustrations, fears, fatigue and then take the actions necessary – we don't really have choices during times like these.

(For example: In the first two years, when live-in caregiver and parent personality-related conflicts regularly arose, I used to catch myself whispering, "Oh no, not again." I really didn't want to address that huge issue of finding a new live-in caregiver, once again – but it sure didn't take long to learn that any procrastination on my part exacerbated the problems.)

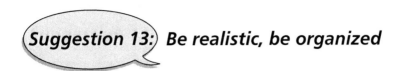

Suggestion 13: *Be realistic, be organized*

What can I do in order to get myself organized prior to care-years or immediately after a turning-point health incident has occurred indicating our care-years have started?

As daughter/son-caregivers, we need quick access to family information during **three specific situations:**

1. When we have to tend to our parents' legal, financial and household affairs on a regular or annual basis or updating basis.

2. When we want to apply to special community programs for care purposes (e.g. to supply the required data to gain financial assistance).

3. When we have to settle our parents' affairs upon death.

Thus, it makes sense that prior to care-years beginning (a turning-point incident) or as soon as possible after a crisis, we should take precautionary steps:

☑ Gather the important information.

☑ Develop a simple way of organizing that information.

☑ Up-date the information often/if necessary.

How do I keep track of valued information?

Since we usually require the same vital information over and over again, it is important to organize easy systems to save ourselves countless hours and give us quick access.

The following is a list of useful ideas:

☑ Keep a directory.

We need to organize a directory of sorts – the names of the main persons in our parents' present-day support network; include postal addresses, telephone and fax numbers, and e-mail addresses. We must keep the directory current.

Rather than list people, companies or agencies in the usual manner, that is alphabetically, it is better to list by what they do or provide (e.g. community health agency, medical supply stores, support groups) and by specialization (e.g. heart, eyes, throat, hearing) because when information is required, it is often difficult to recall surnames of specialists and companies'/agencies' names.

For example, my directory for my parents followed this type of pattern for easy reference purposes, list:

- *Under 'doctor': the family physician only plus medical health care numbers.*

- *Under 'eyes/ears/heart/orthopaedic'…: the specialists.*

- *Under a variety of headings that relate directly to tasks (e.g. health unit, housecleaning, pharmacist, medical equipment and supplies, hospital, yard work…): contact persons and relevant agencies.*

- *Under other individual headings: bank advisors, insurance specialists, pension contacts, income tax , and household maintenance companies.*

- *It is important to have the SIN and the Health Card Number close at hand at all times as these numbers are asked for constantly as they link to all sorts of files (note the numbers in your daily planner also).*

☑ Use a daily planner.

We need to put only the more important, most frequently contacted persons from the general directory into our personal daily planner for immediate, on-the-spot access. These names, thus, will be available when at work, away from home on business, on vacation; the idea is to be prepared at emergency times.

The most important contact persons can be listed on one separate page in a daily planner under "P" for Parents.

For example: My daily planner included: the obvious, such as my parents' family doctor and certain specialists (e.g. Mum's cardiologist). It also included some of the more unusual information that I found useful to have readily available:

- *My parents' local hospital address and numbers.*

- *Main banking contacts (should we need help arranging special $ matters, in a hurry) and legal representatives.*

- *The memorial home chosen by our family (immediate contact with the memorial home is urgent, no matter where one is, as some important arrangements have to be made instantly at time of death, for example, when I was in Mexico and my Dad died unexpectedly and the funeral home needed contact ASAP).*

☑ Keep clippings.

We can get into a habit of being our own clipping service, that is, clipping/ ripping out of newspapers or magazines any helpful articles (on medication side-effects, health problems) which will remind us to ask questions of various professionals or offer us a new piece of information which may be of value to our parents' health.

We should always date and reference the source of the clipping. *(For example: During the first two care-years, I jotted questions on post-it notes regarding articles clipped and placed the notes plus the articles in my daily planner on parent-doctor appointment date pages or in my travel file, so I would be ready on my parent's appointment days.)*

☑ Keep a banking notebook.

For further information, refer to Topic 3, Suggestion #19 – Obtain an Understanding of the Documents.

If banking is one of the responsibilities we are assuming or assisting our parents with, we should consider purchasing a small (e.g. 2" x 3") notebook in order to record the dates and all details (major or otherwise) of every banking transaction undertaken by us for our parents (i.e. any transfers of

$ from one account to another; large items purchased; closure of accounts, transaction verification numbers).

This valuable booklet keeps us accountable to our parents, and others (e.g. accountants and siblings perhaps). It offers a quick overview of the banking business undertaken on behalf of our parents each month. *(Note: It is important that our parents and other family members be able to review this notebook on a regular basis if they want, to feel confident that all is being done carefully. This review should not pose a problem or question their trust in us – we are accountable, it is not our money. As time went on and care complexities increased, I found it useful to hire a small local bookkeeping company to do the work and I set up a 'care account' at the bank.)*

For greater detail, refer to Topic 3, Question: What Should I Do Regarding Banking Matters.

☑ Organize a filing system.

We need to put together a simple filing system or box for papers relating to our parents' affairs – we should keep the files in the location where we tend to our parents' business (e.g. home office).

Since undertaking some aspects of our parents' business and contacting people critical to their daily health are not one-off events, but constant responsibilities, being able to access documents will prove invaluable.

The following outlines some of the file categories required, with folders labeled accordingly:

- Master file folder: Title: Parents

- Examples of sub-folders:

  1. Income tax and Accounting
  2. Pension plans
  3. Medical plans
  4. Banking/Funds
  5. Insurance policies
  6. Legal
  7. Caremanors/respite homes
  8. End-of-life wishes, Funeral Memorial plans

9. Agencies including health units
10. Assistance programs
11. Clippings/other information

Note: Cross-reference to Suggestion #19 and complete the table in that section.

Notes

_____

_____

_____

_____

_____

_____

_____

_____

_____

_____

_____

_____

_____

_____

_____

_____

_____

_____

_____

_____

_____

_____

_____

_____

_____

_____

Suggestion 14: *Emphasize the value of emergency services*

How can I get my parents to realize the value of using emergency services?

Long before a health-related crisis occurs and an ambulance is required, we need to help our parents understand the value of using any emergency services available to them in their area.

If care-years have already started, we need to re-emphasize the importance of using emergency services at all times.

To get our points across (gently) concerning the benefits of these services, we need to:

☑ **Walk in their shoes.**

We need to think about what ambulance calls and hospital emergency wards represent to our parents (i.e. illness, commotion, hospital stays, helplessness...) otherwise their unpredictable responses to using the services may surprise us.

(For example: My parents never had much need for ambulance services in their working and regular retirement years, that is the first 80 years of their lives, so their reactions during care-years emergencies now proved unpredictable. Sometimes they would say, "No, no, I'm okay" other times, "If you want, just drive me to the hospital, but I'm sure I'll be okay" or even worse, at other times, they simply said "No, don't call an ambulance".)

We need to approach the discussion without projecting our general fears around their health and safety; we need to emphasize the benefits of obtaining professional emergency care, rather than the negative illness causing the emergency.

✓ Put time aside for 'the daughter/son-parent emergency-services talk'.

Our elderly parents, especially after a turning-point health incident, will most likely require one or more emergency calls in the future; subsequently, our 'emergency services talk' is not a one-time-only discussion that we can have and then feel confident that we've made our points and that our wishes will be understood and followed when unexpected health problems arise. We need to look for time to have these 'talks' at several non-emergency teachable moments. We should keep in mind that our parents may agree with us when they are feeling well ("Yes, yes, of course I'll call the ambulance"), but may hesitate when the services are actually required ("I thought I'd wait and see how I felt"). Our parents may even be able to influence people who know that using emergency services is best, but do not want to overrule our parents at tense times.

"Always behave like a duck – keep calm and unruffled on the surface but paddle like the devil underneath."

– Jacob Braude

What do I say?

✓ Talk in terms of the immediate, on-the-spot professional assessment while still at home, given in an instant, by well-trained, excellent ambulance and fire paramedics.

✓ Mention the instant attention they will receive at the hospital when they arrive by ambulance, which means they will not have to sit and wait for long anxious minutes or even hours in the waiting room such as would happen if a friend or relative transported them.

✓ If our parents are cautious regarding the costs of using emergency services, discuss the fact that on the whole, it is worth it as such help may end up perhaps shortening the length of time ill.

☑ Keep the topic an ordinary one, whenever timely (e.g. when an ambulance passes, during a television show…), discuss the 'quality of the services' and the 'kindness and speed' of the help.

We have to keep in mind that it may take a feeling of familiarity (utilizing the ambulance services more than once) before our parents appreciate the full value of the services.

(For example: In our family's case, in the first years of our journey, we had occasion to use the ambulance services twelve times for both Dad and Mum. Even though the decision to call an ambulance remained a major problem for Dad always, I knew my "emergency-services talks" were finally having an effect with Mum when one day, I heard her telling her friend why it is a good idea to use an ambulance when feeling very sick.)

What can I do to make an emergency team's job easier?

Since emergency services will most likely be used many times during our parents' care-years, we can assist paramedics by having everything in order for each parent:

☑ **A medication booklet** with an up-to-date list of all medications presently being taken, how much (the dosages) and when (breakfast, lunch, dinner, bedtime, before meals…). We can use medications booklets specifically supplied by health units or pharmacists for this purpose (similar in appearance to a small bank account booklet) or we can purchase a small spiral bound booklet for the purpose. It is important to keep the med booklet information current.

(For example: In Mum's case, we titled each page of her medication booklet according to the time of day the medication was taken, so one page was titled "before breakfast", the next page was titled "with breakfast", one titled "lunch time", one titled "dinner time", and finally one titled "bedtime". Each prescribed medication and the doses were then listed on each page accordingly, vitamin supplements were included too. We noted if any changes had been made to the medication type by the doctors and the date that change to any medication was made.)

☑ **A copy of the health insurance card(s)** – if a card is not available, record the care card number/group number of the health insurance plan in the medications booklet.

☑ **A small box or plastic tray** – containing all the pill bottles and medic-kits being used. As well, a note of any particular medication the local hospital doesn't usually keep on hand can be placed in this designated box or inside the medication booklet – this type of info one learns over time since it is important that the specific medication accompany the ambulance attendants for use by our parent at the hospital.

As a rule, all of the medications presently being taken usually accompany a patient to the hospital. *(Note: Remember to pick everything up from the nurses' station upon release.)*

☑ **A list of any allergies or reactions to any medications.** This list can be noted in the medications booklet. If one particular medication was stopped because of an adverse reaction, a notation should be right beside that medication's name and stop-use date.

(For example, Mum wore a bracelet when she went out, which also contained a note on her important health history and medication allergies. As for my Dad, when he relocated to a caremanor, we wrote out a list of the medications to which he was most sensitive and asked that it be attached in a prominent place to his file.)

☑ **A hospital admittance card.** Each time someone enters emergency, a hospital admittance card is made. As these cards are usually thrown away upon departure, we can ask to keep one for future use, since the card lists the family doctor and gives the basic information used by ambulance personnel upon arrival at our parents' home. *(Keep one admittance card with the meds booklet.)*

Health Canada has made it official: taking Aspirin when you have a heart attack will dramatically increase your chance of survival. In fact, cardiologists say that clinical trials show that taking ASA acetylsalicylic acid during a heart attack (chewing a tablet) boosts survival rates by 25 per cent. Health Canada warns that no one should give ASA to a person suffering a possible heart attack without first determining if a doctor has cleared the patient to take the drug. (*Source: The Vancouver Sun, July 6, 2001.*)

Is there anything else I can do to make emergency teams' jobs easier?

☑ In addition to being organized within the house, we can **organize outside the house** too, to some degree.

We can help ensure that our parents' house is easy to find by emergency teams by purchasing a prominent, **night-reflecting address pole** and placing it in a visible location at the front corner of the driveway. These types of signs may be found at many community police stations or fire halls as they are often sold as fundraising mechanisms. (It is easy to find out what is recommended or available in any community by asking at a local fire-hall; if unavailable, a sign-post can be made at little cost using reflective numbers.)

In addition, we can ensure that **outside house lighting is always in good working order** and of course switched on when an ambulance has been called in the evening or night.

We can make sure that our **parked cars are out of the way of an arriving ambulance.** If our parent has to be taken to hospital, a stretcher will be used to transport her/him to the parked ambulance so, it is important that the crews do not have to squeeze through a driveway or entrance-way obstacle course with that stretcher. We need, in winter, **to keep the driveway clear of snow** (e.g. Mum had a yardman who knew the driveway was a priority and cleaned it as soon as possible after each snowfall).

☑ We can **be ready.** We can be dressed and be prepared to leave with the ambulance or follow it in our car (my preference as then one isn't dependent on transport home at a later time). We need to **make our wishes clear to the caregivers** – that she/he is expected to to be ready to accompany and remain with our parent during the whole emergency period.

We can **pack a tote-bag as soon as we call the emergency services** and have it ready to take with us for our parent's use in case of overnight hospital admission (e.g. night gown/pyjamas, housecoat, slippers, comb, coat, hat, shoes, clothing including undergarments…).

If one parent is going to be left alone at home for a brief period of time, the **designated on-call person** should be contacted to come over as soon as possible until a caregiver is able to return from the hospital. (This on-call person should always keep a key, but if not, explain which door to use so that our at-home parent does not have to use any stairs to let that person in.)

McMedicine by John Lorinc – **Welcome to the pressure-relief valve of the Canadian health system (walk-in clinics), also known as McDonald's medicine.** Since they first appeared in the late 1970's, walk-in clinics have been a steadily growing presence in the primary-care sector. They are popular in big cities with transient populations, and tend to be patronized by younger people with small children, or couples looking for family planning advice. Urgent-care clinics, which offer emergency-room type services but do not accept ambulances, are also popping up across the country. Some health-policy analysts see walk-in clinics as a relatively inexpensive means of relieving the strain of crowed emergency rooms. But others regard walk-in clinics as purveyors of quick-and-dirty medicine with little follow-through and poor integration with the rest of the health system. A 1998 report for the Ontario Medical Association (OMA) found most people go to walk-in clinics with standard upper-respiratory infections and other simple ailments. (continued...)

"It's very rewarding for doctors to operate walk-in clinics," says Dominique Tessier, a Montreal doctor and president of the College of Family Physicians of Canada. "But when you only give walk-in clinic services, you're not giving long-term care." The question facing health-care reformers is how to better integrate walk-in clinics with the rest of the primary-care sector, which is now under active review in many provinces. The federal government last year earmarked $800-million for projects and studies aimed at transforming primary care. But for now, there is little hard data on how the clinics function, how much they bill and what standard of care they deliver. "Walk-in clinics developed in Canada not from the deliberate policy decisions of provincial ministers of health but in response to the entrepreneurial opportunities offered by the public funding of physicians' services through fee-for-service payments," Brian Hutchison, a McMaster University professor of family medicine, observed last year in the British Medical Journal. "Having played no part in their creation, ministries of health have remained on the sidelines, taking no policy initiatives to either discourage or encourage their proliferation." Those who researched this sector make the following observations: Many people who go to walk-in clinics are likely to visit their own physicians with the same complaint, raising the overall cost of health care. And because they offer the possibility of quick medical treatment when compared to emergency rooms or regular doctor's offices, walk-in clinics also drive up demand for health care, according to some analysts. There is no consensus as to the quality of care in walk-in clinics. The OMA study found the poor reputation of walk-in clinics was generally undeserved. Other reports have come to the opposite conclusion. A recent survey by Pricewaterhouse Coopers revealed while Canadians do visit walk-in clinics regularly, they tend to be far more impressed with the care offered by their regular GPs. *(Source: The State of Health Care, Quarterly Report, Edition Three, November 2001, The National Post.)*

Should I plan for potential problems – what if my parents resist help from the emergency services?

It is a fact – parents do resist help from emergency services teams from time to time. We have to prepare for those unpredictable times should our parent pose a problem once ambulance attendants have arrived.

Should our parent refuse to be transported to the hospital and/or refuse ambulance attendants help once the paramedics are on the scene (i.e. standing in our parents' house), we will need to have a persuasion plan in place to convince our difficult parent to cooperate. It is important to keep in mind that emergency services personnel cannot assist or transport someone against his/her will.

At the very least, we shouldn't assume that because emergency services have been called that all will run well from that time forward (these are unpredictable times).We need to be aware that our parents' attitudes may present problems to emergency teams and thereby prepare some methods for dealing with specific problem incidences.

What do I include in a persuasion plan?

We can try to reduce potential problems through awareness and planning, since hindsight is useless when faced with emergency situations. It is therefore up to us as a daughter/son-caregiver to establish what may work with each of our parents in case of a poor mind-set and then put methods in place to get around any predictable problems and surprises.

The following outlines some **useful ideas** when establishing an emergency services persuasion plan for our parents:

☑ **Designate one contact person to be called if a problem is unfolding:** Establish whom our parents trust, whose directions will be heeded, or who the problem-solver is in the family (in many cases that may be a particular son or daughter); designate that person as the contact person for these types of difficult emergency services situations.

☑ **Discuss (in advance) any potential resistance-type problems with the family doctor** so he/she is aware.

☑ **Designate an alternative back-up contact person:** If the designated contact person can't be reached, explain that the caregiver is to telephone a back-up family member (known and specified in advance); if these persons cannot be reached, then the last resort is the family doctor. Since the family doctor is someone who has gained trust and authority, he/she can usually reason with our parent at the time of a crisis.

☑ **Inform relevant persons as to whom the contact persons are:** Give the caregivers, relatives, neighbours and the caremanor nursing staff permission to telephone us/the specified contact persons if ever a problem is unfolding between our parent and the ambulance staff.

What are some of the possible situations I might face?

As a daughter/son-caregiver, we cannot be sure how our parents will react at the exact time of an emergency – the following scenarios (our family's) hint at the need for back-up planning:

Scenario # 1 – The "I'm not going" problem.

During one emergency, Mum and the live-in caregiver telephoned me long distance early one morning as the ambulance people had been called for Dad and a problem was unfolding. At that precise moment, the attendants were standing beside Dad's bed unable to transport him because of his resistance. Things were at an impasse-Dad was very sick and being stubborn; Mum, the live-in caregiver and attendants could not persuade him to accept help. I spoke to one attendant, expressing my permission (taking all responsibility) to remove Dad from home and immediately transport him to the hospital. I was informed, to my frustration (and theirs too I bet) that they could not move him unless he also gave his permission (even though Dad suffered from mild dementia, was now terribly confused, and was in danger of falling again due to the severe reactions he was having to a new prescription medication). Because of my 'OK-maker' history with Dad, I then asked to talk to him so that I could be gentle but firm in convincing him to give his permission immediately to the ambulance attendants. (It is a good idea to have a telephone at each bedside or jacks in the bedrooms or one cordless telephone in the house for just these types of circumstances.) I stayed on the line until the attendants confirmed that they now had the required permission from Dad and were proceeding. Dad was then transported to the hospital.

A similar scenario occurred again with Dad while residing in the care manor. One afternoon Dad was suffering from severe congested heart failure and an ambulance was called, whereby the nursing staff (who can't always act without resident permission) then could not convince Dad to cooperate with the ambulance attendants and be taken to the hospital. A nurse telephoned me long distance to receive directions. Since Dad did not have a telephone in his private room, I could not speak directly to him, so the nurse and I played message-relay to Dad for several minutes. I sent firm and loving messages that she passed onto Dad; he finally consented to go to the hospital with the ambulance team.

To plan for the "I'm not going or the permission is needed" predicament does not require in-depth detailed work – just some thinking ahead. As we know our parents well, one of our responsibilities is to alert any caregivers to potential emergency services-related problems. We also may want to try to explain the possible origin of the problem (e.g. Dad's lifelong fear or anxiety about hospitalisation and illness) and emphasize some techniques that may be effective.

We need to put the directions and contacts in writing if a caremanor is involved. This type of situation with our parent can be raised in a meeting with caremanor administration and nursing staff in order that the staff is alerted from the beginning of our parent's residency.

Scenario # 2 – The "Let's wait until later" problem.

On four different occasions, Mum's live-in caregiver telephoned me to seek guidance and direction, as Mum did not want the caregiver to call an ambulance on each of these occasions. The caregiver was very concerned, as Mum had been feeling very ill for many, many hours. Mum's response was always the same, "I'll be fine, let's wait a while and see." In Mum's case, fear (of another heart attack) immobilized her – I learned that once a specific fear is allayed, most people, like Mum, cooperate fully as they truly do know what is the best course of action to follow at such times.

The solution for these "wait until later" situations focuses on observation and repeated discussions. We have to observe our parent carefully at an emergency time and try to identify what the real fear is, a fear that may be impacting their immediate acceptance of emergency services. Later, we can gently discuss the specific fear (which we suspect) and how trained emergency ambulance paramedics can help us quickly with those major health problems. *(For example, during emergency times, the live-in caregiver and I talked to Mum about her worries regarding her heart condition – we needed direct answers about what was happening physically at that moment. We did not treat the heart-fear as an unmentionable, it was on everyone's mind, so it is acknowledged.)*

We should reassure our parent that the correct steps are being followed in each case and that using (911) emergency services is the best course of action. We must try to calm our own fears and concerns and listen to our parent during these times.

Someone must remain with our parent for comfort during the emergency hospitalisation, therefore, inform any caregivers that we would want them to stay at our parent's bedside (until we get there or until a medical decision is made) – no matter how many hours. We can be helpful by being present at bedside, giving relevant medical history information to nurses, getting warm blankets, talking quietly…

Scenario # 3 – The "Rules apply to everyone" problem.

In a twist of circumstance, the truly unexpected happened during the first six months after Dad broke his hip. One mid-morning while Mum was on an outing at a nearby mall (she still drove then) and Dad was in the last few days of a week-long respite stay at an intermediate care home, our live-in caregiver, at home alone, suffered a major heart attack in the house. Even though she knew that she was having a heart attack, she did not call 911 for help, instead, she decided to rest for a while on the living-room floor. As the symptoms increased, she still did not call for emergency services, instead she crawled to the couch to continue to rest. Soon she was forced to struggle to the nearest telephone and from there she repeatedly tried telephoning, no, not 911, but two sets of close neighbours until finally one answered, came to her assistance and called an ambulance. Mum arrived home – chaos.

Since the caregiver and I had often discussed the importance and benefits of using emergency services for my parents and since we had programmed speed dial into all the telephones in the house, I assumed that the caregivers would follow the house-rules. Later, when asked, she said that she understood what to do as far as my parents were concerned, but did not feel the same rule applied to her personally, she felt she could make up her mind accordingly.

One way of covering all types of unpredictable actions is to emphasize to everyone in the household the need to use ambulance services when an emergency happens – since our parents' care is directly affected.

Scenario # 4 – The "Flip side of the coin" problem.

All the while I was attempting to convince my parents to accept emergency services, my cousin was facing the reverse problem. Her mother (my aunt, age 80+) suffering from dementia and depression was telephoning 911-emergency assistance constantly – my cousin was then being called at all hours to come and collect her Mum from the hospital emergency ward. The situation magnified and one caregiver quit as she couldn't control the calls. Finally the family physician had to intervene, as this "cry-wolf" problem posed a dangerous situation for all concerned.

If this type of problem occurs, we have to meet with our parent's physician and work out what to do. In the meantime, we must designate a person who can be called at any time by the local emergency ward to pick up our parent immediately from the hospital.

Scenario # 5 – "Success at last"

By the fifth year, Mum was making appropriate decisions regarding emergency services – she accepted and used the services when necessary. She also realized the value of discussing the symptoms carefully with the attendants. During one midnight emergency service call, upon an assessment by the paramedics (in this case, they determined that she had either food–poisoning or a 24-hour flu-bug and dehydration was the concern), Mum was given a choice by a paramedic, she decided to remain in her home for that night and sleep comfortably. She had learned to trust the attendants fully, knowing that if the symptoms persisted, she could call them again. It turns out that she made the right decision and was pleased with herself in the morning.

In medicine the dictum is: Cure when possible; comfort always. We can't cure aging, but we can offer comfort. We can't make old people better, faster, or quicker, but we can try to assist them on a developmental level. In doing so, we help them stitch together the legacy quilt they are compelled to create. It's their gift to us, one that we can later embellish and hand down to our children. How can we question the value of this legacy coaching process that offers such huge emotional rewards?

(An extract from David Solie's book www.HealthandAge.com Source: David Solie, MS, PA. How to Say It to Seniors: Closing the Communications Gap with our Elders. (2004) Prentice Hall Press, New York.)

Notes:

_____

_____

_____

_____

_____

_____

_____

_____

_____

_____

_____

_____

_____

_____

_____

_____

_____

_____

_____

_____

_____

Suggestion 15: *Obtain neighbours' cooperation regarding emergency services*

What can I do to gain neighbours' cooperation?

We need to gain neighbours' understanding regarding use of ambulance services if/when our parents may require such.

Some points to consider when the care-years begin:

☑ We should discuss a parent's potential problem attitude with immediate next-door neighbours for awareness.

☑ We should give the neighbours our full permission, when a crisis is occurring, to call an ambulance, so that they can feel comfortable about overriding any risky resistance by our parents. (An emergency is not an appropriate time for neighbours to debate the use/non-use question with a problem parent, therefore our discussions will assure them that they can make the correct decision on their own if need be.)

☑ We should give the nearest neighbours our regular and work telephone numbers as they often end up being present or being called upon during an emergency, simply because of their proximity to and history with our parents.

☑ We should be sure that the close neighbours are familiar with the designated location of the medications and health information booklets in our parents' home. (This precautionary measure is important if there is no full-time 24/7 caregiver with our parents.)

☑ We must make an effort to show our appreciation to our parents' neighbours as they form an important part of our support system with our parents (i.e. they respond if telephoned, they wander over for chats, they are there for special days, they help if requested…).

Notes:

"Though no one can go back and make a brand new start, anyone can start from now and make a brand new ending.

– Anonymous

Suggestion 16: Keep in touch

Is constant communication necessary?

During the care-years, our emphasis is on maintaining constant communication with our parents (versus an as-need or once a week or when-I-think-of-it basis of pre-care regular retirement years).

Touching base is important now, constant communication:

☑ Offers peace of mind for our parents and us.

☑ Avoids many surprise situations.

☑ Keeps our parents alert and involved and interested in everyday family and community affairs.

☑ Allows us to test the climate, so to speak; in some cases, if changes are happening quickly, we may need contact each day just to circumvent problems before they turn into major dilemmas.

How can I keep in regular touch?

Telephone

☑ We need to talk with our parents often – define 'often' (e.g. 1 call/day, 2 calls/week, every Wednesday and Sunday) and then commit to that frequency/schedule.

☑ If we live in the same city, telephone communications is easy; should we live a distance away, this activity does not have to generate a large monthly bill if we register with the best available long distance telephone carrier for our circumstances and up-date our plan periodically (probably everyone already does this step).

☑ We should, in addition, register our parents onto a good long distance plan and encourage them to telephone us on a regular basis too (i.e. unscheduled and often).

☑ It is helpful to write down our parent's telephone company PIN number (identification number) in our files for referral purposes so we can easily update their long distance plans periodically with their carriers. (Having the PIN gives us permission.)

☑ We should discipline ourselves to telephone at times which coincide with known daily activities of our parents (e.g. after a nap period; after dinner) or when our parents usually need a mental boost (e.g. first thing in the morning if such is a low energy period).

☑ When out-to-town on business or vacation, we should continue to telephone our parents. Before leaving town, we should mention the best possible times for our calls (perhaps early mornings or evenings as everyone tends to be available and between activities at these times).

Facsimile

☑ This means of contact is especially useful if we have a parent in a caremanor, as it is easy to find time, once a week/in an evening/during a coffee-break, to jot a quick note to our parent and fax it to the manor.

☑ Faxes are not meant to replace the more personal voice contact of telephones (unless one is working in locations where telephone conversation is extremely costly); faxes supplement that contact.

☑ Faxing serves a dual purpose:

It ensures that someone at the caremanor will deliver the fax and read it to our parent if such a wish is written on the top of the fax, thereby spending some time visiting with and learning more about our parent as an individual.

It keeps our parent very much in the family loop, even though he/she may be living outside the family home.

☑ Faxes are tangible proof to our parents that we really are not far away, not out-of-reach. *(For example, when Mum and Dad were still healthy seniors and I was away on a project in Uganda, a neighborhood restaurant-pub in their community was kind enough to receive faxes periodically from me and the staff then telephoned my parents home for pick-up. I continued to use faxes when Dad lived in the nursing home – "instant letters" he used to say.)*

Mail

☑ A radio announcer in Vancouver calls this method of contact 'snail-mail', but if we live in a different location from our parents, snail-mail remains a familiar way to say hello to our parents as they enjoy receiving a note or card in the mailbox.

☑ When traveling, sending postcards often is a good idea as the pictures stimulate discussion between our parents and others and at times puts them at ease about our safety (can see where we are).

☑ We also need to encourage our parents to send cards/short notes to people important to them as well. *(For example, Mum sent fun shaped-postcards to her sister-in-law who was in a caremanor and to a niece several times a month; this activity kept Mum busy selecting these special cards and writing a short note and in turn helped keep everyone in constant touch.)*

Answering services-machines/pagers

☑ Most of us probably already have answering/contact service in place in our homes (if there is anyone who doesn't, it is imperative to organize such a contact system asap). An answering service allows us to be contacted easily (emergency and non-emerg messages) as we can pick up messages anywhere, often, in-town or away.

☑ In the case of an answering system, we may need to explain to each parent the importance of leaving a clear message each time she/he calls – even if the message is simply hello. *(For example: Mum used to call and would leave a very brief message, "This is your mother, call me as soon as you get home". This type of message, due to so many past health incidences (conditioning), would each time put my stomach in an instant knot. Once Mum became aware of my reaction, she changed her messages to, "This is your mother calling, nothing important, just called to see how you are doing.")*

☑ Two telephone lines are often a good idea in our parents' home, one for our parents and one for caregivers. *(For example: There were two telephone lines in Mum's home, the answering machine was attached to the caregiver's line allowing me to leave messages for the household or for the caregiver if I had a concern and wanted to talk with her privately.)*

E-mail

☑ Some caregivers may have computers (otherwise, when updating, give your computer, and printer to the caregiver for use), thus, e-mailing our parents becomes a quick way to stay in contact at any time from anywhere.

☑ The e-mail messages can be printed and either read to or given to our parents to enjoy as letters. (Computer interactive talk programs offer excellent advantages, too.)

☑ Some caremanors are presently teaching the residents to use e-mail (on large screens) so regular exchanges with family are possible and fun (e.g. animated cards).

Relative

☑ If we live out of town but have a close relative living in the same vicinity as our parents, we should encourage family contact as much as possible and constantly show our appreciation for such. *(For example: Mum had two special nieces who gave her a lot of attention; one lived in the same city and telephoned often, visited, popped in for lunch, met for coffee dates, and never missed celebrating a special occasion with Mum; the other niece lived where Mum and Dad lived prior to retirement and sent Mum a bundle of the home-town newspapers every two weeks with articles highlighted — my cousins' efforts were truly appreciated.)*

Designated contact persons

☑ If going out of town, for any reason, (business, vacation), we need to designate one person as a contact person (friend, relative, assistant…) for our parents to call if they want/need be. A designated contact person should be someone whom our parents know and feel comfortable calling should they need help reaching us.

☑ Of course, we need to remember to advise that designated person each time an out-of-town event is scheduled and set out the appropriate information (our hotel, telephone numbers…) for her/his reference.

☑ If our parents have a full-time caregiver, the caregivers automatically are the designated contact persons and have the relevant out-of-town contact information. *(For example, Mum's caregivers left the written out-of-town contact information on the front-room table so everyone felt comfortable knowing where it was.)*

☑ If our parents still live on their own (and have only part-time caregivers) and are friendly with their neighbours, in addition to leaving a written list with our parents of where we can be reached, we may consider leaving all the out-of-town information with those neighbours as well (especially if away for an extended period of time or in a difficult-to-reach location).

☑ If a parent is in a caremanor, the out-of -town contact information should be sent to the attention of the unit's head-nurse or to the manager for attaching to our parent's file while we are away. We should leave very clear directions as to what we want the staff to do if we are away and an emergency occurs. We need to put our wishes in writing if a caremanor is involved – it is important to be very clear with directions each and every time since we want our wishes followed. *(For example: Dad was in his manor for nearly two years and I had signed papers making me the designated contact, the staff knew of Mum's health and I had expressly stated that I was the contact not Mum. They knew me well as I had a strong presence with Dad – I telephoned several times a week, faxed when away, visited often, had meetings with staff to keep updated on Dad's progress, spoke to the nursing staff weekly, was on a first name recognition basis with most of the personnel and so forth. Even though I had established a good deal of communications, making my wishes known on a regular basis and had advised the staff when I was going to be away, it was still Mum (not me) who was contacted in the middle of the night when Dad died. We can only keep trying when it comes to communication.)*

ABUSE OF THE ELDERLY

Source: Adapted from World Health Organization (WHO) World Report on Violence and Health. Abuse of Elderly

INDICATORS RELATING TO THE OLDER PERSON

Physical
- Says physically assaulted
- Unexplained falls and Injuries
- Burns and bruises in unusual places or of an unusual type
- Cuts, finger marks or other evidence of physical restraint
- Excessive repeat prescriptions or under usage of medication
- Malnourishment or dehydration without an illness-related cause
- Evidence of inadequate care or poor standards of hygiene
- Person seeks medical attention from a variety of doctors or medical centers

Behavioural and Emotional
- States has been emotionally abused (belittled, ridiculed)
- Change in eating pattern or sleep problems
- May be isolated by others
- Fear, confusion or air of resignation
- Passivity, withdrawal or increasing depression
- Helplessness, hopelessness or anxiety
- Contradictory statements or other ambivalence not resulting from mental confusion
- Reluctance to talk openly
- Avoidance of physical, eye or verbal contact with the suspected abuser

(continued...)

Sexual
- Says has been sexually assaulted
- Unexplained changes in behaviour, such as aggression, withdrawal or self-mutilation
- Frequent complaints of abdominal pain, or unexplained vaginal or anal bleeding
- Recurrent genital infections, or bruises around the breasts or genital area
- Torn, stained or bloody underclothes
- Sexual behaviour that is out of keeping with the older person's usual relationships and previous personality

Financial
- Withdrawals of money that are erratic, or not typical of the older person
- Withdrawals of money that are inconsistent with the older person's means
- Changing a will or property title to leave house or assets to "new friends or relatives"
- Property is missing
- Older person "can't find" jewellery or personal belongings
- Suspicious activity on credit card account
- Lack of amenities, when the older person could afford them
- Untreated medical or mental health problems
- Level of care is not commensurate with the older person's income or assets

INDICATORS RELATING TO THE ABUSER

In a family or other close relationship:
- Seems excessively concerned or unconcerned
- Blames the older person for acts
- Behaves aggressively
- Treats the older person like a child or in a dehumanized way
- Has a history of substance abuse
- Has a history of abusing others
- Does not want the older person to be interviewed alone
- Responds defensively when questioned; may be hostile or evasive

(continued...)

If married to victim:
- Evidence of marital conflict or marital instability
- Male dominance in the family
- Economic stress
- Poor family functioning

If abuser is a caregiver:
- Appears tired or stressed
- Has been providing care to the older person for a long period of time
- Poor pre-existing relationship

Notes:

Suggestion 17: Take action ASAP

As a daughter/son-caregiver, one desperately trying to keep one step ahead, we need to make it a habit to pause at crucial times during care-years and ask and answer **two fundamental questions:**

1. What is going to change right now as a result of what has happened today (e.g. for Mum, for Dad, for spouse/partner, for children, for close relatives, for me – everyone on our list)?

2. What should I do right now (take an action or a series of actions) as a result of what has happened today?

There are two specific occasions when this habit will pay off if applied, avoiding undue complications down-the-line:

Occasion 1 – After each meeting/discussion/telephone call – with doctor, emergency hospital professional, health/social agency, care manor staff, nurses, caregivers – **when we are given a new piece of information** which could cause a problem (e.g. new medications prescribed or a medication switch or a deletion or a change in the scheduled time for taking the med; new persons scheduled as part-time caregivers or a rescheduling of work hours and days).

Occasion 2 – When a change to expenses or financial agreements is to take place – whether short-term (e.g. the need for weekly rehabilitation therapy sessions) or long-term (e.g. an increase in residency fees); whether paying privately or government controlled.

What kinds of actions am I going to have to take?

As a daughter/son-caregiver, there are three categories of actions we will end up doing on a regular basis:

☑ **Category 1 – The simple and easy action:** such as searching out a consignment wheelchair, solving a small problem by telephone, listening to a complaint (or even hiring a company to comply with city regulations on our parents' property for coddling moth elimination. Ah, that all our actions should be this uncomplicated and easy).

☑ **Category 2 – The delicate and emotionally-charged actions:** such as telephoning a parent's out-of-town relative hinting strongly that a visit soon might be a good idea, explaining a new illness...

☑ **Category 3 – The very complex actions:** such as letting a caregiver go and starting the whole process of hiring another one, asking for a second medical opinion, requesting leave from a job, weighing the benefits of surgery...

If time allows, is there one rule to try to follow before taking action?

There is one rule which may prove helpful – only when possible, appropriate and timely: we should ask our parents for their ideas, listen carefully to their input, present our ideas, discuss what the best action may be for the circumstance. (We should not assume they will not have or want any input!)

Notes:

_____

_____

_____

_____

_____

_____

_____

_____

_____

_____

"If you're going through hell, keep going."
– Sir Winston Churchill, 1874-1965

Suggestion 18: *Become an advocate*

What does it mean to be an advocate?

Being a parent advocate means doing more of and paying greater attention to what we have probably already been doing for a long time on behalf of our parents, that is, coming to their aid and helping them out with specific issues (i.e. pleading their causes).

This particular responsibility, being an advocate, will become more pressing in care-years than in previous years. The results of our advocacy efforts now will have a significant impact on our parents' happiness, calmness and security, as well as their health.

To be an 'effective advocate' means:

☑ Being knowledgeable regarding not only our parents' needs, but also the options available to assist in meeting those needs. (Evaluating what we know about our family dynamics and what may be the best for our parents in each particular situation.)

☑ Eliciting our parents' input (if their input will affect our actions).

☑ Learning what reasonable demands can be made of professionals and service groups and then making those demands.

☑ Asking appropriate questions repeatedly, especially if the responses are not understood fully or the next steps are not clearly given.

☑ Being patient, cooperative, and firm regarding requests.

☑ Drawing the line, so to speak, at certain times regarding what is/ isn't happening and knowing when and how to speak up (and be heard).

☑ Being persistent and then voicing our requests once again.

☑ Using our judgement regarding decisions, expectations, information gained. (Learning not to assume or take things for granted.)

☑ Being directive and expressing our concerns, through meetings and in writing. (Being precise when suggesting alternatives.)

☑ Saying thanks when efforts are successful.

☑ Keeping one eye to the future.

Is it appropriate for me to take an advocacy position when my parent is actually receiving care in the hospital?

The answer is "**Yes**" and the following **example** tells of the need for advocacy efforts at just such times – when our parent is in hospital.

Background information: *Everyone who reads a newspaper or listens to television news realizes hospital facilities and health care services are extremely stretched everywhere. Even special wards, including well-managed geriatric wards, which have fine teams of nurses, physiotherapists, nutritionists, social workers, doctors and specialists are suffering from lack of funding or overworked staff or lack of trained personnel or lack of bed-space…*

Author's Opinion: *One outcome of this hospital crisis situation is that some of the elderly patients, like our parents, may be sent home after some rehabilitation therapy, but before the optimum time, in other words, prematurely. The goal of specialized hospital staff is to give sufficient treatment so that an elderly patient is able to regain some of his/her lost skills and independence, as many of the basics may have to be relearned in light of the new health condition (how to walk, how to dress, use of aids). In reality though what often happens is that more time is required in the ward by the patient than can be given (bed space problems). The result is that the patient is therefore sent home lacking some basic-skills training. The dilemma then is clear – if everyday basics are not mastered by the patient while in the hospital with its special equipment and trained staff under monitored conditions, then these rehabilitation tasks have to be assumed by family members, thereby setting the stage for challenging situations at home and/or costly hospital return events.*

Our situation: *Dad had been on the geriatric ward for just about two weeks relearning basic skills. The rehab treatment's progress was slow as Dad's balance was extremely poor and his hip remained unstable (the surgeon said the breaks were at bad angles and the pins may not hold). During a telephone call to that ward one day, I had learned that the GMAT team, at a forthcoming patient review meeting, was going to set a release date soon for Dad. During this period, Dad had learned how to use a walker well; he had not yet learned how to use any other aids; more importantly, Dad had not been given any training as to how to go up and down stairs using a cane. The hospital team was aware of my parents' home layout with two sets of necessary stairs which obviously had to be used by Dad often (when he first arrived home and then weekdays whenever he was to leave home for therapy, adult daycare and outings). The decision of the hospital team members was that the morning shift of government scheduled caregivers would be used as trainers at-home, in addition to undertaking their regular daily home care duties (dressing, exercising, bathing) – it was assumed that somewhere in the one hour allocated to our family they would be able 'to fit in' the required minutes to teach Dad how to use a cane safely and how to go up and down stairs properly.*

My role: *As a daughter-caregiver, it was my responsibility to ensure, upon Dad's release from the rehabilitation ward, a smooth, safe transition for both Dad and Mum to his home situation. Understanding Dad's dominant characteristics with anyone except strong authority figures and realizing that once he left the safe hospital rehabilitation environment, he would resist (strongly) any attempt to teach him to negotiate stairs. I knew that the atmosphere in my parents' home would be extremely volatile regarding any new 'forced' learning – first for Mum, whom he would expect to help him, secondly for our live-in caregiver whose job it was to care for him and lastly for the community care team who were to work with Dad on a daily basis. Thus, I did not agree with Dad being released prior to accomplishing this important stair-use skill (at least).*

Actions taken:

- *Wrote a mini-report, to the staff and doctors of the specialized GMAT ward (a copy was addressed to each team member); the report outlined a series of clear recommendations (with explanations); the package was couriered (to ensure that the documents were received) well in advance of the meeting directly to the ward for distribution to the relevant team* members. *(My goal was to impress upon each member the urgency and dynamics of our family's situation – to give the full picture.)*

- *Later that week, booked a flight in order to attend Dad's review meeting; informed the team committee chair of my upcoming presence; as it was winter, caught a flight a day before the meeting so as not to risk fog/snowrelated weather delays common in that region of the province.*

- *Attended the scheduled meeting and presented our family's case (as written in the report) requesting a longer stay in rehabilitation so Dad could learn the required skills in the well-equipped hospital environment.*

The Outcome: *My advocacy efforts were successful – Dad remained in rehab a couple more weeks, until he had mastered more of his basic living skills.*

By being an advocate, greater confidence and a higher skill level was secured for Dad and major problems were lessened at home for Dad plus all those involved with Dad on an everyday basis.

Demographers have spent the last decade warning that growing numbers of the old-old (85 to 99 years old) and the very old (100 and older) could bankrupt public pension plans and burden the health care system to the breaking point. But Dr. Gloria Gutman, Director of Simon Fraser University's Gerontology Research Centre, and Ellen Gee, Chair of SFU's sociology and anthropology department, disagree with the prophets of doom who, they believe, have been alarmist in drawing attention to the coming problem. Coeditors of a new book, "The Overselling of Population Aging", they argue the fabric of Canada's social programs won't be destroyed by the coming wave of oldsters. Contributors to the book say "voodoo demography" is to blame for unwarranted concern about population aging. "We have some lead time" to plan for it, Gutman said. "Also, people are going into old age healthier than they used to. And we have to remember that old people do contribute to the economy through their taxes, both before they retire and after. When they take out those RRSP's, they've got to pay tax on them." *(Source: The Vancouver Sun, June 14, 2000.)*

Notes

"Honest disagreement is often a good sign of progress."
– Mahatma Gandhi 1869-1948

"Whatever you are, be a good one."
– Abraham Lincoln 1809-1865

TOPIC 3

Let's Talk: Understanding legal documents, financial matters and household budgets

How can I begin to understand my parents' affairs?

Personal Anecdote: "Oh my _ _ _ , what do you mean, you redid your wills...again?"

Suggestions:

19: Obtain an understanding of the documents

20: Organize an easy-to-manage household budget

21: Set up a designated "care account" to administer all aspects of care

How can I begin to understand my parents' affairs?

Personal Anecdote:
"Oh my _ _ _ , what do you mean, you redid your wills... again?"

It took many (many!) years for me to convince Dad and thus Mum to see a lawyer to write their wills. A couple of years after Dad's retirement in 1972, good sense won out and together we undertook the task - until then Mum and Dad were part of the statistics, 50% of adult population without wills.

Many many years later, it was time to revisit the wills and see if all remained as they wished, so we looked into any necessary revisions.

In our situation, as I am an only child, I wanted to ensure, during that revision, that there was a 'two-tier clause' in my parents' wills - just in case something happened to me before them or to all three of us at the same time when on an outing or holiday together. When nuances of the inheritance rules were explained carefully to my parents, they willingly revised and up-dated their wills outlining the distribution of their assets to cover various scenarios. All was in order - finally.

A couple of months after the revisions, Mum said that Dad, reflecting upon the process, "became nervous" and forgot "exactly why the specific revisions were made." Rather than bothering me, he convinced Mum to return immediately to their lawyer and "undo" the revised portions. Dad later told me that he wanted to be really sure that I inherited everything so he didn't want to cloud the will by even mentioning anyone else (eek).

Nearly a year later, while drying dishes and chatting with Mum, I casually commented on one aspect of my will, prompting her to comment offhandedly that she and Dad had "redone" their wills again some time ago. Needless to say I was at first confused, as we had spent so much time, not to mention dollars, doing their revisions in order to cover all possible circumstances - then it dawned on me what she was saying. ("Oh my ___, what do you mean you redid your wills again?") A family conference was quickly called - it was decided that we, of course, had to revise the wills one more time - and put the tier clauses back in place.

I learned from that day onward to check periodically on the status of certain documents. One never knows.

Notes:

___

Suggestion 19: Obtain an understanding of the documents

This section offers daughter/son-caregivers some basic organizational ideas and has been written to kick-start the work involved in understanding a parent's business and personal affairs and related documents.

Since every family's legal and financial and household affairs differ in complexity, a greater in-depth review than offered here, in most cases, will be required.

It is recommended strongly that every daughter and son contact the proper professionals, that is lawyer, chartered account, financial planner, insurance representative, notary, bank advisor, estate planner…to discuss her/his parents' matters.

What does a review of the documents entail?

Upon completion of the review, we will know if any important documents are not in place, are missing, or need revising – we must make every effort immediately to get our parents' affairs organized.

There are many good books and articles written on understanding and organizing the legal and financial documents of our parents, we should make time to browse through them periodically to gain new bits of knowledge.

As daughter/son-caregivers, we have to start our review somewhere – these are the steps we can take:

    ☑ **List** – We need to make a list of the documents we think we should have knowledge of (brainstorm). Refer to the table in this topic.

    ☑ **Gather** – We must go about gathering copies of the documents for individual review (contact the source if necessary, e.g. the insurance agent).

☑ **Read/Review** – When we feel somewhat comfortable that we have all the documents at our fingertips, we need to put a few days aside to read/skim the papers and reports (the findings may prove interesting and in some cases, alarming).

☑ **Note-Take** – We need to write down names of contacts, addresses and telephone numbers for each document; we need to list any questions we have if in doubt as to the nature of the contents.

☑ **Contact** – We need to contact the appropriate professionals if we have any questions and make an appointment with each to discuss the documents; if we do not know the contact name, we must place a call to the company/agency and request that a representative be assigned.

☑ **Question** – We should not assume that our parents have undertaken their own reviews in the past – we should ask questions if we feel there may be oversights or if we want information for our own understanding; the aim is to understand the contents (and implications) fully.

☑ **Seek help** – The more complicated our parents' affairs, the more time we (with professional experts) will have to dedicate to the task of understanding these affairs.

☑ **File/Record** – We may want to make copies or request copies of some of the important documents and place them in a safety deposit box/safe for security and ease of access.

☑ **Attempt to keep up-to-date** – We need to check the status of any new initiatives affecting our parents affairs (e.g. new legislation).

Our elders already deserve our respect because they once took care of us. When I was a child, I was regularly admonished to "respect your elders".

...Let's respect and listen to them when they have something to say about the most important things. Nearly two decades ago to this day, my grandmother was lying in her hospital bed during her final hours. In a quiet moment in the middle of the night, she whispered to me, "When you were in the hospital, were you afraid?" She was talking about my childhood experience with polio, when I was taken miles from my home and my parents. I was, of course, terrified nearly the whole time.

Listening to the deeper meaning of her question, I nodded and then asked, "Are you afraid?" "No," she said–and she was fully aware of her fate. She then took a small ring from her little finger and asked me to give it to my daughter.

These moments and others shared that evening showed that she had come to a point in her life when the most important thing for her to do was no longer about herself and her own projects, but about us, her loved ones, and the lives that we had still to live...

She stayed with us through the next morning before she passed on, but I will never forget the lesson she shared with me about moving without fear from this life to the next. It is in our own interest that we give our elders their due respect. Even more than respect, we need to give them our time and our listening, our interaction and our gratitude. This is true no matter our present age, not theirs – a win for both.

(Allan J. Comeau, Ph.D. is a licensed psychologist on the clinical faculty at the University of California at Los Angeles. (March 8, 2005))

The potential for family fireworks is on the increase as the Baby Boomer generation—and its elderly parents—head into an era where the largest transfer of wealth in history is about to begin.

A recent Ipsos-Reid study for Lawyers.com found that just 69 per cent of Canadians at least 55 years old have had a detailed discussion with their family about their final wishes.

Wills and estates lawyer Les Kotzer offers the following tidbits for thought with regard to estate planning:

- Don't assume that equality is always fair. How is it fair to leave the same to the son who got $100,000 to go to university during your life-time when the other son didn't?

- Don't assume goodwill between your children. You have to talk to the children and discuss individual items.

- Don't assume that one of your kids wants to be an executor. It's an issue of power, so be very careful whom you appoint

- Be sure to update your will on an ongoing basis. It should be done every three to four years or sooner if a change in the family has occurred.

- Talk to your children now, because you are the referee. Once the referee is gone, all bets are off. (Kotzer's book, "The Family Fight: Planning to Avoid It" is available through his website for $29.99, www.familyfight.com)

What are the basic documents I should review?

Prior to care-years, or as soon as possible if a turning-point crisis occurs, we should dedicate a block of time for checking that all of our parents' legal and financial documents are in order. We need to gain awareness of the contents and directions of each.

We have to make the necessary telephone calls, schedule the necessary meetings and attend to the follow-up paperwork involved. *(Think of the popular NIKE slogan, "Just Do It".)*

For obvious reasons, we must not put these tasks off 'until tomorrow', even if complex or delicate – we need to attack the most important documents first, not necessarily the easiest.

The important legal documents (with simple descriptions) we should be able to access may include:

☑ **Will (and codicil)** – states wishes about a parent's assets after death.

☑ **Living Wills** – tells a designated person (could be us as daughter/ son caregivers) how to care for a parent if he/she has a terminal illness or ends up in a permanent coma, what to do, that is, the medical procedures.

☑ **Power of Attorney and Enduring Power of Attorney** – gives authority to another person to act on a parent's behalf; only valid while our parent is alive, the power terminates upon death, as a will takes over then. (Also check 'alter ego trusts')

☑ **Living Trust** – used if a parent has a rather large estate, transfers ownership of the assets (e.g. properties) to a 'trust' (similar to a company); a trustee then controls the trust.

Thou Shalt Honour Thy Parents - Helping aging parents is more than just a moral obligation for adult children - It's The Law!

Most adult children would expect to help parents in need because of age, illness, infirmity or economic hardship, but most would be surprised to learn they could end up in court if they don't.

Parental support where necessary is the law in most provinces. It doesn't get the same media attention as child support and spousal support because very few parents have gone so far as to seek a court order compelling a child to fulfill his or her family obligations. (continued...)

Christine Van Cauwenberghe believes the issue is a sleeping giant that will come to haunt Canadians as our population ages. It is a potentially huge responsibility for baby boomers who may still be supporting their own children as well as themselves. "Most children feel a moral obligation to care for their parents but the issue does, sometimes, go to court when there has been a breakdown in the relationship," said Ms. Van Cauwenberghe, Ottawa-based director of tax and estate planning with Investors Group.

"If there is a court order, then it would be enforceable like any other support order. The province might start to garnish some of the adult child's wages or take away his or her driver's licence."

It rarely comes to that because most families work something out – often at extreme cost to the younger generations that might have been avoided with some foresight. Adult children need to know if mom and dad have taken care of their financial future because it can have ramifications for them, Ms. Van Cauwenberghe says.

The challenge is initiating a conversation when parents are often loath to talk about their own finances, which they reasonably consider to be private. At the same time, children may fear coming across as gold diggers trying to figure out how much mom and dad are going to leave to them after they are gone. "It is more than just financial planning," Ms. Van Cauwenberghe said. "It is also planning for disability and estate planning, and again, the conversations can be difficult because they require an admission of mortality on the part of the parents, and that can be somewhat sensitive."

Discussions may be further complicated by blended families and common-law relationships, which can lead to conflicting demands on matters as seemingly straightforward as funeral arrangements. "Talking about matters in advance may be awkward, but talking about them after the time of death can be explosive," Ms. Van Cauwenberghe said. "It can be very traumatic for the survivors and cause permanent damage to the families."

First, talk to your parents about their plans, she said. Do they have a pension or other retirement savings? If not, do they have a plan for supporting themselves? (continued...)

If they are still in good health, consider whether long-term care insurance is appropriate while they are still insurable at a reasonable price. Some children may be willing to pay the premiums if that means they will not have to find enormous sums later to care for ailing parents.

Estate planning questions for parents include:

- Do they have a properly drafted will and power of attorney in place?

- Do they have adequate insurance in case of critical illness or long-term incapacity?

- Who has been named executor of a parent's estate and do they know where to find the will and other important documents when the time comes?

- Have funeral arrangements been made?

- Do they have a health-care directive or living will that would provide guidance in the event of illness?

Ms. Van Cauwenberghe cautions against do-it-yourself estate planning and tax avoidance, which can do more harm than good. "Some people use will kits which are not recommended under any circumstance," she said. "They just cause a lot of grief and a lot of litigation and I would not recommend them."

Techniques to avoid probate, such as transferring homes and retirement savings to joint ownership with a child, can lead to severe inequities between beneficiaries and unintended tax consequences. Professional advice is recommended.

(Source: Michael Kane, The Vancouver Sun, Sunday, August 28, 2005)

Some of the more important financial documents (in no order of priority) may include:

☑ Bank Accounts – savings, checking, certificates

☑ Retirement incomes – pension plans

☑ Bonds, Mutual Funds, Stock Portfolio

☑ Tax information – past year's filings, accountant records

☑ Insurance plans and policies (universal life and the living-benefit plans – disability, long-term-care, critical illness)

☑ Portfolios – assets and liabilities

☑ Shareholders' agreements

Although we avoid talking about money, research by American author Daniel Goleman suggests that 80 per cent of financial decisions are made emotionally *(Source: The Vancouver Sun, April 24, 1998.)*

The following lists additional general documents/information that we should become familiar with and be able to access quickly:

☑ Social Security Information

☑ Pension plans information (past employers)

☑ Health-Medical Plans

☑ Rental properties' agreements

☑ Safety deposit boxes

☑ Credit cards

☑ Birth certificates/Death certificates

☑ Adoption information

☑ Marriage certificates

☑ Divorce papers

☑ Passports

☑ Citizenship papers

☑ Funeral wishes (written) and related information

☑ Funeral plots' deeds, if purchased

☑ Deeds to all properties owned

☑ Automobile information (insurances included)

☑ Military/veteran information (if applicable)

Financial advisor Clay Gillesie of Rogers Group said **wills can be complex documents** that can work against the intentions of the under-or ill informed. The most common pitfall he sees in his practice is a parent arranging his or her estate in joint ownership with the eldest son or daughter to avoid probate (a tax). "The idea is that upon the parent's death it will pass to the son or daughter, who can pay the tax on the estate and then divvy it our to the remaining children"

"But there are four things that may go wrong. He or she may get divorced and the marriage partner gets half; he or she may get sued and lose part of the assets; he may go bankrupt and lose it to creditors; if there is a falling out among the family members, and he or she decides not to give out the assets to one or more of the family members, they have no legal recourse" "None of this is about money; it's about being fairly treated," said Gillespie. *(Source: From Estate Planning, "Ready A Will While You're Able" by Jim Jamieson, Business Reporter, "The Province", December 4, 2005)*

What basics should I look into regarding wills?

As the daughter/son-caregiver, we must be strong enough/brave enough (perhaps loving enough is what I am searching for) to enter into discussions with our parents regarding their wills. *(Question to ponder – Why is death such a forbidden topic in our society today?)*

From time to time, we should check the following:

☑ **Possible revisions:** Once wills are made, we should review them periodically with our parents so that the wills are up-to-date and always set out in accordance with each parent's wishes *(Note: It is advantageous to specify the exact beneficiaries for 'each' item, each policy...each asset no matter how small it seems.)*

☑ **Special advice:** We should introduce ourselves to our parents' lawyer and his/her personal secretary or assistant (it eases communications in the future when needed).

As time goes on, we may need to discuss with that lawyer, any special clauses relating to changes in the mental capacity of each parent (e.g. the impact of dementia-related conditions if we are wondering about responsibilities for some financial affairs). If a will is complex, we should keep their lawyer apprised of a parent's health status so advice with his/her affairs can be offered.

☑ **Inheritance rules:** It is important that our parents understand fully how inheritance rules apply to their situations and set out conditions in the wills that take those rules into consideration. *(Note: It is wise to check what relative in the family hierarchy inherits and under what circumstances if directions are not stated precisely in a legal will. Check the inheritance rules for your province/territory.)*

Here is what happens if you die without a will. Someone must apply to be the administrator of your estate. This creates the potential for disagreement among heirs, regarding who will best handle the estate in a fair and impartial way. If need be, a (B.C.) Public Guardian and Trustee will step in to administer your estate, thus adding to the cost and time necessary to settle your affairs. Your spouse will receive the first $65,000 of the assets and a life estate in your principal residence. A life estate is a charge against the title that ensures your spouse a place to live for the rest of his or her life. It also means your spouse will receive any rental income from the property, should he or she decide to live elsewhere. (It does not preclude your spouse from entertaining a new partner.) The rest of the estate is divided between or among the spouse and children, in varying ratios, depending on the number of children. For example, if you die, survived by a spouse and two children, your spouse would receive the first $65,000, the life estate, and one-third of whatever is left (commonly known as "the residue"). The two children will each receive one-third of the residue. The children will also share equally the value of the real estate, once the surviving spouse has died, or has voluntarily released the life estate. Normally, the person receiving a life estate is responsible for payment of taxes, strata fees, etc. Repairs and maintenance are the responsibility of the ultimate beneficiaries, which might be onerous on children. If the children are minors, the Public Guardian and Trustee will take over management of their legacy, for a sizable, non-negotiable fee. If you have no children or spouse, the estate goes first to your parents, if living. If they are not alive, the estate goes to your siblings, nieces, nephews, and so on, down the line. *(Source: The Vancouver Sun, Article: Engage a professional to prepare your will for you, by L. Salvador, Notary Public, Sidney, B.C. February 10, 2001.)*

What about a living will?

We should have a 'living will' done by a legal firm to let our loved ones know what we want…just in case. Our parents should have a living will as well as a regular will.

What if you are incapacitated as a result of an injury or illness; what if you are on life support...does someone in your family or a close friend know your financial, health, legal and personal wishes...who will make decisions on your behalf? A living will simply sets out your care preferences.

What are the basics regarding powers of attorney?

We should have a power of attorney document for each of our parents.

If we have had a power of attorney in place for many years, we must check with our parents' lawyer to find out if this document has to be updated. *(For example: In our family's case, the government of our province had made changes to the requirements and formatting of the document over the years and we were advised to have each power of attorney redone so that no questions could ever be raised.)*

Any group with which we may want to communicate regarding our parents' business affairs will require a copy of the power of attorney-type document. For example:

- ☑ We need to place a photocopy of the document on file at our parents' bank(s).

- ☑ We need to send a copy to the relevant income tax departments so that we can discuss our parents' taxes with personnel there.

- ☑ We need to send a copy to relevant government departments (e.g. Human Resources for Old Age Pensions) so that we are allowed to discuss information on these specific matters with personnel there.

- ☑ We must send a copy, for file purposes, to the company responsible for doing our parents' income tax returns. *(For example: I eventually had the chartered accounting firm responsible for doing my taxes also assume the work for my parents, as it was easier to coordinate and discuss the family's situation with one firm.)*

- ☑ If a parent is receiving pensions from former employers/ military/ disabled, we must send a copy to their pensions departments for filing there, as we will have questions in the future regarding parent pensions.

☑ If a parent still drives/owns a car, we need to deliver/send a copy to the insurance company agent's office.

We can request the lawyer who has undertaken the work for our family to forward copies of the powers of attorney, to particular departments or agencies when required – a telephone call giving the addresses and contact names is all that a legal firm usually wants in order to forward documents.

We don't always need to use a legal power of attorney – in lesser important situations a written letter of permission from a parent to a company will suffice, such as credit card companies or airlines for points transferring.

Finally, we need to keep a copy of each power of attorney/agreement on file at our own home.

What should I do regarding banking matters?

We should get a very clear understanding of the purposes of our parents' bank accounts/agreements, the banking locations used and the bank contact person for each account.

Accompanying our parents (if possible), we should:

☑ Visit the banks' branches where they do their banking business.

☑ Make appointments to meet the account representatives responsible for our parents' accounts; note names in our files and contact numbers of these persons.

☑ List the account numbers in our files.

☑ Discuss monthly incomes to and disbursements from the appropriate accounts.

☑ Gather relevant information regarding managing all the accounts.

☑ Pay particular attention to any savings/investment growth accounts – we should not assume that banks will inform our parents if 'better' options come available to gain interest. *(For example, Dad had one particular general account with several thousands in it when I reviewed his banking (1996) – this account had sat since his retirement (1972) – it was a non-interest bearing account – 24 years on $ with no interest! When I confronted the bank representative asking why the bank didn't inform customers over the years about these 'old type' of accounts, she responded that information was sent out years ago, but she added, as if to make me feel better, "Many seniors have accounts like this still, they don't seem to like change". The interest on this account alone over the two decades would have amounted to a healthy sum. I blame myself somewhat as I should have paid closer attention to my parents' banking affairs not only at the time of retirement but also as the years went on.)*

☑ Discuss signing authority on each of the bank accounts.

We need signing authorizations on file, even with a power of attorney document on file because a power of attorney is only valid while someone is alive. If a parent dies unexpectedly and our other parent's name or our name, at the very least, is not authorized on a specified account(s), that account(s) becomes frozen and cannot be accessed until probate, resulting perhaps in undue financial complications, depending on circumstances. *(For example: As the main caregiver of my parents, when their health problems became obvious, within the first three months of Dad's fall, my parents' financial affairs became my responsibility. It was then that I took the precautionary step, with their permission and had my name added for signing purposes to their bank accounts. If you are not an only child, a decision amongst brothers and sisters will have to be made as to whom will be responsible for financial matters of parents, perhaps the one with the greatest background in financial/legal issues or the one who lives closest to the parents. Suggestion: If siblings are involved, the sibling responsible for banking matters might photocopy statements each month for his/her brothers and sisters understanding and awareness or each may access on-line information.)*

☑ **We should take precautionary measures whenever possible in order to simplify banking matters.** With some simple banking methods in place, we will be able to respond well when care-needs arise.

☑ We can set up **methods (e.g. authorization forms on file) so that we can access information** regarding the status of our parents' accounts via telephone, fax, computer, as often caregiving-related dollars are needed on the spur of the moment and should be attended to quickly.

☑ We need to put simple **income deposit measures** in place as soon as possible on behalf of our parents (most seniors probably have all this in place already). We should ensure that all our parents' cheques (e.g. old age, pension, disability, veteran, insurance, interests) are directly deposited to the correctly designated accounts (especially if our parents' physical and mental health/memory fluctuate at times). The bank contact will assist with the organization/paperwork.

☑ We should obtain an **access/interact card linking** one of our parents' accounts to one of our own accounts for ease of money transfers, bill payments, and special needs – this measure is especially useful if we live in a different city than our parents or tend to travel a great amount as their banking needs or emergencies can be met instantly.

☑ We need to set up **easy payment methods** for regular bills through an automatic debit system (e.g. television, electricity, natural gas, newspaper subscriptions, telephone, insurance policies, hydro, city utilities…). This task can be organized easily via telephone with most companies.

☑ We need to set aside a **designated credit card** (for ourselves) to use exclusively for caregiving expenses so that we are able to take some of the financial burden from our parents if their savings decline rapidly during their care-years. *(For example: In our situation, I* *found a designated credit card to be a very good way of keeping track of caregiving costs.)*

As already mentioned, **we are accountable at all times** to our parents (and siblings) for managing our parents' financial affairs:

☑ We must keep our parents thoroughly informed of any actions we take on their personal behalf with their bank accounts, if appropriate given their health circumstances.

☑ We should have in place, from the start, a method of keeping track of all of the transactions in our parents' accounts – a designated notebook (if on-line banking is not available) for outlining our activities within those accounts is invaluable.

☑ For each banking activity undertaken on our parents' behalf, we need to record the date, the bank and account number, balances before and after, the action taken, any questions, the verification numbers, and the name of the bank person spoken to if such is required.

Important Note: Cross reference to Suggestion #21: Set up a designated 'care account' to administer all financial aspects of care. Refer to the heading titled: "How can I organize all the financial components of a parent's long-term care needs?"

Crime surveys show that more than half the reported victims of deceptive or fraudulent telemarketing (those phony contests and investments) are over age 60, and more than two-thirds are women. People over 60 account for three-quarters of those defrauded of more than $5000 and the vast majority are victimized more than once. Altogether, this type of scam bilks Canadians of an estimated $40 million annually. Here are some of the more common swindles: phony sweepstakes, draws and contents one 'wins a prize and must send money to handle the shipping and transfers'; fake investment opportunities with 'guaranteed returns'; phone frauds with what looks to be a toll free number to claim the prize, but one is actually running up a phone charge; home renovations scams for substandard work at inflated prices or house inspections that turn up 'serious problems requiring urgent repairs'; misleading advertisements such as the 9 x 12 rug you ordered turns out to be measured in inches not feet; retirement estates and property, the proverbial swampland in Florida; medical frauds for mail-order cures; fraudulent or unethical fundraising where none or just a very small percentage of the money goes to the 'good cause'; confidence games by strangers who profess to be in a profession they are not in order to enlist your help. Remember, don't be pressured ('this is your last chance'); don't send cheques or give credit card information or cash in advance; don't get involved if the caller asks for your help in an investigation (banks and police never involve the customers in investigations); never disclose any private financial and banking information such as a PIN or SIN number; and don't let your fears or concerns get in the way (scammers make their pitches right after a death in a family or during a natural disaster or after a widely reported tragedy). Have a line practiced, "I am not interested!" and hang up. The solution, if you have any doubts, can't get enough information or feel pressure, hang up! It is not rude to hang up on a suspicious call. It doesn't pay some times to be polite. And if you have been scammed, don't be embarrassed at having been taken in, report the crime. Don't let criminals get away with it. (*Source: National Advisory Council On Aging, Expression Volume 14, Number 2, Spring 2001, Government Of Canada*)

What should I understand regarding government pensions?

We should know the amounts our parents receive from:

- ☑ Old Age Security (OAS)

- ☑ Canada Pension Plan/Quebec Pension Plan (CPP/QPP)

- ☑ Guaranteed Income Supplement (GIS)

Call Social Development Canada at 1-800-277-9914, English or 1-800-277-9915, French or visit www. sdc.gc.ca

We should know when to review and apply for revisions on behalf of our parents, for example:

- ☑ Upon change of residency of one of your two parents, to a carehome (termed "involuntary separation")

- ☑ Upon death of one parent

- ☑ Upon a large decrease in personal savings (e.g. low income status)

- ☑ If a veteran *(call Veteran Affairs Canada)*

- ☑ Be sure the application is in for OAS and CPP

(For example: When Dad's residency changed to a carehome, Mum qualified, upon application for an "involuntary separation" supplement to her old age pension – a provision available so that one spouse may live independently at home. It is important to note that in this type of situation, one parents' old age pension may be decreased and the other increased as a result of this revised living condition.)

Of Interest?

Seniors sources of income:

- OAS and CPP/QPP are the main source of income for over two-thirds of seniors in Canada.

- On average, 29% of the total income of seniors is derived from private employers' pensions and RRSPs, 27% from OAS (including GIS) and 20% from CPP/QPP

- 35% of seniors receive GIS

- Approximately 65% of GIS beneficiaries are women

- Two-thirds of men and one half of women rely on income from private pensions plans *(Source: Statistics Canada, The Daily, February 14, 2003)*

Old Age Security Programs	Have Not Applied (as of 2004)
– OAS Old Age Security	About 50,000
– Guaranteed Income Supplement (GIS) and Allowance	About 300,000
Canada Pension Plan	**Have Not Applied (as of 2004)**
– Retirement pension	About 55,000
– Disability benefit/Survivor benefit	No estimate available

Source: Aging In Poverty In Canada, National Advisory Council On Aging, 2005 - **For further information, go to <u>www.sdc.gc.ca</u>**

All that for $25!

Frank lives in Ontario and receives the Guaranteed Income Supplement. To improve his lot, he worked for the Census in 2001, earning $1,384. As a result he had to pay $542 in income tax; his OAS and GIS benefits went down $601 and his social housing costs went up $216. Tallying this up, Frank finds that his income of $1,384 has cost him $1359, for a net benefit of $25! *(Source: National Advisory Council on Aging - NACA - "Aging In Poverty In Canada" Report)*

Should I bother to review my parents' employer pension plans?

It is strongly recommended that, as daughter/son-caregivers, we contact any former employers to review our parents' pension benefits.

We should formally request (i.e. write a letter) that someone check that all is as it should be for our parents and request any responses in writing.

(For example: Into the latter half of the first year after Dad's accident, I was reviewing and filing his pension stubs from his former employer. I noted a concern and contacted the company's Human Resource Department, on three separate occasions. Finally I wrote a letter to the vice president voicing my problem. Time went by, then I received an unexpected telephone call from the Human Resources and Benefits Division manager. It seems that the specific concern I had raised regarding Dad's pension had prompted an extensive review of his pension in general by HR. Guess what – the department had discovered a discrepancy (computer error from many years ago) in the monthly pension amount Dad was presently receiving and had been receiving for over a decade. It turns out Dad had not received one increment in his pension as he should have. The good news, Dad received a lump sum amount, plus interest (upon request) as a pension correction. The bad news, this lump sum payment caused tax problems the following years (which would not have happened if he had received the correct amount each month over the past decade). The point being is that the review of just this one set of Dad's documents proved worthwhile – the pension error was fixed, my parents received the back-payment plus the correct amount from that time forward and Mum then later received her share of the corrected pension amount as surviving spouse.)

...If you are counting on the government to take care of your old age, you are counting on a modest retirement. There could well be times when you have to put on another sweater because you can't afford to turn up the heat. The public pension system was never designed to give everybody a comfortable retirement but, rather, to lift seniors out of the poverty that was endemic before the Second World War. Most financial planners see Ottawa as contributing just one leg of the retirement income stool. The other two legs are an employer pension plan and private savings...You might want to shake off the notion that seniors are a non-productive drain on the economy when, in fact, they pay billions in taxes, drive large sectors of the economy and contribute in a myriad other ways. If you are lucky, you will be a senior, too, some day. It's got to be better than the alternative. (Source: The Vancouver Sun, July 3, 2001, Michael Kane's comments on Gordon Pape's bestseller, 'Retiring Wealthy in the 21st Century'.)

Should I also concern myself with other, seemingly less important matters?

We should contact any **clubs/organizations** which our parents had/have membership in and discuss the benefits (if any/small/large, financial/nonfinancial) available. *(For example: Dad was a life-member of an Italian-Canadian Club which, upon application, had a small daily hospital allowance benefit payable for the number of days spent in the hospital. The Club, when notified, also paid a small sum to Mum upon Dad's death, as a benefit.)*

(Note: If a veteran, the program and assistance benefits from veteran-related associations are worth pursuing – the information can be obtained from association coordinators of regions.)

We can also apply for any **city program aids**, such as use of handidarts or disabled-related parking permits, in order to simplify daily living.

Recommendation: Complete the following table for parents AND then for oneself (put into a file).

The BASICS	✓ In Order ✗ To be done	DETAILS
Will (Codicil)		My legal firm is:
Power of Attorney		My legal firm is:
Living Will		My legal firm is:
Living Trust		My legal firm is:
Bank Accounts **Safety Deposit Boxes**		My banks are:
RRSPs/Portfolios/Funds		My financial service company is:
Tax Information		My chartered accounting company is:
Insurance Plans **Life** **Disability** **Critical Illness** **Long-Term Care**		My insurance policies are with:
Birth Certificate		Location:
Marriage Certificate		Location:
Divorce Certificate		Location:
Death Certificate		Location:
Social Security		Number:
Citizenship Papers		Location:
Passport (Number)		Location:
Pensions OAS **CPP** **Supplement** **Allowance** **Employment-related**		With:
Medical Plans		My medical number is:
Credit Cards		Types and with:
Rental Properties		Contracts/Agreements:
Deeds to Properties		Location:
Vehicle Registration:		Location:
Funeral Wishes		Written and Location:

 **Suggestion 20:** *Organize an easy-to-manage household budget*

How do I begin understanding and organizing a household budget for my parents' home?

We need to find out:

- How regular monthly items are being attended to.

- What bill paying methods are being used (i.e. cheque by mail, bank direct payment, six month scheduled payments…).

- Who is/was responsible for what aspect of the household and the costs.

- Where the dollars are going (and coming from).

- What has to be attended to on a seasonal/annual schedule. What are the costs. Who is going to be responsible for that payment. How is the task to be included in the yearly budget.

- Names, telephone numbers, addresses of any agents/companies and individuals to contact regarding monthly/seasonal/annual household needs.

☑ Month by month

At the onset of the care-years, we must gain a quick appreciation of our parents' monthly household budget since we need to be on top of the $$ output for planning purposes (food, power, telephone, household maintenance, cars, luncheons/dinners, lawn, insurance…).

If a parent, one who is unaccustomed to the budget task, is now going to assume the activity, we may need to reorganize how the household items each month will be handled, perhaps organizing a new method to accommodate the circumstances and that parent.

(For example: Since Dad had always handled the main aspects of the monthly budget process and was no longer capable of being involved in the household

budget responsibilities, an easy-to-manage monthly record keeping system was organized for Mum's use in her first few LTC years (when she was still capable), as keeping a detailed monthly record of all the household expenses was a new task for her. We used a household-budget book (e.g. lined, coiled book) and a small storage file-box. She had a designated location for her budget book and filing box – the spot never changed. When Mum paid a bill or received notice of the automatic payment withdrawal, she dated the receipt as to when paid/received, then recorded the item, the date and the amount in her budget book for that month and popped the receipt into the file box – she was very conscientious regarding this task. Using this method, she had an easy referral mechanism when she needed to 'jog her memory' about anything; she was also more aware of the costs as she wrote everything down (there are advantages and disadvantages to this). Mum and I reviewed expenses periodically (e.g. every month in the first two years; once a year at income tax time). Setting up this simple administrative system offered Mum independence, (limited) control of some of the household monthly expenses and some degree of flexibility (e.g. she planned ahead to when she could have larger home tasks undertaken – she had had the inside of the house freshly painted and new linoleum put on her kitchen floor. In this manner, we were a team responsible for running her household.)

☑ Season by season

Just as we need to plan on a monthly basis, reviewing a budget season-byseason means we have less chance of forgetting a task and its cost:

For example, a seasonal list, for summer, could include:

- Tree care: pruning and spraying the fruit trees; tree-trimming (e.g. the same company was contracted annually).

- Yard maintenance: weekly mowing of the lawn; fertilizing; picking, sorting and boxing the fruit; watering the lawns *(For example: We found the installation of an automatic underground sprinkling system on the whole property costly, although extremely worthwhile, thus eliminating the need for a caregiver or neighbours to move sprinklers. As well, in the second care-year we hired a "yard handyman" who performed many of the tasks year-round, he became familiar with exactly what was required each season, allowing for continuity for the household – we also knew what our seasonal budgets were as a result.)*

☑ According to need

We need to record the dates of annual household expenses and plan for the costs so there are no surprises.

Some items to include are:

- Vehicle(s) insurance and maintenance schedules, including yearly membership in an auto-club for roadside emergencies.

- House insurance.

- Homeowner taxes.

- Memberships payments.

- Travel/health insurance.

- Mandatory homeowner check-ups and maintenance (security alarms, fireplaces, furnace, carpets...).

Hopefully by having a general understanding of the overall household budget, we are in a position to decrease our parents' $-worries.

(For example: Mum and Dad knew their costs month by month, but never 'tracked' all of the household costs on a regular basis during their 24 pre-care years of retirement. Mum, in LTC years, since recording the expenses, sometimes became concerned when she saw the outflow and totals. Mum's caregivers and I learned to listen carefully for small signs of Mum's financial-stress. ("Maybe we should begin cutting back on lunches out" or "I don't think I'll buy that right now"....) When we heard these types of statements, it fell to me to re-emphasize in some subtle manner that all was fine. One live-in caregiver made me laugh as she called the 3rd week of every month the "PMS week" – she was coping during that week with both a teen-age daughter (self-explanatory) and Mum (Pre-monthly Money Scare) as Mum started fretting during that week since the pension cheques were not deposited until the 4th week of each month and she "didn't want to run short". Usually caregivers have a great sense of humour – thank heavens!)

Boomers in Canada are waging war on wrinkles. They're eating smarter, exercising regularly and planning for active retirement. Trends suggest the 10 million Canadians born between 1947 and 1966 will live longer than any previous generation. But there is a trap in clinging to a mindset that is forever young. Maureen Maclachlan (Business Gerontologist, president, Vancouver's Age Matters Communications Group) calls it "freeze-frame syndrome", a reluctance among middle-aged children to accept that their parents are getting older. Consequently, they avoid dealing with money and legal matters until there is a family crisis. *(Source: The Vancouver Sun, April 24, 1998.)*

Notes:

Suggestion 21: *Set up a designated "care account" to administer all aspects of care*

It is helpful to set up a designated account for caregiving related costs, both services and equipment. This type of account will make your life easier.

Why do I need a designated care account?

☑ **Accountability:** We are accountable for expenses relating to care-needs; receipts and records are vital when given this trusted care-years responsibility. An account designated for this single purpose, caregiving, also allows us to set aside any required dollars for later needs.

☑ **Income tax purposes:** Having a special account will assist us during income tax time (we need to work closely with our chartered accounting firm); we are not only responsible for our own tax information and records now, but also for providing information for our parents and for the caregivers.

☑ **Health/medical plan reimbursements:** Some expenses are recoverable (percentages) from medical health plans/health insurance plans with submission of receipts. *(For example: Upon contact with Dad's past employer to discuss how employee/retiree benefit plans might assist our family with caregiving costs, it was explained that certain items of equipment were acceptable for partial reimbursement from the company medical plan for retirees – providing we had all receipts.)*

Once all the care-related expenses are known, the main items will most likely remain consistent, thus allowing us transfers of money (automatic) to the designated 'care account' each month or as pre-arranged to cover costs. We can always increase the amount put into the care account if an outstanding care item is required or circumstances change drastically. Using this method, when the designated care account receives dollars from other sources (e.g. a parent's savings account or our own personal account) or accesses other dollars, there is either a record or cheques detailing the transaction (accountability).

How can I organize all the financial components of a parent's long-term care needs?

In the beginning of 2006, I was asked by a family how they might go about organizing the administrative financial aspects of caring for their elderly parent. The following was my email response, which may offer some guidance for your family.

Dear X…

The following may answer your question and provide some clarity–this is what I did in that regard and it worked fabulously:

1. I obtained/hired a **local business bookkeeping accounting firm** (a small company, a local one to where my mother, the care-receiver lived); the purpose: to do all the administrative work, such as paying the caregivers each month, paying for large equipment items, keeping the books and bank records, preparing required monthly reports to the health unit when subsidization was involved; paper tracking for tax purposes to submit to the chartered accounting firm at tax time and finally to report to me, the family on a regular basis and in-between if need be, etc. I paid the bookkeeping company a $100/month retainer to do the work, some months the work was quite complex others not so, thus we decided on a retainer basis. It is important to understand that this bookkeeping company was used for organizational administrative purposes only but not for income tax purposes.

2. I also used **a chartered accounting company** for tax purposes for my parents (the same one that did my tax returns). I strongly recommend that a family use **a chartered accounting firm** for all their tax work especially when caregiving is involved. I used a CA from the beginning of my journey and it proved very worthwhile, as the professionals there were always up-to-date on caregiving deductions and expenses and methods for assisting me with my related care costs as well.

3. I also recommend that the key family caregiver/care-guide become familiar with the **extended care insurance** that a parent has as then

one can apply at year-end for reimbursements for equipment expenses, ambulance trips… I made a habit of doing this reimbursement step annually at tax time (do not leave it as there are expiry time periods by companies and one may be denied claims that are too old).

4. At the same time, as we were receiving some financial subsidization from our provincial government and thus accountability is key, I **registered a provincial-non-profit group** in my mother's name (very easy and inexpensive to do with one application) and set up **a bank account in the name of that non-profit group.** (Note: Some government subsidization programs require this separate bank account be set up in this manner.) If one does not want to set up a non-profit group then having a special, separate bank account in the 'care-receiver' person's name is important (the person being the one receiving the actual care). I had two signatories for this bank account (one signatory went into the bookkeeping company a couple of times a year and signed dozens of cheques for the bookkeeper's use, in advance).

    All **required 'care-dollars'** from each source were deposited into the bank account via several ways: I put some in, the government put in their subsidized amount when it was received and some dollars when necessary went in from my parent (e.g. from her pension source or for some people perhaps from annuities, portfolio etc). All money went into the 'pot' so to speak, then the bookkeeping company used it to pay, as mentioned, caregiver fees, equipment costs, a small stipend even went back to my mother as allowed for food and accommodation as she had a live-in caregiver (only $100 but she felt it was helpful—more a token thing, but we set it up this way and all had agreed). As well, the company paid itself its $100 retainer fee each month. The point being that all sources of dollars were thus accounted for including payments required for the caregiving of my parent. How the money was spent was there for "all" to see (transparency and accountability are important within families).

5. I set up a **4 person Mini Board,** of which two bank signatories had to be a part of (my mother and I were also on that board). There is really not much work for this Board, but it does keep everything transparent, which of course is extremely important. The Board met once a year (as required—could be a quick meeting over the fence with coffee, if

you get the idea)…but this annual meeting goal is communication as everyone gets a (verbal or written) report from the bookkeeping company as to how the dollars have been spent.

Important Note: This Bank account and mini Board method eliminates any abuse of dollars and also any hint of problem that could arise at present or in the future or at death, between family members, not assuming there will be. As for me, I was an only child and I still loved using this method as it made all the paperwork and the reporting and the income tax work easy. It also was perfect for accountability to the local health region/ authority when my mother was receiving a subsidization (from a provincial government financial assistance program for "self-managed care" to keep her in her own home). Note: If one's parent is receiving a subsidization payment when in a care-nursing home then a bank account system is not necessary for that alone as the co-payment portion is paid directly to the nursing home from the government but for all other uses of care payments, a designated account is of value.

Special note of interest re: this complete method of accountability: If there are 'any' and I repeat 'any' dollars coming from more than one source; perhaps from an insurance company for LTCI claims, and/or from family members who are contributing to the parent's care, and/or from the recipient's own pensions or savings and/or from a provincial government program for subsidization (unless, as mentioned, as in the case of a nursing home, as the home gets the subsidy directly), then I suggest strongly this complete hands-off organizational, administrative method for a family. I feel even more strongly that a method of accountability should be in place **if family members are being paid as caregivers** in order to avoid any family disputes at any time during the caregiving and even later (after the care-recipient has died and the estate is being reviewed by all siblings and lawyers). It is particularly good if long-distance caregiving by siblings is involved as often the nearest child takes on the caregiving duty/obligation – but using this system, all siblings are involved to some degree and all can get the reports from the bookkeeping company upon request. All may even be on the Board. *(My apologies to anyone who may misread my intention here, it is not to suggest abuse or disputes…it is to be clear and open at all times with caregiving responsibilities.)*

Finally, the method outlined is inexpensive; it is effective; it is fair and most importantly, caregiving dollars are going toward the best quality care possible and being reviewed by a Board. In short, there is never any question as to where the money is coming from and where it is being spent—all is administered by a third party. It is also an easy-to-do organizational initiative (takes one meeting with a bookkeeping company to get the ball rolling, one meeting at a local bank/credit union to get all set up, and one simple Board meeting once a year...)

So, the key is two fold: to hire a local bookkeeping company *and* to set up a special care-account in the name of the care receiver with more than one signatory. *(Note: By the way, no one, absolutely no one had access to this account except the bookkeeping firm (not even me, no one—it had been set up that way from the beginning). If my parent needed anything paid from it, I phoned the company and they did it from that account, with the appropriate cheques and signing authorities and the monthly reports available to all (government, Revenue Canada, family members, Board members, my parent, etc....)* This single system needs to be set up from the get-go when care of a parent is involved as dollars are tempting and can go astray with all good intentions. This way, the quality of care for the money available is guaranteed to some degree.

A special note re: Long-term care insurance claims: Again, remember, I am not an agent or specialist in financial services fields, my interest is in the long-term care issue itself, thus I offer this comment as a note for your consideration. There are two 'main methods' insurance companies use to pay the LTCI claims (yet, any type of claim payment can work well for a family that is organized). One, some insurance companies pay the actual care-bills directly when submitted; or two, some companies pay a lump care-sum each month to the family and the family handles the care-bills.

Author's views on each LTCI payment system for your review:

Case One: Some insurance companies pay the care bills directly when invoiced. If the insurance company is paying the bills directly, this has an up-side and a down-side, first the up-side, there is never any abuse of dollars as the money is not going to the family directly but to the bill-payments and all the dollars are guaranteed to being used for 'quality care'; now the down-side, the bills have to be submitted and this can pose an administrative hassle for some families as they must keep bills and invoices each month. For this type of insurance payment, I recommend the use of a bookkeeping company as described previously as the bookkeeping company does all the work and sends all papers into the insurance company for payment. As well, there can be no suggestion of abuse of dollars as the family does not receive cash.

Case Two: Some insurance companies send a specified lump sum payment to the family for the care of the LTCI recipient. Again, if the insurance company is paying a lump sum directly to the family, this has an up-side and a down-side, first the up-side, there are no administrative bill-hassles each month; now the down-side, this lump sum payment system may be fraught with potential problems as you can just imagine in some cases, I am not suggesting all of course, but abuse of the dollars could occur. For this type of LTCI payment, I recommend once again, using a bookkeeping company plus a care-receiver bank account as these methods combined eliminate any of the potential problems–the insurance dollars are paid by arrangement directly into the bank account and no one person has direct access (bookkeeping company only has access) so all dollars once again go where they should, to the quality of care for the recipient ...you get the idea. This easy organizational accountability method works!

Refer to Topic 7, the heading: Do you know the Family Relations Act?

"Experience is simply the name we give our mistakes."
– *Oscar Wilde 1854-1900*

TOPIC 4

Let's Talk: Ensuring a safe and positive at-home environment

What can I do to make sure that my parents' home surroundings meet their care needs?

Personal Anecdote: "But I've been driving for almost 70 years!"

Suggestions:

22: Review the home and prepare our parents

23: Visualize traffic flow areas

24: Organize new care items ready for use

25: Rearrange these two rooms first, the bathroom and the bedroom

26: Pay attention to mealtime needs

27: Remember the importance of telephones

28: Assess vehicle use and driving skills

29: Be neighbourly

What can I do to make sure that my parents' home surroundings meet their care needs?

Personal Anecdote:
"But I've been driving for almost 70 years!"

Mum's regular family doctor was on vacation when her annual driving medical review came due, leaving a substitute doctor to do the evaluation. This doctor, like Mum's own doctor was very thorough in his work, but as he was unfamiliar with Mum's background, he made notes in response to every question on the review form.

These comments subsequently prompted the Motor Vehicles Division to contact Mum requesting that she be tested in order to re-qualify for her driver's license - the retesting involved a vision test, a written test, and a full road, including freeway, driving test. The Motor Vehicle demand caused confusion, "I've been driving for nearly 70 years, I've never had an accident, I only drive up the road to see my brother..."

In the end, Mum was forced to review her driving needs - she was driving very little by this point in time since she went everywhere with her caregiver. Mum opted to quit driving altogether - she was 88 by then and had driven since she was 17 years old.

There were tears reflecting back on so many years of fun and memories. But - she sold her faithful car ("to a good home"), she sold her collapsible garage, she cancelled her car insurance - and she enjoyed spending these extra dollars.

I breathed a sigh of relief - even though Mum drove little and was a very cautious driver, I always worried about her safety on the road. When we reflected on this issue in later years, Mum commented that she didn't miss driving - I believe that to be true, yet, I also know she greatly missed what driving represents - independence.

 **Review the home and prepare our parents**

When we think about what gives our parents pleasure and security, it is their immediate environment – their home. It stands to reason therefore if their home is an organized, safe, relaxing place, that it will contribute significantly to their quality of life in their care-years.

Think about at-home surroundings are extremely important as our aged parents spend approximately 80% or more of their day, almost every day of the year, in that location:

- Watching television.

- Reading books, listening to music.

- Visiting with relatives and neighbours.

- Enjoying meals.

- Having afternoon naps.

- Doing hobbies and crafts.

- Telephoning old friends regularly.

- Writing cards and notes.

- Sitting on the patio.

- Spending time bird watching.

- Tending to the gardening or the plants.

- Celebrating special occasions.

- Sleeping.

Live Longer With Friends

Elderly people who have a network of good friends rather than close family ties have a better chance of living longer, according to a new study. ...Friends may be a beneficial influence on the elderly by encouraging them to eat better, quit smoking or drinking and exercise more, the study says. But they also have a big psychological impact, although less easily defined, by lifting mood and self-esteem and promoting the desire to cope at times of difficulty, it suggests. (*Medical Report, June 2005, The Study appears in the Journal of Epidemiology and Community Health. Agence France-Press*)

Why is it a priority to make changes within the home?

There are two main reasons why we should constantly review our parents' immediate environment and rearrange areas that call out for attention:

1 – We want the house and surrounding areas to meet their new health needs.

2 – We want the home to help create a positive daily environment (i.e. when asked, how is it going, the response we want to hear from a parent is, "I'm having a good day").

(For example: A community health nurse coordinator first drew my attention to the significance of creating a safe, secure home environment, one that would meet the needs of both Dad and Mum. While Dad was still in the rehabilitation ward, the coordinator arranged to have a nurse review the safety of my parents' home environment. It was an extremely helpful exercise as the visiting nurse, on her walkabout, noted many basic changes required in my parents' home. The nurse also mentioned that it was equally important to look for the less obvious – what changes can be made so that regular activities (e.g. meals) remain enjoyable times. During one of the follow-up visits, the health coordinator watched Mum walk around the house, get up off the bed and go about some of her major activities in the house, then further suggestions for changes were offered. She encouraged the caregivers and me to be on the lookout for problem

spots as health levels changed. Ensuring a safe, positive home environment is not a responsibility to be postponed.)

How do I begin?

We need to prepare our parents for the necessary changes required to their home and include them in any home-environment projects:

- ☑ We need to sit down with both our parents (if appropriate) and **discuss the more important changes** we feel may be necessary within their home surroundings including a tentative timeline for starting on the changes (e.g. "When do you think we might be able to do X, Mum?").

- ☑ We must **elicit a parent's input** as it is her/his home and changes may not be easily accepted. We need to be prepared for our parents' hesitations. *(For example: Mum loved her throw rugs around the house, initially she wanted to keep "just a few to keep things clean" – we had to discuss why even "a few" were not possible for safety reasons.)*

- ☑ We should **visit certain suppliers and stores** (e.g. medical equipment stores) to become familiar with their products and services.

We should decide on a store we would like to deal with on a regular basis; introduce ourselves; explain our current situation to the owner/manager; outline what we are attempting to accomplish within a reasonable budget and listen carefully to his/her ideas since experience with the various equipment is valuable.

We should visit the store again in the near future, this time with a parent so she/he may browse around the special products and equipment – while there introduce our parent to the owner/manager. Later, it is wise to introduce the key caregiver as well.

- ☑ We should **remind ourselves to go slowly and to be considerate of our parents' opinions and questions.**

We will not be able (nor should we try) to implement a series of changes rapidly with our parents, as their home may have been arranged exactly as is for many years.

We should be prepared for some resistance if we attempt to make all the changes within a very short period of time (even though making the changes all at once may be the least costly way).

(For example: One week, we had the medical equipment installation technician working in the house two days in a row. During the first day we had several new items installed in Mum's bathroom, but when a shower reach-bar was suggested by the technician, in addition to the rest of the items, Mum became adamant that she didn't want "another" piece of equipment. She needed time to adjust to the changes, think about the benefits of what was suggested. She reconsidered the next day — the technician returned, smiling.)

> ☑ If a parent is hospitalised for any lengthy period, we should discuss with our healthy parent the advantages of having as many of the changes to the house accomplished prior to the hospital release date (less chaos, quicker familiarity upon arriving home).

If a potential problem-parent is at home (versus in the hospital) when changes have to take place, we need to **consider dates/times so as to keep anxiety levels at a minimum** and then schedule the work accordingly (e.g. when the anxious parent is out during day-hospital or therapy visits, during respite periods, or even when on an outing for a morning).

Once the changes have been accomplished, we can invite the local community health unit/CCAC coordinator/nurse to our parents' home for an inspection and further in-put and discussion.

Making a home user-friendly adds very little to the building costs – about $300 in a multiple unit project and about $600 for a standard house – says Vancouver builder Patrick Simpson. Retrofitting later is much more costly but, if you are planning a renovation, that's the time to incorporate Simpson's construction changes. Here are some other relatively inexpensive adjustments that Simpson says will extend the shelf life of your home: a standard door measures two feet, eight inches. Instead, install 36 inch doors. Widen stairways from the standard 36 inches to 42. (Statistics suggest half of all home accidents happen on stairs.) Use lever style door handles. Double the number of electrical outlets in each room, especially beside beds. (Extra plugs mean conveniences like vaporizers, humidifiers, heating pads and even lap top computers can be used in the event someone is bed-ridden for a time.) Raise A/C outlets from 12 to 18 inches above the floor to decrease the need for bending. Lower light switches to 42 inches from 48 to make them more accessible. Run a 2X12 board three feet above the floor around the perimeter of the bathroom wall so grab rails can be installed in the future. *(Source: The Vancouver Sun, January 23, 2000.)*

Notes:

_____

_____

_____

_____

_____

_____

_____

_____

_____

_____

_____

_____

_____

_____

Suggestion 23: Visualize traffic flow areas

We must learn to look at the well-used traffic areas in our parents' home through the eyes of a professional community nurse – are areas obstacle courses or safety zones, which describes each traffic area?

What am I checking for in the house?

☑ **Aids:** If a parent is using a walking aid, we have to do a walk-about throughout all the traffic areas using that particular aid ourselves, be it a walker or cane or wheelchair – we will soon discover spots where are we trying to steer around pieces of furniture and accessories. (It is not as useful 'to imagine the stroll' – it is more effective to actually go through the exercise itself with the aids.)

☑ **Obstacles:** We need to check rugs, chairs, stools, coffee tables, clothing racks – all protruding or unstable furniture pieces/ accessories/ornaments/ plants in each room. We may have to remove all throw rugs, relocate living room hassocks for access only when needed, put away large ornaments or vases, bundle wires…. (We must do the same check in our own home if/when a parent visits.)

(For example: A recliner chair was moved from one location to a new one for Mum's comfort when watching television, leaving a safe wide walking area between the dining room and living room. Mum promptly purchased a large faux tree "to fill the hole" which once again narrowed the passage to its original width – you can't win 'em all.)

☑ **Patterns:** We need to observe our parents' movements throughout the house, discover their pathways and make the necessary changes (e.g. What routes do they use to the bathroom, to feed the cat, to water the plants, to go to the porch, to go to dinner, to sit for television viewing, to go to their desk/closet…?)

☑ **Lights:** We need to check the lighting of each of the rooms. We may need to install night-lights and hallway lights, more plugs and put lamps on the tables (living room, bedroom). We need to pay particular attention to the lighting around telephone locations, as there is usually a rush to reach those places when the telephone rings.

☑ **Special Features:** Finally, we must test any unique features in the home (e.g. non-slip stairs/the sturdiness of the sidebars and banisters on stairwells, will they support weight when leaned upon).

Once modifications have been made to the traffic areas, we must check often for any new problems that may pop up or old ones which may result when items were put back 'where they belong'.

Technology's just getting started…GPS Walkers…. Let's say Grandpa regularly grabs his walker and heads off to bed but winds up in the neighbor's garage. Stanford has built a prototype of an intelligent walker with embedded sensors, voice recognition and Global Positioning System technology. Grandpa might stand in his walker and say "bedroom." The GPS combined with indoor sensors could know where the walker is, map the route to the bedroom and avoid hazards such as stairs, low furniture and the cat while guiding Grandpa to bed. By 2010, you'll see GPS integrated into all kinds of things. (*Source, USA Today, December 16, 2005, article by Kevin Maney, USA Today*)

What do I look for outside the house?

As we did inside the house, we need to discover (i.e. observe) our parents' regular routes outside the house – how do they reach the mailbox, water the planters, refill the birdhouses, go to the patio, visit neighbours, get to the car…

We then need to review each route for:

☑ **Real and potential obstacles** – welcome mats, potted plants…

☑ **Lighting** – automatic on at evening/with motion

☑ **Detail-problems** – bumps in driveways, cracks on sidewalks, loose soil on paths, icy drip-areas in winter. *(For example: Mum's caregivers backed into the garage so that Mum did not have to go around the parked car to get in, the passenger side was thus nearest the door – little things are important to safety and appreciated.)*

In need of an assessment tool?

Reviewing and assessing our parents' living environments is an on-going important job since their health changes will probably be dramatic over the course of many years and their living environments have to be adapted to match these long-term care needs. *(For example, Mum phoned one day in year seven, and told me she could no longer go up and down the eight stairs from the front door entrance of her home to the main living floor, a 1970s home design that had not been forward-thinking obviously. Thus, having no other choice, we installed a stair lift…we laughingly called it the 'Queen Mother lift' as mum used to wave accordingly as she descended and disappeared slowly down the stairs.)*

Note: As caregivers changed from time to time, I was in need of a list of items (i.e. activities) that I could review myself first for safety reasons and later use to outline caregiving duties; a list that I could also review with any new caregivers—this need led me to research CMHC's materials. Canada Mortgage and Housing Corporation (CMHC) provides an excellent assessment tool for family use. The objective of the tool is for each of us to identify specific home improvement areas that will offer a greater degree of independence and safety for our parent or ourselves when going about our everyday activities around the home. *(For example: I found that I truly had a greater understanding of the in-depth level of in-formal care my mother required with her everyday activities, when I went through this CMHC list; as in the last year of her life, she was unable to do or did not do approximately 95% of these activities, her caregivers did these activities with her/for her.)*

I have put CMHC's excellent information into a table format (see following pages) and offer this tool to you now for your use. The list of activities deals with older people who are experiencing a loss in their physical autonomy;

it does not deal with the needs of people who are suffering from mental or psychological problems. It is from: CMHC's *'Maintaining Seniors' Independence – A Guide To Home Adaptations"*. **(To obtain a copy of this excellent free booklet and companion guide, call 1-800-668-2642 or go to <u>www.cmhc.ca</u>)**

Making our homes adaptable—offer an accessible environment, an attractive and practical environment and a flexible environment:

Use this assessment tool

One must answer 'YES' if the senior can perform that activity alone and without difficulty; or 'NO' if he/she is unable to perform the activity, or has difficulty performing it or needs some help or supervision with it.

Answer 'N/A' or non-applicable if the activity is inappropriate for that environment or if the person will never be in that situation for some reason.

RESULTS: Each 'NO' requires a more in-depth look at that activity within the house allowing us to make adjustments.

HINT: At the same time, assess sensory deficiencies too (such as lack of vision, hearing, coordination, strength) as these affect independence too.

...LIST OF ACTIVITIES OF DAILY LIVING.........	YES	NO	N/A
1. GENERAL ACCESSIBILITY			
• Open/close doors			
• Lock/unlock doors			
• Operate light switches			
• Open/close curtains, windows			
• Adjust the heating/air conditioning			
• Go from one room to another, move about in each room			
• Get to the toilet			
• Walk up/down stairs			
• Use the elevator			
• Use the balcony, deck, front porch			
2. GETTING UP, DRESSING AND TIDYING THE BEDROOM			
• Move on/off the bed			
• Take shoes, slippers, clothes out/put in closet			
• Take clothes off/put on			
• Take shoes, slippers off/put on			
• Make bed, change sheets			
3. BATHING AND PERSONAL HYGIENE AT THE BASIN			
• Turn faucets on/off			
• Regulate water temperature			
• Wash hands and face			
• Wash body (basin)			
• Wash hair (basin)			
• Comb/do hair			
• Brush teeth, dentures/use toothpaste, denture cleanser			

...LIST OF ACTIVITIES OF DAILY LIVING.........	YES	NO	N/A
• Shave, using razor/electric razor			
4. **TAKING A SHOWER**			
• Get in/out of shower stall/bathtub			
• Turn shower controls on/off and adjust water temperature			
• Wash/rinse body and hair			
• Reach towel before stepping out			
5. **TAKING A BATH**			
• Get in/out of bathtub			
• Sit down on/get up from bottom of tub			
• Put/pull plug in bathtub			
• Turn faucets on/off			
• Wash/rinse body and hair			
• Reach towel before stepping out			
• Clean bathtub/shower stall			
6. **USING THE TOILET**			
• Sit down/get up			
• Reach/use toilet paper			
• Flush toilet			
• Clean toilet			
7. **PREPARING MEALS**			
• Turn sink faucets on/off and adjust water temperature			
• Use small kitchen appliances			
• Turn on/off hood fan, stove, oven, dish washer			
• Take food out of/put in oven			
• Take food out of/put in refrigerator			
• Open/close drawers and cupboard doors			

...LIST OF ACTIVITIES OF DAILY LIVING.........	YES	NO	N/A
• Take dishes, pots, pans, food out of/put in cupboards			
• Carry food and dishes from place to place			
• Move on/off chair			
• Peel, grate, cut vegetables, fruits, meat,, cheese, bread			
• Open containers, cans, jars			
• Check cooking process			
• Fill up/empty pots			
• Wash/dry dishes			
• Purchase/store groceries			
• Dispose of garbage			
8. DOING THE LAUNDRY			
• Do hand washing			
• Carry laundry bag or basket			
• Fill/empty washing machine			
• Read/work washing machine controls			
• Fill/empty dryer			
• Read/work dryer controls			
• Hang up washing			
• Iron clothes			
9. CLEANING THE HOUSE			
• Dust			
• Use vacuum cleaner/broom			
• Wipe/wash floor			
• Wash windows			
10. USING THE TELEPHONE			
• Answer phone			

...LIST OF ACTIVITIES OF DAILY LIVING.........	YES	NO	N/A
• Dial a number			
11. ENJOYING LEISURE/DOING BUSINESS			
• Move on/off sofa			
• Turn radio/television on/off and select channels			
• Collect mail			
12. TAKING MEDICATION			
• Take medication			

EXTRACT FROM DOUG COPP'S ARTICLE ON THE "TRIANGLE OF LIFE"

My name is Doug Copp. I am the Rescue Chief and Disaster Manager of the American Rescue Team International (ARTI), the world's most experienced rescue team. The information in this article will save lives in an earthquake.

I have crawled inside 875 collapsed buildings, worked with rescue teams from 60 countries, founded rescue teams in several countries, and I am a member of many rescue teams from many countries. I was the United Nations expert in Disaster Mitigation for two years. I have worked at every major disaster in the world since 1985, except for simultaneous disasters.

In 1996 we made a film which proved my survival methodology to be correct. The Turkish Federal Government, City of Istanbul, University of Istanbul Case Productions and ARTI cooperated to film this practical, scientific test. We collapsed a school and a home with 20 mannequins inside. Ten mannequins did "duck and cover," and ten mannequins I used in my "triangle of life" survival method. After the simulated earthquake collapse we crawled through the rubble and entered the building to film and document the results. The film, in which I practiced my survival techniques under directly observable, scientific conditions, relevant to building collapse, showed there would have been zero percent survival for those doing duck and cover. There would likely have been 100 percent survivability for people using my method of the "triangle of life." This film has been seen by millions of viewers on television in Turkey and the rest of Europe, and it was seen in the USA, Canada and Latin America on the TV program Real TV.

The first building I ever crawled inside of was a school in Mexico City during the 1985 earthquake. Every child was under their desk. Every child was crushed to the thickness of their bones. They could have survived by lying down next to their desks in the aisles. It was obscene, unnecessary and I wondered why the children were not in the aisles. I didn't at the time know that the children were told to hide under something.   (continued...)

Simply stated, when buildings collapse, the weight of the ceilings falling upon the objects or furniture inside crushes these objects, leaving a space or void next to them. This space is what I call the "triangle of life". The larger the object, the stronger, the less it will compact. The less the object compacts, the larger the void, the greater the probability that the person who is using this void for safety will not be injured. The next time you watch collapsed buildings, on television, count the "triangles" you see formed. They are everywhere. It is the most common shape, you will see, in a collapsed building. They are everywhere.

TEN TIPS FOR EARTHQUAKE SAFETY

1) Most everyone who simply "ducks and covers" WHEN BUILDINGS COLLAPSE are crushed to death. People who get under objects, like desks or cars, are crushed.

2) Cats, dogs and babies often naturally curl up in the fetal position. You should too in an earthquake. It is a natural safety/survival instinct. You can survive in a smaller void. Get next to an object, next to a sofa, next to a large bulky object that will compress slightly but leave a void next to it.

3) Wooden buildings are the safest type of construction to be in during an earthquake. Wood is flexible and moves with the force of the earthquake. If the wooden building does collapse, large survival voids are created. Also, the wooden building has less concentrated, crushing weight. Brick buildings will break into individual bricks. Bricks will cause many injuries but less squashed bodies than concrete slabs.

4) If you are in bed during the night and an earthquake occurs, simply roll off the bed. A safe void will exist around the bed. Hotels can achieve a much greater survival rate in earthquakes, simply by posting a sign on the back of the door of every room telling occupants to lie down on the floor, next to the bottom of the bed during an earthquake.

5) If an earthquake happens and you cannot easily escape by getting out the door or window, then lie down and curl up in the fetal position next to a sofa, or large chair.

6) Most everyone who gets under a doorway when buildings collapse is killed.   (continued...)

How? If you stand under a doorway and the doorjamb falls forward or backward you will be crushed by the ceiling above. If the door jam falls sideways you will be cut in half by the doorway. In either case, you will be killed!

7) Never go to the stairs. The stairs have a different "moment of frequency"(they swing separately from the main part of the building). The stairs and remainder of the building continuously bump into each other until structural failure of the stairs takes place. The people who get on stairs before they fail are chopped up by the stair treads - horribly mutilated. Even if the building doesn't collapse, stay away from the stairs. The stairs are a likely part of the building to be damaged. Even if the stairs are not collapsed by the earthquake, they may collapse later when overloaded by fleeing people. They should always be checked for safety, even when the rest of the building is not damaged.

8) Get near the outer walls of buildings or outside of them if possible -It is much better to be near the outside of the building rather than the interior. The farther inside you are from the outside perimeter of the building the greater the probability that your escape route will be blocked;

9) People inside of their vehicles are crushed when the road above falls in an earthquake and crushes their vehicles; which is exactly what happened with the slabs between the decks of the Nimitz Freeway. The victims of the San Francisco earthquake all stayed inside of their vehicles. They were all killed. They could have easily survived by getting out and sitting or lying next to their vehicles. Everyone killed would have survived if they had been able to get out of their cars and sit or lie next to them. All the crushed cars had voids 3 feet high next to them, except for the cars that had columns fall directly across them.

10) I discovered, while crawling inside of collapsed newspaper offices and other offices with a lot of paper, that paper does not compact. Large voids are found surrounding stacks of paper.

Spread the word and save someone's life.

Doug Copp, American Rescue Team

http://www.amerrescue.org

 **Organize new care items ready for use**

Our parents, due to changes in health circumstances, may require new personal-use care items in order to create a safer living environment.

Two questions can serve as general guidelines:

1 – What will make life easier/safer for Mum/Dad when…eating? sleeping? dressing? moving around the house? resting? going out? travelling?

2 – Is the item appropriate, simple, useful, safe, easy to handle…?

(Note: Many of the items may already be known, others, not so, as we probably have not had a reason, prior to the care-years, to search them out. Often special equipment is obtained since only one parent needs it, but in truth, it greatly benefits both parents – this was the case with our family.)

How do I know which items are needed?

Dividing the household into categories is helpful when attempting to review needs – less chance of overlooking anything:

☑ **Category 1: Parent with most-obvious needs.**

Initially, we should start by reviewing the parent who has experienced the turning-point health problem and list any new personal items immediately required by him/her.

For example, our 'asap' list for Dad included:

- *Mobility – a walker (with a seat and back support strap), an adjustable cane (for height).*

- *Toiletries – electric shaver.*

- *Clothing – slippers with firm side supports, socks with loose elastic (circulation purposes), sweat suits.*

- *Furniture aids – raised toilet seat with side arms, motorized reclining living room chair (one able to assist with sitting and standing), sheep skin chair cover, piece of porous foam (under a sheep skin to eliminate bed sores from sitting).*

- *Additional necessities – a new sheep skin mattress cover, three large rubber bed sheets, nightwear disposable pads, non-spill urine bottles (for night use).*

☑ Category 2: Other parent's needs.

The list for our other parent may emerge over time in accordance with his/her health circumstances. There could be some duplication of items.

For example, over a period of years, the list for Mum evolved to include the following such items in addition to what was already in the house available:

- *Bathroom aids – bathtub/shower support sidewall bars, outside bathtub support grip pole (when stepping in and out), heavy plastic bathtub chair with back, easy to reach towel rack, lowered bathroom mirrors for make-up, teeth....*

- *Clothing adjustments – sturdier shoes with velcro closures (replacing slipons), warm fleece lined casual house clothes.*

- *Household comfort items – window air conditioner, bedroom ceiling fan with extended pull cords (for easy reaching).*

- *Mobility – walker (around house); stairlift.*

☑ Category 3: Caregiver needs.

A list of items that will make care tasks easier for the caregivers may include items such as:

- For medications – pill-boxes (e.g. 4 kits, enough for a one month's span – less time to fill all at once); a medication dispensing machine.

- Transportation and lifting – lightweight wheelchair, (stored in the trunk of the car, easy on caregiver's back for lifting and collapsing).

- Privacy – own telephone line; computer and printer, optional.

- Alert system for emergencies – a battery operated doorbell system. *(For example: we had two, one placed in Mum's bedroom near her bed, a second in her bathroom and both ring-parts were connected in the caregiver's bedroom.)*

☑ Category 4: Special safety items.

As soon as possible, we should purchase:

- Health alert jewellery – to list allergies, problem medications, adverse medication reactions and health history; it can become a habit to slip a bracelet on before every outing if placed beside an article always worn (e.g. watch).

- A purse/pocket-sized pill-box with compartments – filled with extra pills for the day (when out for the morning, when travelling, when out for dinner).

☑ Category 5: House-related safety items

This list is a common-sense one and many of the items may already be in place:

- The installation of home fire alarms with regularly scheduled test times (e.g. the start of each month).

- Security alarms (deemed necessary) and window locks (especially downstairs/basements).

- The addition of door peepholes (front and back) for clear vision of outside, as many of our parents still live in homes built prior to this item becoming the building-norm.

- The installation of extra lighting throughout the inside of the home, plus good lighting outside the house near the doors and windows including drive-way motion-detector lights (vision, home invasion deterrent).

- Less obvious items – such as rubber on the stair banisters for gripping.

How do I go about acquiring these items?

Since acquiring all the necessary items is costly, prior to purchasing, we should check the following:

☑ **Local hospitals** – for small personal items that the rehab wards often sell to patients at low cost (e. g. clothing grabbers).

☑ **Volunteer agencies** – for rentals (e.g. walker, cane, wheelchair, toilet seats) as such are often available for a limited time (1-3 months) and are useful for transition periods. *(For example: In our situation, we preferred to purchase the aids Dad and Mum were going to need permanently and to rent short-term items as dictated by our budget at those times).*

☑ **Local medical supply stores** – for quality consignment pieces of equipment (e.g. electric motorized recliners, walkers, reconditioned wheelchairs).

☑ **Classified ads of community and city newspapers** – for good second-hand items of a general use (e.g. adjustable beds, exercise equipment…).

Notes:

_____

_____

_____

_____

_____

_____

_____

_____

_____

_____

_____

_____

_____

_____

 **Rearrange these two rooms first, the bathroom and the bedroom**

We need to pace our efforts when attempting to rearrange rooms completely in our parents' home.

We should focus on the two rooms that may require the greatest rearranging – our parents' bathroom and our parent's bedroom(s).

What do I focus on in the bathroom?

Our parents' bathroom may need to be up-dated according to their current needs. When rearranging the bathroom, we need to focus on these factors:

☑ **Accessibility**

☑ **Traffic flow**

☑ **Storage**

We can use the following 'bathroom to-do list' as a starting point:

- Clear walking spaces completely – as the traffic flow will be constant within this confined space.

- Remove any mats around the toilet area – for safety and cleanliness.

- Rearrange countertop space in general or add a small cabinet/table for special items for easy access (e.g. tissues, powder).

- Reorganize storage spaces – clear a storage cupboard very near the toilet for easy safe access of tissue rolls.

- Organize of a storage spot for medications (e.g. the filled and unfilled weekly pillboxes and booklets and prescribed pill bottles).

- Designate a handy under-the-counter storage place for some cleaning materials.

- Organize a designated place on the bathroom counter/in the cupboard for the materials required (e.g. Q-tips, soap, ointments) by part-time community caregivers and therapists if part of our parents' services.

- Check that there is good lighting both in the bathroom and in the access hallways to the bathroom.

- Freshen up the paint (bright and cheerful).

- Place a clock with large numbers on a wall/counter for easy viewing (check for sun glare).

- Add an emergency-alert call system in the bathrooms (e.g. wireless tiny doorbell connection).

- Obtain and install any new equipment for safety reasons.

What do I focus on in the bedrooms?

We need to focus on these needs when reviewing bedrooms:

☑ Physical needs.

- Which side of our parent's body is the weakest/most frail (due to fall, stroke, wound, arthritis, illness); and as a result how has our parent been taught during the rehabilitation process to get in and out of bed? We must arrange the furnishings, especially the bed, accordingly.

- Is morning clothing within easy, safe reach (e.g. undergarments, sweat suits, house coats, pyjamas, slippers…)?

- Is it possible to hang a clock on an easily viewed wall – non-glare clock with large luminous numbers, for easy viewing (day and night) from the bed?

- Is there a telephone within reach on the appropriate side of the bed?

☑ **Exercise needs.**

- How must the bedroom be set up for daily exercise routines (with therapists and caregivers)?

- Is there a place to post exercise sheet directions for review, as the lead therapist will alter exercise routines over time?

☑ **Special needs.**

- What new requirements are there as a result of health problems (bedside aids, telephones, lighting, storage for exercise equipment, chairs…)?

- Is there space for bed pads, special sheets, pillows and bedcovers (i.e. items adapted to fit the new circumstances)?

- What are the special night-time needs? We may eventually need to set up methods (e.g. a bell/ringer, bottles in the bedroom) for dealing with the nighttime bathroom needs as this problem can escalate into a significant one very quickly.

(For example: In the hospital rehab program, Dad learned simply to call out for help to get up to go to the bathroom at night – acceptable to do so in a hospital setting with people working all night on shifts. He then continued to do so when he came home. This method soon proved disruptive as the night-bathroom-calls became more frequent. It was suggested that we change methods, so Dad tried using urine u-neck bottles placed near his bedside for easy reaching. After one month, he became frustrated with the bottles as spills happened and his nightclothes were often wet. Finally it became necessary for him to adjust to wearing strong dependable disposable adult pads at night. Initially, wearing such pads was an affront to Dad's dignity, so it took patience and periodic discussions to help him through this very difficult transition period.)

This is for your reader who is very hard of hearing and no alarm clock can wake him up. I, too am hard of hearing and used to rely on other people to awaken me. Then I discovered an alarm clock attached to a lamp. Now I wake up to a flashing light. I found mine at a local centre for the deaf. Response: Several readers have suggested this type of alarm clock, and have told me they found it at appliance stores, in specialty catalogues, over the Internet and through organizations that sell hearing devices to the deaf. *(Source: Ann Landers, The Vancouver Sun, June 15, 2001.)*

Notes:

 **Pay attention to mealtime needs**

Those of us with elderly parents have long ago noticed that mealtimes are deemed to be important events of the day. Organizing a safe and positive household environment therefore means that we have to pay special attention to all aspects relating to this part of our parents' day.

We mustn't take for granted that mealtimes and all that's involved in their planning and preparation will fall into place – we must discuss some 'guidelines' and periodically check on this part of our parents' day.

What about meal-time arrangements?

We should address meal arrangements early in the care-years journey, as routines and habits may have to be adapted not only to our parents' new health circumstances but also to their new care circumstances.

We should question the basics and organize accordingly:

- Where does everyone eat each meal (location – kitchen, dining room, TV tray)?

- Who else has been added to the household for meals, how many more people; where does the small group eat each meal now (e.g. additional caregivers and walking aids make for a crowd)?

- Is space a problem, do furnishings have to be rearranged?

- Is some reorganization required to simplify regular kitchen tasks (e.g. recycling boxes, garbage bins, additional waste-paper baskets)?

- What happens if there is company for dinner (space, location)? What about needs when visitors arrive (e.g. easy cupboard access for items – to make a cup of coffee...)?

- What about special items now used at meal times, how are these attended to?

- Will the regular kitchen nook/dining room furniture suffice?

(For example: I found out quickly that there is a need to think ideas through from the beginning to the end – in my hasty judgement, a new type of kitchen table chair was needed for Dad, so I ran out and purchased a captain-style with wheels thinking that such would work well – it turned easily to accommodate a walker's position and moves easily into place at a table for meals. But I hadn't visualized the procedure step-by-step – what happens when Dad arrives at the chair, lets go of his walker and because of weak legs, just plops down on the chair – it moves quickly from under him because of the wheels. We went back to using a regular chair at mealtimes and the captain's chair was put in storage.)

What should I do about meal-planning – when caregivers are involved?

If our parents' lifestyle at home has changed due to the addition of caregivers, we must remember to address the topic of meal-planning immediately with the caregivers. Being able to enjoy meals contributes greatly to our parents' everyday attitudes.

We should attempt to help organize meal-planning procedures which our parents and the caregivers can agree upon.

Simple albeit important details should be addressed right from the start as complications can be curtailed before they grow. (Keep in mind that when it comes to food, details count.)

We can begin by making decisions regarding:

☑ **Menu planning:** Who is going to decide on the mealtime menus, especially the main meal of the day (e.g. potatoes more often than rice, meat or poultry or fish, desserts…)? We should explain likes, dislikes and allergies.

(For example: One caregiver experimented and tried a few new foods from time to time; she decided if the main meal was to be a big meal depending on whether lunch was taken at a restaurant/food court or at home. Making weekly desserts was one of the activities done by the visiting community caregiver. I also sometimes tried to introduce (or reintroduce) a variety of food ideas (e.g. a tablespoon per day of yoghurt with acidophilus) during my week of caregiving – note: my efforts often had no effect, but I kept trying.)

☑ **Grocery shopping:** Who makes the grocery lists and how are requests for special foods (e.g. types of cheeses, types of fruits, types of breakfast juice, cereals, sauces, dressings…) accommodated?

(For example: Our caregiver made the main list. Everyone in the house, of course, had input into the grocery lists if and when she felt like something special. The community caregiver also had input if there was something required for baking (and cleaning). We used a simple suggestions method – a piece of paper clipped in the same spot in the kitchen, encouraging all to add individual grocery items to the list.)

☑ **Preparation:** How are foods cooked (e.g. soft steamed vegetables, mashed or baked potatoes, bread or toast or buns, strong/weak coffee, frying, baking, barbequing, roasting…)?

(For example: In the first few months of our care-years, Mum wanted to be involved in the decisions regarding meal preparation, how items were cooked; several years later, she loved having all the meals planned, prepared and ready, with no fuss or concern on her part.)

The part of the house where disinfectant use is most important is the kitchen. "People think the bathroom is the dirtiest part of the house, but it's the kitchen. The cleanest area is the top of the toilet seat; the dirtiest is the kitchen sink. Most pathogens that cause diarrhea enter the house in the food supply." Gerba, of the University of Arizona in Tucson, says research presented at the microbiology meeting found that "you can reduce the risk of acquiring disease by 99% by using disinfectants in the kitchen. The reason you see more consumer cleaning products for the kitchen is because it's a major battle area for germ warfare." Gerba is a respected microbiologist and expert on disease transmission and water treatment; he may be best known as the scientist who alerted America to the microbial perils lurking in kitchen sponges.

What should I remember to include when talking with caregivers regarding meals and their preparations?

If we take time to explain existing meal-time shortcuts, habits, and routines to caregivers, we can reduce the number of stressful situations within the household plus the number of changes being introduced to our parents – keeping some familiar ways is important.

We should, at the same time, explain to our parents that the caregivers have to make some changes fitting their styles of working.

☑ Short-cuts.

We should discuss with the live-in and community caregivers any existing short cuts that may help with meal preparation and care-tasks (e.g. setting the breakfast table the night before).

☑ Habits.

We need to inform the caregivers, as soon as they begin their jobs with us, about schedules and habits of our parents, (e.g. regular coffee-break times, putting mealtime pills out in a designated place, a full candy dish always on a coffee table in case of coughing, meal hours).

☑ Permission to make changes.

We also need to remember to give the caregivers 'permission' to implement space-and-time saving schemes (e.g. adding a hand towel rack near the kitchen sink for use during meals if required versus a long walk by our parents to the bathroom, purchasing a new micro-wave oven, reorganizing cupboards and drawers…).

Grapefruit can be toxic when mixed with drugs...

Evidence also suggest the cabbage family interacts with blood thinners. Put that grapefruit down and back away slowly. Grapefruit tops the list of common foods that can be toxic when mixed with cardiac medications. "A single glass of grapefruit juice can increase the level of a drug in your blood," Nancy Chaytor told the Canadian Cardiovascular Congress (October24, 2005). Chaytor, a nurse practiioner with the Calgary Health Region, said grapefruit inhibits the CYP3A4 enzyme, which metabolizes certain drugs. Potentially dangerous interactions with grapefruit include medications for irregular heart beats, high blood pressure, plus blood thinners such as Warfarin, which is marketed as Coumadin. ...A drug's potency can be also affected by genetics, age, gender, illness, diet or social factors. Evidence suggest that the cabbage family, including broccoli and Brussels sprouts, also interacts with blood thinners, lessening their effect, she said... "That's no excuse to stop eating your leafy greens," Chaytor joked. "Its' all about balance." *(Source: Montreal Gazette, October 26, 2005)*

How do I address nutrition?

☑ We want **to avoid or at least minimize negative situations** when dealing with meals and food preparation – we should keep an eye out for two situations:

1 – A parent slowly eating (picking at) what has been prepared – disliking a meal can be a reminder of dependency (discuss how our parent may propose food preferences).

2 – A parent saying "I don't eat that" or "I don't like that" can prove discouraging for a caregiver who is trying to put together good meals and please our parents and us (discuss how a caregiver may ask for input from a parent without taking orders).

☑ We need to explain to the caregiver any **nutrition supplements** that our parents are taking. These should be added to the grocery list and be part of the regular grocery budget (versus a pharmacy expense).

- We want the caregiver to place these supplements in the pill containers with the prescription medications so none are forgotten.

- We want our caregiver to understand that all supplements must be discussed with us and our pharmacist before use, to ensure that combinations are not problematic.

☑ We have to advise the caregiver of the known **'must have' and 'don't want-type' foods** so that our parents and their caregivers get off on the right foot, so to speak.

(For example: Our initial list was straight-forward – never white bread, only 100% whole wheat; potatoes on a regular basis rather than rice or pasta; desserts are important; neither parent ate between meals; Mum was allergic to head lettuce but loved leafy lettuce and watercress; Dad disliked most vegetables... Over time, our caregivers eventually told me what was/wasn't on the list when I visited – progress.)

With increasing age, the body is less efficient in absorbing and using some nutrients; osteoporosis and other medical conditions common among older people also change nutritional needs. Consequently, an older person is likely to need extra amounts of the following nutrients:

- Calcium to prevent osteoporosis and maintain healthy bones.

- Vitamin D, which the body needs in order to absorb the calcium.

- Vitamin B12 to build red blood cells and maintains healthy nerves.

- Zinc to help compensate for lowered immunity due to aging.

- Potassium, especially in the presence of high blood pressure or the use of diuretic drugs.

- Fiber to prevent constipation.

(Source: Foods That Harm, Foods That Heal, an A-Z Guide to Safe and Healthy Eating, Reader's Digest Association, 1997.)

Suggestion 27: Remember the importance of telephones

The telephone is underrated as a safety item. Telephones serve as our parents' link to us, to friends, to appointments and to emergency services. Our parents' home should have a minimum of two telephones strategically located in the immediate living spaces.

What should I check regarding telephones?

As telephones remain a major means of care-communication, we need to check three factors in our parents' house:

1 – **The number of telephones.**

2 – **Their locations.**

3 – **The types.**

We may need every-so-often to reorganize our parents' telephones to meet their ever-evolving needs (e.g. purchasing a portable one, add/change/ eliminate locations, improve lighting at phone locations, eliminate one memory feature-add another). Reviewing telephone needs is a caregiver responsibility.

(For example, my parents' home, although small, had three telephones upstairs: one in the dining room on a little phone table with quick access from the kitchen; one in the living room on a high coffee table right beside Mum's recliner for easy-reach; and one in Mum's bedroom at arm's reach from the bedside she sleeps on. There was also a jack in Dad's upstairs bedroom (eventually the caregiver bedroom). In addition, the house had a second telephone line/number directly to the caregiver's suite downstairs for the live-in caregiver's personal use. As well, downstairs, there was one telephone connected to the main telephone number of the house for pick-up by the caregiver on that regular line when need be.)

We should make sure that all the telephones in the home (i.e. the ones used by our parents) are exactly the same model.

We should be prepared to replace all old telephones with a type which will meet our parents' new care-years needs (i.e. size of numbers, sight, reach...).

We should look for a telephone that has all these features:

☑ Over-sized (large) number pads showing easy-to-read numbers – to assist with sight-impairments and any coordination problems (e.g. some companies sell what is termed a 'big' phone which seems well suited to most parents' requirements).

☑ Audio adjustments – for any slight or major hearing impairment.

☑ A set of coloured push buttons for emergency calls – for memory storage and quick access (e.g. hit any one of the 'coloured buttons' and a 911 or ambulance-type connection will then occur as it has been programmed to do so).

☑ Lengthy cords – for mobility and stretching if required (of course, all cords must be bundled/fastened out of the way for safety reasons).

☑ A memory system – a must, for frequently called local and long distance numbers. Each telephone's memory of names and numbers should be listed in exactly the same sequence on all of the phones, that is to say, if memory #1 is daughter's number, be sure memory #1 is programmed the same on each of the telephones in the house. The memory button habit is easily formed by our parents. *(For example: One day I asked Mum if she could quickly give me my cousin's telephone number as I was phoning long distance from out of the province and had forgotten the number, Mum responded, "Memory 3".)*

Seniors turn to blogging to stay connected... Web logs let them make new friends, keep up on current events and share their interests.   (continued...)

Forget shuffleboard, needlepoint and bingo. Web logs, more often the domain of alienated adolescents and middle-aged pundits, are gaining a foothold as a new leisure-time option for senior citizens. There's Dad's Tomato Garden Journal, Dogwalk Musings, and of course, the Oldest Living Blogger.

...Bloggers say their hobby keeps them up on current events, lets them befriend strangers around the globe and gives them a voice in a society often deaf to the wisdom of the elderly. "It brings out the best in me, " said Boston-are blogger Millie Garfield, 80, who writes My Mom's Blog with occasional help from her son, Steve Garfield, a digital video producer. "My life would be dull without it."

And it's brought her a bit of fame. In June, Garfield was invited to speak at a Boston seminar for marketers on how to use the Web more effectively. A short video of the event, posted on her blog, captures the professionals laughing at her wisecrack about the benefits of a man who can still drive at night.

Three percent of online U.S. seniors have created a blog and 17 per cent have read someone else's blog, according to the Pew Internet & American Life Project. Compare that to online 18-29 year-olds: 13 per cent have created blogs and 32 per cent have read someone else's blog, according to Pew.

Joe Jenett, a Detroit-area Web designer who has been tracing the age of bloggers for a personal venture called the Ageless Project, said he has noticed more older bloggers in the past two years. "Isn't that phenomenal? And their writing is vibrant," Jenett said. He noted that sites such as Blogger. com give step-by-step instructions and fee hosting, making it simpler to self-publish on the Web.

"It's easy to start one if you can connect dots," said former Jesuit priest and retired newspaperman Jim Bowman, 73, of Oak Park, Ill. Bowman writes four blogs: one on happenings in his city, one a catchall for his opinions, one on religion and one with feedback on Chicago newspapers. "Like any other hobby, you've got to make sure it doesn't take over," he said. *(Source: The Associated Press, Chicago, Illinois, November 11, 2005, reported in the Business Section of The Vancouver Sun by Carla Johnson, an excerpt)*

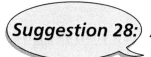 **Assess vehicle use and driving skills**

Should I be concerned about my parents' driving?

We must keep in mind that driving symbolizes independence to our parent, so we have to think carefully as to how we may want to approach this emotionally charged issue. Should a parent be driving, under what conditions, when to give up one's license – all are extremely delicate questions for daughter/son-caregivers to handle. *(Recognize that we may be entering a minefield with this topic.)* What are the options when concerned about our parents' driving abilities:

✓ **The "Does this make good sense" option.**

If we have a reasonable parent, we can discuss driving needs and make timely decisions (e.g. "Does X make good sense Dad?").

✓ **The "Do you feel we should talk about where and when you drive" option.**

If we feel strongly that our parent should be driving under certain conditions only (restrictions), we can open discussions and approach our concerns with our parents (e.g. Can we agree on the times of day you can drive, when you really shouldn't drive as it is not safe – snow/dark/tourist season…). The restrictions must be clearly defined and agreed upon by all.

✓ **The "I think I'll wait" option.**

We can wait until the automatic annual reviews begin for older drivers (check your jurisdiction).

For example: In Ontario, the Senior Driver Renewal Program requires that senior drivers, aged 80 years and over:

- *Pay the applicable licensing fee*
- *Complete a vision test and a knowledge test*

> • *Take part in a group education session every two years*

A small number of drivers may also be asked to take a road test to have their in-car skills assessed

This review consists of a doctor's check-up of our parent and submission of forms stating our parent's competency to drive to the Government Motor Vehicle Department responsible for licensing. The motor vehicle branch may then send a form letter stating that our parent's driving ability has to be fully tested within a designated period.

Usually the prospect of a complete written and road skills driving test will prompt our parent to assess her/his own abilities (if a parent knows that she/he really doesn't have to drive any longer as the caregiver is always the designated driver, the decision to stop driving oneself becomes a little easier).

A checklist on safe elderly driving

Watch for telltale signs of decline in the elderly person's driving abilities.

Do they:

- Drive at inappropriate speeds, either too fast or too slow?
- Ask passengers to help check if it is clear to pass or turn?
- Respond slowly to or not notice pedestrians, bicyclists and other drivers?
- Ignore, disobey or misinterpret street signs and traffic lights?
- Fail to yield to other cars or pedestrians who have the right-of-way?
- Fail to judge distances between cars correctly?
- Become easily frustrated and angry?
- Appear drowsy, confused or frightened?
- Have one or more near accidents or near misses?
- Drift across lane markings or bump into curbs?
- Forget to turn on headlights after dusk?

- Have difficulty with glare from oncoming headlights, streetlights, or other bright or shiny objects, especially at dawn, dusk and at night?

- Have difficulty turning their head, neck, shoulders or body while driving or parking?

- Ignore signs of mechanical problems, including underinflated tires? (one in 4 cars has at least one tire that is underinflated by 8 pounds or more; low tire pressure is a major cause of accidents.)

- Have too little strength to turn the wheel quickly in an emergency such as a tire failure, a child darting into traffic, etc.?

- Gets lost repeatedly, even in familiar areas?

If the answer to one or more of these questions is "yes," you should explore whether medical issues are affecting his/her driving skills.

Aging Roadsters: It's tough for doctors to take away a licence.

You're at risk if….

- Your family and last remaining friend say they are worried about your driving.
- You have trouble seeing signs, including that pesky octagonal one, in time to react.
- Other drivers drive too fast, even with those brake lights on.
- Others honk at you and make gestures that involve flexing several joints.
- You get stressed driving.
- After driving, you feel tired.
- You have more 'near misses' (and near misters) lately.
- Busy intersections bother you.
- Left-hand turns make you nervous.
- Oncoming headlight glare bothers you.
- You have trouble turning the wheel, particularly when having to reach up to grab it.
- You're advised that the 'narrow road' you drive on is often referred to as a sidewalk.
- You have trouble shoulder-checking when you back up.
- Parking is a hassle.
- Only your dog accepts rides from you, and she requests Valium first.

(Source: Dr. David Hepburn 'Good Medicine' column, CanWest, February 19, 2006)

What do I do about my parents' vehicles?

☑ If our parents have been/are a two or two+ vehicle family, we need to **review their present day transportation needs** given the care situation, especially if one or both are no longer driving. We need to make decisions on the best use of all the family vehicles.

We can decide to keep various vehicles for different reasons. *(For example: for a long time, Mum kept her car in good running order and insured even though she used it very little; the larger family car was used on an everyday basis with Mum with the caregiver or other members of the family for errands, shopping, excursions, over-night short-time holidays; our caregivers had their own vehicles for personal activities.)*

☑ We must **check the type of insurance policy** carried on each vehicle, the insurance company's policy regulations on use and drivers.

If the insurance policy has a designation of senior driver use, then we must ask regarding the conditions for that particular designation: what exactly does it mean; does it preclude the caregiver from driving the car, can it be driven by a non-senior age visiting relative, how often can it be used by others if at all.

(For example: When pre-senior caregivers became drivers of the family car, which had up until then had a senior designation because of my parents use only, the insurance had to be changed immediately – no longer senior use driver designation if caregivers were younger than senior age – for the insurance to be valid.)

☑ We need to **revise each of the vehicles' insurance policies** immediately according to the new drivers and uses; we need to **budget for any increases or decreases** (e.g. seasonal insurance for one vehicle if driving it in the winter is to be eliminated).

☑ We should sort and dispose of out dated vehicle documents (e.g. all those old papers tucked away in the glove compartment) and **have current insurance and maintenance papers** handy for future reference.

☑ We may need to **change the registration of ownerships** – put vehicles in both parents names for ease of transfer at a later date, in one parents' name if one is no longer driving or redo if one parent has died and was a registered owner.

☑ We need to **make decisions about co-ownership** – should we, as daughters/sons be registered as a co-owner of our parents' vehicles? We need to introduce ourselves to the insurance agent used by our parents for their vehicles. *(Note: Check the legal liabilities carried by such a co-ownership.)*

☑ We need to **establish who will attend to vehicle maintenance** and budget for that necessity.

☑ Lastly, we may need to **sell** one of our parents' vehicles.

Giving up the pleasure of driving a car is akin for many elderly people to giving up eating, gerontology experts said at an international meeting in Vancouver. "We have to stop demonising older drivers and compromising their mobility and start promoting mobility with an enabling philosophy," said Dr. Desmond O'Neill a gerontologist from Ireland who chaired a symposium on older drivers at the 17th Congress of International Association of Gerontology. Because of the increasing age of the population, drivers over 80 are the fastest-growing group of motorists in the world. **Although statistics show elderly drivers have more difficulty reading signs and seeing lights, especially at night, symposium speakers agreed that age alone is a poor predictor of driving ability and should never be used against people at licence renewal time. Rather, the decision on whether to grant or revoke licences should be based on medical conditions and whether they present a danger to those with them or to others.** Leo Tasca, of the Ontario Ministry of Transportation, said jurisdictions all around North America have been moving away from periodic road testing of seniors when they reach various ages, partly because of the huge costs inherent in testing growing numbers of seniors, but also because authorities recognize that Draconian measures to prohibit elderly people from driving aren't justified. Indeed, research presented by Vancouver Hospital psychologist Karen Tallman showed that even people with early or mild dementia can pass a driving test. (continued...)

Allen Dobbs, one of Canada's leading driving assessment experts, said medical conditions can affect driving ability at any age, whether a person is 20 or 80. Dobbs, a former psychology professor at the University of Alberta who has developed a driving competence assessment program called DriveABLE, said many medical conditions can affect driver competence including cardiovascular disease, stroke, dementia, serious diabetes, psychiatric disorders and certain medications. The DriveABLE program is designed so doctors can refer their patients for an assessment "much the same way as you would send them out for a CT scan or an MRI".

A Saskatchewan study found that despite being legally obligated to report unfit drivers, more than 25 per cent of doctors said they hesitate to do so because of the damage it causes to the physician-patient relationship. Another study published in 'Annuals', the Journal of the Royal College of Physicians and Surgeons, showed that almost 50 per cent of doctors are uneasy about barring their patients from driving and only one out of every 20 doctors surveyed would advise a patient with mild dementia to stop driving or would alert the authorities. In B.C., doctors are asked to assess patients' fitness to drive at age 80, but many are reluctant to prevent their patients from driving. "They don't want to be the one doing the dirty deed, and in B.C., unlike the rest of Canada, doctors are not protected from lawsuits if their patients sue them for reporting them." (The B.C. Medical Association recently passed a resolution calling on the government to amend legislation to give that protection against lawsuits.) Peter McPherson, communications coordinator for the Ministry of Transportation and superintendent of motor vehicles, added, "Many seniors (voluntarily) give up on driving when they feel they shouldn't any more." *(Source: The Vancouver Sun, July 4, 2001.)*

Suggestion 29: Be neighbourly

Just how important are my parents' neighbours as part of a safe environment?

Neighbours form a valuable part of our parent-support circle and help create a safe home environment for our parents.

We need to recognize our dependency on good neighbours and show our heart-felt appreciation when they take time from their own busy schedules to visit or work with our parents.

☑ Next-door neighbours.

We must encourage neighbours to drop over often for a visit, as our parents may feel "confined to barracks" (Mum's exact words when home for several days in a row) – our parents do enjoy catching up on the neighbourhood news especially if they've lived for many years in the same location or region.

☑ Neighbouring relatives.

We can suggest that a relative living in the area take some time each month to visit; or take one parent for a ride, a cup of coffee, lunch, around a mall for a tour, to visit an old friend…(If both parents are living at home together, these outings will allow one parent some free time while the other obtains a little exercise.)

We must reciprocate if that relative has an elderly parent as well – we can also arrange outings together at times.

☑ Neighbourhood teens.

We might be able to arrange for periodic assistance from neighbourhood teens for light chores (unless a caregiver has children willing to help and be paid for the chores).

We should also discuss a potential work-arrangement with the teen's parents to find out if such is possible (e.g. taking garbage bags to the curb on pick-up morning, sorting recyclables into bags and loading them into the car trunk, removing snow from the sidewalks and driveways after each big snowfall). We can then make arrangements with the teens to assist our parents and set a payment schedule.

☑ Skilled neighbours.

We can ask specific neighbours if they are available for short-term contract work (reimbursing for time and energy), as we may need help with home renovations if required.

(For example: An additional bathroom became an important addition to our live-in caregiver suite and two neighbours agreed to do the work to everyone's benefit and satisfaction – and it was fun.)

☑ Special neighbours.

We may want to consider hiring a neighbour as a 'special visitor' for our parent, especially if our parent is shut-in much of the time. This special neighbour may be able to take a parent for a regularly scheduled once a week outing.

(For example, I contracted with a lady in the neighbourhood, who was familiar with Dad's health problems and with whom he felt safe, to take him on Wednesday afternoon ice-cream outings – this activity worked very well for all, especially Dad. He looked forward to his special visitor once a week, he could count on the visit taking place without fail, he felt safe and established a routine he understood, and he was able to have continuity of conversation with this person. Dad was not told, nor was it an important detail for him to know, that his regular visitor was being given a small honorarium each month – he thought she was a great neighbour and she truly was. This happy arrangement which started while he was living at home, continued when he became a resident in the carehome and proved very beneficial. We have to remember that care homes don't provide 'everything'.)

☑ Showing appreciation – thank you.

We should consider inviting neighbours over for a cup of coffee when we are visiting our parent.

We can also organize a neighbour/relative appreciation night in our parents' home, a buffet or dessert get-together – this activity is fun as it gives our parents a reason to have a little party in their home in keeping with our need to make the environment a positive one.

We always want to be on the look out for ways to say special thanks to neighbours for their interest in our parents' well-being and safety.

Notes:

_____

_____

_____

_____

_____

_____

_____

_____

_____

_____

_____

_____

_____

_____

_____

_____

_____

"Friendships are fragile things and require as much handling as any other fragile and precious thing.
— *Randolph S. Bourne*

TOPIC 5

Let's Talk: Using medications, recognizing trade-offs and raising concerns

---

How do I organize my parents' medications?

Personal Anecdote: "I got the message – I understand!"

Suggestions:

30: Become medication-wise

31: Track medications

32: Offer 'extras'

33: Establish exercise routines

How do I organize my parents' medications?

Personal Anecdote:
"I got the message – I understand!"

A couple of years into our journey, I read in a pharmacist bulletin that:

☑ 30% of elderly patients (65 years+) have prescription medication related problems on a regular basis.

☑ 23% of all nursing home admissions are due to the mismanagement of prescription medications.

☑ 20% of all non-elective hospital admissions for patients over the age of 65 are due to mismanagement of prescription medications.

I have no way to verify the bulletin's data, yet the message is clear - medication use can pose a huge problem for our elderly parents. During my parents' care-years, I discovered that:

☑ A medication taken to remedy one health problem can very quickly precipitate another even greater health problem.

☑ A medication used in past years, with no negative side effects, can cause an allergic reaction now as the body has changed in many ways.

☑ Some medications have tradeoffs and decisions have to be made as to when specific prescriptions are necessary.

☑ Medication dilemmas are very disruptive and upsetting.

☑ *Medication problems can prompt drastic decisions.*

And

☑ *Some medications do what they are supposed to do and do it well.*

Notes:

_____

_____

_____

_____

_____

_____

_____

_____

_____

_____

_____

_____

_____

_____

_____

_____

_____

_____

_____

_____

_____

_____

_____

_____

_____

_____

_____

_____

_____

Suggestion 30: **Become medication-wise**

As daughter/son-caregivers, we can't and shouldn't rely solely on the professionals to perform magic when it comes to medication-use with our parents. What prescription medications are used, when they are taken, plus potential reactions must be monitored and reviewed periodically not only by the family doctor (as expected) but also, and equally important, by us!

I'm not an expert, so why is there is a need for my involvement in my parents' medication use?

There are several reasons for our diligence:

- ☑ It our 'job' as daughter/son-caregivers to become involved in decisions regarding our parents' medications, since it is a fact that a large percentage of problems with the elderly are prescription-drug related and we don't want our parent to be a statistic if it can be avoided.

- ☑ Our parents need us to seek information whenever possible regarding solutions to their health problems – this is another area where they are fully dependent on us – if not us, who? *(Note: Do not accept "aging" as a cause of a health problem, since a correct diagnosis accompanied by proper medications together can assist our parents greatly.)*

- ☑ We have everything to gain by actively participating in this aspect of their care (whether living in their own home or in a carehome).

Medications: Seniors often have more long-term health problems than younger people, so they tend to take more medications on a regular basis. Modern medications help us live longer, healthier lives, but with the benefits come some risks. You can reduce the risks by using medicines wisely. (continued...)

The following tips will help you do that:

- Take prescription drugs 'exactly' as they are prescribed. That means taking the correct amount at the proper times in the way the doctor instructs and for as long as the prescription calls for.

- Make sure you understand how the drug should be taken –for example, with food or on an empty stomach.

- Tell your doctor right away if you think a medicine is causing side effects. And whenever you get a new prescription, be sure the doctor and your pharmacist are aware of any medication problems you have had in the past.

- Get rid of drugs that have passed their expiration date by returning them to your pharmacy. Do not put them in the trash or flush them down the toilet.

- Never mix medicines together or mix them with alcohol unless you check first with your doctor or pharmacist to make sure the combination won't cause problems.

- Never take any drug prescribed for someone else or give your prescription medicine to another person. Many things affect the way a drug works in the body, and a drug may not be right for different people even if they have the same symptoms.

- Keep a record of all the medicines you take each day. Include prescription drugs, over the counter products, vitamin and mineral supplements and herbal remedies. Be sure to note any reactions you have.

- Keep a copy of your medication record in your medicine cabinet and carry a second copy with you.

- Ask your doctor to check your drug record every time you get a new prescription.

(Source: From the Healthy Living Guide for Seniors, Medicine Centre)

What should I do?

☑ **Keep an up-dated list of the prescription medications** (including the vitamins and minerals and supplements being taken), why each has been prescribed and the dosages.

☑ **Note the prescription name** of each of the medications, the medications eliminated, those added, those replaced. *(For example: one of the drugs used by Mum was deemed unsafe and removed from the market after years of public use.)*

☑ **Keep in mind that medications have different side effects** under differing circumstances and that changes in overall health, can lead to unexpected adverse side effects.

(For example: In our second care-year, Mum was hospitalised as she had suffered through a prolonged nasty head cold, which had lead to a severe ear infection, which in-turn was causing a very dangerous balance problem. While in the hospital, a specialist placed a small drainage tube in the infected ear and used a standard eardrops medication for the delicate operation. The operation was successful in eliminating the ear infection, but the eardrops medication used during the operation caused a severe allergic reaction around Mum's ear-eyes-neck area for over a month. To counteract the allergic reaction, Mum had to be placed on another medication.)

☑ **Become aware of some of the possible and better-known side effects** of each prescribed medication (common affects, both the long-term and short-term, perhaps even the more rare ones). Make a list of possible side effects by telephoning two different pharmacies when a new medication is prescribed (i.e. the day it is prescribed or as it is being filled). One of the pharmacies contacted should obviously be the one where our parents have an account as the pharmacist there will be able to access a comprehensive list of all the medications our parent is taking (and has taken) and will quickly understand our reasons for questioning. This precautionary action does not imply a lack of trust in our doctor; it represents our involvement in our parents' total care.

☑ **Ask questions regarding any problems** which could result from 'combinations' of medications being taken by our parents (e.g. what to avoid when on antidepressants).

Rethinking Vitamin E

Vitamin E pills do no good for your heart and may even cause heart failure or other heart damage in a significant number of people, says a new Canadian study. Patients at risk of heart attacks or stroke, or who have diabetes, should stop taking vitamin E pills and eat a healthy diet instead, with blood pressure medicine if it's prescribed.

"The focus should remain on a balanced diet rich in fruits and vegetables. This is a recommendation for the general population as well," said the study's lead author, Dr. Eva Lonn, a cardiologist. *(McMaster University study is the third in six months to cast doubt on the health benefits of Vitamin E... from The Journal of the American Medical Association, March 2005)*

☑ **Observe our parent carefully for at least the first month** when placed on new medication (and ask the caregivers to watch) – we will understand rather quickly if the medication is having the desired effect.

(For example: One of Mum's health problems had plagued her constantly most of her adult life – she had for decades suffered from indigestion, and by her mid-eighties, severe 'indigestion' had become almost a daily occurrence accompanied by frequent nausea, unstable balance, sweating, and arm pain. Unable to cope, she became a "regular" in the emergency ward, with the crisis peaking when she required emergency ambulance services for the problem three times in one week. Often we feared that these were signs of a heart attack (due to her history). During each emergency, doctors checked for stroke, heart, flu, and couldn't diagnose the precise problem – the term "aging" was usually mentioned in the discussions. Mum was becoming very frail after one year of coping with this extreme condition. Finally, one morning after being hospitalised the night before for a bad attack, a cardiologist on rounds checked Mum's condition and said (with significant authority I might add as I was present) to the attending doctor on rounds, "This is not heart, check her stomach". Within half a day, our family physician diagnosed a reflux, hiatus hernia, a condition Mum could have had for years (I would say "decades"). The correct medications were quickly

authorized. Mum still continued to have bouts of indigestion, but she and the caregivers knew the trigger foods and recognized the symptoms. She had fewer emergency calls for this problem – the medications did work very well and enabled her to have pleasant days – she was stronger mentally and emotionally because she was not constantly sick. Reflux, it turns out, is quite common with the elderly.)

☑ **Inform our parents' family doctor about our observations** regarding the medications, as some drugs may work well with the majority of elderly patients, but may not with one of our parents.

(For example: Dad's personality behaviours during his care-years became extremely difficult to handle. In the first year, the doctor tried several different types of medications in order to minimize/reduce/control some of Dad's more unmanageable, compulsive behaviours but we discovered the resulting side effects created additional problems. We were soon afraid to try even minimal dosages of any medications. By the end of our first LTC year, Dad's behaviour problems remained erratic, almost impossible to cope with at times. Our family's dilemma around Dad's behaviour and related medication problems was, unfortunately, an influencing factor in the decision regarding Dad's ability to continue to live in his own home.)

☑ **Telephone the family doctor if we are concerned** about any recurring health problems, since a medication for one problem may exacerbate another problem. Ask for tests to determine what may be required.

(For example: At the beginning of our third care-year, a medication given for Dad's persistent congested heart condition was found to be causing liver problems in Dad – later the new medication to rectify those liver problems began hindering the correction of the heart congestion. Changes in medications went on for nearly one year when finally, it was decided to try one specific drug that was known 'sometimes' to aid both problems simultaneously. After a suitable period of time on the new medication, we were very pleased as test results showed that it appeared to be working well on both Dad's heart and liver problems. I was told that Dad would probably live for several more years now – alas, our family will never know for sure if the precarious balancing act was truly achieved as Dad died of a heart attack within that same month.)

☑ **Go to the Internet for information** regarding specific health problems and do a search for solutions for those problems – time permitting. *(For example: For each medication given or new health problem, I found it beneficial to head for the internet right away – a very good use of my time rather than waiting to see what might happen. I always discussed my web findings with my parents' doctor/ pharmacist.)*

Excellent Websites to visit

www.canadianhealthnetwork.ca - one of the best sources of medical information in Canada.

www.mayoclinic.com - renowned medical institution: refer to its Seniors Health menu.

www.cancer.ca

www.diabetes.ca

www.alzheimer.ca

www.merck.com - a pharmaceutical industry source: refer to its Merck Manuals.

www.highwire.org - a Stanford University Service: for medical research.

Under what circumstances might I have to become directly involved in the actual decisions regarding medications?

As part of our parents' team, we are very important decision-makers.

☑ **We need to become involved with how medications are being used when there are tradeoffs involving negative side effects – we have to weigh the options.**

Which will it be, what is best? We must weigh the options and discuss our decisions with the family doctor when it comes to living with a health condition or living with the side effects of the medications prescribed for the condition.

(For example: Three different sedatives, within eight months, in extremely slight doses, were prescribed to help Dad curb his anxieties, which were upsetting for Dad as well as everyone else in the house. Some of the drugs produced results, Dad was noticeably calmer, but at what cost. All three drugs produced obvious, negative physical side effects (shaking, drooling, stumbling, loss of balance, tripping, drowsiness, a vacant look). Decision-time – I did not want Dad on any of the sedatives due to the accompanying unsafe side effects and spoke with the family doctor – we decided to work with the behaviours and seek help from other possible sources. Alas, we were unsuccessful on many levels with his behaviors and the meds prescribed – the problem persisted.)

☑ **We need to become involved when we suspect we may know the real cause of a problem.**

Close personal involvement is critical when searching for reasons for health problems. We can look to a medication as a solution but we must first check the symptoms/signals carefully and try to uncover if any non-medical reasons are causing the health problems noted.

(For example: As Mum had a lengthy history of depression – had been on medications for that condition for almost twenty years – her increasingly tearful and nervous state during one particular six month care period was, at first, attributed to 'nerves'. After a lengthy check-up one day, her family doctor asked me, "What else is going on in her everyday life?" After a couple of months I finally uncovered what might be the root cause of her condition – Mum was feeling trapped and stressed under the present living arrangements. Decision-time – we made two changes – we immediately changed the current live-in caregiver and we slowly altered the rigid schedule of must-do nursing home visits to Dad – problem solved.)

☑ **We need to become involved when we have heard enough excuses and action is required.**

When is it time to disregard what we are being told about our parents' health problems and when do we take action ourselves? The answer, I believe, is sooner rather than later (even if we live in another city) as there are times when we have to draw a line, saying enough is enough – we need to jump in.

(For example: In Dad's second year in the caremanor, during one of my visits, Dad told me that he felt tired all the time and I noticed that he seemed to be nodding off often. When I inquired as to Dad's condition, the care home nursing staff attributed his symptoms to a severe flu virus affecting seniors in the city – the carehome itself had recently been closed to visitors, for a two-week duration, because of the flu bug. The explanation sounded reasonable. I flew home expecting to hear that Dad's symptoms were subsiding – by the weekend, the flu in the care home disappeared but Dad's symptoms of sleepiness persisted. A few days later, I checked again with the nursing staff expressing my concern – they had since concluded that Dad probably did not have the flu, but had a bladder infection and they had started medication for such that very same day as my call; they explained that a follow-up test for the infection had been done but the results were not back yet. This explanation sounded reasonable. Because of my concerns, I started telephoning Dad every day during that week to see how he was feeling – he continued to complain about being very tired. While speaking with the nurses, they suggested that I should not be overly worried, that Dad's fatigue probably was a result of the new bladder infection medication he was on. By the end of that week, in subsequent telephone calls, I was noticing that Dad was beginning to talk thickly and slowly. My concerns prompted even more telephone follow-ups with the nursing personnel, who now felt that Dad might be having an adverse reaction to the bladder medication – they had ordered more tests. It was now one week since I had seen Dad and the explanations were no longer sounding plausible. By the beginning of the next week, I had heard enough – decision-time. I caught a flight the next morning. I went straight from the airport to the caremanor. As soon as I saw Dad (tired, nodding off, talking slowly still, poor enunciation), I became alarmed. I immediately ordered the caremanor staff to stop the bladder medication and scheduled a doctor's appointment for Dad immediately. My decision to take action was indeed the correct one – Dad never had the flu, he never had a bladder problem, and he never had a negative reaction to the bladder medication. By appointment time, he was not only talking thickly and falling asleep every few minutes, but both his legs were very swollen. Dad was in a state of congested heart failure. Our doctor ordered medications to begin immediately, but the congested heart condition was too severe by this point and the medications did not have time to take effect. That evening, Dad had to be rushed to the hospital where he

remained for several days. I feel that the caremanor staff were trying to do their best for Dad, but, I remain convinced that we have to take firm independent actions ourselves when our parents' health is in question, as well as when there are questions as to what is taking place health-wise.)

(Note: When Dad lived in the care manor, I had written a letter to them on file, to the nursing home administrator, stating that Dad was not to be given an medications that had not been run by me first – he was not to be given any drugs to control his behavior, etc.)

Orthopedic patients face long delays – Dr. Michael Stanger, the Victoria-based president of the B.C. Orthopedic Association, said joint, muscle and bone diseases are already six times more prevalent than cancer. The Institute of Health Economics shows the indirect economic impact of bone and joint problems, including arthritis, is nearly $20 billion a year in Canada. "The biggest reason for this staggering number is the result of lost productivity of people who are unable to work and conduct business," he said, noting that in the next 30 years, the aging of baby boomers will mean the number of people with bone and joint-related problems will increase by 124 per cent. "And demographics don't lie," Stanger said. As they say, 'Houston, we have a problem.' *(Source: The Vancouver Sun, May 24, 2001.)*

Caution: Medications! *Some facts to consider from Canada's National Advisory Council On Aging,* "Expressions' newsletter, Volume 15, Number 1

- There are now (2001) close to 22,000 prescription drugs on the Canadian market, an increase of one third since 1997

- Problems issuing from doctors' prescribing practices include 'inappropriate doses' (A Canadian Association on Gerontology forum identified practices such as over-prescribing of tranquillizers and under-prescribing of heart medications for seniors. National Forum on Closing the Care Gap", September 2000)

- An estimated 50% of prescriptions are not taken properly, and as many as 20% of hospitalizations of people over 50 have been attributed to adverse reactions to medications or noncompliance with drug use instructions (Health Promotion Research, 1995)

- Often family physicians aren't aware of all the medications patients are taking. When lists of medications taken by seniors were compared with records kept by their doctors, discrepancies were found in 96% of cases, 60% of them involving over-the-counter remedies and 40% involving prescription drugs prescribed by other physicians.

- Even when drugs are prescribed and taken correctly, side effects are a risk – dizziness, nausea and constipation are among the most common. Side effects can in turn cause further problems, such as falls and fractures.

- Investigators at McMaster University in Hamilton Ontario, the Seniors Medication Assessment Research Trial (SMART) showed that seniors had an average of three drug-related problems, and more than 80% had a least one.   (continued...)

- Research led by Dr. Robyn Tamblyn showed that after the Quebec Government changed its drug plan, introducing annual premiums, fewer needed prescriptions were filled, resulting in a 111% increase in doctor visits, a 47% increase in emergency room visits, and a 66% increase in hospitalizations, institutionalizations and deaths. The study found that people continued to take drugs for acute symptoms such as pain but reduced their use of preventive drugs, such as those that lower cholesterol. Other research shows that people reduce the amount of medication they take when the cost goes up, or stop taking it altogether. There's also evidence of sharing medications with others and taking drugs after their expiry date (Health Reports 10/4 Summer 1999)

- In the first 6 months of 2000, an estimated 5 million Canadians - 24% of those surveyed-took a natural health product (NHP) instead of going to a doctor for a prescription. The percentage was even higher, 41%, among those who had taken three or more NHPs. In addition, 8% of NHP users substituted an NHP for a prescription given to them by a doctor-that's an estimated 1.3 million unfilled prescriptions (from Protegez-vous, consumer magazine, February 2001). Many equate 'natural' with 'safe' but this is not necessarily the case. Consumers are taking a risk when they take a natural product without knowing whether one of its active ingredients could interact with a food or prescription drug.

*(To receive free "Expression' newsletters from NACA, telephone 613-957-1968 or
email **seniors@hc-sc.gc.ca** or visit **www.naca.ca**)*

Suggestion 31: *Track medications*

We must make sure that our parents' medications are very well organized.

What can I do to help keep track of medications?

☑ **Use medication booklets** – by using medications booklets, we are able to:

- Keep an up-to-date list of the all the prescription medications and vitamin supplements presently being taken.

- Make note of any medications that were tried and stopped, with a reason if known, as new doctors (e.g. substitute for family physician on holidays, emergency room hospital doctor) may need to be made aware of this relevant past information quickly.

- Note the major health problems so if asked (e.g. by paramedics, emergency service attendants) the highlighted history is written.

☑ **Use medication-alert jewellery** – by using medic-alert bracelets or necklaces, our parents will:

- Feel secure that their most important medical information is with them always (up-date the information when required).

- Feel safe in that the medic-jewellery is stamped with a universal (health) sign, people understand the significance of the symbol should something happen.

☑ **Use medic-kits** – by using medic-kits, we are able to:

- Organize daily pill-taking times for one-week periods.

- Stick to required schedules easier during the day. In order not to forget other types of (non-pill) prescriptions (e.g. eye drops), schedules can be set to correspond with pill-taking times.

- Refresh our memories as to whether or not the pills for each specific time have been taken (just by referring to the time of day slot in the kit for that week).

- Have pills handy to dispense. *(For example: The weekly medic-kit being used was always in the same location in the kitchen and the caregiver placed the pills to be taken, from the kit into a miniature plastic glass for each meal and bedtime – the routine never varied.)*

- Have pills for an outing or vacation always ready.

- Put the vitamin supplements with the meds for use.

After any change in the medications being taken, we should ask our pharmacist to up-to-date the medications card in the plastic envelope which is located on the backside of the medic-kits. We need to review the card from time to time by telephoning the pharmacist first, then, the doctor, just to check that our list matches their information (e.g. interestingly enough, we once found that our list was the most up to date list).

☑ Use purse-size pillboxes

Purse-size/pocket-size (mini) pill containers are useful when a parent is going to be away from home for a few hours – the pillbox compartments can be filled for the day.

We should encourage our parent to carry the mini pillbox in the same spot each time (e.g. certain side of purse, pocket) as caregivers need to know where to locate the medications if need be. As well, the location can include emergency medications (e.g. nitro glycerine spray).

☑ Medication dispensing machines

Look for new tracking equipment for medications' dispensing (e.g. there exists little machines now that sit on counters like cappuccino coffee machines do).

Emergency Measures – One in five Canadians has a medical condition that should be known in an emergency. But some people don't realize their condition is serious enough to make a difference during an emergency says Shelagh Tippet-Fagyas, president of Canadian MedicAlert Foundation, an emergency medical information service and registered Canadian charity. Commonly under-identified conditions include "many allergies, any metal in their bodies and a lot of heart conditions," Tippet-Fagyas says. "People think if they are on aspirin daily or a blood thinner, it's controlled and won't cause any problems." MedicAlert provides bracelets which identify your life-threatening conditions and a phone number through which emergency responders can access your medical history. For information on MedicAlert, call 1-800-668-1507 or visit **www.medicalert.ca** *(Source: The Vancouver Sun, May 21, 2001.)*

Spending on Drugs Outstrips Cost of Doctors

Almost $28B A Year

Drug spending in Canada continues to rocket upward, hitting almost $25-billion in 2005, according to a report from the Canadian Institute for Health Information (CIHI).

Every man, woman and child now purchases, on average, $770 worth of drugs a year, says the report released May 10, 2006. Prescription medicines account for the lion's share, ringing in at $20.6 billion.

The report reveals huge variations in expenditures across the country. People in Nunavut spend just $482 on drugs per capita par year compared to $836 by Ontarians and $836 for New Brunswickers. The residents of the North-west Territories, Saskatchewan and British Columbia are notable for being at the low end of the drug-consumption chart.   (continued...)

...Freezing Canada's prescription drug spending at $20-billion for just one year would free up enough money to hire 8,000 doctors, or 20,000 nurses, or finance early childhood education or school lunch programs that could have huge health impacts, says Steve Morgan at the Centre for Health Services an Policy Research at the University of British Columbia.

"We now spend significantly more on prescription drugs tan we do on paying every doctor for every service they provide, in the country."

The report details how prescription drug use has doubled from about $10-billion in the late 1990s, and is up 11% from 2004, making it the fastest-growing segment of health spending. It has been proven that vulnerable populations, including the elderly and people living on low incomes, stop taking "clinically essential" medications when faced with higher payments, he said.

The report notes Canada lags internationally when it comes to public payment for medications. Compared to 13 OECD countries, Canada ranked eighth in public-sector drug expenditure per capita and 11th for share of public expenditure in total drug spending, far behind France and Germany.

Many provinces have increased the public share of prescribed drug expenditure in the past 10 years, the report notes, but variations persist. In 2005, the share of total prescribed drug expenditure funded by the public sector ranged from 32.3% in New Brunswick to 50.9% in Manitoba.

There are also considerable provincial variation in how much is spent per person on prescribed drugs by the public and private sectors. In 2005, estimated public-sector spending on prescribed drugs per capita ranged from $194 in Prince Edward Island to $341 in Quebec. The Canadian average was 4295 per person. *(Source: CanWest News Service, with files from Emily Mathieu; article by Margaret Munro, National Post, May 11 2006)*

Suggestion 32: *Offer 'extras'*

☑ We can research good supplements

We should ask our pharmacist if a vitamin and/or mineral supplement would be of benefit to our parents' general health, even if it is just the addition of a good daily multi-vitamin recommended for seniors. *(Note: We should never assume that what works for us is a good idea for our parents too.)*

Two swallowing hints to help our parents:

- If given a choice, purchase easy-to-swallow glycerine capsules rather than large dry pills.

- Suggest having a sip of water before taking a pill, to grease the passage, so to speak.

☑ We can encourage the selective use of over-the-counter aids.

We can suggest that our parents try certain over-the-counter aids (e.g. cold remedies, cough drops, creams…) but only after having checked with our pharmacist regarding the use of each.

We can also apply information in a creative manner.

(For example: During one bad flu season, a news article suggested that people flying keep cough drops in their mouths while on airplanes since the throat is the first level of defence – a large percentage of germs enter through our mouths. As a result, I suggested to Mum that she keep cough candies, with zinc and echinacea, in her purse, handy for when she goes into places with large groups of people, such as the shopping malls – sometimes she remembered, sometimes she didn't.)

Daily Aspirin a good choice for anyone over 50, expert says...Heart attacks, strokes could be reduced, *a researcher claims*

London: Everyone over 50 should take a mini-aspirin daily to reduce the risk of heart disease and strokes, a leading researcher said. While strokes and heart attacks could be reduced by about a third, a low-dose aspirin a day may also help to protect against cancer and Alzheimer's disease, a conference heard.

"People should be given the evidence of the benefits and risks so that they can decide what they want to do," said Professor Peter Elwood of the College of Medicine, Cardiff University, and a pioneer of studies on aspirin and cardiovascular disease. Dr. Antony Bayer, the director of the Memory Team and senior research fellow in geriatric medicine at Cardiff, said 80 per cent of North American specialists thought aspirin should be given to patients with dementia and cardiovascular risk factors. Elwood, speaking at a London conference organized by the Aspirin Foundation, said a study had indicated that only 53 per cent of patients who suffered strokes or heart disease and who should have been taking aspirin to prevent further attacks were doing so.

A research paper calling for a debate on the use of aspirin in older people has been accepted for publication by the British Medical Journal. But the subject s contentious as aspirin also raises the risk of bleeding. Stomach bleeding can be a serious problem requiring transfusions, and can be fatal. Numerous research studies have found low-dose aspirin—normally 75mg a day—reduces the risk of heart attacks by about 30 per cent *(Source: Associated Press, April 13, 2005, Vancouver Sun article by Celia Hall)*

☑ **We can purchase some handy reference materials.**

We should try to purchase one or two good health reference books not only for our general understanding but also to assist our caregivers in understanding our parents' conditions.

Books on food-related topics are often helpful when confronted with identified health-related circumstances. *(For example: We learned that breath mints, such as those offered in restaurants, aggravates the reflux condition, mint is the problem it seems. We were also able to make a list of many of the acid inducing foods to avoid, cutting back on our trial and error time.)*

A Reminder of the Importance Of Maintaining Dental Health As Seniors

A 77-year old man with a history of hypertension was found face down and unresponsive. Initial chest X-rays revealed nothing, but because of recurrent seizures the patient had to be put on a breathing tube. Only after he developed pneumonia did an X-ray reveal the clear image of a tooth in the air passage from the windpipe to the lung. The tooth was removed and the patient recovered. *(From the "New England Journal Of Medicine", 2006)*

Six routes to a ripe old age:

- Eat a calorie-restricted diet.

- Get regular exercise (a 30 year old woman who doesn't exercise will lose one-quarter of her muscle mass by age 70).

- Engage your mind (build up mental reserves that compensate for aging changes).

- Have a spiritual connection (most people who live to 100 have had a life-long awareness of their spiritual side).

- Stress-proof yourself (one trait people 100 and older have in common is the ability to adapt to change).

- Be a blood donor (medical research suggests that lightening the body's iron load reduces the body's production of free radicals and thus slows aging.)

(Source: "Living to 100" by Thomas Perls and Margery Hutter Silver, with John Lauerman. "The Quest to Beat Aging", a special edition of Scientific American. "The Longevity Masters," by Louise Lague, in Modern Maturity magazine.)

Notes:

_____

_____

_____

_____

_____

_____

_____

_____

_____

_____

_____

_____

_____

_____

Suggestion 33: *Establish exercise routines*

✓ We should discuss exercise routines, with caregivers, therapists and doctors, especially if our parent finds exercising difficult or is somewhat negligent about this initiative – the doctor will offer support and reinforce the need.

✓ We should address who will be responsible for the regular exercise programs or short-term strengthening routines, is it our caregivers, the visiting scheduled government caregivers, a rehabilitation therapist…? Our parents must see us as a united team as far as exercise is concerned.

(For example: Upon release from hospital, Dad did not want to attend to his daily exercises as set out by the physiotherapist; he did not like to do his walking laps. He tried constantly to negotiate his way out of the exercise program with the community caregivers responsible for the task. As none of the caregivers wanted to force the exercise routines upon Dad, often exercising did not happen. I soon understood that communicating with the caregivers on a regular basis was necessary, encouraging them to overrule Dad's dismissal of the need to exercise thus forcing Dad, as much as was reasonable, to do a few of the basic required exercises. Later, Mum had difficulty with walking, she needed reminders to use her walker and do some walking in the house for exercise.)

✓ We can encourage the caregivers to incorporate simple exercise-oriented methods into regular activities, when possible.

(For example: When on an outing, the caregiver used to park one or two spaces away from the main entrance of the grocery store so walking just a few steps more would be necessary for Dad. She also added to the grocery list an item that she knew Dad would want to pick out himself, such as a ripe, sweet watermelon or certain Italian salami or cheeses, so it was necessary for him to walk to specific sections. Initially when our caregiver felt Mum needed a prompting, Mum's small portable pedal machine was placed under the footstool in front of her living-room chair. Sometimes the strategy worked, other times, not.)

☑ If our parent is really stubborn about exercising, we must not place 100% responsibility for the exercise program on a live-in caregiver, as that caregiver has to live within the environment and maintain harmony. We can request assistance or we can request that an exercise routine become part of our parent's regularly scheduled adult day-care program (this works well).

After exercising for 30 minutes thrice weekly for four months, a group of people 50 to 77 improved their memory, planning and organization skills, say scientists at Duke University Medical Centre who published their results in the January (2001) issue of the "Journal of Ageing and Physical Activity". "The implications are that exercise might be able to offset some of the mental declines that we often associate with the aging process", said the study's principal investigator, James Blumenthal in a press release issued by the university. "We know that in general, exercise improves the heart's ability to pump blood more effectively, as well as increasing the blood's oxygen-carrying capacity," he said. "so it may be that just as exercise improves muscle tone and function, it may have similar effects on the brain," he said. *(Source: The Vancouver Sun, January 17, 2001.)*

Doing Chores Improves Odds Of Survival In Elderly

People who burned the most energy going about their daily lives had only a 12.1 per cent risk of death over six years, compared with 24.7 per cent for people who used the least energy, according to a study in the "Journal of the American Medical Association". "Any movement is better than no movement," said lead investigator Todd Manini of the National Institute on Aging. *(Reported by T. Barry, Vancouver Sun, July 12, 2006; Source: Bloomberg, with a file from Associated Press)*

Instruments of health...Harps.

Dr. Abraham Kocheril, chief of cardiac electrophysiology at the Carle Heart Center in Urbana, Ill., says he has found signs that harp music might help sick hearts. He has used a harpist as an accompanist in his operation theatre. The theory is based partly on the work by Dr. Ary Goldberger of Harvard Medical School showing that varied rhythms created by healthy hearts are similar to note patterns in classical music. Some enthusiasts believe the harp has special healing qualities, and Dr. Kocheril said resonant vibrations from live harp music may be particularly effective at regulating quivering heart rhythms. Other music instruments and recorder music might offer similar benefits, he told The Associated Press. "Potentially, there could be prescription for music five days a week...to keep the heart healthy in general and to keep rhythm disorders under control."

(Source: Social Studies, A Daily Miscellany of Information by Michael Kesterton, Globe and Mail, January 10, 2006)

Notes:

_____

_____

_____

_____

_____

_____

_____

_____

_____

_____

"Health is the greatest of gifts, contentment the best of riches."
– *Buddhism*

TOPIC 6

Let's Talk: Riding an emotional rollercoaster

How do I cope with the more challenging behaviour changes?

Personal Anecdote: "What a roller-coaster ride!"

Suggestions:

34: Show compassion, manage responses

35: Try to understand 'fixations'

36: Establish membership in the general health team

How do I cope with the more challenging behaviour changes of my parents?

Personal Anecdote:
"What a roller-coaster ride!"

After I raced through the first months following Dad's accident, an experienced social worker specializing in caring for the aged shared with me two insightful ways to try to understand some of the more challenging behaviour changes my parents were already displaying and could display in the future.

She started by offering a simile - she said that my days now, caring for my elderly parents, would feel similar to being on a "roller-coaster ride all the time" and she reminded me that this roller-coaster ride was not going to end until…. Thinking in terms of a roller-coaster ride kept me from being lulled into believing that events might fall slowly into a routine and life could achieve a 'normal' rhythm someday soon. Over these care-years, I continued to think in terms of a roller-coaster ride and it forced me to remain alert and to try to anticipate the next swing of the ride.

That same social worker also helped me understand some of the extreme behaviours I might be confronted with during these care-times. She said to apply "a simple, although illogical formula": Think of an obvious more problematic (personality) behaviour that my parent has had, prior to a turning-point health crisis, then "magnify that specific behaviour several times". Using this formula, I would thus have a much clearer picture of what that particular problem behaviour might become 'after a serious health crisis'. (Apparently, it is the negative-type of behaviours to which this rule applies - wouldn't you just know it!) I was told, that if that general 'rule of thumb' was used, not only would I have a glimpse of some of the challenging behaviours to expect, but also I would have a glimpse of the degree of patience needed to cope with those behaviours.

As well, she pointed out that each of the problem behaviours may not occur in isolation, but could overlap throughout any given day, thus contributing to the overall ride for that day.

I was being prepared....

The following are **some examples of challenging, hard-to-understand behaviour changes we were confronted with in our circumstances, some you may have experienced on your journey, some not - but you will be able to see the formula in action and hopefully begin to think about your own situation.**

Example 1: Magnified behaviours - They are very difficult to manage and seemingly impossible to help.

Prior to the accident, Dad could be easily have been described as being a worrywart with a need to control his immediate environment somewhat (certainly two identifiable personality traits all his life). In the first care-year, as the months progressed, Dad's constant demands to have his surroundings just as he wanted them and his excessive worrying grew, thus presenting a serious problem, one with which we often felt helpless to do anything to alleviate.

Case-in-point - Dad became visibly upset if every person in the house was not within his range of vision. He didn't want the caregiver out of his sight, even if she was on the back porch sweeping (within his view if he turned his head) or in the kitchen preparing lunch (the next room to him). He would ask Mum over and over again throughout the day, where "the lady" was and he would call out "Lady! Lady!" continuously if he couldn't see her. At the same time, whenever Mum wasn't in the same room, he would call out almost non-stop until *she came back into the room with him (she couldn't go for a nap in her bedroom even though the bedroom door was in direct line with his vision from his chair).*

In addition, Dad would question the whereabouts of others who happen to be in the house at any one time, until each person reappeared. For example - during one of my week-long stays, since the caregiver and Mum were sitting in the living room with Dad, I explained to him that this was a good time for me to shovel snow from the driveway, that I would be outside for 15 minutes and I indicated pointing to the clock when I would be back inside. Within minutes of going out the door, Dad started yelling so loudly and repeatedly for me to come in that the caregiver came outside and asked me to return to the living room as Dad was becoming agitated and Mum was growing very upset with the commotion.

As Dad's behaviour had magnified to that of a controlling obsessive worrier now (remembering the formula), a great deal of patience was required by everyone to be with him throughout a whole day (careful explanations and close proximity did not seem reassuring enough for Dad). Even though he was never left alone in the house and even though people around tried to accommodate him, this particular behaviour continued non-stop from morning until bedtime month upon month - there seemed to be no rest for him or others. Just as we were forewarned, a previous personality trait had become a big behaviour problem.

When Dad moved into the caremanor, this type of behaviour lessened somewhat over time, yet, when family members or close friends came to visit, his behaviour took a turn - he didn't want anyone to leave his room, he called out for us to 'hurry up' if we were getting a cup of coffee or talking with a nurse.

In the carehome, Dad did continue to worry, yet, he did not become really agitated unless extremely concerned. Case-

inpoint - For many hours after a morning fire drill practise (residents had to leave the building, everyone being helped down the stairs), Dad questioned all the staff about the use of the elevators; the staff showed him that the elevators did indeed work and kept reassuring him throughout the day that the elevators were still in working order (they tried to explain that the elevators were never broken). That evening while visiting, he questioned me over and over about the elevator use and became extremely upset when I was getting ready to leave as he did not want me to use the elevators (the stairwells were locked for evening security.) Excessive worrying about the carehome elevators 'not working' carried over into the next month.

Long before Dad's health changes, I realized how painful such a worrying nervous nature was for Dad, how much joy he must be missing out on because of this nature. I had always felt so sorry for Dad, but now I also felt helpless as he was unable to control his constant worries and insecurities, and his present behaviours were causing problems for those around him.

Example 2: Behaviour combinations (overlapping as well) - Coping with them is exhausting.

Dad's assertiveness combined with his high need for routine were difficult to handle as individual behaviours but in combination they became impossible and exhaustive to cope with. One recurring daily situation caused immense problems for our family - it was the not-so-simple matter of when to get up in the morning - Dad insisted on getting up the minute he woke up regardless of the hour.

When Dad returned home from the hospital after his accident, our live-in caregiver got Dad up at 8:00 AM since the government scheduled community caregivers arrived at the appointed time of 9:00 for personal hygiene, dressing and therapy. Within the first month, Dad started calling out from his bedroom ("Get up! Get up!") close to 7:30, so the live-in caregiver was getting him up that half-hour earlier and waiting with him until 9:00. By the end of the first couple of months, Dad's calls were beginning closer to 6:00 A.M.

Within six months, Dad loud calls were starting at 4:30 AM with Mum and the live-in caregiver attempting to endure them until 5:00 (even though the hollering grew louder over the half-hour, 5:00 AM was the earliest the caregiver felt she could be ready to start her long day). Dad's forceful nature, his lack of understanding of proper times, and his impatience and strict adherence to routine - all now magnified - together turned into an extremely stressful condition - everyone was awakened every single morning at 4:30 AM and expected to get their day started some four and a half hours before a community caregiver was scheduled to arrive to begin the actual day.

We were told to try some behaviour-altering methods: changing Dad's bedtime having him stay up late (that didn't work, he just became stressed at night wanting to go to bed); to use reason and quiet whispers asking him to wait for "just a half an hour" before calling again, pointing to a certain time on the bedroom wall clock (this technique worked for four to ten minutes maximum). We tried ignoring the calls (they turned into loud hollers and Dad and Mum both became extremely stressed). We even tried very mild medications (they had adverse effects throughout the day prompting emergency calls and periods in the hospital).

We were never able to alter Dad's upsetting morning routine - towards the third quarter of that first care-year, the live-in caregiver was getting up between 4:00 and 4:30 AM and assisting Dad, he would then go to his recliner chair and rest and she would curl up on the couch with a blanket and Mum would be able to go back to bed - until about 7:30. I was now flying in to see my parents at least twice a month for several days at a time and attempting to offer members of the household a full night's rest by helping Dad at the wee hours of the morning. To say that everyone was excessively exhausted would not be an exaggeration.

This behaviour problem continued in the caremanor - but now Dad's calls from his room (he would never use the call button) were routinely at 4:00 AM and were waking neighbouring residents. After trying many methods (except medications as I specified - no medications allowed), the nursing staff (upon agreement with me) decided that the best way to handle his insistence was for the night staff to get Dad up when he started calling at 4:00, dress him for the day, help him with his shaving and other toiletries, at which time, he seemed content to retire to his recliner and sleep until 7:45 AM breakfast time. This was his schedule for the rest of his life.

The brain is like a muscle: Use it or lose it. That's the growing conclusion of research (by Case Western Reserve University Medical School, Cleveland, USA scientists) that shows fogged memory and slowed wit are not inevitable consequences of getting old, and there are steps people can take to protect their brains. Mental exercise seems crucial. People have to get physical too. Bad memory is linked to heart disease, diabetes and a high fat diet, all risks people can counter by living healthier lives. (*Source: Washington Post, reprinted The Vancouver Sun, August 7, 2000.*)

Example 3: Objectionable behaviours - It is tough not to take them personally.

Another warning sign of Dad's changing mental health was his use of abusive language and harsh tone of voice. As a daughter-caregiver, managing the correct response, when faced with these offensive behaviours from a parent, I found, was challenging. Not taking the behaviour personally was even more challenging.

About two years 'prior' to Dad's fall (i.e. turning point health incident), we had started noticing a significant increase in Dad's use of questionable language and an added harshness and abruptness to his normal tone of voice.

Mum voiced our discomfort several times with Dad, but nothing changed. After the fall, this particular behaviour grew noticeably worse and became extremely hard to tolerate. If the slightest thing annoyed Dad (e.g. if someone didn't wait at his side until he finished his glass of water; if his walker was not placed in the exact same spot he expected it in; if an object on the dining table such as the salt shaker was out of its normal placement) we would hear some mumbled swearing, just loud enough that those to whom it was directed got the full impact. Of course, if something big happened that was disagreeable to Dad, the intensity of the language and voice grew.

As a daughter, I had little patience for Dad's nasty manner and as a caregiver, I was unskilled to handle this type of behaviour, so, initially, I chose to confront Dad with his behaviour, hoping that, if pointed out immediately, he would recognize its inappropriateness. Upon seeking help, I found out that my technique for handling these situations was inappropriate and ineffective at "Dad's point of health". I was advised that Dad couldn't curb this behaviour, such was the nature of his dementia-he really wasn't always aware when he was swearing or being nasty. I was told that we shouldn't take the behaviour personally. (Note: I since learned that use of abusive language" is an all too common behaviour change among persons with dementia.)

Soon, I switched to a very quiet approach, gently asking Dad not to say those things, all the while, reminding myself to stay calm in the process. It was especially difficult not to react when others were the targets. The behaviour was hardest on Mum and our caregivers as living with Dad full-time, they had nowhere to escape to during these eruptive, frequent moments throughout each day.

When he moved to the carehome, Dad's tone of voice remained harsh and he still mumbled his displeasure and had mini temper bursts when forced to do something that was not part of his routine, but his outbursts of bad language decreased, happening less frequently.

In truth, coping with this particular behaviour often required more patience than I could muster - I learned that the best I could do was to walk away for a few brief minutes - it was too unsettling, I had to regroup.

Example 4: A behaviour showing up all the time - Gently questioning the behaviour is at times the only option.

For Mum, tears and a plummeting attitude usually accompanied a physical ailment of any magnitude - Dad used to say, "She's down in the dumps". In her LTC care-years, Mum was tearful often and easily - when discussing a memory (this makes sense) or even, listening to/reading a special news article or purchasing a gift/card for someone special.... Mum also reacted immediately with tears if she was offended (One afternoon, I dictated an address quickly to her live-in caregiver rather than to Mum herself as there was chaos going on around me in my office and I was feeling rushed - Mum's response, annoyance plus tears "Don't you think I am capable of doing anything?" Ah yes, independence is indeed important).

Initially, I became alarmed with the frequency of the teary times, feeling I should be doing something about them at every occurrence. Later, even though concerned, I tried to ignore some of the occurrences, letting Mum work her feelings through. I also tried the questioning approach, I would quietly interrupt the tears to ask if there was anything wrong (physically) or if there was a problem at home - this approach allowed Mum to think for a moment, to compose herself and even to respond in fun ("Oh, you know me, I am such a ball-baby."). I understood that Mum could control this teary behaviour to some degree and that understanding decreased my anxiety when the tears started.

Conclusions:

Initially, in the first part of the care-years, it is probably normal for us to focus all our attention on our parents' actual physical ailments and those related needs, but we learn rather quickly that our parents' behavioural problems (if they exist and when they become problematic) can be much more difficult than the physical problems to manage throughout the day. Unreasonable, demanding behaviours can extract a toll on a family.

The mental health of older people, the group with the highest rate of depression and suicide in Canada, frequently is ignored by their doctors, a report says. Their report (in the Canadian Family Physician) says depression among the elderly exceeds 11 per cent, with the rate as high as 50 per cent in nursing homes. One-quarter of suicides involve the elderly. Yet, many family doctors surveyed said they're ill-prepared to spot mental illness, and so don't offer treatment. Most disturbing is that many doctors wrongly believe older patients won't benefit from help. With the over-65 population expected to rise to 6 million from 3.7 million in 20 years, "this is a significant health challenge we as a society face," said Dr. Tony Reid, scientific editor of the journal. Dr. Nathan Herrmann, head of geriatric psychiatry at the University of Toronto, agreed that psychiatric disorders in later life are one of the greatest public-health challenges of the next generation. Many older people tend to view mental illness as taboo, so they don't seek help, and doctors and society have contributed to the problem. The authors of the Kingston study want physicians to update their thinking and hone their diagnosis and treatment skills. Medical-school students are being versed on the needs of the aging, Herrmann said. "Family doctors will have to assume more of a leadership role," Reid agreed. *(Source: The Calgary Herald, May 11, 1999, taken from Queen's University, Kingston, Ontario study.)*

Suggestion 34: *Show compassion, manage responses*

As daughter/son-caregivers, we must understand that we have parents who not only are trying to adjust to their new dependencies and lack of freedoms, but also are undergoing rapid physical and mental health changes that they cannot do anything about. This understanding alone should prompt us to respond to our parents with compassion and empathy (and lack of complaint) at this time in their lives.

Through discussions with professionals, we can learn how to manage our responses when challenging behaviours occur. The professionals could include:

- Local social workers with responsibilities for seniors

- Support groups for family-caregivers

- Health specialists with geriatric training

- Family doctors

- Local seniors' associations

- Day-care hospital/therapy program staff

- Psychiatrists

- Nurses

- Trained, experienced caregivers in carehomes or extended care facilities....

Managing our responses means thinking before reacting:

☑ We have to acknowledge our limitations – understand that we may not be able to handle a parent's questionable behaviours in a regular manner or at all.

☑ We have to adjust our reactions to the severity and frequency of our parent's behaviour on any given day.

☑ We have to try to model good coping skills and assist others in the family, including all caregivers, in learning such.

During care-years, whether a health crisis is of a physical nature (e.g. hip break, stroke, disease, illness), an emotional nature (e.g. depression) or mental nature (e.g. dementia), we must ask questions about any possible personality changes that could go hand-in-hand with that particular health crisis (i.e. what warnings to look for, what to expect, how to respond, what accompanying changes are common, where to seek help...).

We need to remind ourselves that difficult behaviours are posing problems for our parents too – compassion and patience are key.

Music can take care of the pain.... Music has long been know to calm and relax. But a University of Montreal study suggests it doesn't merely provide a distraction from pain, it induces an emotional reaction among listeners that can diminish their pain by up to 15 per cent, the study found. The impact reflects an individual's musical tastes. Jazz fans may be best soothed by the trumpet sounds of legend Miles Davis while classical aficionados may find comfort in an orchestral masterpiece.

"Our analyses showed that music the subjects liked had a significant effect on reducing their pain," said Mathieu Roy, a doctoral student in neuropsychology. *(Ross Marowits, Canadian Press Service, January 17, 2005*

Think you're too old? Meet Clarice…Clarice Rummel will be 87 when she graduates next month (May, 2005); she hopes to inspire other seniors. (Clarice received her UBC degree, retired in 1972 when she was in her 50s. She began university at age 81)

It's never too late to go back to school, says Clarice Rummel of Vancouver… "one of my goals is to get other old people to realize that they do not need to be sitting there watching soap operas and rotting: They can off to school," said Rummel, who is getting a bachelor of arts degree with a major in religion studies.

Until she graduates and can take it easy at her daughter's Shawnigan Lake home on Vancouver Island, Rummel will be busy in her sparse university residence preparing for her final examinations on the Koran, the beginnings of Christianity and pre-modern India.

…She said she had become bored with retirement, even though she had taken an extended solo trip to India. It has taken her five full years to complete the four-year program because she needed one year off for rehabilitation after hip-0repacement surgery.

Rummel credits her "supportive daughter" with providing the assistance she needed to enable her to attend university. She had intended to go to university earlier in life, but the Second World War got in the way. "At the time I should have gone to university, but at the time I graduated from grade school in England, World War 11 came along," she explained. When her brother died early in the war, Rummel felt it was her duty to enlist. She joined up. And her ability to speak German meant she was destined for important wartime work. She was stationed on the southeast coast eavesdropping on communications between German flyers and forwarding the information to intelligence. That sometimes-critical information was used to intercept bombers and fighters attacking Britain. *(Source: Vancouver Sun, April 12, 2005, an excerpt)*

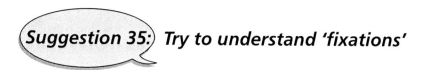

Suggestion 35: Try to understand 'fixations'

'Fixations' (I have been told) is quite a common problem among the elderly with dementia.

From day to day or week to week, our parent may fixate on a variety of different concerns – in other words, our parent may show extreme anxiety over what he/she thinks needs attention and dwell upon that topic continually despite our on-going efforts to eliminate the concern or to redirect the train of thought.

Managing the correct responses to fixations (whether large or small concerns) is very challenging.

What can I expect when 'fixations' occur?

We can identify a 'fixation' (my description) as:

- ☑ The **same topic** (usually in the form of questions) popping up over and over again within a single discussion, sometimes for hours (even days) at a time; accompanied by...

- ☑ **A high level of anxiety** on the part of our parent who doesn't want us to leave until the fixated topic-problem is put to rest to his/her satisfaction; including...

- ☑ **Verbal orders** to take a specific action immediately around the concern (growing more demanding if not followed).

Fixation-days are very hard to deal with for the person with the fixation plus the caregivers and family members trying to respond. When we find ourselves in the midst of a persistent fixation time with our parent, we need to practise any instant self-relaxing, stress-buster technique that works for us, especially if we are getting frustrated when all our efforts to end our parent's fixated anxiety have failed.

(For example: On a fixation-day, I used to go into the bathroom, lean, arms outstretched on the counter, look closely in the mirror at my reflection and

repeat in a whisper, "Take a deep breath Patty, be patient" – after three deep breaths, I would venture forth again and listen one more time to the questions and try various means to put Dad at ease. At the same time, it would help to remind myself that the 'fixation anxiety' is harder on both my parents, than it is on me. I faced the opposite with Mum in that she would not mention her concerns outright; she would become very quiet and occasionally allude to the problem.)

We may notice some fixations during hospital recovery and rehabilitation periods. We may find ourselves unconsciously thinking that the nursing staff will work with these newly manifested fixated behaviours and that they will disappear altogether (like magic?) as our parent becomes healthy enough to return home. Such may be the case – or not. We may notice 'fixation behavior' when change is occuring as frail seniors feel safe with routine and dislike change as it raises anxieties.

Caring for a parent may mean mum or dad may have to move in with you and your family

Just over half (55%) of parents are being cared for in their children's homes. Overall, most family care-giving is provided in the caregiver's homes (77%); this is almost always the case when the care-receiver is a spouse/partner (97%), a child, or someone with a mental disability (Note: As well, most Alzheimer patients are cared for by a loved one at home). *(Source: National Profile of Family Caregivers in Canada - 2002: Final Report, Statistics Canada, Health Canada)*

What can I do when fixations are going on...and on?

☑ **Learn coping skills, responses asap:** If we are noticing fixations while our parent is still in the hospital recuperating, as a precaution, we should immediately ask about the conditions we are seeing and the skills we should be learning (e.g. what to do) – if fixations are showing up at that point, we will more than likely be forced to deal with them when our parent goes home.

☑ **About our frustration:** Will power is required as, it is natural, that tones of voices (ours and our parent's) may tend to become a bit ragged (due to both parties' frustration levels) when dealing with a nagging question asked over and over again (all day long). Remember louder doesn't make for better understanding. *(For example: The sprinkler company crew had to quit working at our home several times one week as they could not handle Dad's repeated question of them, called out through the living room window, they just didn't know what to do and we couldn't curb Dad's behaviour and questioning and worry during those weeks – ignoring Dad's yelling was not an option as Dad became louder.)*

☑ **About our guilt:** We should not beat ourselves up when we experience brief periods of annoyance with our parent during fixation episodes. It is (nearly) impossible to be attentive to the same concern hour after hour, to alleviate our parent's repetitive concern time and time again, to keep trying to move the question aside and not grow impatient in the long process.

☑ **With our other parent:** We need to help our other parent cope with fretful fixation-days since she/he has to remain in the same environment (i.e. cannot escape if living together). We should watch for signs of stress within our other parent as a result of living with fixations of a partner. We should also watch if a parent doesn't seem to visit for long with her/his spouse in a carehome due to the inability to manage good responses on a fixation-day. *(For example: Mum really never did grasp these behaviours, summing up her challenge one day by saying, "He just isn't interested in anything else and I can't seem to change the subject." I think it must be a lonely time for both partners when visits are unsatisfactory.)*

☑ **About topics:** We should watch for occasions when fixations occur with our parent and identify, if possible, the process by which the topics become concerns. In doing so, we can be somewhat prepared. *(For example, Dad developed one constant daily fixation beginning in the hospital rehab ward that lasted the rest of his life, both in his own home and in the caremanor. Dad would ask, first thing* *every morning, the name of the person who was going to help put him to bed that evening (then he had to be reassured repeatedly as the day went on that the identified person was correct and would actually show up). While in the caremanor, he would wait outside the nurse's office until the morning shift change meetings were finished, he would sit, in the mid-afternoon, near the office to confirm the caregiver or nurse was going to be on duty — I often wondered if Dad was fixated on this concern because he recognized complete physical dependency, yet he had never gone without help for one day since his turning point, breaking his hip.)*

Memory—Forgetfulness is part of aging, but scientists say there is hope

...There is no doubt memory starts to deteriorate as we age, says Graf, who is 53 (a University of BC psychology professor who specializes in memory). Memories are stored in neuro networks and throughout life we lose them, he explains. While science has proven we regenerate neurons throughout our lives, what we lose as we age are the cells that insulate the neurons. Researchers believe that as this insulation thins, the speed at which neurons communicate with each other slows and memory just isn't what it used to be. That's the biological explanation, but there is also a psychological reason why middle-aged people suffer memory lapses. Our brains are so full of stuff that nothing we add stands out anymore. The whole world is a cliché. Children learn so quickly and remember so well because everything is new to them. But as we age, it gets harder and harder to differentiate between two similar items. This gives us the ability to consider things in a bigger context and to respond more thoughtfully to events than children can, but it's train wreck for memory. (continued...)

There is what experts call a lapse in prospective memory—forgetting what is in the future (e.g. an appointment). It's the opposite of retrospective memory, or what is in the past. While older people have been known to have prospective memory lapses, statistically it's a phenomenon of youth. Children and youth are terrible at remembering what they have to do (homework, household chores, meetings..) whereas adults have a harder time remembering what they did, says Graf.

Not to worry. Like abs, memory can be toned up, with work. Guy Pilch, a mental fitness consultant based in Victory, says protecting your memory needs a holistic approach, involving both mental and physical fitness. There are lots of mnemonic techniques, he says, but equally important are efforts to reduce stress, improve concentration, increase physical activity and improve diet.

"Memory is something that needs a multi-faceted approach," he says. "You can't remember if the brain is flabby." Pilch adds that the brain loves humor and rudeness, so he uses them to help him remember. One facet you can forget right now is that old standby, rote. It was proven not to work 30 years ago when psychologist Gus Craig discovered that the brain has various levels of processing information. He found that the more a person thought about the meaning of a word, the better they remembered it, even if they didn't know they'd be tested. "Thus it is not that you want to learn that is critical. It's what you do to remember," says Graf. With our brains so cluttered with facts, figures and episodes, what w need is a good filing system, explains Graf. We need files that stand out from the crowd, that are sorted by context and that can be accessed when needed. Hopefully, that will ensure we show up for appointments on the right day. If not, mark them in your planner—and remember to read it. *(Source: The Body And Health Section, the Vancouver Sun, April 18, 2005, article by Karen Gram)*

"No one can avoid aging, but aging productively is something else."
– *Katharine Graham*

How can I try to help to alleviate the effects of fixations?

☑ **Understand the origin:** Realizing that certain conditions can trigger a fixation may help us understand how to reduce the fixation. *(For example: We found that Dad's fixation-of-the-day might be linked to a visitor he had that day since something said during their conversation would remind him of an issue – e.g. one day the fixation was house insurance as an old friend visited early in the morning on his way to pay his house insurance and that started the concern and anxiety.)*

☑ **Look for factors that help in certain circumstances:** Certain factors may work to reduce fixation behaviours. *(For example, we found three important factors had to be 'in place, at the same time' to reduce (not eliminate) the intensity of some fixations:*

- *Easily understood care routines with organized sets of guidelines, accompanied by specific schedules; plus…*

- *Clear rules for activities (e.g. going to the caremanor barber every x days; signing in and out of the manor); plus…*

- *Non-family persons in positions of authority.)*

☑ **Ask for help:** We may need to seek professional advice and join support groups if fixations (with all the unwanted emotional baggage that goes with them) are seriously affecting our parents' quality of life.

Mental gymnastics help you get a grip on details…Three basic steps form basis of memorizing tricks

Unless you are an advertising executive called to testify at the Gomery inquiry into the sponsorship scandal, memory loss is very annoying. If you want to remember something, there are lots of tricks you can employ, but experts say they all rely on three basic steps. First make it distinctive (encode); second, connect it to something you already know (recode); and third, figure out how you will retrieve it when you need it (retrieve).

Here is a sampling of some of the tricks and the types of memories they are good for:

LOCI: This mnemonic device connects what you want to remember to a specific location you have memorized. So if you have a grocery list, including eggs and bread, visualize the eggs smashed on your door and the bread on the top step. So, when you are at the grocery store, you can mentally work through your house and see what object is in each spot. The locations serve as retrieval cues for the desired information and the visual image strengthens the memory, especially if you are a visual learner. This technique is limited only by the number of locations you have embedded in your memory. LOCI is useful to remember any set of information, such as a list of chores or points in a speech.

PEGWORD: An offshoot of loci, developed to adapt to modern society's tendency to move around a lot. People learn a series of words that serve as "pegs" on which memories can be "hung". For example, the peg words could rhyme with numbers to make the words easy to remember: One is for gun, two is a shoe, three is a tree, four is a door, etc. To learn the same grocery list, one might associate gun and bread by imagining the gun shooting the bread. Two is a shoe, so one would imagine a milk cartoon sitting in a giant shoe and so on. When you need to remember the list of groceries, you simply recall the peg words associated with each number; then these serve as retrieval cues for the groceries. Peg methods such as this one permit more flexible access to information than does the loci method. (continued...)

For example, if you want to recite the items backwards for some reason, you can do so just as easily as in the forward direction. If you need the eighth item, you can say, eight is a plate: and mentally look at your image for the item on the plate.

The PQ4R: This acronym stands for preview, question, and the four Rs: read, reflect, recite and review. It's a mnemonic technique used for remembering text material, based on the understanding that the brain becomes very focused when faced with questions. The first step is to preview the text by skimming quickly through the chapter and looking at the headings. Then form questions about the information by simply converting the headings to questions. Then go through the four Rs. Read the text carefully, trying to answer the questions. Reflect on the material by, for example, creating examples of how you cold apply the principles you are reading. Recite the material after reading it. Then review–go through the text again, trying to recall and to summarize its main points.

MINDMAPPING: This modern organizational thinking tool developed by Tony Buzan, author of "Mind Map, The Ultimate Thinking Tool", exploits brain research showing that the brain responds to visual images, color and links to other memories. With mind maps, you shape your thoughts into a diagram with the main idea in the center and secondary thoughts radiating out from there. It's good for note taking, planning, memory and creativity. The idea is that the diagram reflects the way the brain works anyway. It claims to be the easiest way to put information into the brain and to retrieve it. The natural formation helps you remember, but also helps you make connections you might not have thought of, thereby increasing your creativity.

MEMORY SOFTWARE: These computer programs offer a variety of games and tests to build memory skills. *(Source: The Vancouver Sun, April 18, 2005, by Karen Gram)*

 **Establish membership in the general health team**

(Refer to Topic 2, Suggestion # 18, Become An Advocate.)

A parent's on-going health team could be defined as individuals who assist in the care of and offer attention to the health of our parents – that description therefore includes any daughter/son-caregivers/care-guide.

It is to our whole family's benefit if we become an active participant (rather than an observer) in decision-making around health and caregiving issues for our parents. We need to make time to offer details, which may be relevant to our parents' care, to other team members. Once again, we must know who the other members of our parent's health team are, such as the family doctor, cardiologist, optometrist, day-hospital staff, social workers, community care workers, ear-nose-throat specialist, pharmacist....

We should realize that each of the health professionals forming our parent's team only see and thus make decisions based on a limited perspective of our family, usually one part rather than the whole. They cannot be expected to know a family's interactions – yet they do need to be made aware of family dynamics since the decisions these individual members make are ones that our family has to live with on a daily basis.

Our job as one team member is to inform other decision-makers of our family's broader picture.

What can I do?

We can do the following:

- ☑ **Use memos:** At any given time, a health professional may know only of the progress of one parent, the patient, and remain unaware of the present physical or emotional condition of the other – if important, we can write a memo to the doctor or specialist prior to the next appointment giving a broader picture of the family. *(For example: my parents' family physician joked that he had to purchase a new fax machine due to the volume of information I sent him during the first three care-years).*

☑ **Advise all caregivers of a health history:** Specialists, substitute doctors, emergency services often need to know the length of time a medication has been taken (e.g. how many years on an antidepressant) or past health history (e.g. when did open heart surgery take place, a stroke, a fall…) – we need to advise the caregivers of these facts. It is very helpful to write an outline of our parent's health history if necessary and have it ready for all caregivers to review upon being hired or scheduled.

☑ **Use notes-to-file:** If our parent is in respite care for any period or residing full-time in a caremanor, the nursing staff of the home need to be fully informed regarding that parent's past health history including any special health requirements (e.g. the degree of vision or hearing impairments). It is useful to write a note-to-file for the carehome nursing staff and forward it in advance of the residency period.

☑ **Introductory letters:** Assistance-related groups/departments, such as regional health unit coordinators, are not usually privy to the past health history or behaviour patterns of a parent prior to their first visits, therefore providing them with this type of information in advance of the first assessment visit enables each to make more appropriate decisions regarding the type and frequency of assistance to offer. When requesting services from any special program or group, take time to write a confidential introductory letter describing the family to the responsible contact persons to add to their files – such will save time later and could increase the level of assistance given.

How can I demonstrate my interest?

Being an active participant in a parent's health team or committee (if committee methods are used in your region) is a guaranteed timesaver over the long-term.

We can demonstrate our involvement by taking these steps:

☑ **Attend the important health-related meetings** which are set up to discuss our parent's health problems and well being (to be included from the start, we must be sure to inform the family doctor of our interest to participate). If possible, we should try to attend the very first meeting to establish our role right away as an active/involved daughter/son-caregiver and/or care-guide, especially if government program assistance, financial or services, is being requested.

☑ **State our role on the team.** We need to come prepared to participate, not to observe and listen only. *(For example: We can state in meetings with health professionals, "I believe that the more informed you are regarding my family as a whole, the better your decisions will be for us; my role here therefore is to offer relevant information to help you make those decisions.")*

☑ **Take a position when necessary** – even if it flies in the face of what is being recommended by the professionals at that point. We must maintain our confidence in a medical-oriented environment (not become intimidated), be polite and be firm when appropriate, make requests (not demands) and remind ourselves that the experts present also want the best and most efficient care for our parent. *(For example, "I would like my father to be able to attend day hospital twice a week rather than once a week for three reasons, one he needs more therapy than he is presently receiving, two, he needs a greater social time with others now, especially men, and three, my mother and caregiver need some personal time. Day hospital two times a week will help with these goals, will the change be acceptable?" Note: although they agreed with my reasons, space was limited thus twice a week was not possible.)*

☑ **Take notes** during each meeting and ask questions (as many as need be) to clarify the what's and when's. As in any meeting, a summation of the decisions arrived at during this current meeting is a good closure technique.

Fax/e-mail any agreed upon understandings as follow-ups. As we have made notes regarding what was discussed during the meeting and what the next stages of therapy/assistance/care are to be (as a result of the decisions made at the meeting), we need to be businesslike regarding our immediate follow-up. *(For example, I discovered that the very next day we need to fax or e-mail our understandings of the decisions made, as any later could prove too late since health decisions are implemented quickly.)* Our memorandum of the results of the meeting should be addressed to the family doctor, as he/she is often the committee's leader for his/her patients. We need to add a copy to our files also.

The following is a sample format for a follow-up memo – the style worked for me and may for you also – actually, any style is acceptable, just as long as the follow-up is done and done quickly.

Memo to: Family Doctor *(insert name)*

Re: Meeting to discuss X's care plan

Paragraph one (as a beginning): Upon review, the following was discussed during our meeting yesterday (always include the date) – list the main topics discussed: 1, 2...

Paragraph two: The following decisions were arrived at – list the decisions: #1, that such and such will be taking place and when it is to begin, #2...

Paragraph three: Further to that meeting, Dr. X, our family doctor, is going to do A, the therapist is going to do B and our family is going to do C – list each responsibility arrived at during the meeting, person by person, and the dates these are to go into effect (e.g. one week from now, next month).

Paragraph four – an ending: I trust we agree on the contents of this e-mail/memo/ letter/fax, but should there be any discrepancy, please contact me immediately – state contact numbers including telephone area code, e-mail address, fax. I look forward to our next meeting, please advise me in advance of the date and location in order that I may have time to arrange my schedule.

Thank you for your cooperation (include a contact telephone number.).
Sign and cc a copy to each of the persons who were present at the meeting.
List all the persons being copied.

Aging doesn't mean mental fitness has to decline–seminars such as Train Your Brain make believers out of the formerly forgetful

"There is absolutely no question that you can improve your mental functioning with training," adds psychologist David Hultsch, director of the Centre on Aging (University of Victoria)...Research in the past decade has turned previous assumptions about memory loss upside-down, says Pilch, 48, whose interest was galvanized by glitches in his own memory. "I was curious, how could I tune myself up?"

When brains get flabby, their owners become anxious and self-doubting, which narrows their world. "They stick to the familiar, and that's the one thing you can do. You've got to get out of that safe environment and be stimulated."

"The loss of mental function is not inevitable with age, he says. While old brain cells inevitably die, there's evidence that brain cells renew themselves and that the connections between neurons can strengthen and multiply. "The absolute key point is that it's not a quantity of brain cells issue; it's the number of connections between brain cells," said Pilch.

Bill Spriggs, 74, now brushes his teeth with his left hand instead of his dominant right, and is memorizing the phone numbers of his friends a s a mental exercise and time-saver"

(Guy Pilch, Master's degree in counseling psychology and previously worked in psycho-geriatrics and mental health, holds Train The Brain Workshops, sponsored by the University of Victoria Centre On Aging www.trainthebrainconsulting.com)

"An ounce of emotion is equal to a ton of facts."

– John Junor

TOPIC 7

Let's Talk: Working with caregivers

How do I go about finding that all important someone to care for, respect and laugh with my parents on an everyday basis?

Personal Anecdote: "There are no guarantees!"

Suggestions:

How do I go about finding that all important person(s) to care for, respect and laugh with my parents on an everyday basis?

Personal Anecdote:
"There are no guarantees!"

As soon as our turning-point health crisis occurred, the term "caregiver" became part of our family's daily vocabulary as caregiving became a priority in our lives.

Understanding one's family's need for and growing dependency on caregivers is one of the most critical issues a daughter/son with elderly parents will have to address. Yes, we have to pay close attention to the overall health of our parents, yes, we have to learn to balance our time to include new responsibilities - but - finding good caregivers, that's the wild safari part of our care-years journey. In the first three years, our family had four privately hired (by us) live-in caregivers, as well as over a dozen different homecare government scheduled community caregivers in our home.

What does caregiving include? Who are caregivers? How are they categorized and trained? What can we expect of each type of caregiver? What are the costs? Are there any special assistance programs available to help pay for caregivers? How does a family go about hiring caregivers? What are the employment rules? What do caregivers expect of us? Finding the answers to these questions makes for a steep learning curve. (It is also crazy-making too at first.)

Given that both Dad's and Mum's health after Dad's turning point fall prompted our first intensive experience with caregivers, given that there are many different kinds of caregiver categories and many private and public agencies involved in the issue, our family needed a start-point, so I began by sorting out the roles and functions of the different types of caregivers. By categorizing the caregivers, we at least had a point of reference when discussing our needs with others.

We learned that:

☑ The types of caregivers and services required by a family are defined by 'our parents' health or aging problems at any one moment' and the types required will change over time due to evolving care needs (e.g. full time live-in caregiver; scheduled weekly community caregiver; specific task caregiver such as home-maker; respite caregiver; nurse caregiver...).

☑ A family usually requires the services of more than one type of caregiver, at the same time (that is, combinations working together).

☑ Caregivers of varied types may be supplied by a provincial/territorial government health authority or community care access center.

☑ Caregivers may be hired privately (newspaper ad, church group...) by a family or hired by going through a for-profit business.

Caregivers come and go... this is part of any 'care-journey'! Over the course of ten years, our family had a variety of caregiving circumstances; many caregivers overlapped depending on the type of health problems of my parents and the government assistance available at the time. We used, over the ten years: live-in caregivers, government care-aides and home-makers, daily/hourly shift-caregivers, part-time live-in shift caregivers, respite caregivers, family members, as well individuals hired for specific home-related tasks.

We found various caregivers via word-of-mouth recommen-dations, newspaper advertising, agency searches, long-time friends, family connections, and local community groups and of course, through government assistance programs.

As the years went by, we found we could not rely on the same type of caregiver as changing health needs of my parents demanded a more qualified or more-time involved caregiving situation. As well, I had to keep reminding myself that this is a 'job' to a caregiver and as in other jobs, this worker too may change as circumstances evolved.

We went through scores of caregivers - sometimes we changed because the working-relationship demanded change; other times we changed because the caregiver's health changed (e.g. one live-in caregiver had a severe heart attack a few months into the job); other times we changed because the caregiver went to another position (e.g. pay was better, job less demanding, change of location of living, caregiver became better skilled and more educated...); other times, we changed because we could only get the caregiver for a specific duration.

Changing caregivers is very stressful on a parent who is counting on you to 'get things organized'. My mother found this aspect of her life extremely disorienting and upsetting (I would make sure I was with her for a few days before a change in caregiver and a few days after; I would also make an extra trip that month when a new caregiver was hired just to ensure all was going along well for all parties.) Looking back, I am unsure if I could even today 'read' the exact time when change is forthcoming, but after ten years, the best barometer was always my parents' levels of joy and acceptance (and my 'intuition').

The following is a breakdown of the caregiver categories including brief descriptions that our family developed for our own use when faced with the caregiver-puzzle.

Over the years, by attending conferences, meeting with professionals, and reading articles, I learned other names for each caregiver category, but for this practical guidebook, I will use the terms first devised for our journey - as they are self-explanatory and made sense to us in our beginning care-years.

We had 6 Categories:

Category 1: Care-guide (i.e. 'care-manager').

This is a fairly new term for Canadians, but a very important designated person in one's lifestyle and retirement planning. A care-guide ('your' careguide) is the key manager of the level of care and the kind of care to be received. This person is responsible for all of the decisions and actions taken (when you are no longer able, due to usually physical challenges) — the big decisions involving the long-term care of a loved one. Often this person is a spouse or an adult child or a sister/brother. The care-guide may also be a caregiver (dual roles) that is, the person who does the hands-on care duties on a regular/respite basis.

This person may or may not live in the same house or even city as her/his parents, yet, remains the person who is the main contact, the one who tends to the necessary activities and the one who is responsible for creating a comfortable, safe living environment for the parents. As mentioned, this person of course, could also be the on-the-spot, everyday caregiver who assists with our loved ones' everyday activities of living.

Category 2: Daughter/son-caregiver (daily basis or respite basis).

This is often the key caregiver (and, as mentioned, may also be the 'care-guide'), the child of the senior parents who is designated as the person responsible for their overall everyday care/activities. If there are no children involved, the main caregiver may be a relative - it is common now to find siblings looking after siblings, grandchildren looking after others in the family and so forth. Of course there could also be a 'spouse caregiver' category (self explanatory).

Even though we know caring for our loved one is our responsibility, we may also feel we don't have a choice as there is no one else available or there are no home care services to help out.

67% of caregivers are looking after family members because they see it as a family responsibility or because they simply choose to do so (63%). Overall, the population is divided on whether or not they had a choice, with just over half (52%) saying they did have a choice, while 44 percent felt they did not.

(Source: National Profile of Family Caregivers in Canada - 2002: Final Report, Statistics Canada, Health Canada)

Do you know the Family Relations Act?

There is an 'obligation to support parent'

Adult daughters and sons in Canada should understand that we have maintenance and support obligations and that one of those obligations is an 'obligation to support parent'.

- We need to check the 'Family Relations Act' in the province or territory in which our parent resides.

For example, my parents resided in British Columbia and the Family Relations Act in BC states the following:

Obligation to support parent

90 (1) In this section:

"child" means an adult child of a parent;

"parent" means a father or mother dependent on a child by reason of age, illness, infirmity or economic circumstances.

(2) A child is liable to maintain and support a parent having regard to the other responsibilities and liabilities and the reasonable needs of the child.

91 (1) A person may apply for an order under this Part on his or her own behalf.

(2) The Attorney General may designate in writing those persons who may make applications for orders under this Part on behalf of a parent described in section 90 or on behalf of a spouse.

(2.1) A designated agency, as defined in the *Adult Guardianship* Act, may apply for an order under this Part on behalf of a parent described in section 90 of this Act after an investigation is conducted under Part 3 of that Act.

(2.2) A representative, substitute decision maker or guardian may apply for an order under this Part on behalf of a parent described in section 90 of this Act if the representative, substitute decision maker or guardian is authorized under the *Representation Agreement Act* or the *Adult Guardianship Act* to make decisions about the routine management of the parent's financial affairs (1966, c. 128 (supp), 7)

(3) Any person may apply for an order under this Part on behalf of a child.

(4) A spouse or parent affected by an order under this Part or a person described in subsection (1), (2) or (30 may apply for an order altering, varying or rescinding the order or canceling or reducing arrears under it.

(5) If the right to apply for an order under this Part is assigned to a minister under section 24.1 of the *BC Benefits (Income Assistance) Act,* section 15.1 of the *BC Benefits (Youth Works) Act* or section 13.1 of the *Disability Benefits Program Act,* the minister to whom the right is assigned may apply for the order in the name of the government or the name of the person who made the assignment. (rep.& sub. 1997, c. 15, s.16)

Stress levels are increased significantly when one becomes a caregiver

Seven in ten (70%) acknowledge that providing care has been stressful, and this is even the case among half of those who say they have been handling the responsibility very well. One in six (17%) of caregivers fit into the 'high stress group' (a rating of 4), and this group is more likely to include women – the most significant predictor (or indicator) of care-giving stress is the lack of choice in taking on this responsibility. *(Source: National Profile of Family Caregivers in Canada – 2002: Final Report, Statistics Canada, Health Canada)*

Jobs and careers are affected when caregiving is added to one's responsibilities—the decisions may require quitting, retiring early or making serious changes to the pre-caregiving conditions of our jobs.

More than one in four indicate their employment situation has been affected by their care-giving responsibilities, either in terms of quitting/retiring early (9%) or having had to make other changes in their work situation (e.g. schedules, role) (18%).

Among those currently employed, care-giving has been disruptive to their work, either to a significant (19%) or some (33%) degree.

More than four in ten (42%) believe it would be very helpful to receive flexible work hours, while an equal proportion express similar interest in short term job and income protection through the federal government Employment Insurance (EI) program (42%).

One in five (21%) feel this would not be helpful to them, while another 11 percent say it would not apply to them because of self-employment or because of other reasons.

By comparison, fewer than one in five (18%) see a significant benefit in having access to a leave of absence without pay, likely because they could not manage without their employment income. *(Source: National Profile of Family Caregivers in Canada - 2002: Final Report, Statistics Canada, Health Canada)*

Category 3: Community-based scheduled home-care caregivers/workers/aides:

These types of caregivers are qualified health-care individuals who are:

☑ *Employees of or on contract to a provincial government community-based health authority/community care access center or*

☑ Employees of or on contract to a private for-profit company that provides homecare services in a city/area.

The job of this category is to provide specific caregiving services to our parents on a regularly scheduled basis, for a specific task. This category of caregivers forms an important support group to our parents if still living on their own in their own home/apartment/retirement community/condominium. This type is also support for us if our live-in/shift/family caregiver must be given scheduled time-off.

This category of caregivers provides a broad range of at-home, care services defined by the level or type of care our parents need 'at any given time':

☑ Environmental Care: Helps with some housecleaning services; prepares some meals.

☑ Personal Care: Assists with bathing and other personal hygiene needs; prepares a parent for bedtime; assists in the mornings.

☑ Other Care: Administers an exercise program; provides companionship.

☑ Could provide scheduled relief for hired live-in/shift/spouse caregivers (e.g. during the week and holiday) and could be available for emergency relief.

☑ If provided by the government, this type of caregiver can provide supplementary care for a parent even if you have hired some support privately on your own.

Category 4: Specialized community-based formal caregivers

There is another category of caregivers that provide specialized skills (e.g. occupational/physical therapy) and/or nursing skills. These are formal caregivers usually supplied by your regional health authority - upon request (depending on the health need) or maybe hired privately by a family.

Category 5: Lead agency or department responsible for coordinating homecare services for seniors in the community.

This is a designated government department, usually community-based (if not, it is regionally-based), whose mandate it is to assess the level of need of our parents (i.e. do an assessment) and provide care services in one's home matching the assessment's findings. (Note: For your further information: This is the same government department that also assesses nursing home subsidization requests)

As soon as a crisis (turning point) occurs with one of our parents, we should ask the hospital social worker or the hospital staff about "the lead government department responsible for caregiving services in our community" and immediately contact that department to discuss possible caregiving assistance for our parents. In most cases, the department/ division is part of the local health unit or contracted to the health unit, therefore one could telephone locally/regionally for information. (One should also ask for information about any private for-profit companies/agencies offering at-home care services.)

This designated government department hires and/or contracts qualified individuals to work as caregivers.

The appropriate department/center/authority assigns community caregivers on a daily or weekly or as-need basis to our parent's home. The cost of these services often depends on the level of income of our parents; some families receive fully paid services, some cost-share. (An option is to hire homecare services on one's own and not go through government services.)

At-home care performs a vital role in the caregiving of our parents and as such is a critical part of a family's support network.

(For example, after Dad's release from the rehabilitation ward, the regional health unit organized two one-hour shifts, one hour in the morning and one in the evening, for community caregivers to assist Dad in his own home. Later, the agency coordinated a roster of community caregivers to assist our live-in caregiver with Mum's care - we received two half-days, 4 hours each, and one full day, 8 hours, giving our live-in caregiver time off in the week; during my visits, I telephoned the department well in advance to cancel the scheduled services for the actual days only I was spending with Mum.)

Note: It is a good idea to identify the department responsible for care services for the elderly in the area prior to a health crisis with a parent - just takes a phone-call or two, begin with the local health unit. As mentioned, one also should investigate the private companies available in the area and telephone the local health unit/department/center for advice on these companies, to get further information.

Note: For further research, go to www.longtermcarecanada.com and click on the "Government Programs" menu and then the "Provincial/ Territorial Government" tabs; the "Care programs and services offered by each province and each territory" are listed, click on your province.

Category 6: Live-in and/or shift caregivers.

These are key care persons in establishing and maintaining the ongoing security and happiness of our parents.

These persons are critical members of a family's care-team and the most difficult type to find when searching for quality, reliable everyday assistance.

This is the caregiver who either moves fulltime into or does a partime shift in our parent's home (with family and/or without furnishings) on a permanent basis or shift basis (eg. 4 days on, 24 hr, and then 8 days off) and for that period may consider our parents' home her/his/their home too. The job responsibilities are vast:

- ☑ *Offers daily 24-hour care, both general and emergency.*

- ☑ *Understands and distributes medications.*

- ☑ *Attends to parents' hygiene and safety.*

- ☑ *Plans and prepares meals.*

- ☑ *Organizes and participates in outings, appointments, exercise, special occasions....*

- ☑ *Shops for groceries, household items, clothing, gifts....*

- ☑ *Is a companion - discusses news, sports, nature, new ideas, shares coffee breaks....*

- ☑ *Networks with small circles of relatives and neighbours plus other types of caregivers required.*

- ☑ *Becomes a 'type' of friend/companion (note: even though an employee) offering support, laughter, respect, dignity, and attention.*

In addition, it is the responsibility of this type of caregiver to undertake planning a full orientation program if/when a government scheduled caregiver is assigned to homecare work with our parents, in order that a smooth transition of some of the duties occurs and all tasks and routines are undertaken properly and safely with as little disruption to our parents as possible. It is also the responsibility of the caregiver to organize the household (e.g. groceries available for baking, pills set out for the day, cleaning materials in correct places...) so that the tasks to be done by the scheduled caregivers on their scheduled homecare days can be accomplished.

If there is no live-in caregiver, but shift caregivers only, then one of the shift caregivers may be designated as the central caregiver for supervisory purposes. Of course, the daughter/son-caregiver and/or care-gude may also assume the orientation training for any caregivers who may periodically work with our parents.

This type of caregiver's job is large in scope, large in responsibility and large in importance.

Special Note: The importance of caregivers (in general, all types) should not be underestimated by any family member, especially a daughter or son living in another city depending fully on those caregivers to be attentive to one's parents.

Notes:

_____

_____

_____

_____

_____

_____

Suggestion 37: Hire live-in and/or shift caregivers

Hiring live-in/shift caregivers is one of the most important duties we will undertake on behalf of our parents in their care-years, as this person becomes a focal point member of the daily caregiving team for our parents.

Hiring a caregiver is a task, which if done properly and carefully, can prevent heartache and problems in the future for the whole family and offers great joy to our parents' everyday world. The very nature of caregiving demands that everyone involved is able to work together (easier said than done).

As a daughter/son, we can try to cover as many conditions as possible in order to establish a harmonious mutual living arrangement for all parties involved – but personalities play a huge part in how caregiving duties are actually carried out, how the everyday work is perceived by our parents and how well the caregiving services are accepted by each party. (To get a feel for the dynamics involved, imagine being together 24 hours a day, 7 days a week/30 days a year/year after year.)

Note: Even when all steps are followed carefully, there are no guarantees that a caregiver-parent interaction will be a successful one.

The study (Health Services Utilization and Research Commission, Saskatchewan Branch) findings suggest **seniors' living arrangements and social contacts** may play a larger role than receipt of care services in keeping them healthy and active, said Cecile Hunt, Chair of the study panel. *(Source: The Vancouver Sun, May 30, 2000.)*

Is there a process I can follow?

The assumption in this section is that a daughter/son-caregiver or care-guide will be undertaking this hiring task on her/his own therefore a step-by-step process is given. (Of course, for a fee, one can also contract with a private company to do the actual hiring of caregivers <u>or</u> one may also contract with a private company to supply the actual caregivers through their own efforts to recruit such) – these options are somewhat more costly than doing the hiring on one's own.

Note – try not to rush a hiring because of a crisis situation.

The following outlines the steps recommended when setting out to hire caregivers on our own for our parents (i.e. it is based on our family's hiring experiences as this is the pattern we used.)

Step 1: Put the word out.

☑ Think of people already known to our family and contact them, they may be interested. (Don't forget to ask our parents if they can think of anyone. This is a very important and possibly a time saving step.)

☑ Contact family members, friends, doctors, health unit professionals, care home staff, church leaders, volunteer organizations, pharmacists… and inform them of our need to hire caregivers (i.e. the type – live-in/shift/part-time/respite…).

☑ Let groups and associations in the immediate community know (e.g. use e-mails …) that we are beginning to search for caregivers for our parents.

This Step 1 is an extremely important one as word-of-mouth is an excellent way to find prospective candidates – people who may be perfectly suited but may never have thought of this type of work.

(For example: We hired one live-in caregiver, in this manner, by simply 'putting the word out' – she was known to Mum and my cousin and had always been very kind and friendly with Mum in the past when they met at the mall. When her company downsized, we approached her for the position, she had not thought previously of being a caregiver – it proved itself to be a good arrangement for all involved at the time.)

Step 2: List the personality characteristics/traits preferred.

☑ Outline the characteristics of people we think our parents now enjoy being with and the type whom we think our parents will work well with on a daily basis (e.g. patience, an interest in nature, kind and gentle, speaks X language, positive energy, laughter…).

Note: Try to be thorough, as these traits can be more important than the actual list of care duties to be performed.

☑ Also write down the characteristics of people who may work well with our own personal style since as the daughter/son, we will be the actual employer (e.g. flexible, calm – doesn't get in a flap, open direct attitude…).

☑ Outline special requirements (e.g. non-smoker, age preference, drivers license, gender if important).

☑ List any special qualifications/training relating to caregiving needs (e.g. experience with dementia, first-aid training, care certificate…).

☑ In addition, we need to ask our parents if they are prepared to accept a caregiver with a child/children, a spouse, a pet. All of these 'details' must be considered prior to interviewing.

(For example: Initially our family would not have considered hiring a caregiver with children – for Mum – because at the beginning I placed too much weight on the companionship aspect of the job, so looked for a retiree. Knowing what I know now, I would not be age-conscious, I would look for a person who is compassionate, one capable of caring for my parents, one with the correct attitude and one with energy and enthusiasm – with or without children. One of Mum's live-in caregivers had a teenage daughter and a cat, both of which added a new dimension to the home environment; needless to say, the cat was spoiled and well loved and spent hours on Mum's lap, this lasted for one section of our LTC years… then all moved on, as change happens.)

Step 3: Brainstorm and set out a list of duties.

☑ We need to think in terms of the detailed needs of our parents over each section of a regular day, include everyday living activities plus once-and-a-while duties in the list.

Regular duties may include medication needs, attending to appointments, meal preparation, grocery shopping/baking, short drives and outings, chatting, picking up prescriptions, grooming-hygiene needs.

The once-in-a-while duties may include: some household chores (e.g. washing and ironing), organizing seasonal tasks, training part-time caregivers when necessary…

☑ Upon completion of a duties-list, discuss the items with each parent (if capable of good input) or assume the responsibility for an all-inclusive list.

Step 4: Plan for caregiver needs and desired conditions.

☑ Take a good look at our parents' home and consider the caregiver's future full-time/part-time living conditions: bathroom, bedroom and private quarter surroundings, storage for belongings, telephone/television hook-ups, furniture requirements – list what needs to be built, added on-to, removed, adapted.

(For example, we redid the lower half of my parents' house for a live-in situation – we adapted a large recreational-room into a living quarter, left one bedroom as is except for adding a television outlet, built a downstairs bathroom suite, reorganized part of the basement for storage purposes, sorted closets, added a second telephone line, extended the television cable, painted the rooms…. When we switched to shift caregivers rather than live-in, we re-did an upstairs bedroom.)

Step 5: Decide on hiring package guidelines.

We should be very clear on our package (and the details) – it should describe the following:

- Salary (in dollars/month) including bonuses/extras; *Check with your province's Employment Standards Branch to gain an understanding of the salary scale – what it really comes down to is what the family can afford and what the caregiver requires as a base salary (i.e. negotiations with fairness and in accordance with your province's employment standards). (Note: Often Employment Standards only give hourly rates based on an 8 hour day, one must then calculate a month's salary within reason as with any other job.) **Cross-reference to Topic 9: Eliminating surprises, knowing the costs of care and planning for future care-years.**

- Responsibilities; specific duties; and expectations of the position.

- Weekly time off (hours/days); paid vacation periods and relief time.

- Living quarters arrangements.

- Food arrangements.

- Furnishings (existing, new or bring own).

- Vehicle use.

- Telephone use (separate telephone numbers and billing statements eliminate confusion).

- Visits by caregiver family members and friends (sleeping arrangements, dinners, rooms available).

- Television needs (in the living quarters); computers (Internet charges).

- Education and training costs. *(For example: One caregiver and I agreed that paid educational courses would be a beneficial part of the compensation package – we agreed on one course per semester – the arrangement worked well, and Mum was very proud of how well her caregiver was doing in these courses.)*

The complete hiring package will have a value – we can calculate that full value/cost for our own purposes.

Step 6: Write a detailed newspaper advertisement (only when all is ready) for placement in both the smaller local and regional papers.

☑ Give as much detail as possible (e.g. I found that a lengthy ad served as part of the first-level screening process since people can truly judge if the position is one they would like).

☑ Use a newspaper box number to ensure privacy (remember, the last thing we want is a series of letters or calls to either our parents' home or our home nor do we want to draw attention to our parents' circumstances – elderly are an easy target).

☑ Do not state any personal telephone numbers or addresses (parents or own) for security reasons (safety of parents) – just give the newspaper box numbers.

☑ Note at the end of the ad that a criminal record check will be done on the successful candidates.

☑ Have the ad run for two weeks, allowing for a good response time.

☑ Try to be precise in the overall wording of the ad as it is the first impression a candidate will have of the family and our manner of conducting business.

(Note: It helps to keep in mind that this position is a paid one, that we are the 'employer', searching for the best 'employee' possible, that the job is an extremely important one.)

Step 7: Prepare a simple candidate-review table for the interviews (to fill in at the end of each candidate's interview).

On a large piece of paper (e.g. I used poster size paper), design a table in order to record the results of each interview; use columns and headings.

The table allows us to compare/contrast the candidates in an orderly, efficient manner.

A screening-interview 'table' may be set out as follows (i.e. it worked for me):

☑ List all the applicants' names down the left hand side of the page in the rows, with their present addresses and telephone numbers for contact purposes (written under their names).

☑ Across the top of the page, in the columns, put the following titles to form columns: experience, age, education/ training, skills, hobbies, valid drivers license, nationality, smoking/ non, marital status/family, references, knowledge of area, involvement with organizations or associations and volunteer work with seniors, background in healthcare, will live in or not (e.g. some people respond to the ads wanting the position but not wanting to live in even though living in part-time as a shift caregiver or full-time as a live-in caregiver is stated as a firm requirement).

☑ Lastly, leave a wider column space on the far right hand side for 'impressions' – this is a note-space to write down feelings, reactions, problems noted, good points, etc. regarding the candidate (this column turned out to be a very important column when decisions were being made).

Step 8: Prepare a series of 'what if' questions for use during the interview:

These questions are scenarios realistically based on our parents' present health and emotional conditions:

• What if my father does this…?

• How would you respond if such and such happened?

• What would you do in the case of…?

• What will you say if my mother wants to do… and it is unsafe?

• What would you do if there were a problem with…?

(Note: These questions are more essential to our understanding of our candidate than the factual information, as we are attempting to gauge the candidates'

methods of working with the elderly, especially the characteristics we listed as important in Step 2 – patience, kindness, quickness for forgiveness, tone of voice, dignity working with the elderly, quick-thinking, energy levels...).

Step 9: From the long-list of applicants, develop the short-list of candidates.

☑ First, fill in the table based on the contents of the letters from the applicants.

☑ Next, review the candidates (the long-list) based on their responses to our newspaper ad. (If a family member or friend tells us about a possible candidate, he/she must also write a letter if interested, as you want to be able to screen 'all' the applicants based on their own letters.)

☑ Highlight the best candidates – these candidates become the short list, that is, the persons to be interviewed (e.g. 4 maximum).

☑ Set a schedule for stage one interviews – time, location (e.g. a quiet restaurant, coffee shop) – do not use one's own home or parents' home, again, for security reasons.

☑ Contact each candidate on the short-list by telephone and arrange the appointments (do one/two interviews per day); set aside one full week for the stage one interviews.

Step 10: Conduct Stage-One interviews.

During the interview, listen carefully (try hard to listen and observe more than talk).

Be friendly – but again, keep in mind that what you are doing is conducting a 'job-interview' for a very important position (hint – be very thorough).

☑ Begin the interview by asking, in detail, about previously held positions – especially caregiving positions or other jobs interacting with the elderly – ask about the physical, mental and emotional health of those with whom they worked, as often the type of experience the candidates have may be totally different than what is needed for our parents (e.g. companionship care and dementia-care require very different skills and temperaments).

☑ Present the 'what-if scenario questions' – resist falling into the 'interview-trap', that is, spending too much time on the factual questions (many of the facts have been gleaned from the response application letters so no need to go over what was given unless it was unclear).

☑ Question references (who they are, how long they have known them, are there others we can contact, such as the family doctor and especially a college teacher if the person has a care-certificate) – we are attempting to establish a full understanding of the candidate's personality and abilites and strengths (very difficult to do – no surprises later).

☑ Conclude by telling each candidate when she/he will know if she/he has made it to the next interview stage (have a very short time frame).

☑ When the candidate has left (it goes without saying, not during the interview), immediately fill in the table, especially the 'impressions' column (memory will be fresh at this time).

Step 11: After the Stage-One short-list interviews.

☑ Upon completion of the interviews, narrow down the list to the best possible candidates (e.g. two).

☑ Discuss these potential candidates with our parent (*e.g. in our first hiring go-round, Mum and I made the decisions as Dad could not be involved in this type of judgement at the time*); ask for comments and input from parents and close relatives.

Step 12: Stage-Two parent involvement interviews (if possible).

☑ Arrange for these interviews (in the same location) with each of the selected candidates so that our parent now may meet each of the finalists (one close relative may also consent to attend for some added input – but set the ground-rules ahead of time.)

This meeting is key as it is our parents who will be sharing their home and private times with this employee and our parent must feel part of the process for greater acceptance.

☑ After each candidate's interview, discuss with our parent(s) their impressions and then add their comments to the columns on the table. *(e.g. I found out that I had to remind my mother to be open-minded and not select one until all had been seen.)*

Step 13: Make decisions

☑ Decide on the finalists in order of preference.

☑ Very carefully check the references of the one - three finalists/ candidates being considered. (Organize open-ended questions to ask the references ahead of time – e.g. how would you describe X, what duties did X do for you, were there any problems, describe all the duties performed, how did she respond when….) Make notes while speaking with the references and add these notes to the screening table. (Note: I found professionals associated were very candid, such as professors, teachers, past larger company employers…)

☑ Select a caregiver for the position.

☑ Contact that person to advise her/him of the decision AND to check that her/his employment status has not changed since the last interview (remember, each have been job hunting). At the same time, advise that candidate of the final check to be done.

☑ Do the required (criminal) check on the candidate.

Step 14: Do the proper follow-ups now with the all the applicants.

☑ Send a letter/note card to every person who responded to the newspaper and other advertisements, thanking each for her/his interest. (Telephoning is not recommended as a discussion is not necessary, nor desired; return addresses were not placed on the thank-you envelopes – again for security reasons.)

☑ Make special mention of the fact that their letters will be kept on file in case there is a need in the future to contact them.

☑ Telephone only the few finalists who were selected for Stage 2 interviews and thank them personally for their interest.

☑ Keep the table and response letters on file – as we just never know when we may need to go back to our notes and find anther caregiver. *(For example, in our situation, courteous follow-ups proved of value as in the first year, we had to go back to other candidates and offer them a job, when the first live-in candidate suffered a heart attack while caregiving, and later when a shift caregiver quit with no notice.)*

Step 15: Contract the position with the successful candidate

☑ Have a written letter-contract ready which states the expectations of the job; job duties, salary, time-off, all items covered in Step Five (e.g. There are sample contracts in many reference books or contact a law firm and have one drawn up – recommended as you never know what to expect down the line – what if you have 'to fire' a caregiver, etc.)

☑ Have two copies of the contract signed and dated.

☑ File a copy of the contract in our caregiving master file box/drawer.

☑ Up-date the letter if/when things change and file the revised contracts.

Step 16: Before taking any action, think about whether you want to hire caregivers on one's own or go through an agency

We need to understand all the factors involved in hiring on one's own or working through a private agency and using its caregivers:

☑ Budgets – Fees – Dollars available.

☑ Our Tax responsibilities/Our Unemployment Insurance responsibilities/Our Workers Compensation responsibilities…etc: as a private employer, you are required to pay the taxes and EI and CPP for your caregiver employees, full or part-time…You will want to discuss with an accountant this question and arrange for a bookkeeping company to do this type of work if that is your choice (e.g. we did and it was 'well' worth it).

Or, you may decide to hire shift caregivers as consultants and they then are responsible for paying what is required.

☑ Supervisory Responsibilities: Unfortunately there is a potential for abuse, mental and physical and even financial when people are working with a frail elderly person. Most persons, we found, work with seniors out of a genuine desire to help and care and contribute, but there will always be others who may take advantage when there is an isolated home with little supervision. Families must address supervision at all times but especially when a daughter/son key caregiver lives a fair distance away and cannot make weekly visits. (Often we may be so grateful for care provided that we neglect to see the manipulation or verbal abuse…). Supervision is, thus, very important – meaning, regular supervision.

(For example, when it became necessary to use a combination of 3 shift caregivers, I designated one as the supervisor and paid accordingly for that additional service; when we had both a live-in caregiver and shift caregivers, the live-in caregiver also had supervisory and training duties for the shift-part-time caregivers. In addition, close contact by the careguide/key daughter-son caregiver is necessary at the very minimum of once a week—things can go off track very quickly making the everyday working and living conditions strained. The bottom line

is that constant supervision is a must and should be built into any caregiving situation.)

If a home care agency which is licensed has the responsibility to provide the caregivers on a regular basis, then that agency automatically assumes the supervisory responsibilities of its employees' actions. It is responsible for the training and providing information on an on-going basis about the client (i.e. elderly needing care). The agency can provide the resources and the guidance in some cases to the family as well regarding the health of the parent. The agency does not replace the responsibility of a child key caregiver though.

If a family cannot or is not able to assume all the various responsibilities involved with caring for a parent (or spouse) then the family may want to work through an agency recognizing that the question of costs is often a factor for this service.

Recommendation: At all times, one is advised to consult both a lawyer (re: employment law) and a chartered accountant (re: taxes) when beginning the process of hiring caregivers. These professionals may just get you started or they may stay involved throughout from time to time.

SAMPLE CONTRACT LETTER
(A guide only, as this is the formart used by our family)

Address: Date:

Dear _____X (name)_____,

RE: CONTRACT FOR CARE-GIVING SERVICES FOR ___Y (name)___

This correspondence will serve as a contract between you and the family of *Y*. As discussed previously on (*date*), the terms of the contract will be as follows:

Part One: Position and Salary.

Your job will be a (*type of*) caregiver to *Y*; by that assumption, your hours will be (*state the hours/day*)—as required.

Your salary is (*state dollars per month*) for (*state if certain nights and/or weekends you are hiring for*) plus (*amount if for anything extra and why*). You are to be paid in two allotments on the 15th and the 30th of each month. Your paycheques will be issued to you directly from (*state by whom, bookkeeper/accountant/family*). Your salary is calculated using the appropriate guidelines for the Employments Standards for (*give your province*). The amounts are as follows:

List the months and salaries (based on 30 or 31 days or whatever).

Part Two: Benefits.

1. The benefits paid by the family to you include WCB, CPP/QPP and UIC. These contributions will be discussed by (*the bookkeeper/accountant/family—whomever is responsible for the bookwork*) as to what applies to you personally—the result will be your net salary per month.

2. Food and accommodation will be provided within the home.

3. The family's vehicle for caregiving purposes will be available to you.

You will receive (*state the number of*) days a week, 8:00 AM to 4:00 PM off and a regular shift-caregiver will undertake the duties at this time. These are to be scheduled days, (*name the days of the week*), unless agreed upon by the shift-caregiver and yourself. Should that caregiver be unavailable for planned or emergency purposes, then it will be expected that you will work that period.

Part Three: Vacation and Time Off Days.

You are to receive paid vacation days each calendar year in accordance with the Employment Standards legislation. These may be taken as separate days or in one-week spans unless otherwise agreed by the family and yourself.

You are to receive additional time off days as scheduled by the family of *Y* if/when a family member assumes caregiver respite duties. In order to plan, time off days should be scheduled early for each month, although flexibility may be required due to work and travel-related commitments of members of the family. For special events, such as Christmas, time off days will be discussed between you and the family, well in advance.

Part Four: Duties -List duties for your family situation

Example: The general duties of the position for *Y*'s care are as follows:

- Establish and maintain the on-going safety, security and well being during everyday periods and emergency periods
- Offer daily 24-hour care, both in general and in emergency situations
- Attend to medication needs and health (doctors, specialist) needs as required
- Attend to hygiene needs
- Plan and prepare meals and any special baking
- Organize and participate in outings, appointments, exercise and special occasions and holiday times

- Shop for groceries, household items, and special items when necessary
- Attend to vehicle maintenance for the family vehicle, if required
- Serve as a companion—discuss news, nature, stories, share mealtimes…
- Network with small circles of family relatives, neighbours plus other types of caregivers (including the orientation and training and on-going management of relevant caregivers when certain aspects of homecare are to be undertaken)
- Organize and undertake the household chores (e.g. seasonal routines, some cleaning, washing, ironing …)
- Serve as a friend offering support, laughter, respect, dignity and attention
- To be attentive, always, to the needs and signals shown regarding health, happiness and daily care.

Part Five: Duration of Contract

It is understood that this contract is a term contract from (*state beginning and end dates*) and to be revisited by (*give date*) in order to discuss the continuation of the contract beyond the end of (*set a deadline month*). It may, however, be terminated at any time by providing written notice to you in accordance with Employment Standards legislation or by providing to you compensation in lieu thereof. You may resign upon providing two weeks written notice to the *Family of Y/CareGuide*. It is also understood that you will discuss any matters of importance regarding this contract and your duties and your continuation with the position with the family at any time whereby an important decision has to be made that influences the health and care of *Y*.

Thank you for your cooperation and consideration.
Signature of CareGuide/Person Hiring
Name of CareGuide for Y
Date
Name of Caregiver and Date

A major study completed in 2002 for our federal government concluded that even at the highest levels of care, the cost of caring for people in their homes is less (than building, operating and maintaining nursing homes). What is surprising about the study is that home care is still cheaper even when the labour of family caregivers is accounted for at the equivalent of minimum wage. The savings are as much as 75 percent for low needs home support clients and 25 percent for those needing the highest levels of care. *(Source: Home Care Cheaper Than Care Home, D. Braemhane, Vancouver Sun, 2006.)*

Notes:

"Kindness is more important than wisdom, and the recognition of this is the beginning of wisdom"

– Theodore Isaac Rubin

Suggestion 38: *Organize living arrangements*

We must keep in mind that our parents' home will have to be reorganized to accommodate caregivers' personal living needs. Large-scale changes may pose an obstacle initially with our parents. We may need to discuss the impact of caregiver space requirements carefully, repeatedly and gently with our parents (especially if there is to be a 'live-in' situation).

(For example: Mum, an extremely organized person concerning all aspects of her home – a place for everything and everything in its place is one of her mottos – was unprepared for anyone living with her who did not share a similar philosophy; initially she was also unprepared for the storage requirements within her basement to accommodate the number of boxes (e.g. caregiver's items) which would eventually fill that one downstairs area – Mum learned to be somewhat flexible, as I did too.)

We should plan for the basics:

- A good-sized bedroom, unless hiring the specific live-in caregiver means more than one person moving in (e.g. children/spouse), then two bedrooms may be required.

- A private full bathroom (e.g. we learned that sharing bathrooms with parents does not work).

- An entertainment-work-hobby area.

- Ample storage space (for possessions).

As a minimum, a caregiver, full-time or lengthy shift, requires a large room as her/his own living quarters and a private bathroom. *(Note: All the candidates, we interviewed, tended to simplify this need, mentioning that they would require 'just' a bedroom for their personal things – we found this was definitely not the case – in reality, everyone has 'stuff' and needs 'space'.)*

Prior to a caregiver moving in, we need to set aside time for rearranging some of the rooms, including closets (storage, regular, hallway closets), shoe/boot racks, and shelves. The process will probably mean sorting and storing some of our parents' belongings and delivering the unwanted items to non-profit organizations (e.g. we had two full car loads for the SPCA).

After the reorganizing phase, we may need to contract to have built/renovated whatever is required.

Notes:

_____

_____

_____

_____

_____

_____

_____

_____

_____

_____

_____

_____

_____

_____

_____

_____

_____

_____

_____

_____

_____

_____

_____

Suggestion 39: Channel communications with all caregivers AND your parents

If possible, our parents must be our first significant level of contact/ discussion when it comes to assessing our caregivers' progress — as our parents' health care, daily happiness and overall satisfaction are the main reasons we undertook hiring caregivers in the first place.

What can I do at the beginning?

During the probationary months, it is important that we set aside short periods of time for private one-on-one 'how-are-we-doing' discussions, first with our parents, then with the caregiver (and with other family members if any are involved directly in the care responsibilities).

Three tips:

1. We shouldn't assume that we truly know how things are progressing in our parents' home.

2. We shouldn't try 'to fix things' each time we get a hint of a problem.

3. We need to listen carefully and be alert during this probationary period and always (as time alters behaviors).

How can I build good everyday communications?

Think of communications as a tall stool — without all three legs it will topple quickly. We have to build three channels of communications:

Level 1.   Between our parents and ourselves (given their new health situation our past style of communicating with them may be forced to change).

Level 2.   Between our parents and their caregivers.

Level 3.   Between the caregivers and us.

There is much we can do:

- ☑ Offer hints to our parents and the caregiver (e.g. how to handle various delicate situations with one another).

- ☑ Help our parents and the live-in caregiver develop satisfactory methods of dealing with ordinary problems *(For example: At first, I tried to act as a conduit between those in the household, but, this method of communicating did not work well as it takes on the appearance of interference; it also signals to the parties that they cannot solve the problems.)*

- ☑ Check with our parents before taking an action – meaning before we offer advice to a caregiver regarding very specific situations that our parents may have mentioned *(For example: "Do you want me to raise this little problem with X? How do you want to handle this?").*

- ☑ Offer very clear directions and explanations to the live-in caregiver when making suggestions; try not to be over-protective of our parents as we may give incorrect signals to the live-in caregiver re: how she/he is doing the job.

- ☑ Listen for signs of miscommunications between our parents and the live-in caregiver and us.

(For example: During a regular telephone call one afternoon, I mentioned to our (then) live-in caregiver that I would like her "to keep an eye on my mother for the next month" – I explained that I felt Mum needed some rest and had been under a lot of stress prior to Dad's relocation to the carehome. The live-in caregiver didn't ask what I meant and I didn't elaborate on my explanation as it seemed a logical request. It turns out that she interpreted the message literally – she took it to mean that I did not want Mum left alone at all – thus for the next three weeks, the caregiver was constantly with Mum. A problem erupted when both had had enough of each other's constant company and Mum telephoned me upset that she couldn't do anything on her own – without any warning, she then had let her caregiver go. Her house! Her decision! My miscommunication!)

✓ Agree to communicate as one household unit so that all persons living in the home have the same pieces of information and understandings. How a family communicates depends on the circumstances, but be clear on who really needs the information (e.g. we often did not include Dad in our regular discussions due to the complexities of his behaviours). *(Note: This is a very useful hint as our parents may not 'hear' what we are saying and the message can get skewed — so be sure all are 'in the loop'.)*

✓ Try to set reasonable goals (for outings, exercise, nutrition), yet, at the same time try not come across as being rigid with those goals since complications may set in when the caregiver tries to carry out our wishes precisely.

(For example: In the course of a conversation with a past live-in caregiver, I had indicated that it would desirable for Dad to have an outing/car ride perhaps every second day. Carrying out this direction soon proved impossible for the caregiver as Dad who had a habit of settling comfortably in his chair in the living room each day, found it a problem to move around and resisted going out. My wish for fresh-air outings every two days soon resulted in a push-pull argument between the caregiver and Dad, with Mum serving as referee; everyone became stressed — the key was to be reasonable in my wishes and to let the caregiver be the final judge of what is working on a daily basis.)

✓ Check back often with each party (asking if X is happening or being done, and so forth). We should remind ourselves that a caregiver will learn our parents' boundaries in a slow and methodical manner over time and will obviously take longer to put some actions into effect than we would.

✓ Try to understand what we are being told by a parent or a caregiver, also try to understand what is being implied — we can't assume that the messages we are receiving are completely correct either (i.e. we must ask what our parent is implying by a statement and remember that there are two sides to a story — even a very small-detail story can get off-track quickly).

(For example: Mum was to have a quick foot-massage before bedtime as she suffers from leg and foot cramps – during my visits when I would rub her feet, she would say, "that helps so much"; when questioned about the frequency of the activity as done by the caregiver, Mum's response was usually, "I don't like to ask". Concerned, I approached the caregiver who responded, "I try, but your Mum often says not to bother as she wants to go to bed". The real obstacle – Mum didn't think the caregiver should have to 'rub feet' even though the caregiver wanted to and knew it was helpful. I learned that I often didn't have the full story until touching base with each party. I also learned that all of us could come up with workable solutions to small problems 'sometimes' using a touch-base round-the-table everyone-present communications method.)

✓ Look for non-verbal communications, as these are often a major means of communicating in caregiving situations. We need to watch for signs that all is proceeding well (or not) within the household. (Hint: Non-verbal methods may be used by an unhappy parent who doesn't want to rock the boat.)

✓ Lastly, in our on-going desire to establish peace and harmony, we should never dismiss any feelings expressed by our parents or our caregivers. We need to stay alert during care-years journeys (i.e. tip-toeing around a problem is not a good communication strategy, I found).

Notes:

_____

_____

_____

_____

_____

_____

_____

"Good communication is as stimulating as black coffee, and just as hard to sleep after."
– *Anne Morrow Lindbergh*

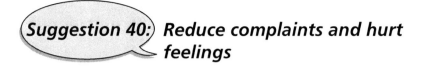

Suggestion 40: Reduce complaints and hurt feelings

During care-years, **we can reduce hurt feelings if we remember to ask our parents' their opinions** and include them in decisions affecting their everyday lives if/when appropriate. **They want their voices heard.**

We want our parents 'to feel' independent, that is to say, even though our parents are now dependent in many ways, they still may be capable of participating in what is happening around them. They expect to be involved, therefore, from time to time, we should re-emphasize that wish when talking with the caregivers. **We should also try to remember the high value placed on independence by our parents as we go through our day.**

(For example: Mum sometimes jumped into the conversation when she felt her input was not being sought especially when house maintenance was the issue – she felt strongly that this is her home, she had looked after it for years, she was capable of understanding what is going on, and she should at the very least be asked if she had any questions or ideas. Case in point – during one of my monthly respite visits, our caregiver asked me to follow her downstairs in order to show me the location of the new on-off switch for the yard's automatic sprinkler system as the lawn maintenance company had recently changed a few things around. Mum, who was standing beside me at that moment, responded quietly but firmly, "This is my home, shouldn't I know that too." Of course, Mum was absolutely correct, in that I live hundreds of miles away and she lives on-the-spot, but setting lawn sprinkler schedules was a task which she wouldn't be tending to ever, so the caregiver and I didn't' think to involve her – never-the-less, Mum wanted to let us know that she was interested. Point made.)

(Another example: Quite the opposite happened, independence applied without discussion – Mum made a spur of the moment decision without any consultation about her fruit trees in the backyard when she asked the yard maintenance man to cut down her only plum tree – days later when Mum asked her caregiver how the plums were ripening, the caregiver gently responded, "I don't know, you had the tree cut down." Shocked, Mum realized what she had done and

commented, "How could I have been so stupid, what was I thinking, darn." It was quite funny, as every subsequent year during the summer season when she was eating 'purchased plums', she wondered aloud about her actions and we laughed together. In her own manner over the years, Mum reminded us on many incidences, even though she required caregiving, that she was very interested in all aspects of her own home, that her independence, such as it was, was important.)

What should I emphasize to all the members of the household in an attempt to avoid hurt feelings?

☑ That problems do not disappear magically.

We need to emphasize that if disagreements (of any size) occur they should be discussed in a respectful manner before they become a touchy subject – the aim is to get back on track fast.

☑ That some types of criticism convey a wrong message.

We need to emphasize with our parents that they should not voice a criticism about any current or past caregivers (live-in or visiting community caregivers doing home care services) to another caregiver as she/he will naturally begin to wonder what is being said about her/him to the others within the home.

☑ That casual remarks are often misunderstood.

We need to discourage our parents plus other family members (i.e. relatives who visit or call often) from making off-the-cuff remarks during family conversations about household or caregiving affairs as these remarks can be overheard (even if the caregiver is not present but somewhere in the house) and the intent could be misunderstood by our caregivers.

We may have to stress with our parents that they can speak quietly to us about problems at all times (but not to use whispering tones during telephone conversations as such indicates secrecy). We can suggest that they should use their bedroom telephone if they want to talk privately about a caregiving concern.

☑ **That it is not necessary to be included all the time.**

It may prove important to emphasize occasionally to our parents the fact that they should not expect to be included in the caregiver's personal activities at all times. We can use the example of our own time spent together, just as we like and need one-on-one private family time, so does our caregiver.

☑ **That the first level of contact is our parent – unless a problem.**

The first point of contact for our caregiver, if appropriate, when a solution is needed to a 'small' problem, is to be our parents not necessarily us. Problems may arise, none-the-less. *(For example: Although we never talked in terms of employee/er, the caregiver will view us as a daughter/son as the 'employer' (technically that is so) and may want our advice, but our parents may feel they are the also 'employers' as I found out when Mum 'dismissed' two of her caregivers – so it is a delicate balance when obtaining input during problem-solving times. Note, I did not interfere once the dismissals had occured, it was a decision I felt my mother made and I respected such.)*

☑ **That private telephone conversations are necessary – we must take care with the use of answering machines.**

Our parents, if they have a full time live-in caregiver, really have little privacy, thus a telephone conversation represents such to them. We need to discuss with our live-in caregiver the use of telephone answering machines (i.e. the record feature should only be switched on when no one is at home or better yet, the answering machine can be hooked up to the caregiver's own private telephone number).

How can I offer little hints?

There are many acceptable ways to offer hints to ensure that household interactions continue on an even note – over the care-years, these techniques have proven themselves workable for our family's sitations:

☑ **Scripts.**

We can help our parents find/try out appropriate opening lines if need be. *(For example: when Mum did not know how to begin a delicate conversation or raise a small concern with a caregiver, together we would think of ways to broach the topic – we would 'try out the words'.)*

The caregiver and I also discussed ways to approach topics with Mum. *(For example: Mum did not really like any air conditioning on in the house, so when the temperatures soared to 30+ in the summer months, the caregiver and I discussed ways to reinforce the need for air-con.)*

☑ One-liners added to the grocery-list for likes and dislikes.

One or two line hints can be added onto the weekly grocery list by anyone giving an indication as to likes/dislikes. *(For example: tin of French-cut green beans – a favourite type of bean; yams – she loves them mashed; would you please buy some vanilla ice-cream for Dad... I found this method of lists worked with some caregivers but not all when one said to me one day after reading a list of suggested grocery items, "....do you think we are stupid." (Oh, oh!). I subsequently learned to ask caregivers first what method they would like, if any? I kept trying to give hints as we must all do to get our points across—it was just a matter of finding what worked for each caregiver.)*

☑ To-be-discussed if you see fit – type notes.

A brief note may be clipped to the designated note spot to raise a possible question or to remind one of an appointment.

(For example, I looked for notes written by the caregiver as soon as I arrived for my respite caregiving days, as there were often appointments scheduled for Mum to coincide with these days. As well, the caregiver had the option of using her own judgment regarding the contents of notes I leave, e.g. Mum's live-in caregivers were very aware of nutritional needs so when I wrote "no processed foods" on a note one day, they understood my general concern, but did not raise the issue as each caregiver made decisions based on that day. As time went on, I did not use notes unless truly needed.)

☑ Special chat time.

It is advisable to have informal chat times with the caregiver. *(For example: our caregivers picked me up at the airport and dropped me off so we would have regular chats then – at the beginning of my visits, she could raise a concern and at the end of my visits, I could emphasize something I may have noticed; we also chatted in the late evenings when others were in bed.)*

☑ Separate telephone numbers.

It is recommended for our parents and our caregiver to have different telephone numbers so that we may speak to each privately (spontaneously or with or without the other knowing or caring).

When we want to check on how our parent is doing, it is helpful to be able to wait until evening or early morning and call our caregiver on the separate line to ask questions which she/he may now feel more free to answer as our parent is not present.

☑ Email.

Quick messages can be exchanged allowing all to keep in touch often. *(For example: Our caregiver often alerted me to little problems – "When you phone today, just so you know, your Mum isn't feeling well today – she won't admit it is probably the fish and chips, donut and coffee she had for lunch while we were out today." Smile-smile)*

Notes:

_____

_____

_____

_____

_____

_____

_____

_____

_____

_____

_____

_____

_____

_____

_____

_____

 *Organize the grocery budget responsibility*

Grocery shopping guidelines need to be addressed as soon as we have caregivers working in our parents' home as the job involves carefully worked out budgets plus meal planning (mealtimes are very important to our parents).

We need a method for shopping for groceries that doesn't involve the caregivers asking a parent for money each time an item is required. We also need a method that is accountable.

As new factors are being introduced (new person's likes and dislikes, more persons for meals and new diets for our parents), the emphasis is on flexibility and organization of new procedures for food shopping.

Each household will differ, but a budget format should be put in place as soon as possible in order to set some guidelines right from the beginning.

The following example outlines one procedure for establishing a grocery budget for a family with live-in/shift caregiving *(Note: These are the preliminary steps we followed and the method worked very well for our family):*

Step One: At the beginning

- Right from the start at contract stage, when a caregiver becomes involved, grocery responsibilities are assigned to the caregiver and listed in the contract.

- Estimate the amount of money that might be required in terms of a monthly grocery budget, fix that amount, advise the caregiver.

- Decide upon a trial period for the 'set amount' required (e.g. we used four months) .

Step Two: Run a trial period

- Each month, for the trial period, put the agreed upon dollars in a monthly grocery envelope; these dollars are allocated for groceries only (i.e. meals eaten out are not paid for from these designated grocery-dollars).

- Set simple rules: all receipts and any change must be placed back in the envelope and no IOU's allowed.

Step Three: Do a review

- Each month during the trial period, the caregiver tallies the receipts for a monthly total and records the amount on the back of the envelope (with explanations if warranted).

- Review the budget quickly with the caregiver during monthly visits and discuss any pertinent questions (are we short, how did it work out this month, any major items needed?).

Step Four: Set a fixed amount

- Track the grocery expenses in this manner for four months; at the end of the trial months, average the costs.

- Discuss the trial period (e.g. we now felt we understood more clearly how much should be budgeted for groceries for the complete household each month).

- Set the amount.

Step Five: Readjust the amount if required

- Continue tallying the monthly receipts for one full year and then once again review the budget averages.

- Discuss larger additions to the budget when major dietary needs have to be considered *(e.g. cases of Ensure were purchased for a few months to supplement nutritional requirements, as suggested by the pharmacist)*.

- Readjust the fixed amount if warranted after one year.

Later:

- An amount was set and remained that unless the caregivers needed a particular item – they had been given discretionary spending for what she felt would benefit the home situation. The caregivers tracked these items and kept the invoices and each of them was reimbursed for any 'extras' for that month; or they took the extra dollars from a cheque left for just such needs. Budgets I learned were simply good guidelines. *(For example: Some caregivers feel free to replace kitchen/bathroom equipment and this type of action should be discussed upon hiring (acceptable or not). I found it was best to work carefully with the caregivers when budgets were concerned.)*

Notes:

_____

_____

_____

_____

_____

_____

_____

_____

_____

_____

_____

_____

_____

_____

_____

_____

_____

_____

_____

_____

_____

_____

_____

_____

_____

_____

_____

_____

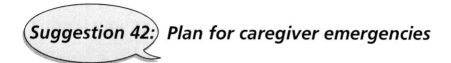

Suggestion 42: *Plan for caregiver emergencies*

Caregiver health-related emergencies can and do happen (e.g. one caregiver had a heart attack and another required major surgery).

During these types of emergencies, as daughter/son-caregivers, we have to tend to the needs of two groups – our parents plus the caregivers.

What do I do in case of a health emergency of a full-time 'live-in caregiver'?

No, we don't throw our hands in the air asking, "What next!" (well, maybe we do, but it won't do us much good!).

We do become super-efficient – attending to our parents' immediate needs and safety first and then the live-in caregiver's needs.

(Note: It is wise to go to our parents' house as soon as possible if a live-in caregiver emergency occurs, as the household disruption is immense and our parents' insecurities will surface – they will be asking, "Now what is going to happen? What are we going to do?")

We need to prepare for live-in caregiver emergencies if/when they occur:

☑ **Attend to our parents' care needs immediately.**

We should always have a backup plan in place with an emergency part-time on-call caregiver – a neighbour or relative, who is able to drop everything and stay with our parent on the spur of the moment when called. *(For further discussion, refer to Topic 1, Suggestion #2, Don't Neglect Our Other At-home Parent.)*

We can also contact the provincial government community health unit responsible for home care services and request a relief caregiver if possible to help with these types of emergency situations (do not expect an instantaneous response as schedules and union rules are involved). Another option (and may be the easiest in a situation like this) is to consider hiring a short-term caregiver from a reliable agency. (I also found that telephoning those that applied for the job initially was helpful, so don't throw out the list.)

☑ Attend to our live-in caregiver's needs.

We must obtain a list at the time of hiring (placed on file) of contact persons (relatives, friends) and telephone numbers relating to our live-in caregiver, so that in an emergency these persons may be called immediately.

We need to keep in constant touch with our live-in caregiver (e.g. in the hospital) until she has her own family members with her.

☑ Attend to our family's future needs

We should not guarantee the caregiver her employment position until we have assessed the whole care-situation – we need to be honest and advise her/him (when timely) of our process, as our parents' care is our priority.

We need to be prepared (always!) to start the search process again for a new caregiver – we have few options.

Many "boomer" women can expect to have a more financially secure old age than the generations preceding them. This will be particularly true for those with higher education, full-time jobs, good incomes, good pension coverage and disposable income. Others will not share these advantages. A significant number of "boomer" women will reach old age widowed, divorced or separated. Whether women in these categories will have adequate finances by 2011-2031 when the "boomer" cohort retires remains to be seen. In order for that to be the case several issues will have to be addressed:

- Persistent occupational and wage discrimination, which affects current finances and pension benefits, must be resolved.

- Social policies such as the C/QPP and the OAS/GIS which have decreased, but not eradicated poverty among seniors, must be maintained.

- Measures are required to alleviate financial and retirement hardships for the increasing number of women who will give care to their parents/spouses.

(Source: Perspectives on Aging – Briefing Papers on Aging and Policy, No. 2, August 2000, Gerontology Research Centre at Simon Fraser University, British Columbia.)

Notes:

_____

_____

_____

_____

_____

_____

_____

_____

_____

_____

_____

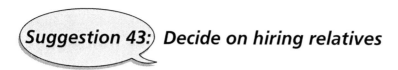

Suggestion 43: Decide on hiring relatives

Is it a good idea to hire a relative?

This suggestion focuses on hiring a relative as a 'full-time live-in' 24/7 caregiver. It does not discuss using relatives as paid casual or 'on-call part-time' caregivers, which we did do with satisfactory results. It also does not discuss our parents and our relatives agreeing to move in together for mutual benefit. The suggestion only discusses on 'hiring' a relative for a full-time 'live-in paid' position.

If/when/how relatives become involved in the live-in caregiving of our parents is an individual family's decision. Of course, often financial and location circumstances leave few avenues – statistics indicate that family members are indeed the main group of informal caregivers, but statistics do not tell us the per cent of families who have 'hired' relatives as 24/7 live-in caregivers.

To begin – a personal bias: I have concluded that if we have choices, employing a relative, as a 'full-time paid live-in caregiver', is not a good caregiving strategy, nor is it a good family relations decision. We did so on one occasion – the end-results were not positive for any of the parties involved (the relative, Mum, me). I do want to add though, in fairness, I have not met with many daughters or sons who are doing so, thus I cannot question their overall experiences employing relatives as full-time live-in caregivers for parents. I realize that I may receive criticism from many sources for the contents of this section – but in keeping with the guidebook, this is one experience in our family's long journey – our findings will not apply to every family – consider it more food for thought, before you act.

If I am thinking of hiring a relative, what should I do?

The following set of guidelines (alas, gained mostly through hindsight) may offer some direction when considering hiring a relative (or perhaps anyone close to the family) as a live-in paid caregiver:

First – Look at the relative as a caregiver, that is through a new pair of glasses. *(Note: The relative should be doing the same – looking at our parent(s) as a care-receiver now.)*

We need to ask ourselves some challenging questions:

- Am I hiring this relative because I am desperate right now?

- What was the previous relationship between the relative and our parent?

- How has the relative responded to our parents' health problems in the past (shown interest or not)?

- Does she/he take time to visit our parents now?

- Has she/he 'volunteered' in any manner in the past to help with our parents?

- How did the relative treat her/his own parents as they grew older and needed care?

- Does the relative have other family commitments within the surrounding area, what do these consist of, will those obligations helpful or a hindrance?

- What is our own relationship like with the relative prior to this point?

- How has the relative handled general job responsibilities in the past?

- What is her/his work background/experiences?

- What is the general personality of the relative (e.g. tone of voice, laughter, energy levels, companionship ability, physical and mental health)?

- How will our parent and our relative react if the arrangement doesn't prove satisfactory (e.g. sever all ties, anger, acceptance…)?

Second – Discuss the 'job'; develop a written employee contract for the position.

We need to follow the same procedures as we would with anyone else, as we are now hiring a very important employee to do a job for our parent:

- ☑ Set a defined probationary period of 6 months maximum for the first contract as a short period allows each party to leave with dignity (at the end of the contract) should obstacles arise.

- ☑ Go over each of the contract conditions verbally before putting them into writing so that a discussion can be held on points before they are put into black and white on paper.

- ☑ If there are flags of concern based on a personal knowledge of each other, clear up these concerns one-by-one, ahead of time.

- ☑ If having an open, two-way conversation with the relative is currently difficult, establish ahead of time a suitable method and time for 'talking business' once a month.

- ☑ Discuss expectations (i.e. work expectations) as the relative may feel that all was well before when dealing with our parent and expect the same conditions to exist now.

- ☑ Discuss any assumptions regarding past methods of doing things between the relative and our parent, as these methods may not work in the same way on a 24-hour a day live-in basis (i.e. health conditions and care expectations are different now than in the past).

Third – During the initial probationary 6-months, listen for "interaction indicators". *(Note: This listening/observing step should also be done at the start of any new caregiver job.)*

Interaction-indicators (my term) give us clues as to whether this relative-parent relationship is really working out.

These indicators describe care-related interactions between our parent and our relative (e.g. all is going well or we have a problem between two people who think they know each other well and can't agree at this point).

Conversations containing these types of comments are what may be characterized as 'indicators':

- Caregiver-relative to us when we pose a question: "You aren't here, you only know part of what goes on."

- Parent casually comments "So-and-so has changed."

Upon hearing these comments, we need to seize the moment and ask for specifics (examples of why such was said) – a problem may be implied and one party may not be willing to say more about it – until questioned (a red flag is being waved, do you see/hear it).

We can try to give sound advice to the relative, as we actually do know our parent better than the relative (do take note on how this advice is received and more importantly, acted upon).

We can also give advice to our parents, reminding them that our relative is now in a different role than the past.

Fourth – Think ahead about how to handle 'delicate situations' which could arise based on family familiarity.

Our relative may take a few liberties when talking with our parents and vice versa, based on their past histories together – would we allow these same liberties if this was a non-relative caregiver? (This can present a very *touchy* situation to handle.)

Our parents and our relative, both, have relationships with mutual family members, so we must be aware that 'talk' is going to be exchanged regarding this 'job'. What feeds a family rumour-mill and what is harmless talk – we should be prepared for such dilemmas when hiring a relative?

Fifth – Before hiring, be very clear on how either party can end the employee-relationship (put that understanding in writing).

Surprises may occur around how caregiving duties are being handled. Unhappiness between the parties is a definite possibility.

If a contract is in place and understood by each person, then each of the parties may terminate the job properly.

We need to address how either party can give notice without pinpointing cause (e.g. "The arrangement is not working out, I am going to look for another caregiver." Or " I am not happy and made a mistake in taking this position, could you find someone by….")

If the hiring was a parent's idea, then the parent may be reluctant to want to tell us of any problems – ahead of time, at hiring, in case this happens, we have to explain to our parent, from the start, that she/he needs to discuss all the care situations with us – we have to be able to step in quickly and relieve a parent's stress and awkwardness if/when such occurs.

Should termination by either party take place, determine how all concerned will get back to a normal family relationship over time.

Sixth – Should the probationary period prove successful (for everyone) plan a contract extension – for six-month periods.

When reviewing the employment situation, it is our duty to try (as much as possible and to be fair to our relative) to view our relative's role as a family member separate from her/his role as a caregiver.

Notes:

_____

_____

_____

_____

_____

_____

_____

_____

_____

_____

_____

_____

_____

_____

_____

Suggestion 44: Keep constant contact

As daughter/son caregivers, once we have completed hiring caregivers (even very good ones – whew!), we can't let ourselves fall into the trap of feeling that "finally, all our worries are over". Of course, some of our big worries will definitely be reduced, but our overall responsibility, as a daughter/son caregiver/care-guide, will not decrease – it remains – our duty is to our parents.

In fact, by hiring caregivers, we have created an additional, important task; that is, keeping constant contact with our caregivers as they interact with our parents.

How do I keep contact?

☑ During the initial months:

We should check that our first impression of the caregiver when interviewed for the position (e.g. strengths, weaknesses, interests) was correct – if not, we need to review the situation quickly – and find out what is really occurring in the home.

(For example: When interviewing, I felt that one candidate's assertiveness in potentially difficult situations would be an asset with Dad. Instead, what I perceived to be an assertive manner actually turned out to be an argumentative style, completely opposite to what was needed to work agreeably with Dad – and to make matters worse, Mum was constantly being forced to intervene between the live-in caregiver and Dad. This characteristic proved unsettling for all concerned and the working relationship, at an appropriate point, was ended.)

☑ Each week:

As the caregiver is providing an important service, we should ask (directly or indirectly):

- How is it (the job) going?

- How is the household (functioning) today?

- How is my parent doing today?

- What did you both do this morning/afternoon?

- Any concerns/problems?

(For example: When Dad was living at home, I telephoned once a day and talked with each person in the house – the caregiver, Mum and Dad – and each of those people had a different perspective on the conditions of the day. Several years later, I still spoke with Mum daily and Dad every second day in the nursing home, but only touched base with their caregivers once or twice a week unless there was an issue developing.)

☑ As time goes on:

Keeping constant contact does not necessarily eliminate potential problems but it certainly reduces the surprises.

We should be aware that hiccups can develop between parents and the live-in caregiver, and if left unresolved, as time goes on, these minor annoyances have the ability to cause disruption of the overall harmony of the home – it is our responsibility to continue to touch base – always.

With good contact, as daughter/sons, we will come to appreciate our various caregivers' skills and manners more and more.

And, with constant contact, we will continue to be amazed by our parents' flexibility and adaptability to their care-years situations!

"Well done is better than well said."
– Benjamin Franklin 1706 - 1790

Food-for-thought: Who Would Take Care of a Loved One with Alzheimer's if Something Happened to You?

It is important to have a plan in case of your own illness, disability, or death.

✓ Consult a lawyer regarding a living trust, durable power of attorney for health care and finances, and other estate planning tools.

✓ Consult with family and close friends to decide who will take responsibility for the person with AD. You also may want to seek information about your local public guardian's office, mental health conservator's office, adult protective services, or other case management services. These organizations may have programs to assist the person with AD in your absence.

✓ Maintain a notebook for the responsible person who will be assuming caregiving. Such a notebook should contain the following information:

- emergency numbers

- current problem behaviors and possible solutions

- ways to calm the person with AD

- assistance needed with toileting, feeding, or grooming

- favorite activities or food

✓ Preview board and care or long-term care facilities in your community and select a few as possibilities. If the person with AD is no longer able to live at home, the responsible person will be better able to carry out your wishes for long-term care.

(To order free copy of *"Home Safety For People With Alzheimer's Disease"* call 1-800-438-4380, USA-based. Also call CMHC Canada Mortgage and Housing Corporation, 1-800-668-2642 and ask for their booklet, "At Home With Alzheimers.")

TOPIC 8

Let's Talk: Organizing nursing home living

Just in case – How do I tend to nursing home living for my parent?

Personal Anecdote:"I never thought I'd have to make this decision!"

Suggestions:

45: Select a care residence carefully

46: Add value to nursing home/carehome living and stay in close touch

47: Understand how we may unintentionally contribute to new problems

Just in case – How do I tend to nursing home living for my parent?

(Stop! Don't even think of skipping this section – as no daughter or son/or spouse knows where a care-years journey will lead.)

Personal Anecdote:
"I never thought I'd have to make this decision!"

When the health of our parents calls for drastic changes in the types of care required, each daughter/son-caregiver has no choice but to decide on the best place to receive that care. Is a change of residency now required, is nursinghome living an answer?

I believe that as long as all of our caregiving actions are based on our love for our parents and our desire to provide them with an excellent care environment, we can feel confident that the decisions we have to make along our journey are the best ones possible for our parents given their health circumstances. Having said that, any decision involving a change of residency remains fraught with conflicting emotions for all involved.

It seems that when seriously considering carehome living for a parent, we are thinking and acting as responsible caregivers (i.e. what is best for my parents in these conditions). Yet, once the decision to move a parent into a care residency is actually made, we abandon our caregiver logic and re-examine that same decision over again with our hearts, as daughters/sons only- thus a colossal conflict ensues.

After the decision period, we scold ourselves with rhetorical questions-"How can I do this, move my Dad from a home he worked hard for, built and loves? How can I separate my parents? Is it fair that he has to learn new routines this late in his life?"

As guilty feelings engulf us, we begin wondering time and time again, "Maybe I need to try doing more; maybe we can try one more time to solve these problems; maybe I should move closer to them; maybe Dad and Mum could relocate and move in with my family..."

And even while organizing the final arrangements for the move, we will catch ourselves viewing the new residency itself negatively, thinking, "My Dad/Mum doesn't belong here!" and we continue to think in emotional terms.

As our feelings fluctuate between sadness and futility, we will find ourselves wishing that we weren't the one with such a responsibility- we will keep wishing that "things could be different."

It is during these moments that we come to understand the real meaning of the word 'hard' - I look back on those particular residency decisions regarding Dad's and Mum's care as one of the most heart-wrenching periods in my life.

Making a firm decision regarding carehome living for a parent is not where any of us thought we would be at this time in our lives. Still anyone who has had to make that decision will attest to the fact that there are two related, even more devastating times- one, introducing the decision to our parent(s) and trying to explain the reasons why we can no longer care for him/her at home; and, two, carrying out that decision - the actual move day, packing up a suitcase and personal belongings, helping our parent into the car, driving to the home, settling things in and finally looking back as we leave our parent in a new environment. I remember that return drive from the caremanor, alone, back to comfort my mother now and deal with her new living situation - I remember whispering to myself, "Dad and Mum, I love you and I am so sorry, I wish I knew another way to help" while wiping away streams and streams of tears.

Our story

I offer our family's very personal story around this emotional care-related dilemma in order to demonstrate the need for some of us as daughter/son-caregivers/care-guides to take a most extreme action, that of moving a parent to a nursing home at a late point in life for health and safety reasons. "I just never thought I would have to make this decision."

Part 1 - Making the decision - We had run out of choices.

It was nearly one year since Dad's fall and by the time Christmas season rolled around, it was apparent that I had to look seriously at care alternatives for both my parents (Mum 86, Dad 85) since their health was deteriorating rapidly and regardless of our organizational efforts for their care, their home life was in crisis.

Our family situation was very fragile and my parents' total care was being compromised due to conditions linked to their health, ones they could neither alter nor control.

I discussed our dilemma with my parents' family doctor; he called a health team meeting consisting of the hospital social worker, the physiotherapist, the rehabilitation day care coordinator, himself as chair and me.

The team reviewed our family's care initiatives at the time:

- We had a full time live-in caregiver 24 hours a day to care for both Mum and Dad.

- We had two shifts of community-based government scheduled caregivers coming to the house to work with Dad twice a day, one hour in the morning and an hour in the evening, for personal hygiene and exercise needs.

- We had regular housekeeping assistance once a week; we also had a yard/lawn maintenance worker for outside jobs.

- We had one relative, Mum's favourite niece, as a regular social visitor (weekly); she also telephoned often in the week.

- Dad went on regular outings with the live-in caregiver a minimum of twice a week.

- We were accessing the hospital bath program on a weekly basis for Dad.

- Dad was attending an adult day-care program one day a week for social therapy and some physical rehabilitation.

- We had the proper equipment/aids installed in the house and regular assessments were done for safety purposes.

- On a monthly basis, Mum and Dad separately were seeing the family doctor for varying updates and some on-the-spot counselling.

- We had used our allocated government carehome respite time of one week per year offering Dad more social interaction and structured physical exercise and Mum guaranteed rest.

- We had tried various prescription medications with Dad to reduce excessive behaviour problems and tracked the side-effects.

- I was serving as the relief caregiver for one-week periods per month to help the live-in caregiver with my parents' care and give her time-off; Dad and I went out daily for lunches and Mum and Dad and I together, went *out for at least one dinner together during each of these weeks. We had family time.*

- *We had meetings as required with members of Dad's health team to discuss our family's progress/issues of concern.*

It was agreed that we did indeed have a comprehensive care program in place.

The team then reviewed our family's problems and concerns:

Dad:

- *Dad's anxiety-type fixations, accompanied by temper outbursts, parts of his dementia, were growing more difficult.*

- *Dad remained weak and very lethargic; he had lost extreme amounts of weight.*

- *Dad's walking was very poor as his hip breaks never allowed for proper balance - he could not stand up alone nor walk without a firm grip on his walker/ wheelchair for balance and support.*

- *Dad's morning wake-up calls were at 4:00 or 4:30 AM and the live-in caregiver and Mum were exhausted.*

- *Dad was not responding well to medications (i.e. too many negative dangerous side effects) to curb his anxieties (he had several very serious falls within six months) and we had several emergency ambulance services situations with him.*

- *Dad was less than cooperative at times with both the live-in caregivers and with the government scheduled morning/evening caregivers.*

- *Dad required that Mum (and the live-in caregiver) be present with him at all times, thus coping was difficult for both of them and a restful day could not be achieved.*

- *Dad's eyesight was very poor, he had lost almost all vision except for slight grey blurs in one eye due to glaucoma and the other eye required immediate cataract surgery (to date, he had vigorously resisted this simple surgery).*

Mum:

- *Mum's physical and general mental health had deteriorated substantially over the last year as she found it stressful balancing the varying schedules and care demands of her spouse of each day (even though there was a caregiver present).*

- *Mum was becoming ill often with colds and bronchitis and flu; she also had numerous ambulance emergencies that year with severe reflux condition.*

- *Mum developed shingles on her legs.*

- *Mum was suffering from sleep deprivation on a regular basis and could not catch a nap in the day due to Dad's demands for her presence.*

- *Mum was 'confined' to the house, even certain rooms for six days a week (to keep Dad peaceful), except for the one morning a week when Dad attended the adult day-care program or was on outings.*

- *Mum was serving as negotiator and peacemaker during confrontations between caregivers and Dad.*

Daughter:

- *As a daughter, I was averaging two trips most months, and sometimes up to fifty per cent of my time at my parents' home to attend to either medical emergencies* or household emergencies. Balancing caregiving, work, family and the responsibilities seemed impossible - emergencies dictated.

It was agreed that the carefully organized care program we had in place in our home was not "doing the job" - that is, it was not meeting the care needs of either of my parents.

The team then reviewed my parents' levels of need:

- Dad required 24-hour a day nursing care.

- Dad needed an extremely structured daily lifestyle with well-defined routines and schedules.

- Dad required a care environment that he would not attempt nor be allowed to control - one conducive to working with his behaviours.

- Dad should be on as few medications as possible (due to the negative reactions to the ones tried).

- Dad needed to feel truly safe (perhaps ending some of his unspoken fears) with round the clock help available (on duty).

- Mum required her own full-time (24-hour) set of caregivers.

- Mum needed a safe, non-threatening calm living environment in order to become stronger, physically and mentally.

- Having my parents relocate to live with me or having me relocate to live with them were not options as not only did they not want to do this (leave their city and friends and relatives) but also, little changed when I was present except that my parents felt more secure with me right in the house with them (Mum felt that things were more under control).

- My parents and the caregivers needed to know that a stable daily acceptable routine was in place and working.

The team weighed the possibilities:

Our family was using or had tried all the care resources available and had exhausted the avenues recommended by health professionals, there seemed only one option left - a change in residency-patterns for my parents offering 'each' of them the best care possible, in keeping with each's needs.

Two recommendations were made:

1. Dad should be relocated to a nursing home where he could receive the level of nursing care and attention his health demanded, a residence (of our choice) near his home where he could live comfortably and safely in a regulated environment.

2. Mum should remain in her own home as long as possible, with a full-time caregivers to meet Mum's growing health needs.

These recommendations had many ramifications. They meant separating my parents after 60+ years together, establishing a new care regime for Mum (with yet another set of strangers), and moving Dad from his own well-loved retirement home to a carehome environment. Necessary changes, yes, as I wanted to give them more quality years - yet upon reflection, rivers of tears still overwhelmed me, my parents were elderly and so dependent now because of their health and age. I felt helpless and we each felt robbed - their health needs seemed like a thief to me, robbing them of their independence.

Part 2 - Informing my parents - I hated what I had to do.

Dad's present mental health, his aggressive personality and his lifelong avoidance of "taboo topics" (i.e. all topics relating to illness, aging and death) pointed to the fact that introducing the idea of "living in a carehome" to Dad was going to be a very, very traumatic moment for Dad (and me). Mum, tired and in a borderline depressed state, could not be involved.

I approached my parents' family doctor for assistance - given that he knew my parents' histories, understood our family's caregiving efforts over the past year and was concerned with each of my parents' present health problems, he agreed to help me 'open' the discussion with Dad. We decided that he would raise the topic when I next brought Dad for a check-up.

The appointment day arrived, the three of us met - it was a disastrous session.

Even while the doctor was examining Dad, Dad wasn't listening to anything regarding his general health or care nor would he answer any questions directly - Dad was behaving as he always had in the past when health problems arose ("Nothing's wrong, I'm okay, everything will be fine..."). Dad was truly unprepared for what was coming next. (To this day, knowing Dad as I did, I still don't know what I could have done differently to reduce this bombshell.)

The check-up proceeded, finally, when the doctor suggested that Dad's health needed "nursing care" and that Dad might have "to consider changing residency to a carehome," Dad became instantly alarmed and angry. He told his doctor in no uncertain terms that our family could manage as we had for the past year, that his "wife would help take care of him".

Dad told me to explain to the doctor that our family was doing fine, and when I didn't readily agree, he looked betrayed - he pointed an accusing finger asking if the doctor and I had set this up together. He struggled up from his chair several times during the session, grabbing his walker repeatedly, heading for the office door. Dad was not having anything to do with this distasteful topic, but as he liked his doctor a lot, he kept saying, each time more loudly, "Sorry Doc, I'm not going!"

As the tears dripped on my blouse, I watched Dad in the doctor's office feeling trapped and scared. I wanted to help him, as I always had in the past- as he had always trusted me to do.

Dad expected me 'to be there for him' and during those precise moments, seeing his hurt and confusion, I wanted to put an end to his anger and fear and pain by saying, "Okay, okay Dad, let's leave it for now and see how things will go". But I didn't, I couldn't (the door was 'open' - I had to proceed) - Mum and Dad's complex and urgent health problems demanded a change in each of their caregiving methods.

I knew without a doubt that I had to remain committed to this residency-decision or I would never get to revisit the topic again with Dad. On this very disturbing afternoon I knew that if I relented (like I wanted to do), there was nothing more that could be done in terms of improving the levels and conditions of care in their own home and thus, I could expect to watch both my parents' health deteriorate rapidly.

Part 3 - Obtaining agreement - Not much left to say.

In total, I don't think we were in the doctor's office more than twenty minutes, when I came to the realization that Dad and I, at this stage in our lives together, would have to work our way through this issue as 'father and daughter'. As Dad grabbed his walker one more time and headed through the office door, I nodded to the doctor, thanked him and caught up to my father.

I helped Dad into the car, we didn't speak, we started for home. Even though Dad and I were both feeling drained, one kilometre or so from the doctor's office, I decided that we had to come to some sort of agreement. I also knew that we couldn't arrive home with the status being undecided, as he would most certainly bring Mum into the uproar and I knew she could not handle it well, she was too fragile by this time.

Pulling over to a side road, stopping the car, I told Dad again how much I loved him, how worried I was about his health and how I knew we all were trying to do our best for each other. I then quietly added, "Dad, you have to go, you have to give it a try, there is no choice, what I want you to decide is when." We continued- in silence and deep thought.

When we arrived home, of course Dad immediately questioned Mum as to why she couldn't take of him herself - I did not allow Mum to be brought into this highly charged dilemma and reiterated several times to Dad that Mum could not be expected to be his full time caregiver, as she is his age, had heart history problems and needed help too.

It was only one hour since Dad and I had left the doctor's office and as one would expect we were exhausted emotionally. I was feeling a sadness beyond words, as if I was betraying a loving trust that Dad had in me, that is to care for him and Mum always (he would never understand that is what I was attempting to do).

I asked Dad to think about what we had talked about and finally, he closed his eyes and asked that he be given a couple of hours to do so. Dad did just that, he later that afternoon called me to his side and said quietly, "I will move in two months" (this would schedule the move at Mum's birthday).

Dad and I discussed what the move would mean and we compromised - we agreed that he would try a 'trial residency period' with the following three conditions attached: he would try living in the carehome for three months and see how it went; he would do his weekly exercise program (with proper assistance) in order to strengthen his walking ability; and he would have his cataract surgery done during these three months as the specialist told us the procedure should not be left much longer (after the cataract surgery Dad was going to be without sight for a short period and would require special care so this was a good time for the corrective surgery to be done to restore sight to this one eye.)

We cleared three hurdles that day - one, Dad had agreed to try a new residence with agreed upon conditions; two, a firm date was set for the move and three, once Dad had some input into the process, he 'appeared' no longer angry (just resigned).

As I had selected a 'preferred' care home, I immediately telephoned to arrange a meeting with the owner-manager in order to organize the agreed upon date for admission. The next day, I learned that room space was available now and could not be 'saved' for two more months and that there was no guarantee that we would have a room at the time we wanted it. So, to keep to the schedule as agreed with Dad and to guarantee availability, I rented the room immediately and paid for this extra time. (Note: Our family offered the room as a respite care room during this period it was not being used but the carehome did not allow such, I am not sure as to why not.)

Part 4 - Waiting - Getting ready mentally.

My hope during the time period preceding the residency move and all the care changes engulfing my parents was to have Dad and Mum shift their thinking, that is, to have them focus not on how much life was going to change but rather how much would remain the same. I didn't want Dad or Mum to think of these changes as a final chapter, one living in an 'old age home' and one 'dependent on strangers' - so our talks were open and honest.

I listened for each of my parent's feelings when they began skirting some aspect of the topic (will I get to do this, I wonder what I will do all day...). For the month of January and the first half of February, Dad, Mum and I talked on many occasions of Dad's new "apartment" and Mum's "new living arrangements" and what each could expect. (I started right from the beginning using the terms "apartment" when referring to Dad's place at the carehome and still used the term "home" when referring to his own house.)

A break-through came one morning, in late January - Dad asked me to take him for a drive to see the carehome, "I don't want to go inside, can we just drive around and see the place". I knew then that a small but important shift was occurring, that Dad and I had made some progress together.

Also by the beginning of February, Mum had arrived at a choice for her personal live-in caregiver.

Part 5 - Move day - My parent trying to cope bravely with the massive changes happening to them.

Move-day, change-day arrived, February 17, 1997. We celebrated Mum's 86th birthday in the morning and just before lunch, as agreed, Dad and I drove to the nursing home/caremanor and he moved into his new room, his "apartment". Mum said she just 'couldn't come with us', she sat in her easy chair, alone, reflecting on... I will always remember them standing together in the living room - the last time they would ever live together... (I can't find the words to describe that emotional moment!)

As agreed, that this period was to be a three-month trial run in the caremanor, Dad brought only one suitcase of clothing, his favourite comforter for his bed, and his shaving kit with him. In addition, since I knew Dad would love his motorized reclining chair and as I wanted him to feel as comfortable and settled as quickly as possible, my cousin and I moved his favourite chair into his room and placed some family photographs onto his dresser, while Dad was at lunch that same day. After lunch I explained these additions to Dad by telling him the truth, the people-in-charge required that new residents bring some of their own furnishings when they move in. After lunch, I watched as Dad very quickly settled into his familiar recliner.

The twists and turns of our family's care-years journey really struck me as I prepared to depart - I was actually leaving my Dad in a carehome. As I stood in the hallway and looked back at Dad resting in his chair, I felt such pain. I knew that Dad was in pain too. I also recognized then that we were going to have to work our way through the next stage of nursing home relocation - as I had been warned- Dad was depressed during the first few months.

I kept thinking, so here we are as a family at this significant juncture in our journey, now what. As I turned back to Dad to say our goodbyes, we could not see past our tears- when I returned home to Mum still sitting quietly, we could not see past our tears.

There is a passage in the best seller novel 'Memoirs of a Geisha' that reads something like, 'we cannot go forward walking backwards', I am reminded of this passage from time to time when I catch myself dwelling on the most troubling moments of our journey, moments like this.

Part 6 - The trial months - I couldn't help but wonder how our family would make out during this period.

I was counting on Dad's high need for routines and structure to help him settle into the manor's daily life. I also knew that if we could manage the first three months successfully, Dad might be amenable to staying on (indefinitely).

I telephoned Dad every afternoon, during this trial time, to touch base, just as I had done in the past when he was living at home. I flew in regularly for one week a month caregiving (and most months still made two trips as Mum's health was requiring emergency attention by now). Dad and I went out every day during those weeks for lunch and a drive; Mum and I had private time together and as well the three of us went out for drives and early dinners as a family when we could.

Mum visited Dad either every day or every second day, staying most of the morning. Dad had weekly outings with a 'companion caregiver' I hired for him one a week. During this period, I constantly checked with the caremanor nursing staff to make sure he was adjusting to the new surroundings. Dad's doctor visited him when passing through the caremanor, his favourite treats and desserts were brought to him weekly, we talked about his new frirends... In these months, Mum and her new caregiver seemed to be developing a pattern for working-living together.

When the three-month trial period was over, although Dad had not participated in any exercise programs nor had he had the cataract surgery, we discussed 'living in the caremanor'- I asked him directlywhat he thought he should do now, what he wanted to do now. Dad chose to stay living where he was "for a few more months" mentioning that he remained committed to the exercises and would "think about" the cataract treatment. A daily lifestyle was slowly taking shape for both parents.

Part 7 - Living day-by-day, month-by-month, care-year by care-year, in a nursing home.

Dad seemed to adjust to a caremanor lifestyle, although according to a staff review it took six months for him to work his way through a depressed state - a common length of time apparently.

Dad's days remained as they were in the trial period. Over time, Dad 'allowed' us to add a few more items of familiarity to his room (paintings and pictures, the occasional plant, his own afghan which Mum had crocheted).

Each month, we drove to the house so that he would remain familiar with his property and continue to relate to it. We went to the house for occasional lunches or spaghetti dinners and of course for holidays and family events. He was told about property/house-related needs when he had questions.

I think that Dad settled into his new lifestyle to the best of his then abilities. At the manor, Dad enjoyed Saturday ice-cream socials and the monthly birthday celebrations; he made two special friends in the home; he looked forward to his schedule of appointments with the barber and podiatrist and for bathing; he liked most of the staff and joked with some on a regular basis, especially the male staff.

Dad joined others in complaining about the food once and a while; he had his normal treats of Purdy's and M&M's always at hand in his candy dish - when I was there each month, we continued to go out everyday of that week to restaurants or even an occasional pub for a beer and burger. As a family, we celebrated special occasions with a few relatives and on those occasions, he looked forward to dressing up for dinners out.

Dad was informed as to neighbourhood and city news and the outcomes of the national hockey league games. Mum continued to visit (later switching to every third day for her own health reasons); a niece visited both Dad and Mum often. Mum's caregiver dropped in for chats on her days off; Dad had a couple of old friends visit occasionally. Dad went for ice-cream drives with a caregiver-friend every Wednesday afternoon. (Note: We quickly realized that we shouldn't rely on old friends as visitors, since Dad's long-time friends were elderly also and finding it a challenge to get around; we also felt we shouldn't rely on relatives for regular outings as everyday work demands make it difficult for people to juggle schedules - so, right from the start, we made special arrangements, by hiring a familiar caregiver to visit one afternoon every week so Dad could have an outing to look forward to - it worked out very well.)

In addition, Dad's 'apartment' was adjacent to the main activity room so he listened to the Sunday services and concerts and called out to passing residents to say hello and visit. Dad's location was also close to the main nursing desk where he would go and sit on his walker twice a day for chats with a few other residents and the staff members.

In the manor, Dad had the 24-hour daily nursing care he required; he had social activities around him; he had some new friends and kept in touch with a few old ones too; he had routines he could count on; he had guaranteed security and safety offered by the large number of staff; he had familiar items in his room and he had Mum (and me) close by, always.

Even though Dad remained on very good terms with his doctor, he would comment from time-to-time when asked by his friends about living in the manor, "Doctor X tricked me, you know." Perhaps by believing this, Dad was sparing my feelings and never had to acknowledge that moving to a nursing home was in part his daughter's decision - I raised the topic at times, but will never really know Dad's level of understanding or full feelings. On the other hand, Dad also maintained, "But now, the decision to stay is my own". Eventually Dad started to refer to the caremanor, as "home" too. (But in truth, I know he knew differently and given a choice, well, this would not be where he would call 'home'.)

I had to remember, as a daughter, I remained Dad's key caregiver/careguide even when he was in the nursing home - my role remained as part of his new team, perhaps its increased even in importance.

Our journey continued - I know Mum and Dad wished it could have been different somehow - I do too - another care-year passed.

Part 8 - Continuing with the journey.

By mid of 1998 Dad began to lose interest in all daily activities and events and his health problems escalated - he developed liver problems and severe heart congestion requiring emergency attention on several occasions.

Like Dad, Mum suffered a variety of health problems that year and required emergency attention on several occasions. She went through both care-related plus health-related difficulties.

Dad lived in the caremanor for almost two years until October 18, 1998 when he died - we missed him always. Mum was at that time in her late eighties and continued to live with full-time care in her own home - as she used to say when asked "How are you", "I am doing as well as can be expected".

Throughout our care-years, when in the midst of major changes, my parents and I learned not to dwell on "I wish" or "If only" sentences - as we were unable to change the aging and resulting health circumstances which shaped our care-years journey together.

"Old" myths die hard!

Yet they are a powerful influence on our attitudes and actions (or lack of such). Some myths and stereotypes are rooted well back in time—think of Shakespeare's portrait of old age: "sans teeth, sans eyes, sans taste". In our society where youth is prized and we are in denial about aging and there is a fear of dying, some of the myths persist. We must work hard to correct our assumptions and change our negative attitudes as myths can harm.

MYTH: Most seniors live in nursing homes

REALITY: Just 5% of men and 9% of women over age 65 live in health care institutions in Canada; and most who do are 85 years old or older. These percentages have declined since 1991.

Long-term care does not necessarily mean nursing home care!

The Soapbox

It's been a while since I've stood on this particular soapbox, so forgive me if I am not as subtle as I could be when I say that the notion that you are no longer a caregiver when your loved one is living in a care facility is pure Poppycock! (Please forgive me for the profanity).

At a recent event, I heard from a caregiver who had been slapped in the face with this thoughtless opinion from some of her relatives. So, let me reiterate, over 90% of all caregiving happens at home, but once appropriate facility placement is made, you are not only still your loved ones caregiver, but you may have added to their lives as well as saving your own. The other thing you have accomplished is to add members to your loved ones care team.

As far as I am concerned, you are still the captain of that team, responsible for seeing that your loved one receives the best care possible from the facility. But the value you have added by your carefully determined decision is the realization that it sure would be nice to be able to spend some time with your loved one as loving son, daughter, husband or wife again, as opposed to emergency medical expert, pharmacist, nutritionist, as well as incontinence specialist. *(Source: Gary Barg, Editor-in-Chief, Today's Caregiver Magazine (on-line),* **www.caregiver.com***)*

Notes:

_____

_____

_____

_____

_____

"We do not remember day; we remember moments."
– *Anonymous*

Suggestion 45: *Select a care residence carefully*

There are many types of care residences, such as: assisted living complexes, private group homes, independent living community care complexes, nursing homes or caremanors, extended care units (usually as part of hospitals), Alzheimer care units, disabled living complexes, culturally-oriented carehomes, veteran care facilities…

Choosing a care residence requires time and diligence, not to mention an abundance of energy and attention to detail.

We shouldn't attempt this task when feeling rushed or pressured, therefore prior to a turning-point health crisis with a parent (just in case), we need to enquire as to the choices for residences in our parents' region (or in our own area if we plan on moving our parents closer to us as time dictates).

We should steer away from boldly stating, "I'd never do that to my parent" – who knows where a caregiving journey will lead (I didn't know, my cousins didn't, you won't).

Check for Accreditation

- An accredited facility does its best, not because it has to, but because it wants to. Seeking accreditation shows a desire to achieve excellence- a wish to be 'quality minded.' No better attitude can be brought to the care of the aged and frail.

- An accredited facility has shown that it meets a set of national standards set by the Canadian Council on Health Services Accreditation. While many good facilities are not accredited, an accredited facility is almost certain to deliver satisfactory care.

- Because accreditation must be regularly renewed, it keeps facilities on their toes. It also offers them benchmark scores against which they can measure the growth of their delivery of excellence *(Source: National Advisory Council On Aging, Expression, Volume 18, Number 4, Fall 2005, 'The Changing Face of Long-Term Care')*

How do I begin the nursing home review and selection process?

Step 1 – Take a little time to become familiar as to what nursing home living means.

☑ Visit and walk around two or three homes in the immediate area (if you have many choices) to obtain a general feel for care home living and to become familiar with the types of carehomes in the area (no invitations are necessary, just go on in).

☑ Talk to your parents' physician and ask his/her opinion of the various residences.

Step 2 – Find out what government health-care professionals think of the residences in the region and organize a preliminary list of homes.

☑ Discuss, with the government regional coordinator of health care (i.e the person responsible for carehome placements), the strengths and weaknesses of every carehome in the region as persons in these positions are extremely aware of each home's benefits. (Ask particularly about any of the near-by homes visited in step one if interested.) Do this step even if you are not going to apply for government subsidization as these persons are in constant contact with nursing homes.

☑ Be direct – ask the health unit coordinator, "Which residence would you select if making a decision for one of your own parents?"

☑ Discuss the levels/types of care given in each carehome (which meets our parent's needs, which are not options).

☑ List the possibilities, eliminating the more obvious based on the information gained during the discussion with the coordinator; include the managers' names of each of the carehomes on the list.

☑ If there are many choices, make a list consisting of two or three of the highly recommended carehomes.

☑ If the choices are few, make note of the most recommended one and the least recommended (and why).

Step 3 – Make contact.

☑ Telephone the managers of the carehomes on the list and state the main purpose of the call ("I would like to set up an appointment to look around, become familiar with the carehome"); also ask specific questions (relating to the needs of our parent).

☑ Organize with the managers a roster of visits (dates and times over a one-week span) to each of the carehomes on your list (e.g. in our case, I visited five homes, Mum came with me to see a couple).

Step 4 – Prepare the selection criteria.

☑ Prepare a list of 'first-impression' criteria *(refer to the next section – "What should I look for?")* to be able to compare/contrast each of the homes visited (don't even try to rely on memory).

☑ When writing our carehome selection criteria, we need to keep in mindthat we are selecting a 'home', that is a home to match our parent's care needs and personalities (versus our own likes and dislikes) – we need to look at the home through our caregiver's glasses. *(For example, Dad needed round-the-clock nursing attention so only carehomes with such could remain on our list, he would never accept a roommate nor a shared bathroom, so the number of single rooms in a home was important; he needed help getting in and out of bed and dressed so he required a certain level of care...)*

Step 5 – Gain an in-depth understanding.

☑ Take notes when visiting each of the carehomes on the list, gather brochures; ask costs, ask if public funded and/or private pay or both types of rooms exist; be sure to write down contact names for call backs.

☑ Ask questions for each selection criteria item *(again, refer to the next section – "What should I look for?")* if the answer isn't obvious.

(Note: A paramedic once said to me, "all nursing homes are not created equal". His comment reinforced the fact that as a daughter/son our task is to seek out a nursing home with excellent staff, an excellent residence environment, superb care. Quite simply, we are to provide excellent quality of life for our parent when in a nursing home.)

Sex, Statistics and the Older Person

A study by John DeLamater of the University of Wisconsin-Madison and Morgan Sill of the University of Michigan, published in the May 2005 issue of "The Journal of Sex Research" found that the sexual desire of older people is influenced more by attitudes toward sex than by biological factors such as medication.

As expected, they found that increasing age was positively correlated with lower sexual desire. Illnesses, such as high blood pressure, and the use of medication, such as anticoagulants, also resulted in lower sexual desire.

However, psychological factors were just as important. Negative attitudes toward sex were correlated with low sexual desire, and people who rated sex as important to their relationships had higher sexual desire. Besides age, attitude was the strongest predictor of desire.

Other social factors that predicted high sexual desire were a greater level of education the presence of a sexual partner. Conversely, people who were less educated and did not have an available partner reported lower levels of desire.

These findings contradict commonly held beliefs that older people are not sexual and that sex is only for young people.

DeLamater and Sill conclude that "negative attitudes about sexual activity among older persons need to be challenged so that future cohorts are not influenced by such attitudes".

They also suggested that assisted living communities should be restructured to allow elderly residents to engage in intimate relationships.

(Source: University of Wisconsin-Madison Study, Madison Wisconsin, June 2005)

What should I look for?

First-impression selection criteria may include the following (these are not in any order of priority):

☑ How open does the communication seem between the manager and staff and clients (me) – this is an important question as we will want constant contact with that manager and head nurse if we have a parent living there?

☑ How do the residents appear to be getting along (personally and with others)? The best way to find out is to sit for a few relaxing minutes and talk to a few residents, ask them for their opinions of the home, ask them about their likes, dislikes, the meals, ask how they spend their days; talk to any family members visiting.

☑ What is the staff-resident ratio?

☑ What is the nurse-resident ratio on each shift/how many nurses full-time?

☑ Who is responsible for the 'plan of care' to be written for each resident, can we review our parent's care plan at any time?

☑ How are staff hired – qualifications, experience required, are checks done on candidates…?

☑ Is there a 'residents' committee' that has input to the everyday care rules/regulations/events/living conditions?

☑ How spacious are the rooms, hallways, dining areas, and yards/lawns/recreation areas?

☑ Do the residents' rooms have windows, their own large bathrooms, good closet space, well-maintained furniture, safety features…? Are the rooms air conditioned?

☑ How light and bright and welcoming is the whole home (dark brown wood panelling and low ceilings versus brightly painted walls and skylights); are the walls decorated for mental and visual stimulation (e.g. paintings, large notice boards, billboards with menus...); are there plants around and colourful furniture...?

☑ Who owns the home (private, company, franchise); how old is the home, what are its immediate, long-term plans (find out if its being sold, is it unionized).

☑ How close is the carehome to our parent's house (for quick visits by our other parent and neighbours)?

☑ Does the home give preference to any special group and why (e.g. main language spoken; foods...)?

☑ Are pets allowed?

☑ Will a resident be allowed to stay if his/her health deteriorates to the next level of care or will the resident be forced to move once again to another carehome that offers that next level of care (i.e. we don't want to have to move our parent if possible)? In other words, is this nursing home part of a larger 'community care retirement center' complex? Can services be 'added' as age and health demand more care?

☑ What is a sample week menu (it might be a good idea to pay for a meal, then sit and chat to residents)?

☑ What types of activities are held on a regular basis? Do residents have a say? computers? etc.

☑ What is the mission statement, goals of the home; are they posted for all to read?

☑ Is the carehome operated like a home (open-door policy) or like an institution, meaning, can residents receive visitors at anytime as in a personal home, can residents use the main telephone or be notified of a call at any time of the day? *(For Example: Both Mum and I wanted to be able telephone Dad each day to chat, and we wanted to feel comfortable with that procedure since we did not feel it was a good idea for Dad to have a telephone of his own in his room)*

☑ What is the actual physical layout of the home, that is, the configuration of the rooms to the dining, activity and nursing station areas? Sketch it.

(For example: Most of the homes we visited had the residents' rooms down both sides of hallways (hotel style) or along specially designated corridors (spoke-like) with nursing stations at the center of each wheel and the dining areas and entertainment areas far away like lobby spaces. At first I thought these wheel-hub style configurations were a very good idea as the design would force residents to leave their rooms for social exchanges; but, after a respite experience with Dad in a carehome which was designed in the hub fashion, I realized that this particular layout could prove more detrimental than encouraging for some people like Dad who would choose to stay at the nurse's station and never venture to the actual entertainment area. I thus looked for a carehome where the residents' rooms circled the outside perimeter of large activity spaces, now knowing that Dad, who liked to sit in his recliner most of the time, might be beckoned to venture more often into the visible activity area when entertainment occurred. The nursing home's room layout turned out to be a very important criterion for Dad as he was forced to interact due to the proximity of his room to the home's activity area. This architectural design also proved a good one for safety reasons (e.g. Dad fell one day, could not reach his bell, but was very quickly noticed by someone in the main activity room.) As mentioned, I may not have recognized the importance of the physical lay-out of the building had I not observed my father in a respite situation before he relocated to a carehome – Dad had always been very social and out-going, so I was interested during respite to discover that, with the changes in his health, he didn't go out of his way to be with people – in short, we required a carehome design which would suit Dad's 'present' personality. I then understood why I was told, when our journey began, that the parent I used to know, the one I had dinner with, sat around and chatted with, was not the same parent who will require care — my parent had changed.)

Depression? Although most seniors enjoy good mental health, as many as 20% of people age 65+ suffer mild to severe depression, ranging from perhaps 5 to 10% of seniors in the community to as many as 30 to 40% of those in institutions.

(Source: Mental Health Problems Among Canada's Seniors; Demographic and Epidemiologic Considerations, Health Canada, 1991)

Notes:

"Being seventy is not a sin."

– Golda Meir

'Teddy Tapes' spark legal war…Elder Care: Judy Sillin took charge when she sensed her dad had been neglected, setting up a secret camera at his care home to find the truth.

The teddy bear that sat above Stephen Piccolo's bed in a Kamloops nursing home last fall got to see it all. For two months he sat there on top of the dresser looking innocent—and looking down on what it's like to spend your twilight years in government care. Right down to the diaper changes.

If the staff at Overlander Extended Care Centre wondered why the grumpy, 90-year old former rancher had developed a sudden fondness for small stuffed animals, none of them thought to check. This was the kind of teddy you buy at Radio Shack.

Hidden inside was a tiny camera that, for eight hours a day, transmitted sounds and images from the old man's private room to a remote receiver and, ultimately, to a VCR. The teddy cam was placed in the private room by his daughter and her son. Just the previous year they had formed an advocacy group to campaign for a Royal Commission into what they see as the declining state of residential care for the elderly.

..The tapes contain what the Sillins say is powerful evidence that some seniors are neglected and even abused in the overburdened system that has encouraged low staff morale. What teddy saw, however the public cannot…But it will be up to the courts to settle the exchange of lawsuits between the Sellins and the nursing home staff. Apart from the allegations of neglect, abuse and defamation, the case will involve one of the most complex legal and ethical dilemmas of the 21st century—how to balance the desires of families to monitor the care of their loved ones against the privacy rights of employees.

According to an affidavit entered by the Sellins, and to people who saw the preview that was briefly posted before it was banned, the preview shows:

- Her father being fed bacon and eggs in spite of the fact that, according to the Sellins, he is unable to eat solid food. He can be seen either coughing or vomiting the food back up while repeatedly being given more. (continued...)

- A care aide handing Piccolo a glass of milk and, when he asks what it is, replying: "If I told you it was horse pee would you believe me?"

- Piccolo lying on his bed just 48 hours before his death— unclothed and uncovered from the waist down for nearly two hours. He can be seen trying to pull a sheet over his legs.

The affidavit also alleges that Piccolo's requests for fluids were repeatedly ignored and that he was admitted to hospital to be treated for dehydration.

(For the full story, read "The Province" archives, section B3 Sunday, May 29, 2005 – Cover Story, by Peter Clough, Investigation, "The Province", Vancouver, B.C. May 29, 2005; more on the same story in "The Province" December 8, 2005)

How do I make a final selection?

Step 1 – Discuss the findings

☑ Arrange a follow-up meeting with the health unit coordinator (again, even if you are not applying for government funding) and discuss the findings and impressions of each of the homes – listen to her/his perspectives. Be sure to ask if there have been any reported problems in any of the carehomes in the region (e.g. thefts, abuse, harassment...).

☑ Ask the health unit coordinator in your area, the one responsible for nursing-home placements the following question, "If your mom/dad had to go into a nursing home here, which one would you select (and why) ;and which one would you avoid?"

☑ Discuss, if appropriate, our findings with our other parent, and close relatives in the area.

☑ Decide on two care homes as 'finalists'.

Step Two – Gather information on the two carehome finalists:

☑ Contact other sources to ask questions regarding the two care homes (e.g. our parents' family physician, the regional health unit and/or social workers, and the hospital geriatric ward/rehabilitation ward). Ask their opinions of the two carehomes; ask if they know of any families with parents residing in those homes and what the family has learned; ask specifically about any reported abuse or major problems they may be aware of in the homes.

☑ Telephone the government department that has the mandate for homecare licensing – ask for copies of the latest reports and rankings of the carehomes in the region; if unavailable or too costly, ask at the health unit if it would be possible to review their copies. If copies are not available, ask to speak with someone who can discuss the results.

☑ If close family members are not aware of these two selected homes, then perhaps a small group of family members (e.g. 3) should visit the two care homes together at this time and offer their opinions of the two finalists.

☑ Judge if our parent (the one who is going to be changing residences) should visit the homes, if yes, do a walk through with him/her and listen for his/her impressions (but do think carefully about this parent involvement step before doing it – you don't want it to back-fire).

Step 3 – Investigate the details.

☑ Investigate the two finalist carehomes to confirm your understanding of these basics:

- Room availability

- Levels of care provided – general staffing and nursing care

- Costs/funding

- Comfort fees monthky and 'extra' charges

- Transportation means

- Pharmacies used

- Staff-resident interactions

- Resident-resident interactions

- Equipment available within the care manor and what special items the family is expected to provide.

Step 4 – Select the caremanor desired.

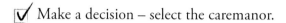 Make a decision – select the caremanor.

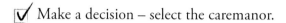 Inform family members so everyone is aware of the decision and the reasons for this selection.

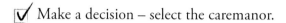 Telephone the caremanor manager and arrange a meeting to discuss specifics.

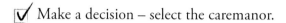 Set a date for taking up residency or if residency is in the future, make arrangements for the manager to call each time a room comes available to check on our needs at that point in time. If waiting until a government funded subsidized bed space becomes available, contact the health unit coordinator often to check on status.

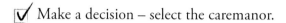 Place deposit if required.

"Life consists not in holding good cards but in playing those you hold well."

– Josh Billings

The first study of how caregivers respond to placing loved ones with dementia into care shows they experience high levels of depression and anxiety. Previous research has shown that when someone with dementia dies, their caregivers tend to experience an improvement in emotional health. Death gives a sense of 'closure' and there is relief that the suffering of the person with dementia is at an end. And the burden of caregiving is lifted, leaving the carer to get on with their own life.

Now a study from the University of Pittsburgh reveals how the opposite is true when a caregiver has to let someone with dementia go into institutional care. The researchers studied 1,222 caregiver-patient pairs, where the patients had moderate to severe Alzheimer's disease. The caregivers reported high levels of anxiety and depression linked to the transition.

The reasons for this distress may relate to the fact that the person with dementia often suffers physical and cognitive decline on going into care. The caregiver may, without foundation, blame themselves. They also have to give up control over their charge's care, which is difficult. And they have to cope with making frequent visits. All of this suggests that caregivers need lots of help and support when they make the decision to transfer the care of the person with dementia to an institution.

(Source: Journal of the American Medical Association, August 2004)

Poem

The following anonymous poem has been attributed to several sources. It is generally described as having been found among the possessions of an older woman who died in a geriatric ward of a hospital.

What Do You See?

What are you thinking when you're looking at me?
A crabby old woman, not very wise,
Uncertain of habit, with faraway eyes.

Who dribbles her food and makes no reply
When you say in a loud voice, "I do wish you'd try?"
Who seems not to notice the things that you do,
And forever is losing a stocking or shoe.

Who, resisting or not, lets you do as you will
With bathing and feeding, the long day to fill.
Is that what you're thinking? Is that what you see?
Then open your eyes, nurse; you're not looking at me.
I'll tell you who I am as I sit here so still,
As I use at your bidding, as I eat at your will.

I'm a small child of ten with a father and mother,
Brothers and sisters, who love one another.
A young girl of sixteen, with wings on her feet,
Dreaming that soon now a lover she'll meet.

A bride soon at twenty-my heart gives a leap,
Remembering the vows that I promised to keep.
At twenty-five now, I have young of my own
Who need me to guide and a secure happy home.

A woman of thirty, my young now grown fast,
bound to each other with ties that should last.
At forty my young sons have grown and are gone,
but my man's beside me to see I don't mourn.

continued...

At fifty once more babies play round my knee,
Again we know children, my loved one and me.
Dark days are upon me, my husband is dead;
I look at the future, I shudder with dread.....

For my young are all rearing young of their own,
and I think of the years and the love that I've known.
I'm now an old woman and nature is cruel;
'tis jest to make old age look like a fool.
The body, it crumbles, grace and vigour depart,
there is now a stone where I once had a heart.

But inside this old carcass a young girl still dwells,
And now and again my battered heart swells.
I remember the joys; I remember the pain,
And I'm loving and living life over again.

I think of the years; all too few, gone too fast,
And accept the stark fact that nothing can last.
So open your eyes, nurses, open and see,
Not a crabby old woman; look closer - see ME!!

Anonymous.

"Age does not diminish the extreme disappointment of having a scoop of ice-cream fall from the cone."
– *Jim Fiebig*

Suggestion 46: Add value to nursing home / carehome living and stay in close touch

Prior to an actual change in residency for a parent, we need to ask ourselves, "What can I do to make caremanor living more enjoyable for my parent?" (Having a parent reside in a nursing home means that we must be committed to the responsibilities attached, that is giving time, energy, consistant contact, adding value…)

What can I do to add quality and love to carehome living?

We can visit, call, write, visit, visit, visit:

☑ **Telephone** – the afternoon often is a good chat time, as personal care schedules with nurses and aides consume morning hours leaving the time between lunch and dinner as slow time.

If in the same town, if a parent has a telephone in his/her room then keeping close contact is simple – telephone at the same time each non-visit day establishing a routine. If long-distance, telephoning two-three times a week should work well to maintain close contact.

If a telephone is not installed in our parent's room, it is easy to request that a staff member find our parent to receive our telephone calls. (Discuss preferred times with the staff, being sensitive to the carehome's busy schedules.) Once the staff becomes used to our request, calls will be quickly handled (in addition, staff members will use this time to tell us about our parent's progress, an added benefit).

If distant relatives and family friends are visiting us in our own home, it is fun, at that time, to telephone each of our parents so that these visitors can have a chat with our parents too.

☑ **Plan for private, normal time together** – at a meal, on a drive, in his/her room; plan time to read the newspaper headlines and some articles aloud, talk about neighbourhood events, sports, gossip…

As a daughter/son, we need to spend quiet one-on-one time with our parent, time to chat when there are only the two of us – this can be in his/ her room, at a restaurant, in the activity room over a cup of coffee...

When both parents are visiting, they need some time together without anyone else hovering (daughter, son or caregivers) – they need to be able to chat as they used to. *(For example: when Mum no longer drove, she with her caregiver together would visit with Dad and after a few minutes, the caregiver would go into the activity room to read leaving Dad and Mum to visit the rest of the time on their own.)*

An Ann Landers' letter from Liz in Sacramento: My cousin suggested I bring a small cassette recorder with me when I visit my father (in a convalescent center). This way, I can state the date, and let my father know we are taping his conversations for others to enjoy. Some days, he understands, other days he doesn't but the visit is there for all the grandchildren, nieces and nephews to treasure and be able to hear Dad's voice. The tapes are easy to send in the mail and will serve as a living diary. *(January 15, 2000.)*

☑ **Write a letter or card or fax at least once a month in the right font size and color, if living out of town** (in addition to telephone calls) – note on the outside of the envelope or top of the fax page a request for a staff member to read the contents to our parent if eyesight is in doubt. *(Note: If a staff member reads the letter to our parent, usually a discussion follows – the staff will get to know our parent as a person beyond the carehome, with family and interests.)*

☑ **Scheduled weekly outings** – set a firm schedule with a special friend or a hired caregiver 'companion' so your parent can have some time away from the caremanor, to go on drives...(i.e. one can't be expected to stay in the same environment, day after day, week after weeks, month after month—happiness and stimulation are needed).

☑ **Make plans to celebrate, recognize special days,** as there is a heightened awareness on the part of the residents since there may be decorations for special calendar occasions, (e.g. Thanksgiving, St. Patrick's Day) around the home. Go out for luncheons on those days, bring baking to share with tablemates, go for a ride to watch fireworks, see street sights.

☑ **Go to restaurants often (again, remember meals-times are very important)** – take time to ask as to the choice of restaurant/type of cuisine and telephone the restaurant ahead if a special request is necessary (e.g. special diet) or if a ramp/equipment is available. *(For example: When I visited each month, Dad and I had our usual 'restaurant week', that is lunches for the whole week in different restaurants of his choice. I recognized the importance of meals to him.)*

☑ **Make the room personal, cosy,** showing individuality (e.g. family pictures, paintings on walls, comforters, pillows, plants, treats, own furniture).

☑ **Make special requests of the carehome staff and to some degree, at times, involve them in some way in our parent's activities.**

(For example, we often brought fresh fruit and pastries for Dad and his tablemates for lunch and asked the kitchen staff to set them out. We bought boxes of chocolates for him to share with the staff and other residents when they visited him in his room. We encouraged Dad to ask the staff's opinions on a restaurant we could try and he then returned with a sample menu from the place.)

☑ **Drop a note to the carehome administrator for special matters or concerns** – follow-up at all times on each concern as the administrator can make changes if necessary to assist our parent. Drop in at least once a month to the administrator's office to say hello.

☑ **Stop at the nursing desk during each visit** to hear of any of the staff's concerns, to follow-up on their requests and to place any special requests through them.

☑ **Check on 'little things'** too – Always check on our parent's water-intake (dehydration can contribute to dementia problems) and ask the care staff to serve water also to our parent during the afternoon cart service; request that a multi-vitamin be given once a day (again malnutrition can contribute to dementia – malnutrition does not necessarily imply poor quality of meals but how our parent's body is using its food). Request that the staff note these needs on our parent's file.

☑ **Take time to find out how our parent is adjusting** – listen to the staff, as they are present always. Ask specifically about our parent's interaction with others in the care manor, both staff members and residents as the staff may not report any non-health issues to family unless the behaviour is highly problematic.

(For example: On one occasion, I was told that Dad had not been getting along with another (male) resident ("they are grouchy together"), the nurse suggested to me that both were "strong-willed" so the staff was keeping an eye out and not seating them together at meal times. One day when I asked, the nurse reported that the man had been "baiting and bullying Dad across the tables during lunch" and so Dad "pushed the man who landed flat onto the dining room floor". I was stunned hearing this story from the carehome staff as I always knew Dad had a temper, but never in all my memories do I ever remember hearing of him striking anyone, physical violence of any degree was not his nature. Dad never mentioned the incident except to hint in passing that he didn't really like "that fellow" and that he got "fed up" with him one particular day. And yet, another time, during a casual stop at the nursing desk, I learned that a female resident had become a special friend and that she visited Dad several times a day – I then made it a point to meet her, she was a delightful well-spoken kind person whom I welcomed as a friend for Dad. She used to tell me that "he was the most handsome man in the home" and that the visits were 'fun' for her.)

☑ **Be prompt for important appointments** when a special request is made by the carehome (e.g. purchase equipment, schedule tests for our parent…).

☑ **Leave (some/a little) spending money** in a designated spot for fun-use. *(For example: We always left a few dollars in the bedside dresser so Dad could 'treat' occasionally on his weekly ice-cream excursions.)*

☑ **Treat the carehome staff well and with humour,** as these are the people who interact with our parent on a 8-hour everyday shift; share with them little anecdotes which have occurred on outings; say thank you in writing (and actions) when something special has been done for our parent.

☑ **Become familiar with the carehome** – make it part of our family's immediate environment and participate in the activities (e.g. teas, bake sales, church services, raffles, monthly birthday parties…)

☑ **Advise a staff member when we are leaving after a visit** – if we live out of town or if our parent is emotional – ask a staff member to go in for a chat with our parent as soon as we leave his/her room – a very helpful idea.

☑ **Post reminders** – when out-of-town family members are scheduled to make visits – the dates can be marked on a large monthly calendar posted in our parent's room (e.g. in our case, my schedules were always lined in on Dad's calendar and written on Mum's kitchen calendar). Special outings can be marked on the calendar several months in advance. *(Note: Calendars serve as reminders, giving our parents something to look forward to when they glance at the dates marked off. The calendars also help keep the carehome staff informed as to our visits and any up-coming family events.)*

☑ **Agree upon regular visitations for the other parent** – when one parent still lives at home, regular visits should form a pattern (e.g. Sunday afternoons, every third day in the morning).

☑ **Continue familiar activities** – we should continue familiar activities with our parent now living in a carehome – just like 'before.' *(For example: When Mum was still driving, she spent several mornings a week with Dad and she often brought her crocheting – Dad was comfortable with Mum doing this activity while they chatted as this was the same as their routines at home used to be.)*

The following was written by Judy Vekasy, a registered nurse and director of activities at a nursing home in Savannah, Tennessee – it originally appeared in Ann Landers column in the "Memphis Commercial Appeal".

Here are some suggestions for those who need someone to allow them to give of themselves. **Nursing homes are full of opportunities.** You say you can't do anything. Can you read? Good. Read to me. My eyes aren't what they used to be. Can you write? Good. Write a letter or a card for me. My hands are shaky. Can you sing? Good. Help me with words, and I'll sing along. Can you tell me about your job? I was a nurse once myself. Can you listen? Wonderful. I'm starved for conversation. Can you bake a sponge cake or zucchini bread or angel biscuits or make fudge? They aren't on the nursing home menu, but I remember how good they were, and I would like to taste them again. Do you play checkers or dominos or rummy? Fine, so do I, but there is never anyone who has the time. They are understaffed around here, you know. Do you play the violin or the flute or the piano? My hearing is poor, but I can hear any kind of music. Even if I fall asleep, you'll know I enjoyed it. Once we were somebodies, just like you. We were farmers and farmers' wives and teachers, nurses, beauticians, stockbrokers and electricians, bankers and sheriffs, and maybe a few outlaws, too. We're not all senile – just old and needing more help than our families can give us. This home, whatever its name is "home" to us, and you're an invited guest. Please come. The welcome mat is always out.

I hope you will keep this, and read it again in January, February, and every other month of the year. We'll still be here, and our needs will still be the same.

Notes:

_____

_____

_____

_____

_____

Suggestion 47: *Understand how we may unintentionally contribute to new problems*

We should be aware of how and when we can unintentionally create new problems for our parents, given their current health conditions.

What can we do so we don't add problems?

☑ **We have to train ourselves to act versus react** – We have to tune into the fact that some of our unconscious actions could now, unknowingly, under these new health and living circumstances, have an instant impact on our parent – a conditioning effect setting off a new series of problems and worries that our parent and others who work with him/ her (us included) will have to cope with from then on.

☑ **We must try to second-guess the consequences of events,** especially if something we are doing could play into already existing anxieties of our parent.

☑ **We must learn to take our time** (again, don't get rattled, take a deep breath, go slow, practise a calmness) when interacting with our parents – perhaps we need to concentrate on going slowly. *(For example: Mum's caregivers took it upon themselves to remind me of this need often – they were right as it maintains a calm demeanour around Mum and it helped.)*

The following anecdote is offered in the hope that it will assist other daughter/son-caregivers in their understanding of the far-reaching effects of some of our innocent actions – learning from our mistakes:

Beginning with a very early morning alarm wake-up, rush-hour driving to the airport, and a 55-minute commuter flight to my parents' hometown, as well as,a long list of urgent medical-related errands requiring my immediate attention upon arrival, I later found myself by four-thirty in the afternoon running "in high gear" (as Mum so aptly described my usual state) – and I was only half a day into one of my scheduled monthly respite visits. We were, that evening, to have a family dinner, thus, I was rushing to help Mum get ready and then hurrying to pick up Dad at his caremanor so we could all enjoy an early dinner. (Mistake #1, too much planned on arrival day.)

We enjoyed our leisurely dinner together. Upon finishing our desserts and chatting, it was time to leave, we got as far as the exit door of the restaurant, but as it had no disabled persons access ramps or railings, I had Mum sit at the exit while other restaurant patrons kindly assisted me in helping Dad (with his walker) down the outside stairs safely.

I asked Dad to wait at the bottom of the stairs and promptly returned to assist Mum down the stairs, as she requires a guiding hand and firm help at all times. While I was occupied helping Mum, Dad became impatient (I might have guessed) and promptly set off on his own, across the busy parking lot, wheeling his walker to our car which was by now wedged in between two other parked vehicles in a very crowded lot. (Mistake #2, misreading a parent's state of agitation.)

Seeing this, I rushed Mum (as much as possible) across the lot to the car, asking her to hang onto the back door as I turned my attention to help Dad once again - he was by now standing by himself at the car. (visualize two wobbly parents!) I unlocked the doors of the car, threw my purse in, got Dad positioned properly, lifted his legs, and once seated correctly, buckled him in. (Mistake #3, getting rattled.)

At this precise moment, as I was attending to my parents, a ruckus broke out near us in the parking lot with teenagers throwing ice cubes and spraying water and generally having summer fun - this disturbance proved very unsettling for Dad and he started calling out "Hurry up! Hurry up!". I turned quickly back to Mum, arranged her comfortably into the back seat and buckled her up. (Mistake #4, getting more rattled.)

Right then, adding to the disruption (as if on cue), an impatient driver wanting our soon-to-be vacated parking spot stopped his vehicle behind us and started honking. His actions created a traffic jam in the parking lot and the noise caused Dad to become even more agitated ("Hurry up!"). As the parking lot antics escalated (more kids throwing more ice cubes and playing, the car honking, other cars waiting, Dad yelling), all I wanted to do was get us out of there - I sprinted around the back of the car to the driver's side, jumped in, buckled up and took off. (Mistake #5, reacting, not thinking.)

Realizing Dad became concerned and worried, each and every evening, about 'time' (a fixation - he wanted to be present at the exact time of the night-staff shift change so he would be assured that someone would be assisting him with going to bed - "I want to be there"). My mind forgot about the restaurant and started to focus on the new challenge - getting Dad back on time before he became upset further. Because I knew that he became restless due to this fixation, we headed directly back to the caremanor from the restaurant - I had timed it so he wouldn't be late. (Mistake #6, Not looking at consequences of all fixations.)

Arriving at the residency parking lot, I had a nagging feeling that I had forgotten something during the confusion in the parking lot, then it hit me - during the chaos, I had zipped around the back of our car to get in after helping Mum and therefore didn't see Dad's walker left along side the far passenger door - in my haste, I had forgotten to put his walker in the trunk of our car, I had left it sitting in the middle of restaurant parking lot. (Mistake #7, not taking time, not being calm.)

Oh no! I had left Dad's walker unattended, we were going to have to go back to the restaurant immediately and to make things worse, Dad was now not going to be able to be at the manor 'on time' for the shift change. I knew that these mistakes were going to cause an explosive reaction, aimed in my direction.

Without a word, I pulled a U-y and headed back down the highway. I explained quietly to Dad why I was turning around - he almost hit the car roof in disbelief ("How could you forget my walker?!?!") I felt so badly for Dad - he was completely dependent on his walker as his major means of transportation and was instantly convinced that we'd never find it again, that it would be stolen by now.

So on an evening that was planned to be a pleasant one for my parents, we ended up zooming down the road on a very hot summer day, Dad in a state of panic-temper and Mum absolutely still in the back seat, watching the whole picture play out. (As for my state of anxiety, well during one brief moment, I started to laugh - to myself, of course - I just could not believe this day so far.)

As expected, the walker had been turned into the office of the restaurant for safekeeping and Dad and his walker were united once again - but my carelessness and rushing had now unknowingly created a new behaviour problem.

From that evening onward Dad was 'conditioned' - his walker could not be allowed to leave his sight (under any circumstances). That episode, due to a combination of factors (my unintentional mistakes), caused him to develop a fear of losing his walker. At the manor, it had to be beside him always; the equipment repairman had to go to the manor to attend to the maintenance of the walker with Dad present (rather than taking it to the shop and waiting for it); and without exception, on every outing, with every person, he asked repeatedly for an entire drive, "Did you put my walker in the car?" (Whenever possible, we ended up putting the walker in the back seat of the car, just for everyone's peace of mind.) No matter where he was, for the remainder of his life, he never again let that walker out of his sight and everyone had to accommodate his fear of losing it. We now had another 'fixation' to deal with...and this one ended up being a lasting one, it never went away.

There will be no nursing home in my future.........

When I get old and feeble, I am going to get on a Princess Cruise Ship.

The average cost for a nursing home is $200 per day. I have checked on reservations at Princess and I can get a long-term discount and senior discount price of $135 per day.

That leaves $65 a day for:

1. Gratuities, which will only be $10 per day.
2. I will have as many as 10 meals a day if I can waddle to the restaurant, or I can have room service (which means I can have breakfast in bed every day of the week).
3. Princess has as many as three swimming pools, a workout room, free washers and dryers, and shows every night.
4. They have free toothpaste and razors, and free soap and shampoo.
5. They will even treat you like a customer, not a patient. An extra $5 worth of tips will have the entire staff scrambling to help you.
6. I will go to meet new people every 7 or 14 days.
7. TV broken? Light bulb needs changing? Need to have the mattress
8. Replaced? No Problem! They will fix everything and apologize for your inconvenience.
9. Clean sheets and towels every day, and you don't even have to ask for them.
10. If you fall in the nursing home and break a hip you are on your government's health plan. If you fall and break a hip on the Princess ship, they will upgrade you to a suite for the rest of your life.

Now hold on for the best! Do you want to see South America, the Panama Canal, Tahiti, Australia, New Zealand, Asia, or name where you want to go? Princess will have a ship ready to go. So don't look for me in a nursing home, just call shore to ship.

P.S. And don't forget, when you die, they just dump you over the side at no extra charge.

Anonymous

"Life consists not inholding good cards but in playing those you hold well."

– Josh Billings

Notes:

TOPIC 9

Let's Talk: Eliminating surprises, knowing the costs of care and planning for future care-years

When care is needed, what major costs should I expect, how will I cover these costs and how can I plan for this time in our lives?

Personal Anecdote: "A FINANCIAL TSUNAMI!"

Suggestions:

48: Become familiar with the various costs associated with care

49: Face the facts – Be realistic when planning for care-years

50: Find out well-in-advance about the options available to cover the costs of different care situations – we need a LTC financial literacy program in Canada

Personal Anecdote:
"A FINANCIAL TSUNAMI!"

Pre-Long-Term-Care Times: January 3, 1996 - I had two parents both in their mid-eighties, retired for 24 years, living comfortably - they owned their own home, drove their own vehicles; they had their own bank accounts for personal activities, a basic monthly household budget as low income seniors and still had some small savings remaining for larger annual and unexpected expenses - their later retirement years had been going along as expected.

January 4, 1996: The Beginning: What a difference a moment makes! 9:30 AM icy driveway - my Dad fell, a lifestyle turning point - our family's long-term care years officially started.

February 1 -Within the one month, I had two dependent parents requiring care in their own home with a live-in caregiver (home renovations of approximately $3,000 were required immediately to accommodate a live-in caregiver and $3,850.63 of special equipment was required for 'first stage' home safety and health needs- —as time went on, $6,000 - $10,000 more for special equipment was also necessary); our roles changed, mine went from loving daughter to loving daughter-caregiver-care guide. Budgets were established as the costs of long-term care aging needs, I thought, were becoming apparent, but the real financial challenges were yet to come.

1996: Care-Year One: Our family's budget for Care-Year #1 (1996) increased over 200% from the pre-care retirement times. Not surprising, my parents' retirement savings were going down rapidly just when their care-needs were increasing rapidly- —as a family we had become 'financially interdependent' now.

1997: Our care-years journey continued: Both my parents, requiring care on a full-time basis, had two distinct sets of care expenses now. One parent (Dad) now needed residency in a nursing home caremanor and the other (Mum) remained in her own home with a full-time live-in caregiver. Our family's budget for Care-Year #2 were still going up from the pre-long-term care retirement times. The long-term financial challenges were becoming obvious.

The 'care portion only' of our household budget started to explode at this point in time. What were our family's choices —together we now had to budget for: $869 of on-going 'extras' required; plus Dad's 'basic monthly nursing home cost' of $3,400+; plus Mum's 'at-home care-related caregiver fees and care expenses' of several thousand per month in order for her to remain in her own home (over the years, the fees varied from $1000 - $5000/mo). Added to those costs, of course there were the regular living expenses that we all have in order to run a household.

What about two parents in living in two different care-environments — an 'involuntary separation'? I was totally unprepared for care costs for two parents living in two separate environments -- two budgets each month, one for my Dad to pay for his nursing home care and one for my mother to pay for her at-home care...at the same time! You do the math if you want to estimate these costs per month for a family with both parents needing care in two locations; now do the math for one year; now several years!

2005 —Year #10: Our budget had kept increasing over the years, as more and more care was required (this makes sense but is often forgotten when calculating the cost of care overall). We have no choices; our parents need care -- a financial tsunami indeed!

Our care journey ended: Dad died in 1998 and Mum several years later, in mid 2005.

My conclusions regarding the costs of care:

- *Care in one's own home and in an nursing home is costly*
- *Care without government assistance is costly*
- *Care with government assistance, which is very helpful, is still costly (A family must recognize its dependency and its high risks when relying on government assistance services and programs for long-term care needs)*
- *Because of the costs associated with care, adult children for the most part will probably have to assist with care costs of an elderly parent(s)*
- *The financial costs of care, without planning, strike Canadian families like a tsunami*

To this day, I believe that as Canadians we are ill prepared for this time in our parents' lives and our own. I know I was and have since learned that there are many more families just like mine across the country - we all are in need of an education on the long-term care phase of our lives and what that stage entails emotionally, organizationally and financially.

We want to be independent, we want information, we want to do the right thing...we need to know the facts since we are living so much longer now, we need to be educated about this new issue in our country—long-term care

"Extended health care services (i.e. home care and nursing home care) are not and never were insured health services under the CHA (Canada Health Act)"

Source: Canada Health Act
For more information, refer: www.hc-sc.gc.ca/hcs-sss/medi-assur/transfer/index e.html

"Home care is included in the federal Canada Health Act as an 'extended health care service'. However, home care services are not publicly insured in the same way as hospital and physician services. Provinces and territories provide and publicly fund home care services at their own discretion."

Source: "A Study On Home Care in Canada"
For further information, refer to: www.hc-sc.gc.ca/hcs-sss/pubs/care-soins/1999-home-domicile/situation e.html#fundy

The Study goes on to address how our publicly funded home care programs work, it states:

"Home care is not subject to the five principles of the Canada Health Act. Nevertheless, each province and territory has established its own publicly funded home care program, and some provinces cover some home care services as part of their provincial health insurance plans. Specific features of provincial/territorial home care programs – including program policies, services, and delivery mechanisms – differ from jurisdiction to jurisdiction."

DETAILS FOR PLANNING AND DISCUSSION PURPOSES

NURSING HOME/CARE MANOR LIVING:

Below is a copy of our family's Dec 1997 invoice from Dad's nursing home...note our basic fee per month, the little incidental costs one must consider and then finally our cost per month when accepted for government subsidization upon application and assessment.

Living in a nursing home is costly

Subsidized ✱ Free

date	description	debit	credit	balance
Dec 1/97	opening balance			$ 3487.49
Nov. 30	ice cream socials	$ 1.00		$ 3486.49
Dec. 12	pharmacy	$ 6.49		$ 3480.00
Dec. 13	barber	$ 5.00		$ 3475.00
Dec. 29	barber	$ 5.00		$ 3470.00
Dec. 31	ice cream socials	$ 2.40		$ 3467.60

$3,120.40+ (private care/month) and
$1,141(subsidized care/month)

---

*From Patty's seminars on LTC Planning

CARE IN ONE'S OWN HOME/AGING IN PLACE:

The box below gives an overview graph of the cost of care when one 'ages in place' (i.e. stays in one's own home with 24/7 care)

·   *$1,507/month*
Mum's income as a senior each month from all the sources

·   *$7,117/month*
Our total budget to be considered each month

- $7,117/month

Our budget minimum each month 'without government financial assistance/subsidization'.

- $3,480/month

Our subsidization allocation from a (B.C.) provincial government program for Mum's care each month--once we had qualified and kept qualifying (assessment of need is done each year)

Government assistance per month: $3,480 from a special provincial subsidized program for disabled and seniors called Choices In Support for Independent Living (CSIL)— most provinces have such a financial assistance-type program designed to keep people in their own homes managing their own care versus moving into a nursing home; we did not receive this assistance until the last few years as it is very specialized, but when we did, this was the amount we were allocated and it was deposited into a care society bank account for use with Mum's care fees each month

- $3,637/month (minimum)

Our family's portion of the budget each month 'with government financial assistance/subsidization'

That is, $7117 (total budget required) - $3,480 (subsidization allocation) leaving $3,637/month for the family input (these costs per month varied at times as one would expect with the unpredictability of care needs).

Monthly shortfalls in the care-years for at-home 24/7 care:

- $5617/month

Mum's shortfall without any government financial assistance (i.e. before we qualified for the government assistance; if we would not have qualified; and heaven forbid, if the program was to be cancelled)

That is $7117 (total budget required) - $1,500 (her income amount) equaling $5,617

· $2,137/month
Mum's shortfall with government assistance

That is $7117 (total budget required) - $3,480 (government assistance amount) - $1,500 (her personal total income as a senior) equaling $2,137

Question to consider with 'shortfalls': Whom do you think makes up the extra amounts required each month for a parent(s)?

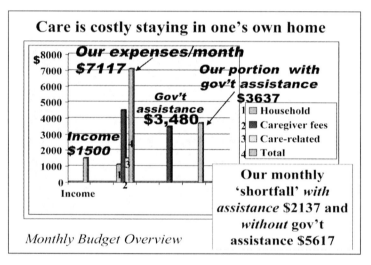

*From Patty's seminars on LTC Planning
Explanation: An overview of our monthly care-budget

The following outlines our budget items considered each month for at-home care (2004/5):

> Caregiver fees per month: ~ $4,500 includes: ~$82 minimum wage fee for 'an 8-hour day' plus CPP, EI, WCB payments and miscellaneous costs (Note: costs varied somewhat from

month to month and this fee was often not acceptable--we
had caregivers refuse the work)

> Other care-related costs per month (averaged): $1507/
month includes such major items as: equipment; caregiver
paid holidays of 14 days; additional caregivers to fill
holiday time; respite care of 4 days/month and evenings;
accommodation and food

> House hold regular expenses per month: $1,110 includes:
hydro, house insurance, groceries, telephone, natural gas—
the usual costs to run a home that all of us have

> Total expenses per month: $ 7,117

What are our choices for funding our long-term care years

Caregiver now, care-receiver tomorrow

*Because of our family's financial experiences in these care-years, I feel
confident advising any reader of this guidebook to plan wisely in order
to cover the costs of taking care of one's parents – and to do so in advance
– I definitely wish that I had done so a long, long time ago.*

*I also strongly recommend that each reader consider discussing with
her/his own financial advisor how to put a care plan in place for one's
own care-years, to cover the costs.*

*It is wise to keep in mind that lifestyle/retirement years may have two
chapters – the pre-care years and the long-term care-years – it is my hope
that at the very minimum, this section of the guidebook will prompt
every reader to review her/his personal and family's financial plans –
now – for the up-coming care-years stage of life.*

Self-Funding –Wealthy	Personal Savings	Annuities	Life Style Planning Long-Term Care Insurance
Life Insurance –Whole universal	Home Equity –loans –Reverse mortgage	Viatical Settlement (not in Canada yet)	Government Programs –Cost Sharing

Our Choices

> Long-term care (whether in one's own home or in a health facility) is the single largest out-of-pocket cost for adults over 60
> —therefore it is a significant risk!

Retirement...Financial planners say people underestimate how long they will live. A person 65 should be planning for another 30 years.

Floyd Murphy, a financial planner (Vancouver) says, "People vastly underestimate how long they will live. A person of 65 should be planning for another 30 years. And the most expensive years will be the last 10, when costly care may be needed."

(Source: RRSP Extra, article by Rosemary McCracken, The Vancouver Sun, February 15, 2006)

> **FACT**
>
> **Who Pays LTC Costs?**
>
> **Families do**, no matter where LTC is located...
>
> **With some assistance** from provincial government programs...
>
> **That assistance varies** in terms of 'services' and/or 'financial help' depending on one's care needs and income

Notes:

_____

_____

_____

_____

_____

_____

_____

_____

_____

_____

_____

_____

_____

_____

Suggestion 48: *Become familiar with the various costs associated with care-years*

Each family situation will differ with care-costs, depending on the number of parents in need of care (e.g. 1-4*), the levels of care required by each parent and the choices that, we, daughter/sons and other family decision-makers, select around the whole issue.

(*For a boomer couple, there may be two sets of elderly parents, requiring some level of care, at some point in time, or heaven forbid, at the same time, then the resulting costs can be significant.)

Once we become fully informed regarding our parents' health circumstances and needs, once we become knowledgeable regarding our parents' savings and financial status and once we develop an awareness of care costs and our funding methods, only then will we be able to develop a monthly budget and discuss methods of meeting our parents' care needs.

Examples of long-term care costs one may encounter

These are examples of the types of long-term care expenses we incurred throughout our family's care-years; each may be used as a guideline for your planning –they are, I feel, the 'basics' for planning. As well, you must check in your own province or territory for these costs when doing your planning for your future needs (and don't forget to factor in inflation each year of 2%-5%).

1. **LTC expense: Safety Equipment:** Each family must budget for this type of cost. My parents' home had to be 'safety-proofed' adding such items as: support bars, bathroom equipment, recliner chair with lifts, walker, wheelchair, exercise items, more telephones... Over time, as health changes took place, we continued adding equipment as required: bedroom equipment, then an electric stair lift *(i.e. as Mum could no longer go up and down the 8 stairs from the front door to the living level— when they retired in the 70s the house they had built was not designed with an aged-future in mind.)*

Cost Guidelines:

☑ Some of the costs of equipment items, in part, may be reimbursed annually from a family's extended health plan upon submission of receipt.

☑ Some of the equipment may be rented from the Red Cross for short periods or from local associations, check in your community.

☑ We found we needed approximately $4,000 for house-safety equipment at the very beginning (prior to hospital discharge) – to assess your home, refer to Topic 4.

☑ Later the costs climbed in relation to the care needs – equipment is an on-going cost one must budget for each month/year – visit your medical supply stores to get an idea of costs of care-related equipment and supplies.

2. **LTC expense: Home Modifications for Caregivers AND Care-receivers**: In order to accommodate our new need for caregivers, we now had to have renovations done to my parent's home – the downstairs recreational room was converted to a living quarter and a bathroom was added downstairs as well. If the house is not set up with a suite or a second living quarters (bedroom, bathroom, some living space, some storage), then this expense must be budgeted for from the beginning if one is going to use a live-in caregiver or over-night caregivers.

Cost Guidelines:

☑ The basic home modification cost our family approximately $2000 as we had two neighbors who were carpenters and 'handy' to do the work. The costs would have been significantly higher had we used a construction team – ask organizations for locally donated help or approach neighbors.

☑ Check/call CMHC Home Modifications guidelines for financial assistance - 1-800-668-2642 or www.cmhc.ca

☑ Cross reference to Topic 4 "Ensuring a Safe and Positive Environment at Home".

3. **LTC expense: Home Maintenance and Up-grades**: A quick note of caution – my parents' retirement home was built in the 1970s and so, here we were some 20 odd years later into their care-years, just as the house started to need some expensive maintenance (e.g. complete new roof, new furnace, air conditioning...). One must be prepared for these home maintenance expenses as well in later years if one is going to remain in one's home for care, that is if we want to 'age in place'.

4. **LTC expense: Emergency Expenses for unexpected situations**: In 2003, the city where Mum was living experienced a brutal forest-fire fire-storm *(Cross-reference to the Personal Anecdote, Topic 11)*, which resulted in costs for yardwork and emergency living conditions (as we were evacuated and moved to a motel for the period of time). Do not think, "that won't happen to me"...as my point here is that every family on LTC journey has to be able to access dollars quickly for unexpected situations. *(Note: I sometimes wonder how I might have handled two parents needing care in this fire-storm emergency, one evacuated from a nursing home and one evacuated from her own home, both requiring significant attention...I would have had to scramble to hire caregivers for the situation as our then live-in caregiver had moved into her own mother's apartment to help out in the same threatened city.)*

Cost Guidelines: Along the journey, we had varying emergencies that any family might encounter.

☑ Caregiver-health-realted emergencies

We had emergency caregiving problems when one of our live-in caregivers had a heart attack (yes, I couldn't believe it either when I got a telephone call to jump on the next plane as Mum was now tending to the caregiver's needs and Dad was leaving respite the next day!).

☑ Caregiver-job replacement-related emergencies

We had need of emergency caregiving when Mum 'let her caregiver go' right on the spot one day and then again, when another announced she was quitting, with no notice (again, I was jumping on a plane).

☑ Travel emergencies - if a 'distance' care-giver/care-guide, one must budget (each month) for travel emergencies.

My message: be prepared for the unexpected—emergency preparedness is not just for a city it is for a family too during its LTC years.

5. **LTC expense: Hiring Expenses: To find live-in or shift caregivers:** There are many 'hiring' expenses around a decision to hire on one's own, such as newspaper advertisements, interviewing, part-time caregiving (i.e. while you do the work of hiring full-time you still need someone in the home to care for parents); time commitments away from one's job obviously have to be considered. Your other option is to use a home care agency instead of hiring on your own, as the company is then responsible for the screening, the everyday schedules; but this option has an added cost attached that a family has to consider as these are for profit businesses *(Note: at times I felt that perhaps the added cost of using an agency might be offset by the responsibility and time commitments spent doing all the work on one's own—you will have to decide based on your situation. I never did use a company as when I checked, the costs, for our family, were too high, but the option, if affordable, is a very good one.)*

6. **LTC expense: Live-in/shift caregiving basic fee and conditions** – At first, I was inexperienced with hiring for this type of position, did not know the rules and regulations for this type of job–no excuse, but I offer this note as an explanation and a warning. I thus 'negotiated' a set monthly salary of $1000 with the first live-in caregivers, plus offered a place to live for her and her family; covered all the food and accommodation and extras required (e.g. television, internet…) for the family and offered to assist with any adult education courses that might want to be taken for skills upgrading. I found this arrangement worked well for a time, but after understanding the employment standards and subsequently educating myself on caregiver hiring practices, I strongly do *not* recommend this method of 'negotiating a fee' – why do I mention it then? I mention it as a heads-up, because some provinces have vague employment guidelines for hiring '24/7 live-in caregivers'

and so families may tend 'to negotiate' salaries (just as used to be done for nanny care in the 80s). There could be a problem with this method as the live-in caregiver when applying for unemployment later (after leaving your employ) may be told that she/he was 'underpaid' and can come back to the family for a pay-settlement (a family on a care-journey doesn't need any more surprises believe me).

I recommend strongly that you check the "Employment Act" for your province (as I finally learned to do) and read the guidelines for caregiving. Unfortunately the guidelines are for workers doing 8-hour jobs and do not give good direction re: a 24/7 caregiver situation. By reading the act, one is able to judge what could be expected as a reasonable salary and use that as a guide for full time live-in/shift employment. I would also suggest that you telephone a couple of local home care agencies and ask what they are charging for a 24-hour day of caregiving, but do keep in mind that these are businesses and they don't usually fill full time live-in/shift positions; nonetheless, the discussion may prove of value as a guideline (e.g. when I telephoned two companies, I delicately asked what would be the 'best fee I could expect' if I used their agency and workers for a 24-hour situation on a monthly basis).

Cost Guidelines: For 24/7 caregiving, I finally settled on (and I repeat, these are just guidelines):

- ☑ A salary of $3,000 – $4,500 per month for a live-in caregiver and all that entailed

- ☑ A budget of $5,000 for several shift caregivers (replacing a live-in situation; for example, 4 caregivers, these are 3 days on, 24/7 shift workers)

- ☑ Living and accommodation expenses (i.e. these amounted to an estimated extra $350-$400/month);

- ☑ Unemployment Insurance payments

- ☑ Canada Pension Plan payments

- ☑ Workers Compensation payments

☑ Use of family vehicle for all work-related tasks with the correct insurance in place (e.g. appointments, grocery shopping...).

☑ I later found that if I were to hire the caregivers as 'consultant-type positions' as they may be 'self-employed', then the UI, CPP, and other compensations and deductions (e.g. book-work) did not have to be done by our family—the caregivers were thus responsible for their own.

Cross-reference to Topic 7, Steps 16 and 17 for 'Managing the administration of a care-situation.'

7. **LTC expense: Respite time** is required if you have caregivers. I offered 4 days a month off for a live-in caregiver, in a sequence allowing the caregiver to 'go home' or to visit family or.... The cost of a respite caregiver will differ for each family, our estimate was a fee of $95-$100 per 24 hour per day as a guideline for a respite care.

Cost guidelines: Unless impossible,

☑ I would do these respite days per month myself as it allowed me time with my parents and time to see how all was working out each month.

☑ I recommend a daughter/son caregiver consider taking on this extra respite commitment especially if in a distant caregiver/care guide role. It may mean time off from a job and the cost of lost wages and lost benefits were not taken into consideration in our costs at any time—but the days each month will be significant and should be budgeted for by a family.

☑ As well note, a family can apply for one week a year respite, through their local health department/authority or CCAC for respite help – apply early in the calendar year, January if possible, for the week you may want as there is little choice available the longer you wait. *(For example, when Dad was still living in his own home, he spent one week in respite care in a nursing home so that Mum and their live-in caregiver could have some time for a break—alas, that is the period that the caregiver had the heart attack so little respite happened for any of the parties.)*

8. **LTC expense: Days off for full-time live-in caregiver—** These days off are required if you have a live-in caregiver. I suggest two or three days off (8 hours) each week (8:00 AM to 4:00 PM worked for us) with caregivers hired for these time slots (we had three persons who would rotate days weekly). We used a budget of $85 per day for these 8 hour shift days.

9. **LTC expense: Holiday pay**—Each caregiver in a live-in situation is entitled to a paid holiday (for example, 14 days after a year of employ). When this caregiver is on paid holiday, one still needs to have a caregiver in place. See Employee Act for your province. (Note: It is the same as running a business – check the Employment standards Act in your province/territory.)

10. **LTC expense: Shift caregivers**—Using shift caregivers offers some flexibility. Our family used them in the following varied manner throughout our journey: as caregivers hired for 8 hour shifts to relieve the live-in caregiver; as respite caregivers when the live-in caregiver needed a full day off; as emergency caregivers in urgent situations due to caregiver illness, flight delays for a returning caregiver, etc; and finally, to replace the live-in caregiver method completely (we were set to use a 3 day on 4 day off rotational system, a shift defined as 24 hours).

Cost Guidelines:

☑ One must take UI/CPP/WC taken into consideration with shift caregiving. *(For example, when I planned for this, our total caregiver fees budget of $5,000/month was allocated to the shift caregiver scenario.)*

☑ When planning on using a several person shift caregiving method versus a live-in caregiver method, one may be able to combine several of the costs, that is the live-in caregiver salary, the days off shift caregiver fees, the 4 day respite fees and then put these dollars together to cover this method of care.

The pros and cons of 'live-in caregiving or rotational shift caregiving' will have to be weighed by each family. *(For us, the cost per month for shift caregivers fees on a monthly basis ranged between $4,500 and $5,000 per month and that amount was considered too low by 2005 as I told by some caregivers; as well, by 2005, it was becoming more difficult to locate people willing to live 'full-time' with a family, especially qualified people who had 'care-certification' as they had the option of working in nursing homes with all the benefits attached.)*

11. **LTC expense: Self-Managed Care or Independent Living (Financial) Subsidizations**—Each province has a type of 'independent living' program. This type of program enables a senior (or other in need due to a wide range of disabilities) to live in one's own home with the family 'managing their loved one's own care program'. These government subsidization programs have strict guidelines and accountability built in (good!). Call your own home care health authority or CCAC or health unit and ask about "self-managed LTC programs" and their criteria for application; ask to discuss the possibility with a care nurse coordinator. *(For example, our family used the Choices in Support for Independent Living CSIL, program in BC, once I found out about it and 'applied', for my mother's care—an assessment of the care level required is undertaken and helps the health unit care coordinator set the subsidized amount a family is to receive).* One more note, when seeking assistance, do not limit yourself to asking about services and programs for 'seniors' only, ask also what is available as 'disability programs'. *(With the self-managed care program, I used to say that what I really set up was a 'mini-nursing home' for my mother in her own home—and that was the truth as that is exactly what families must be prepared to do when a loved one wants 'to age in place').*

For further information, go to www.longtermcarecanada.com click on the 'Government Programs' menu and then on the 'Provincial Programs' dropdown menu and select the 'Care Programs' for your province and territory. Most of these programs give access to contacts and information plus the self-managed care subsidy program criteria.

12. **LTC expense: Nursing home care** – The cost of nursing home care is easy to discover. You can visit (as I did) several nursing homes in the area required and ask for their private-pay fees. *(For example, in 1997, our*

costs were $3,120 per month basic for Dad's carehome living–one must also ask what this basic fee covers and what 'extras' a family must budget to pay for over and above the basic accommodation fee, in our case, these extras ranged from $250 and up each month depending on Dad's needs—ambulance costs, ice-cream socials, hair-cuts–all the little things). It is estimated that inflation is approximately 5% for nursing home living (my research findings in Canada haven't found that (I've found 2%), but it does depend on the province and the type of home and the type of care required—therefore check!). The fee range charged by nursing homes vary greatly…do your homework. Some nursing homes still offer only specific levels of care (although most now recognize that they will lose their client-base if they don't offer many levels of care). Some nursing homes have no subsidized beds; some have a mixture of public subsidized beds (i.e. government subsidized) plus private pay beds/rooms. Nursing homes are not to be confused with "Assisted Living" residences, whereby some services are offered and some can be 'added' as needed – but not 'full care' (assisted living is not discussed in this guide book).

A note on Nursing home subsidizations: First of all, let's be clear, subsidization does not mean 'free'. I suggest that people think of subsidization like a 'partnership' for the care of a loved one, the government may pay part and the family pays part. Subsidization means that the provincial government will, upon assessment of 'annual income' (find out the definition for your province/territory as some provinces/territories also assess 'assets') and upon meeting set criteria, assist families with the cost of nursing home care for a loved one. The subsidization covers some of the cost of the room and board but does not cover it all—that's where the individual and family comes in as they must pay the balance each month. Each province offers a nursing home subsidization program based on a formula, which is reviewed often (usually quarterly, but as a minimum annually) in accordance to the cost of living—this subsidization, as mentioned, is to assist families with the financial costs of the care of a loved one in a nursing home situation. The subsidization formula in all of the provinces in Canada is based on income testing, and some on asset testing–but 'asset testing' is not always the rule, so do check by calling your local health authority or seniors' advisory group. There is some 'baggage' attached to applying for and receiving subsidizations for nursing home care—can you get into the one you want; will you have to share a room; is there a wait time before you can get a loved one placed; what do you do in the meantime…? *(For example, Dad could no longer be cared for at home so we applied for a subsidization for his nursing home care, such was not available (i.e. no beds) at that time in the nursing home we selected; thus, we had a choice, he could move into that nursing home and we would assume the full cost or we could keep him at home until we were able to get a 'subsidized bed'. We chose to have Dad move to the nursing home and we assumed 100% of the costs while we waited for a subsidized spot to come open…we did not feel we had any choice due to his health demands.)* I would not recommend, at any time, that any family 'count' on government subsidization—just in case it is not available when one needs it, or at all.

13. **LTC expense: Extra companion-caregiving when in a nursing home:** This particular care-related cost is, in my opinion, not an optional one although at first glance, it may appear so. It covers 'companionship', for example, the one-day a week caregiver you may hire for 4 hours or more one day each week as a 'social companion' for your parent to take him/her on outings or be present. *(For example, Dad knew the lady we hired; we arranged that she would take him out Wednesday afternoons every week for a drive, an ice-cream cone, a burger…a change of pace. This extra outing worked out well for Dad as he felt special and considered her a good friend, and she was; he truly looked forward to this time.)* The cost of this care companion was discussed ahead of time and a constant 'retainer' was set and paid monthly by the family *(Dad never knew we 'paid' for this service, it wasn't necessary that he know).*

14. **LTC expense: 'Extra' costs to a monthly budget for a daughter/ son caregiver:** These expenses each month now must be added to a family's monthly budget, they include: travel costs; extra groceries while visiting each month; restaurant costs as you will want to take your parents out for a break; miscellaneous you will now provide more often as they will need 'a lift' at times –chocolates, plants, florist treats; as well there are tax accounting costs as income tax now will demand a full understanding of care-deductions; long-distance telephone costs (e.g. to parents, to caregivers, to pharmacy, to doctor, to specialists, to hospitals, to health authority care coordinator…).

Statistics Canada's research on caregivers tells us that we should budget between $300 - $500/month for these 'extras' when we become caregivers of parents. My own findings over the first six years of our journey put my 'extras' for this category only at $550 - $869. (Of course, where one actually lives in relation to one's parents will determine the monthly costs.)

15. **LTC expense: Loss of Income**–Job-related costs were not calculated nor tracked on our care-journey, as the costs away from the job whether employed or self-employed are not only difficult to calculate but also difficult to guestimate...alas, they are real and must be accounted for as part of a care-related budget. Note: Remember for each day off the job as a 'working caregiver', not only is monthly income affected, but alas CPP and other benefits are affected.

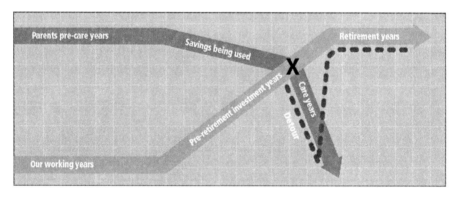

This graph illustrates what happens when parents' care years begin (X) and intersect an adult child's retirement savings plans.

The parent's savings drop rapidly as their savings are now going to LTC needs.

As well, their child's savings go on what I have termed a 'care detour' (author's words). The 'care detour' is obvious as an adult child has to start helping with LTC costs and is usually able to do so from two areas: time off from work or withdrawal from our retirement savings (RRSPs, etc.)

The scenario also makes one question what happens if the adult child is already retired when a parent(s) requires financial assistance for care. Again, this trend in Canada, senior children looking after senior parent(s) – with both sets now in their retirement years possibly, is becoming more and more common. (Calculate your age when your parents are 88 or so years old.) This graph makes it apparent that one has to prepare well in advance for one's own long-term – care years too.

Use the budget page following for your calculations – don't procrastinate – plan for your LTC-years and enjoy life now with no worries as to later.

FAMILY CARE BUDGET SHEET

HOUSEHOLD ITEM	MONTHLY AMOUNT	NOTES
HOUSEHOLD BASICS–MONTHLY Vehicle, light, telephone, heat, groceries, etc		
ANNUAL HOME COSTS		
AT HOME CAREGIVER COSTS - Live-in/Shift • Fees, full-time • Fees, shift • Workers Comp • Unemployment Insurance • CPP • Respite • Holiday Pay • Accommodation & Food • Extras		
NURSING HOME • Nursing Home room and board • Miscellaneous costs • Companion caregiver		
EXTRAS • Extra needs		
ORGANIZATION • Accounting • Bookkeeping company, monthly • Chartered Accounting firm, annually, taxes		
FAMILY EXPENSES ('Extras')		
MEDICAL NEEDS AND SUPPLIES		
EQUIPMENT		
HOUSE RENOVATIONS/REPAIRS/MAINTENANCE		
ASSISTANCE—yard, trees, lawn….		
TOTAL		% change from last month

Author's Conclusion: *I would say based on my family's care experiences and my own research and training, over the years that a Canadian family should plan to have approximately $400,000 for their potential care-years journey – depending on the number of persons needing care and the number of years spent in long-term care – as this is guideline.*

Let's do the math:

Scenario: One couple in their own home, one or both needing care eventually, for a short period spanning 5 years; using a modest $6,000/month for at-home care (that is running one's house and paying fees and all other requirements) $6000 x 12 months x 5 care-related years =$360,000

Scenario: One couple in their own home, one or both needing care eventually, for a period of 2 years; using a modest $6000/month for the complete at-home situation (as above): $6000 x 12 months x 2 years = $144,000 for that 2 year period; then one of the couple needs nursing home care for a period of 2 years due to a frail state and let's use a modest amount of $4000/month for nursing home care: $4000 x 12 months x 2 years = $96,000 but the other spouse stays at-home with care for the same 2 year period (overlapping care-years): $6000 x 12 months x 2 years = $144,000. The amount needed for this 4 year span of care-years for a couple who eventually experiences 'involuntary separation' is now: $144,000 while they are together needing care+ $96,000 for one spouse+ $144,000 for the second spouse at the same time = $384,000

But long-term care often lasts for a much greater span than 5 years! So, you do the math for yourself....don't procrastinate, just plan...you are going to live a long life, so plan now and enjoy all stages!

Note: 22% of Canadians have been caregivers for 10 years and 22% for more than ten years, thus you can see that 'long' term care is well named.

I think it is fair to say that this is a very large amount for most Canadians and because I don't have such myself put aside for my very own care-years, I have become an advocate of long-term care insurance. I have policies in place for myself and my husband and even though I dislike the idea of more taken from out of our monthly bank account for insurance, I feel we have no other way to plan well for the financial aspects of our future care. Thus, combined with pensions and savings, these LTC insurance plans will allow us the quality care we may require.

I've learned, peace of mind, protection of assets, quality care and most of all independence are important when planning for one's future. I also want to enjoy my lifestyle now without having to fret over tomorrow and what it may/ may not bring.

To me it is the same as house, car and other insurance policies. I don't self ensure these two large assets and the risks of anything happening – I purchase policies in case something happens – so why would I want to risk self ensuring my long-term care when I can now buy a policy for that risk as well?

*Talk to your financial advisor or call Advocis to ask for a list of planners in your city/area (**www.advocis.ca**). Or call your insurance agent to discuss an LTCI policy.*

Cross-reference to Topic 13 for further thoughts on LTC insurance.

As I am not an advisor or insurance agent, this discussion on LTC insurance I have written from an educated consumer's point of view. Also go to www. longtermcarecanada.com for a further review on the topic. Note: Wouldn't it be wonderful if your provincial government decided to offer the public (us) an LTC education program <u>AND</u> an incentive program such as deduction of LTCI premiums now with no penalty when we receive the premium later – since LTCI reduces our dependency on government programs (sort of like our RRSP program incentive at tax time). Just a thought – perhaps a post-card written to your MLA would receive attention? At the end of this book, such is provided – just clip, sign and send to your elected representative.

*Financial planning is very personal, what works for one person or family can not be applied to another—my message is to put a care-plan in place for yourself...**while there is still time.***

Canada Customs and Revenue Agency

April 2003

Seniors who are eligible to claim the disability amount can claim attendant-care expenses paid to a retirement home as a medical expense

Starting with the 2002 tax year, seniors who are eligible to claim the disability amount and who live in a retirement home can claim attendant care expenses as a medical expense.

There is no change to the basic rules to claim the costs of attendant care (guide RC4064, *Information Concerning People with Disabilities*).

What's new is that for 2002 and later tax years, the rules also apply to seniors who are eligible to claim the disability amount and who receive part-time attendant care in a retirement home. This is not reflected in the 2002 version of the guide, but it will be part of the updated guide for the 2003 tax year.

The following must be provided for a claim to be allowed:

1. Proof of payment, such as a receipt, that shows the actual amount paid specifically for attendant care (as opposed to rent, for example). As the service provider, the retirement home should determine the amount paid specifically for attendant care.

2. The senior must be eligible to claim the disability amount by having Form T2201, *Disability Tax Credit Certificate*, certified by a qualified person and approved by the Canada Customs and Revenue Agency (CCRA).

Generally, attendant care covers the salaries and wages paid to employees of a retirement home who provide the following:

• health care

• meal preparation

• housekeeping for the resident's personal living space

• laundry services for the resident's personal items

(Continued...)

- transportation driver

- security (in secured units)

The claim for attendant care is the portion of the salary and wages of all such attendants that can reasonably apply to the senior, but is limited to $10,000 per year ($20,000 in the year of death). The claim for attendant-care expenses can be made in addition to amounts claimed under the Disability Tax Credit.

Eligible seniors who have already filed their 2002 tax return can request an adjustment by visiting our Web site at ccra. gc.ca/tax/individuals/faq/t1adj-e.html.

A request for adjustment can also be made by sending in a completed Form T1-AJD, *T1 Adjustment Request* or a signed letter that explains the request. The letter must include the senior's social insurance number, address, a daytime phone number, and the supporting documentation.

In addition, this attendant-care change applies to past tax years if a *Notice of Objection* (an appeal) has already been filed but has not yet been ruled on, or if a *Notice of Objection* can still be filed for the tax year(s) in question.

For information on appeals, visit the CCRA Web site at ccra. gc.ca or see the pamphlet called *Your Rights*.

The pamphlet is available on our Web site www.ccra.gc.ca or you can order it by calling 1-800-959-2221.

For general tax enquiries, call 1-800-959-8281.

What if I don't have a plan in place yet to cover the costs of my parents' care-years, what do I need to consider?

As alluded to in the very beginning of the guidebook, for planning purposes, it is wise to divide lifestyle but especially our retirement years into two parts or passages:

- The regular retirement years which we all look forward to, save for, see advertisements about, these are our independent years, the pre-care years – these may be the years your parents (and you) are enjoying right now.

- Then there is another possible part to retirement, one which we rarely acknowledge, hardly ever talk about, plan very little for, these are our increasing dependent years, our long-term care-years – these are the years when 'caregiving' shapes our lifestyles.

It is necessary to talk about retirement planning in terms of these two sections or chapters as the financial planning for each of these two times is very different and 'both' require special thought.

(As mentioned, my parents' care-years began when my parents were in their mid-eighties living on a fixed income supported by careful savings – they are a classic example of what usually happens with the elderly – when their savings are going down, their living costs are going up dramatically due to the expenses associated with care needs. My parents had not considered the care-years chapter of their lives in their retirement planning (they retired in 1972). Given that the life expectancy then was calculated to be in the low 70's age range and given that retirement pensions did not become a priority with employers until later in our parents' working lives, not only were their pension incomes very small, but also they were living longer now due to advances in medicine.)

Public purse covers 70% of Canadian health-care bill, study shows

It's no secret that health spending in Canada has soared in recent years to $130 billion in 2004 from $37 billion in 1984.

In the 20-year period examined, population increases accounted for 14 per cent, or $13-billion, of new spending, while inflation accounted for 45 per cent, or $42-billion.

The balance, 41 per cent, or $38-billion, was because of changed in health-care practice, including new drugs and other innovative therapies, according to the study by the Canadian Institute for Health Information, an independent non-profit organization that provides data on the health-care system. "This is the first detailed break-down of where the new money is going," institute president Glenda Yates said...

"About 60 per cent is due to more people in the system and inflation, and 40 percent of growth is because we're doings things differently." "Hopefully, this kind of data will inform the debate."

Of the $130-billion in annual health spending, about $95.5-billion is paid out of the public purse and $34.5 billion privately.

The private monies include insurance and out-of-pocket expenses, which are split about evenly.

That means that about one in every seven dollars spent on health care in Canada–$17-billion a year–is paid directly out of pocket, a figure Ms. Yeates said most Canadians will probably find surprising. More surprising still is that out-of-pocket spending in Canada is similar to that in the United States. The U.S. system, however, has only 45 percent public spending and relies much more heavily on private insurance.

(continued...)

...While 70 per cent of Canadian's health spending comes through the public sector, it is less than the amount spent in Britain (83 per cent), Germany (78 percent) and France (76 per cent) but more than in the Netherlands (62 per cent) and the United States (45 per cent).

"I don't think anybody can say what is the right public-private mix, " Richard Saltman, a professor of health policy at Emory University in Atlanta, "It's really a values question."

Canada finances almost all hospital and physician services with public dollars, while prescription drugs, dental care and nursing-home care are paid principally with private funds.

In France, which has a similar public-private mix overall, a far greater percentage of public money is spent on drugs and dental care, but citizens pay for a good chunk of hospital and physician services.

"Asked how Canada stacks up against other developed countries, Dr. Saltman said "decently." He said Canada is essentially "middle of the pack" in terms of per capita spending on health, and its overall public-private mix of funding.

According to the report, higher spending does not necessarily translate into better access to care. The CIHI report cited a 2004 study that shows 40 per cent of Americans went without care in the previous year because of the cost, while in Britain the figure was 9 per cent.

In Canada, 17 per cent of those surveyed said they had gone without care because of the cost, but for the most part they had skimped on drugs and dental care, not basic medical care. The CIHI has offices in Ottawa, Toronto, Edmonton and Victoria.

(Article by Andre Picard, Public Health Reporter, National Post, 2005)

What is involved in planning?

Planning requires that we address four questions – honestly:

- The first looks at our parents' present and on-going financial status.

- The second addresses our financial ability to help our parents with the expenses incurred during their care-years.

- The third focuses on helping our parents prepare for their future care needs.

- The fourth centers on our personal initiatives for our own care needs.

Question #1 – Will my parents' present retirement finances cover their care-years?

☑ Can my parent's income/savings/investments/assets cover the monthly costs of caregiving for both of them/one of them?

☑ For differing levels of care as needs change and in different locations (if required)?

☑ For how long?

52% Back Private Care

More than half of Canadians believe they should be allowed to pay for private health care, as long as there is also free care available for all who need it, a new poll finds (Leger Marketing) Quebecers were most likely to support a private system along side the public one, with 65% saying yes, followed by British Columbia at 56%, the poll found. Ontario and Alberta leaned slightly to the no side, with 46% and 45% in favour of private care. Only 37% of respondents in the Atlantic were in favour of private care. *(Source: National Post, April 26, 2005)*

Question #2 – Will I be able to help with the costs of care for my parents – immediately if need be? In the near future?

☑ Can my own personal budget cover all/part/a little of the monthly costs of care for each of my parents/one parent? (Can my present monthly budget expand to absorb more expenses?)

☑ What types of care duties can I offer to help with (i.e. do myself) in order to offset the costs? How long can I expect to be able to offer that assistance? What then? (What of help from siblings? Relatives?)

☑ If I have to help (with $) during my parents' care-years, what will be the financial impact on the rest of my immediate family (i.e. spouse/partner, children)? On my future?

☑ How will taking care of my parents affect my job, my pensions, my benefits and long-term savings?

☑ How will taking care of my parents affect my retirement plans? Possible relocation plans, if any?

☑ How will taking care of my parents affect my everyday activities – would they have to be revised due to these new on-going financial responsibilities, care emergency costs?

Question #3 – How do I go about preparing for my parents' care-years?

☑ Can I do something now to prepare for some of these inevitable care-years expenses for my parents? Who can help me? Where do I begin?

☑ Do I understand some of the programs and services for care available in my province/territory (research/call a health unit, don't rely on neighbour chatter for accurate information)?

☑ What are my financial planning options? What are the costs associated? What exactly should I ask?

☑ What plans have they in place to safeguard their hard-earned assets/savings if/when they need part-time or full-time care and attention?

Question #4 – Is 'my own house' in order? *(Cross reference to Topic 13)*

☑ What about my own care if required as many are dependent on me?

☑ Have I a well-thought out 'care plan' in place for myself (my wishes, my documents, finances…)?

☑ Do I need/have a long-term-care insurance (LTCI) plan in place (the younger age the purchase, the less the monthly costs)? (Health is a factor in planning at any stage.)

☑ Do I have/need a critical illness (CI) policy in place?

☑ Have I a disability policy (DI) with my employer in place? What is my option if I am self-employed?

☑ Do I have a life policy in place designated for my parents' care? *(For example, as I was somewhat financially responsible for my parents care, I had to have a plan in place should something happen to me, thus I had a life insurance policy on myself with my parents as beneficiaries. When my parents were fairly capable, this was made payable directly to them; when their care-years started, this policy was in a type of trust situation for their care with my husband and my best friend as directors.)*

☑ Am I prepared personally for my own long-term care (if needed now due to some catastrophic health event, think of Christopher Reeves, or later when I am in my late 80's)? If yes, should I do a review of my plans? If no, why not and what am I waiting for?

A care-plan = LTCI policy, a CI policy, a Life insurance policy, a written financial plan, documents up-to-date, a well-informed care-guide in place…
– P. Randall 2006

"You don't waste time fixing the car, so why would you wait to fix your body," orthopedic surgeon says

Cost* of going private (e.g. at the Cambie Surgery Centre, B.C.) for some operations:

(*Prices re approximate and depend on severity and complexity of the case, time in recovery and tools or implants required. * Fees are for the facility. For (B.C.) patients, the surgeon's fee is paid by the Medical Services Plan)

- Ankle and foot surgery: $800 - $5,500
- Ankle replacement: $16,000 to $17,000
- Cataract: $900
- Elbow repair or ligament reconstruction: $2,400 - $3,950
- Gallbladder removal: $3,800
- Hand or wrist surgery: $2, 250 - $4,500
- Hernia repair: $2,500
- Hip arthroscopy (minimally invasive cartilage repair): $6,000
- Knee cartilage or ligament repair or reconstruction: $3,00 - $7,500
- Should dislocation repair: $2,900 - $6,000
- Spinal surgery: $6,300 - $12,500 (discs, fusions)

(Source: Body degenerates as patients wait, The Vancouver Sun, June 3, 2005, Special Report, Stories by Pamela Fayerman)

"Beware of small expenses; a small leak will sink a great ship.:
— *Benjamin Franklin 1706-1790*

Would you want to live to 100? From cost of living to responsibilities of care giving, retirement is not always playtime

Although we've gamely gauged middle age as beginning some time close to 50, it's only recently that living to 100 has become a real possibility. The number of over-100s in Canada is increasing every year. Nearly a million Canadians are now 80-plus and the over-80s are the fastest growing segment of the population, up 21 per cent in the past five years.

We're not all going to make it to 100, but if you want to check your chances, there's an age calculator at **www.livingto100. com** It certainly makes you re-think what middle age is. And that's just the start of the re-thinking.

...all sorts of interesting and unexpected questions (arise). What if you end up like 73-year old lawyer Bill Landau...he can afford to retire, wants to retire but this dad and law partner won't let him! What if you decide to be the good child, start taking care of your 80-year-old mother but 20 years later she's still going strong?

The growing group of oldsters is now important enough that marketers have come up with some cutesy names. There are the "go-go years" the "slow-go years" and the "no-go years" – the ones no one is looking forward to. Grey-haireds in the go-go years are being targeted by the advertisers selling time shares, vacation homes, cycling tours, walking tours, anti-inflammatories and, of course, Viagra. They're the darlings of the people who sell motor homes, expensive sports cars and motorcycles.

The slow-goers are tempted by ads for "gracious living" in assisted-care homes with beautifully appointed restaurants, call bells in every room and –in small print–the convenience of being just steps away from the next level of care, which is what we used to call nursing homes.

Even the no-goers are targeted. Sadly, mostly by funeral homes and lawyers offering to do or re-do their wills.

(continued...)

BUT, as "The Sun's Smart Money" columnist, Michael Kane has been reporting this week, the problem isn't so much what are we going to do with all of this extra time, but how are we going to afford it.

As Kane pointed out, if you do live to 100, you need to have $5,433,160 in the bank at 65 to have even $3,000 a month to spend.

Yet the average Canadian only has about $60,000 in a registered retirement savings plan (which is probably the reason most Canadians list winning the lottery as part of their retirement strategy).

The reality is that instead of winters on snow-white beaches, most Canadians will-of necessity- spend their "golden years" as greeters at Wal-mart, ticket-takers in movie theaters, doing some other low-paid, part-time job.

It's almost enough to make me consider taking up smiling or skydiving in my 80s because most of those greeters will be women. Not only do women live longer, they have earned less and saved less than men.

Sadly, women's failure to break through the glass ceiling in large numbers means that the only ceiling most will likely be poking their heads through is the "silver ceiling". Female baby boomers will be the largest group of Canadians ever who – out of necessity – will work into their 70s and possibly beyond.

It makes a lie out of virtually everything they were told. Growing up in the 1950s, they were encouraged to be stay-at-home-moms like their mothers. But few had that choice. Housing prices rose too quickly. Many studied hard, got an education but didn't have a realistic chance at the really high-paid jobs. Times just didn't change that quickly. Many of those with well-paid jobs took time off to have children, cut back their hours to look after them or in middle age, to take time out to look after elderly parents. Everybody assured them they were doing the right thing.

Yet, single, divorce and widowed women over 65 are already four times more likely than men to live in poverty. Increased longevity will only add more years of scrambling and scrimping to pay the rent and buy groceries. (Daphne Bramham, Columnist, Vancouver Sun, January 14, 2005)

Suggestion 49: *Face the facts – Be realistic when planning for care-years*

We must take our blinders off – we can't remain 'in denial' about ageing – it doesn't mean we need to think 'old' it just means that we are aware and have 'all our ducks' in a row. A 'let's wait and see' attitude is a recipe for disaster within a family – we can begin by facing some facts.

What about long-term care-year one?

Face the facts – Providing good care is expensive – even with some government assistance.

Face the facts:

- ☑ How much money will my parents and I need to cover **one year's care expenses** for one or both of my parents?

- ☑ Do I have any financial resources at hand to cover my own **'extras'** portion that is often required during caregiving, approximately $500-900/month?

- ☑ What about the costs of **crisis care situations**, do I have a reserve fund tucked away to help me during those emergency times (which unfortunately are frequent during care-years)?

- ☑ What will my family do if we cannot access **government services** right away or only partially – what if our financial assistance application is accepted but does not become available at the precise time we need to put care into place for our parents – how do we manage in the meantime (e.g. months or one year)?

...Only 36 per cent of Canadians have discussed long-term care plans candidly with their parents or in-laws

The (Ipso-Reid) survey found that 63 per cent of Canadians say they will feel guilty unless they can adequately provide parents or in-laws with the kind of help or social assistance they will need at some point.

The societal challenge of aging is enormous Mindszenthy said... Nearly three quarters of all Canadians have living parents or in-laws, and 22 per cent of all Canadians are 60 or older. With the first of 10 million baby boomers turning 60 in 2006, those numbers are set to explode over the next two decades.

"And then you have today's multi-family connections," Mindszenthy said. "My daughter got married two years ago, and she has seven parents as a result of divorce and remarriage." At the same time young adults are increasingly moving back home when their job or relationship goes awry. That's the "boomerang" component squeezing the Sandwich Generation from the other end of the age spectrum.

"You've got pressure from both ends and then there is workplace pressure," Mindszenthy said. "All of a sudden you have people saying "I have to take my mother to a doctor's appointment," and they are using up holidays and sick days which, more than ever, they really need for themselves."

A Statistics Canada indicates that more than 4 million Canadians aged 45 through 75 are providing informal care to those 65 and older who are experiencing long-term health problems. Workplace consequences range from reduce hours and lost income to turning down job opportunities or actually quitting work.

(Source: "Parenting Your Parents", authors, Mindszenthy and Gordon, citing Ipsos Reid polling; article, "Few discuss long-term care plans with parents, in-laws", Michael Kane, The Vancouver Sun, January 13, 2005)

What about care-years three to five?

Face the facts – The financial demands involved in caring for parents for an average of three years seriously impacts any family's resources and a daughter or son's personal savings.

Face the facts:

☑ Do I know what financial plans my parents have in place at present that could assist with the cost of three to five years of caregiving? What if care is required longer – 10 years?

☑ Does our whole family have the combined resources to cover three years of caregiving in a nursing home? In their own home? A combination of both (what if there occurs 'an involuntary separation')?

☑ How dependent are my parents going to be on me financially over three to five care years? What if something happens to me during their care-years – have I got that covered? *(For example, I had a life insurance policy on myself payable to my parents for their monthly care, just in case something happened to me.)*

Face the facts – Hidden care expenses add up.

In addition, which care costs do I have to include in an on-going monthly budget? What will these extras total each month and who will have the available resources to pay for these care requirements as they are required?

☑ Renovations to the house.

☑ Special equipment.

☑ Prescription medications/Over the counter drug store needs.

☑ Special dietary needs.

☑ Supplies for each parent (e.g. briefs for incontinence, foam for beds, sheep skin on chairs, bedding pads...).

☑ Transportation needs.

☑ Rehabilitation treatments.

☑ Eyewear, dentures, hearing aids.

☑ Adult day care programs.

☑ Home care services.

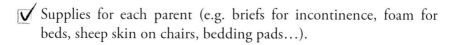

According to Statistics Canada, 20 per cent of women and 13 per cent of men aged 45 to 54 reduced their work hours to meet eldercare demands.

(Source: "Caregiver leave program lacks heart", column, Second Opinion, Andre Picard, The Globe and Mail, September 29, 2005)

What about a longer period?

Face the facts – Taking care of our parents over a long period of time often means putting our own saving plans on hold (or even using our own retirement saving RRSPs for parent-care).

Planning for several years care scenarios is very difficult:

☑ What if eventually we have two parents in need of carehome residency, will our family be able to cover the costs? (Will we have to sell our parents' house to do so... or what?)

☑ Am I able to review their financial resources and care-plans and judge what is available for long-term? If need be, can we access some assistance programs in our region to help my parents as their resources are gradually depleted – are we confident that the programs will even be offered when we need them? When would we need such financial assistance to kick in 'if' we qualify, in year one of their care, in year three or later? *(Question to ponder: Are Canadians relying somewhat on our government to take care of our parents/us?)*

☑ Will my financial support for my parents' care be able to continue beyond five or more years?

☑ Will I be willing to/be forced to move in with my parents or move my parents into my own home to help with the caregiving?

If, at any time of the year, you (either alone or with another person) maintained a dwelling where you and a dependant lived together, you may be able to claim a maximum amount of $3,848. The dependant must have been one of the following individuals:

☑ Your or your spouse or common-law partner's child or grandchild; or

☑ Your or your spouse or common-law partner's brother, sister, niece, nephew, aunt, uncle, parent, or grandparent who was resident in Canada.

You cannot claim this amount for a person who was only visiting you.

As well, your dependant must have met all of the following conditions. The person must have:

☑ Been 18 or over at the time he or she lived with you;

☑ Had a net income of less than $16,989 (line 236 of his or her return, or what line 236 would be if he or she filed a return); and

☑ Been dependent on you due to physical or mental infirmity or, if he or she is your or your spouse or common-law partner's parent or grandparent, born in 1940 or earlier.

Source: Canada's Revenue Agency, December 2006; updated annually; for further information go to:
http://www.hrsdc.gc.ca/en/lifeevents/caregiver.shtml

Face the facts – As caregivers of our parents, there are few tax benefits we can claim to off-set the costs. The following article explains. Note: It is important to call a local charted Accounting firm to get up-dates yearly.

If, during the year, you (either alone or with another person) maintained a dwelling "where you and a dependent live", you may be able to claim the caregiver amount ($3,848 as of 2005). The dependent must have been one of the following individuals:

- your or your spouse's (common-law partners) child or grandchild;

- your brother, sister, niece, or nephew, parent, or grandparent (including in-laws) who was resident in Canada; or

- your aunt or uncle who was resident in Canada.

In addition, the dependent must have met "all' of the following conditions. The person must have:

- been 18 or over at the time he or she lived with you;

- had a net income (or would have had a net income if he or she filed a return) of less than $16,989 (2005); and

- been dependent on you due to mental or physical infirmity or, if he or she is your parent or grandparent (including in-laws), born in 1940 or earlier.

If you and another person support the same dependent, you can split the claim for that dependent. However, the total of your claim and the other person's claim cannot be more than the maximum amount allowed for that dependent.

You cannot claim this amount for a dependent if "anyone" claims an amount for infirm dependents age 18 or older for that dependent or "anyone other than you" claims an equivalent amount for an eligible dependent. This means "you" can claim this amount for the same dependent. *(Source: MacKay LLP, a western and northern Canada based firm of Chartered Accountants, April 2005.)*

Face the facts – I cannot afford to overlook putting some plans in place for myself, now that my parents are somewhat dependent on me.

☑ What if something happens to me (accident, illness, death), how would that impact my parents (care-wise)?

For example, as an only child with dependent parent(s), I had personal plans in place for two reasons:

1 – Taking care of my parents became my financial responsibility and these plans were to help me meet that obligation, to some degree, if a problem were to arise.

2 – I have learned my lessons well when it comes to planning, for my own care needs, if they occur unexpectedly and in my retirement years. I want to be able to enjoy my savings without worrying about keeping large sums of dollars aside for the care-years possibility).

*I have a **critical illness policy** worth $50,000 in case of a critical diagnosis. This policy would be able to help me for a short-term while trying to grapple with the consequences of my health condition and my parents care previously.*

*I had a life **insurance policy for $250,000 designating my parent(s) as sole beneficiaries**; it was set up as a type of trust for their/her care (contact a lawyer to handle the details for this type of arrangement). Having this policy in place 'lightened my worry-load' – I considered it one component of my planning (I simply changed beneficiaries when both of my parents had died, keeping the policy.)*

*And, of course I have **long-term-care policies for myself and my husband** – hopefully for use a long time in the future or better yet, never, but who knows? Do you agree that life takes many paths?*

"In this world, nothing is certain but death and taxes."
– Benjamin Franklin 1706-1790

Suggestion 50: *Find out well-in-advance the options available to cover the costs of different care situations – we need a LTC- financial literacy program for Canadians.*

Planning for long-term care-years requires discussions with professional financial planning/insurance advisors – we must be able to understand our options and put the most appropriate plans in place for our family members and ourselves.

What are my options when planning?

We have **three basic options** for covering care-years expenses (as far as I can determine – and – hoping to win a lottery isn't one of them).

Option: Assume 100% of the costs within our combined family unit—self ensure (note my comments in suggestion 48).

☑ We can use our parents' income/savings/investment portfolios. *(Reminder, once again – We must keep in mind that these caregiving-related costs may be coming at a point in time when our parents' retirement financial resources are dwindling.)*

☑ We can access our own personal monthly income (e.g. salary, pensions) as well as our own long-term savings (portfolios/RRSPs).

☑ If our parents own their own home completely, we can apply for what is termed a reverse mortgage with the government agency responsible and use those funds (a percentage of the assessed value). *(Note: If for estate planning reasons, we are listed as co-owners with our parents on their home, then a reverse mortgage may not possible as the requirement states that the home must be 100% owned by the actual 65 year old owner applying.)*

☑ Depending on the level of care required, we can have our parents move in with us and take care of them in our own home or we can move in with them to help with their care. We can also share the care duties and time allotments with other family members.

☑ We can use a combination of the above methods.

Why care-for-life contracts can be a 'disaster' for the elderly - As our population ages, more of these kinds of agreements are being made between family members and friends - At the start, it seemed to be a sensible arrangement between loving family members. Juliana, a retired Surrey businesswoman, was finding it increasingly difficult to live alone so she sat down with her daughter Maria and son-in-law Hugh and together they crafted what lawyers call a "care for life" contract. She would transfer her house to the young couple in return for their promise to provide food, lodging and care through her old age. At the start, such arrangements often do appear to make good sense. If only life were so predictable. They simply could not "get along." Juliana commenced legal action against the young couple, seeking to have the contract set aside on the basis that it was unconscionable and involved undue influence. This of course made a bad situation much worse around the house and Hugh and Maria asked her to move out for the duration of the hearings. Juliana moved in with her other son, and added a breach-of-contract allegation against Maria and Hugh for kicking her out. The case landed in British Columbia Supreme Court four years ago (1997), and the judge sent all parties packing to their tarred nest and their messy (but still binding) contract. Rewarding the young couple 80 per cent of their court costs, the judge admonished them to continue performing their duties despite hardship and inconvenience. "Living together for the parties, particularly after this litigation, will be awkward and difficult, but not impossible," he wrote in his July 1997 decision. Awkward and difficult are among the mildest terms Vancouver lawyer Margaret Hall uses to describe the fallout from poorly conceived care-for life agreements. "Dangerous" and "devastating" are often closer to the mark, Hall says... As our population ages, she notes, more of these kinds of agreements are being made between family members and friends. Often they are driven by factors such as tight real estate market and the increasing rarity of stay-at-home daughters. "Older people of otherwise very modest means are living on extremely expensive real estate," she observes.   (continued...)

"The family home, which the senior is reluctant to sell, may be hotly coveted by adult children, who may themselves be priced out of home ownership – let alone in the old neighbourhood." Add to that scenario a pair of rose-coloured glasses: "Nobody wants to imagine that living with your mother (or if you're a mother, living with your grown son) may turn out to be anything less than mutually enjoyable." Now add a stroke, or chronic depression, or pressure from other family members, or a financial crisis arising from overloaded caregiver's inability to carry on paid employment, and there you have it: danger, leading to devastation, perhaps even to death. Indeed, an "incentive to hurry death" is the way one American lawyer, a specialist in elder abuse, describes a worst-case scenario, in which the caregiver, exhausted and stressed by the demands of the agreement, neglects the senior – perhaps subconsciously. "These arrangements are a disaster for the elderly," writes criminal lawyer Stephen Taylor in a submission to Hall. "Overnight they go from being in control of their estate to being penniless, submissive and dependent." And even in death, such agreements can continue to wreak havoc. As in the case of Simpson v. Simpson, which went to the Supreme Court of B.C. in 1997. The elderly Mrs. Simpson signed the deed of her Burnaby house over to her eldest son in 1987, with the stipulation that he and his wife would pay rent back to her and provide a ground-floor suite where she would continue to live. They also made a verbal promise to care for her in her old age. The plaintiffs in the case were Mrs. Simpson's three younger children, who brought action against their brother shortly after their mother's death. "Disgruntled heirs" in legal parlance, they wanted the 1987 deed set aside and house returned to the estate. They claimed that their mother had been subjected to undue influence in signing her house over, and that the verbal promise of care had been breached when she was admitted to a geriatric hospital in 1991. The judge called their allegations groundless, calling all such "care-for-life" agreements into question by noting that "the time may well come in anyone's life when institutional life is a practical necessity. Short of outfitting the suite as a quasi-hospital, such was the case with Mrs. Simpson," said the judge. (To contact the B.C. Law Institute's Project Committee on Legal Issues Affecting Seniors, call 604-822-0142 or check the website www.bcli.org) *(Source: The Vancouver Sun, July 18, 2001.)*

Option: Rely (fully/partly) on government assistance health programs for seniors—become dependent to some extent.

We can apply for financial and services assistance – at the correct time – and if/when accepted, cost-share using available government assistance programs.

Cross-reference to Topic 1, Suggestion #9, Investigate Potential Assistance Programs; browse www.longtermcanada.com clicking on the 'Provincial Government Programs' tab.

Note: I do not recommend relying on this option as some government services and programs may not be available when you need them.

What might be available?

☑ **Assistance with cost-sharing of residency in a nursing home:**

If our parent requires residency in a caremanor, we can contact social services or the regional community health unit (i.e. the department administering our provincial government financial assistance programs), apply for financial help and go through the 'assessment process' for placement eligibility.

Most of our assistance programs are based on two factors:

1. Financial status using income tax returns (1-2 years returns) as proof, an income-formula is then applied (i.e. a means test).

2. If found eligible for cost-sharing assistance, the second factor comes into play, bed availability in designated nursing homes.

Even when a parent is deemed eligible to receive financial assistance to help cover a portion of residency costs in a carehome, if our parent needs a space before his/her name 'reaches the top of the funded bed assistance-list' the family will be forced to pay 100% of the carehome costs at that point in time while waiting if your parent needs to be there, in a nursing home. *(For example, when Dad's name was first accepted, we were advised that there was judged to be a three year wait for a government-funded bed/room in the carehome we selected – in reality, the time turned out to be less.: but we decided to pay the full cost ourselves until a bed became vailable. Little choice.)*

If permitted by your health unit/care center, it might be a good idea, while in care-years but prior to a major crisis, to apply and to list a parent for subsidized residency assistance – just in case. This safeguard measure, of registering our parent for a selected caremanor room, is preferred, rather than queuing up later for a space or making alternate arrangements for a parent's interim care when a health crisis 'forces' a decision. Of course, the desire 'to age in place' (i.e. at home) may eliminate the need to take this action (what of the future?).

☑ Assistance with at-home care services:

While our parents are still able to live safely in their own home, either independently or with a live-in caregiver, we can contact our regional community health authority or community care access center (i.e. responsible department for home-care services) and make an application for help with at-home care needs.

An assessment is undertaken, reviewing the level and hours of care our parents require, assessing their financial status and determining their eligibility for home-care services (i.e. personal care and housekeeping care).

☑ Assistance from special programs:

No matter where our parents live, we need to research the special programs available in that particular region of their province/territory.

Usually there are many programs to help seniors maintain their independence in a safe manner, such as CSIL 'Choices in Support for Independent Living' in British Columbia and 'Choices' in Alberta… These special programs have been designed in response to interest expressed by seniors and families advocating for greater choice and control while living in their home within their own community – direct funding for home support services to eligible clients is available.

Another special program is SAFER, Shelter Aid For Elderly Renters – it provides direct cash assistance to eligible residents (of B.C.) who are age 60 or over and who pay rent for their homes. In Alberta there is a special 'subsidy program' for elderly residents – check your province for its subsidized rental programs for seniors – all offer some type.

Special Note – Different locations may have similar programs with different titles – ask probing questions, outline personal circumstances and simply ask often, "What is available to help my family?". Refer to www.longtermcarecanada.com (government programs tab – click on provincial governments) to find a contact in your area for seniors services and call and ask questions.

"Oil takeover talk sign of dependency society"

One of the most troubling results of the rise in energy prices is the demand by so many Canadians for the government to do something. Actually, the really frightening part is that, for about half of Canadians, the demand is for government to do EVERYTHING. Perhaps we shouldn't be surprised, given we're raised in a culture of dependence, that the first response of so many of us is for government to take care of us. *(Source: Article by Andre Picard, Public Health Reporter, National Post, 2005)*

Author's question: Do you think the same could be said for Canadians' attitudes towards our health system when addressing 'care' of seniors? Does 'dependency' go hand-in-hand with an 'undying faith in government'? "Is independence important to you? If so, how do you plan to fund your long-term care years?"

Caring for terminally ill loved ones

Canadian workers can claim up to six weeks paid leave, under the Employment Insurance (EI) Program, collecting a maximum of $413 a week, but only if they are caring for a dying spouse, child or parent. Siblings do not qualify (2006).

Option: Have a long-term-care insurance policy in place for each adult member of the family — co-share the risk.

Cross reference to Topic 13, Suggestion 60 for more information on long-term care insurance, also go to <u>www.longtermcarecanada.com</u> to research insurance companies with this LTCI product.

We can apply for and take out a long-term-care insurance policy for each parent (usually can be purchased up to approximately 80+ years of age); we need to discuss such a policy with a licensed insurance agent-financial planner as there are many variations and costs and differing scales of benefits for care. The policy is health-related (i.e. your current health and health history to date are important – don't plan on waiting 'till later' as many have regretted that decision as their health changed making it either more difficult or impossible to get coverage – as the US slogan says, "don't wait till your health goes south and your premium goes north.")

Managers who are quick to talk "flex" with new parents have little patience for employees torn by elder-care demands. This is having a marked effect in the Canadian workplace. A recent survey found that one-quarter of business and professional workers refused transfers that would take them too far from aging relatives. Women, who make up 73 per cent of elder-care providers, are more than twice as likely to report not seeking career promotions for this reason. Which is not to say it's a women's problem. The research shows that when women are not around men provide the same level of care and get even less support from employers who believe that's "women's work". The problem in today's workplaces is not a lack of policy but a lack of will (to implement). *(Source: The Vancouver Sun, 1998.)*

Personal Anecdote:

"I felt I had/have no choice, I incorporated long-term care insurance into my care plan – but I also 'read' the policy carefully asking questions about the 'terms' used." (No surprises later, please!)

As my understanding of the magnitude of the caregiving problem grew, I decided to apply for and own a long-term care policy for myself as part of my personal 'living benefits insurance package' (e.g. disability, critical illness and long-term care). I now own two LTCI policies for myself.

I consider a LTC policy equally important as a life insurance policy, as it also is a type of protection for my family. Who will care for me? Will my care impose financial problems on my husband/others in my family? What if an accident happened to me whereby I needed care in my own home or in a facility, how would such be provided and for how long would I be able to pay for such care? When a senior, I plan on living a long life, how are my care-years going to be financed?

No one likes additional monthly payments of any kind, but as we grow less sure of what our government health services will be able to provide when we actually will have need those services, we must begin to look more closely at our responsibilities for our own care and immediately put in place some plans for our own security (like RRSPs, as this is a way to participate in our retirement savings with government help). I feel that I can't afford to be without a policy for my own care-years.

For example: One of my LTC policies when purchased cost me $84.65/month or as I prefer to think of it, only $2.82 per day - I equate this cost to less than a latte a day, which I love. As I have so often said to my friends, perhaps all we have to do is put things in perspective and relate the cost of a policy to *something we enjoy (e.g. nice wine, dinner out, new clothes, a round of golf, a concert, plants for our garden, doing a hobby/attending a sports event...) and simply recognize that the cost of LTC is more than acceptable for the benefit and peace of mind gained.*

A long-term-care policy enables us to have the financial flexibility to select live-at-home care and/or facility residency care; depending on the company you select for their policy, it covers nursing needs, therapist needs, adult day care needs, equipment, respite...

Ask the following types of questions of an Advisor/LTCI Specialist/Agent and take good notes!

☑ What is a long-term-care policy?

☑ What do the terms 'imply' (e.g. use of an 'agency'; can a family member provide care...)?

☑ How exactly would my parents and I benefit from its purchase? (Remember, LTCI is not only for the benefit of a care-receiver, it is for the care-givers as well.)

☑ Describe what we are purchasing (i.e. details, such as benefits, elimination period, equipment coverage, respite care, etc)?

☑ What about inflation? (A very important factor.)

☑ Will I lose all the money I've paid if it is never used? (But remember, LTCI is not there as a savings plan, it is like other insurance policies you own, house, car, etc., it is to cover a possible 'risk'.)

☑ How long do I have to pay on the policy (many are until age 65 or 20 year pay, some you pay for life)?

☑ Is it better to buy a policy if I have many of assets or if I have few (Again, LTCI can prevent an erosion of assets)?

☑ Can I get a better rate through my employer and when/if I no longer work there can the policy come with me (without an increase)? (Note: Employers in Canada don't offer full group LTC insurance as a benefit – yet.)

☑ What happens if I can't continue to pay the premiums (is there 'forfeiture protection' or could I receive limited benefits then)?

☑ Is there a return of premium (estate reasons), if so, do costs go up? (Again, LTCI is not a savings plan.)

☑ Could my children purchase a policy for me (a type of gift)? Who would own that policy then?

☑ Is there a discount for couples/persons living together or persons purchasing at the same time?

☑ Are the premiums fixed/locked-in or can they go up? (A very important question) Ask: will the cost of the premium go up over the years and if so to what extent? You want to be able to keep this policy even when your dollars may be limited in your 'old-old' years, you do not want to have to give it up just when you might need to use it. So, ask about the future, a guarantee of what you can expect to be paying.

For further discussion go to www.longtermcarecanada.com then to the 'Long-term care tab' and the dropdown menu on 'long-term care insurance'. Or browse the web pages of the insurance companies that distribute this product – the companies and their links are listed on that website as well. (Do your homework; be prepared to ask questions on this relatively new product being offered to Canadians.)

Special Note – Don't forget – we must to plan for our own care-years as soon as possible in order to feel secure in our future retirement and of course, to obtain lower costs. Odds are that a long-term-care policy is a plan that we most likely will use and benefit from within our lifetime. It is what I call a positive policy in that if life treats us well and fairly, we will be around to claim from the policy!

Let's look to the 'future' in order to understand the circumstances surrounding 'the present' long-term care issue in Canada.

"Although home care is not currently considered a medically necessary service under the Canada Health Act, provinces and territories recognize its value and have taken steps to expand home care under provincial and territorial health care plans. But there are wide variations across the country in terms of what types of home care services are covered and how much individuals pay to cover a portion of the costs. Because home care has become a partial substitute for care that was previously provided primarily in hospitals or by physicians, and because of the value of effective home care services both to individuals and the health care system, a strong case can be made for taking the first step in 35 years to expand coverage under the Canada Health Act. As outlined in Chapter 2, the Commission recommends that the definition of what is covered under the Canada Health Act should immediately be expanded to include medically necessary home care as well as diagnostic services"

Source: "The Future Of Health Care In Canada" or as it is commonly called, "The Romanow Report"-- Section 8: For further information, refer to "The Future Of Health Care In Canada" www.hc-sc.gc.ca/english/care/romanow/hcc0023.html

"Ask a man which way he is going to vote, and he will probably tell you. Ask him, however, why, and vagueness is all."
– Bernard Levin

TOPIC 10

Let's Talk: Saying Goodbye

What do I do when my parent dies?

Personal Anecdote: "How do I say goodbye?!"

Suggestions:

51: Plan for this time well in advance

52: Organize the details of the actual day of the service plus immediate follow-ups

53: Be there for our other parent—a priority now

54: Enjoy and appreciate memories—always

What do I do when my parent dies?

Personal Anecdote:
"How do I say goodbye?!"

Dad

On October 18, 1998, at around 3:20 AM my Dad died.

Dad and Mum and I had spent the previous week together. Dad's medication had been changed several weeks before in order to help with both his congested heart condition and the problems with his liver and the follow-up test results indicated he was responding well. I'll always remember the doctor giving me the good news then, "...your Dad could live for another five years...".

All seemed as well as could be with Mum and Dad, all care-related details had been attended to - so I flew home and then left for Mexico, for an over-due vacation. Exactly one week later, I received a telephone call in the night that Dad had died. The caremanor nurse had telephoned Mum to tell her that Dad had suffered a heart attack in his sleep, Mum's caregiver called me.

I spent those next early morning hours in Mexico, anxiously rearranging flights and packing and contacting close relatives and contacting the funeral home. During the many quiet hours on the planes, my thoughts were with Dad and all the little things he loved and all the things we had done together. Of course, I cried, clouds and memories swirling around as I flew homeward.

Upon arriving at my own home late that night, I packed once again - I remember trying to concentrate on what I would need for my own father's funeral and to attend to his business affairs. I caught an early morning flight to go to my parents.

As arranged, I went directly to the funeral home to spend some private time with Dad. I wanted to tell him one more time how much I love him and what a good father he was.

Strange what comes to mind during those heart-wrenching minutes with a much-loved parent - memories are both powerful friends and powerful enemies. I noticed Dad's large hands and snippets of yesteryears returned - always holding onto two of his fingers as a little girl as we strolled down the 'Gulch' - Dad waving his hands in the air passionately while watching hockey or giving a speech at the Colombo Lodge.

Was it only a week ago that I placed my hand on his while he was resting in his recliner in the nursing home? So there I sat, one last time with my Dad, holding hands, reminiscing and saying goodbye - I love you Dad.

Mum

On August 17, 2005, at 9:36 AM my Mother died.

One month previously, Mum was aware and involved in most aspects of her everyday life. In July I had been married, Mum was very pleased for me; my husband and I spent that weekend in July visiting with my mother. She had had a cake prepared and a few relatives came to visit while we were there. Mum, although fairly quiet, was in good spirits. My husband and I left for Turkey the following week for a three-week vacation and I spoke to Mum almost each day while I was away (except for the period of time we were in Cappadocia region and those of you who have been there will know why as communications is not always easy).

Upon my return, I immediately within three days flew to visit Mum. It was an important time as we were training a new set of shift caregivers and Mum was very anxious over this pending change. Mum and I spent our days together as we usually did when I was there, I took her to the hairdresser, we had dinners together, I held a training period and she met the potential caregiver candidates...all flowed as it should.

My main concern at this time was that Mum was very tired and very quiet and seemed even slower than usual; as well, I noticed that she wasn't as interested in her surroundings as she normally was. In part, I attributed this to her worry over the change in caregiver structure and in part to her ever-changing health—she was 94.5 years old now—an amazing age (she used to say, "How did I get this old?" and we would laugh).

I left on a late Friday flight that week; then, on the Sunday just after 3:00AM in the morning, the caregiver called and said that she had called the ambulance as Mum had had a heart attack a few minutes earlier and they had taken Mum to emergency; the caregiver was going to sit with her until I arrived. I caught the earliest morning flight possible and went straight to the hospital. Mum was very glad to see me there and in tears told me that she felt 'miserable' and asked what was wrong with her. (I did not lie, I just chose not to tell her all the details at that point.)

The doctor and cardiologist arrived sometime that morning and of course, told me what I already knew. My Mother was not going to be able to survive this event. I stayed with Mum over the next days sleeping in her room at her side; she was rarely awake during these final days.

I felt that we had said our long-goodbye throughout all the care-years we had spent together and so, just being a little family unit unto ourselves, being with her on our own felt natural although unbelievably heartbreaking.

The night before Mum died, she showed her love and concern for her daughter, as she had done all her life; she looked at me late that night and said, "Patty, you must be tired, why don't you get some sleep." I held her hand and climbed on *to the bed with her that evening and lay until the hours of the morning cradling her, she died in my arms—as I had always prayed would happen. And now ...well, now, it was time to spend remembering all the wonderful years together as mother and daughter, including those special care-years together. I love you Mum., as always*

Note: I am not sure what each of us does the moment a parent dies—for me, it was the most intensely personal time of my life and I wanted to be alone. Dad and I had only few years together on our care-years journey. Mum and I had ten years on her care-journey together. My parents were incredibly brave and thoughtful during their journey and my love and respect for my parents grew even more as I watched them become 'elderly'. They grew old with 'dignity'.

How each of us handles the death of a much-loved parent is intensely private. What motivates us to make decisions in a certain manner about each aspect of a parent's passing is also very private. This topic was written not so much as suggestions, but as reminders - to take one step at a time, one day at a time.

Notes:

_____

_____

_____

_____

_____

"Those who do not know how to weep with their whole heart, don't know how to laugh either."
– *Golda Meir 1898-1978*

Suggestion 51: **Plan for this time well in advance**

Planning our parents' funerals/services well is one more way we can show our love – we want to do everything in accordance with their wishes.

What do I need to know?

Our parents, over the years, will have given us opportunities to enter into discussions with them regarding their end-of-life wishes – thus, when these 'windows of opportunity' pop up, we have to listen for the cues, not curtail the conversations (e.g. "Oh Mum, let's not worry about that now") and encourage discussions.

(Note: Hospice care is not dealt with in this guidebook as it was not part of our journey – I do encourage readers though to become familiar with hospice services within the community – as a planning measure.)

It makes sense that our parents will rely on us to carry out their wishes at death, so we must ask, **"Do I have a full understanding of my parent's end-of-life wishes?"** Our answers will range between:

☑ Yes – my parents and I have discussed their wishes fully and they and I have already made arrangements in advance.

And

☑ No – I will have to think carefully regarding what my parents' wishes may be as this is not a conversation they will enter into – I will make the arrangements in advance or at the time of death based on my best understandings of what their wishes may be.

For example – at the beginning of our caregiving journey, I decided to make funeral arrangements for my parents in advance, thus, in April 1998, I signed prearranged funeral services agreements with a local funeral home, for both my parents. After careful thought on their wishes and some research, I selected the basics only for a service, as I knew I could add to those basics if so desired at a later date.

How did I make these important decisions? Dad would not discuss his end-of-life wishes no matter what, although from time to time I had heard him mention that he wanted to be cremated; I made sure that was his ongoing wish by checking with him when the moments seemed right. Mum had not said much either in the past but when Dad died, we had a chance to talk more about her wishes. For the most part, by listening carefully to my parents' comments over the years, I was able to get an understanding of their general wishes for something "simple" (e.g.. a "small reception" following a "very short memorial service" in a comfortable "cosy place"; something with "nature" incorporated into the service, no limousines for the family, just "regular cars"…).

I chose to do this planning for both parents, prior to their deaths, for several reasons – because I would be less emotional, less rushed, less in turmoil, more efficient, and more considerate of their wishes and lifestyles. I took my time to think about the actual services and the need for the merchandise being offered as part of the funeral agreement (For example: I ordered small shrubs from the local nursery as I wanted special items in keeping with my parents' lifestyles and values rather than have the funeral home do the floral work on my behalf; I used the service folders as acknowledgement cards and chose to write personal notes inside the folders to send to friends who couldn't attend rather than order two different cards.)

I wanted to say goodbye in a fitting manner, to do this end-of-life activity well and have choices – which I don't think I would have had if I had to do such organizing within a day or so of their deaths. Within two months of completing the prearranged planning of my parents' services, I made a point of visiting the selected funeral home in my parents' city, introducing myself to the manager of the funeral home and looking around the neighbouring area to become familiar with it. I then reviewed the arrangements once again to make sure that I had selected what would be in keeping with each of their wishes and lifestyles and left feeling that all these particular plans were in order.

The more you learn about funerals, the happier you'll be. That's the message in a new print and radio advertising campaign by the Ontario Funeral Service Association, aimed at encouraging people to plan ahead and lend a personal touch to their finale. The funeral directors are disheartened to think that no more than one in five people have pre-planned their funeral services. "Preplanning can be as simple as discussing your preferences with your family or your executor. Or you can prearrange your funeral with the funeral home of your choice," says Michael Fitzgerald, Association president. And, of course, "There are even several prepayment options." *(Source: The Vancouver Sun, May 15, 1999.)*

Notes:

"We have two ears and one mouth so that we can listen twice as much as we speak.

– Epictetus

What should I keep in mind?

☑ **We should not leave issues or arguments unresolved with our parents.**

At the time of the death of a parent we do not want to have to cope with any unresolved feelings, as grief itself is unsettling.

It is difficult enough to say our goodbyes without wishing that we had settled an old argument. If we focus on the need to keep good communications with our parents ('better late than never' applies), then there should be few regrets.

☑ **Whenever we find ourselves doing this type of planning, we should focus solely on our parents' wishes and the manner in which they lived their lives.**

If we have discussed end-of-life wishes with our parents, if they are very clear as to what they want, it is easier to direct our planning and not be distracted by our own wishes if different from theirs. (We begin to think about pre-arranged planning more often while actually on the care-years journey.)

If we plan our parents' funerals well in advance we can focus 100 percent on their wishes. If we do not plan in advance and have to make arrangements while they are very ill or within a day or so of their deaths, we run the risk of blurring their wishes with our pain and anxieties.

If we haven't had any straightforward talks regarding end-of-life wishes, when planning, we need to focus on what our parents believed in and how they lived their daily lives. *(For example: Even though my parents did not make many of their wishes known in words, they made them known by their everyday actions – my job was to translate their lifestyles into their end-of-life wishes.)*

Note: What do you think? Read the following thought-provoking quotation by world famous environmentalist David Suzuki.

"If people think cardboard is tacky, perhaps they could rent a fancy casket with a trap door. Then the casket could be used again and again." – Environmentalist David Suzuki on why he plans to be cremated in a cardboard casket. *(Source: The Vancouver Sun, December 30, 2000.)*

(For example: I too chose 'cardboard caskets' in 1998 when arranging in advance for the cremations aspect for my parents. I did so because of my parents' general love of nature and especially Mum's life long love of trees and large forests (similar reasoning expressed by environmentalist David Suzuki). I want to add though that when I visited Dad and Mum privately in the chapel, it was, at first glance, difficult to look beyond that 'cardboard' – I guess I would have preferred to see each in a beautifully carved wooden casket – but I stayed focused on what was important to my parents during their lifetimes. I feel confident that they would approve of this particular decision. As well, I did not have any cut flowers at Dad's or Mum's services except two small arrangements on a table at the front of the chapel. In place of cut floral arrangements, I arranged with a local nursery to have small shrubs (fruit and berry) in pots brought to the chapel for Dad's service and rose trees for Mum's service and placed them at the beginning of each row of pews and all along the front wall of the chapel, again in keeping with my parents' love of nature. At the end of the service I asked those in attendance to take a shrub/tree home with them – to this day, I still have people say to me, "Your Dad's/Mum's tree is doing so well". I even had a photograph sent to me that first year of Mum's rose shrub blooming.)

"Count your age with friends but not with years."
– *Anonymous*

Last wishes for those with little time left – Edmonton's Comfort Care – by Brad Evenson – Palliative care, also called comfort care, is mainly directed at providing relief to a terminally ill person by managing symptoms and pain. The goal is not to cure, but to provide comfort and maintain a decent quality of life until death. In many parts of North America and Europe, dying people have, for decades, been cared for in expensive hospital beds. The practice is a huge drain on scarce funds. The problem became a crisis in the early 1990s when the federal Liberals cut payments to provinces, forcing them to slash the number of acute-care beds. "So the idea was to look after people in a more appropriate environment. There's no necessity for people to die in an acute-care hospital if they no longer need acute-care services, the diagnostic imaging, the operating room and so on. And it's not an ideal environment; they're big, noisy places with lot of hustle and bustle." (Dr. Robin Fainsinger, clinical director of the Capital Health Authority's palliative care program.) At the time, palliative care in Edmonton was a patchwork of programs offered by hospitals with separate governing boards and no co-ordination of services. This made it difficult to create a city-wide system of care. When the province changed to a district system in 1992, it dissolved hospital boards, creating a new opportunity. Under the leadership of Dr. Eduardo Bruera, an internationally recognized expert in palliative care, Edmonton's health authority hired doctors and nurses to provide end-of-life care. Other Alberta councils, such as Calgary, developed their own systems. Since Edmonton already had the staff and bed capacity, the new system needed no startup money, just re-organization. Dr. Bruera guided the development of continuing-care centres – the new term for nursing homes – to open more palliative-care beds. *(Source: The State of Health Care, Quarterly Report, Edition Three, November 2001, The National Post.)*

It is important at all ages to discuss end-of-life wishes:
While 90 percent of respondents (1997 Angus Reid poll) said
they would like to die at home, only 6 per cent felt they
could care for loved ones without hospice or palliative-care
support.

In fact, only 15 per cent of Canadians die at home or in
hospices, while 75 per cent draw their final breath in acute-
care hospital beds or extended-care facilities.

(Source: Statistics Canada)

Notes:

"Forgiveness does not change the past, but it does enlarge the
future.

– Paul Boese

Suggestion 52: *Organize the details of the actual day of the service plus immediate follow-ups*

How can I make sure that I have absolutely everything organized?

While grieving, we still have to attend to the details of the actual day of the service – a very difficult duty for each of us.

I found that an effective method of undertaking the organizational aspects in a thoughtful manner was to **'visualize' that day in sections and plan the details accordingly:**

Section One: Out of town family accommodation and transportation – Prepare carefully especially if many of the family members are elderly or disabled.

☑ Which relatives from out of town will want to stay with our other parent at home?

☑ Is there a hotel near the location of the service for out-of-town family members – what can be arranged there (rates/meals/reception)?

☑ Will I need taxis, limousines, private vehicles? (The proximity of the hotel to the service location is important.)

☑ Who will go with whom to the service – 'partnering', especially for seniors?

☑ What are the transportation arrangements – family members to/from the actual service, other sites, the reception, parents' home…?

☑ If some persons are coming from a carehome, what are the transportation and care-related arrangements for each of them? Has the nursing home manager been advised?

Section Two: Service venue – Is all as we want it to be.

☑ Does the location for the service have spacious parking nearby, if not, where else may people park close by?

☑ Does the venue have stairs/elevators/access for disabled?

☑ What arrangements have been made for the hearing impaired, sight impaired?

☑ Have the seating arrangements been planned? For immediate family, for wheelchairs or walkers or motorized chairs?

☑ Is there a private room for the family prior to the service?

Section Three: Details of the service – Plan all aspects.

☑ Will we have a video/CD? If so, prior to the service (e.g. one week or so, ask the funeral director/planner) we must access photo albums quickly and gather pictures plus decide on accompanying music *(e.g. I decided on a CD for my mother's service and was very pleased with the result; everyone loved the glimpse of this amazing lady and will remember her as a vital individual as a result; anticipating who might attend the service, I was mindful to try to include photographs of them with Mum as well.)*

☑ Will we have a picture of our parent in a prominent spot, where will it be placed, how will it be presented, what will be beside it? If cremated, will the urn be in view, where/if a casket, will it be in view, what will be placed on it?

☑ What service items will be required:

- Service folders (choices may be supplied by the funeral home or place of worship) – the service folder may also be used as an acknowledgement follow-up to those who could not attend but sent best wishes or flowers or donations.

- Prayer cards, hymn books.

☑ What music will we want, if any/who will sing/when are selections of music to be played?

☑ What of flowers/plants/shrubs and locations of such? When will they be delivered (hint: double-check the day before if a nursery is being used and is to deliver).

☑ Who will greet guests prior to the service beginning? At the reception? *(For example: rather than use the memorial home staff, my cousin and husband greeted all guests at the doors at both venues, the chapel and the reception.)*

☑ Who is going to be involved directly in the service: who will speak and say what, who will begin the service and how?

☑ What type of service atmosphere do we want to create – religious, friendly, casual, long, short?

☑ What is my role as the daughter/son – will I speak? *(For example: I felt that Dad and Mum would want me to do their services, so I lead almost all aspects assisted by my parents' favourite nieces and nephews. My memories given during each of the services were anecdotes and offered a daughter's view of each of her much-loved parents.)*

☑ How do we want to end the service? What is done with the urn/casket (if present)? *(For example: I, with my husband's assistance, handed every couple/individual present a large potted shrub and said 'thank you'.)*

☑ What are the other less-noticeable items to be considered:

- Fees – funeral home, church honorarium

- Major merchandise: casket/urn

- Clothing for burial, cremation – the family selects the garments; a fee may be added for dressing.

- Obituary notices for newspapers – decide on the number of newspapers for the announcement, the number of days for placement, and if a picture is going to accompany the writeup – have all these ready to give to the funeral home who can handle such for you.

- Notarised copies of the death certificate are required for legal purposes later *(Note: three may be the bare minimum needed, six preferred)*.

- Permits

- Records fee for vital statistics

Section Four: Reception – if a reception is to follow, select an appropriate venue very close to the service (convenience, parking, less confusion…); a church hall or private home may be preferred – **Preview the site ahead of time.**

For example: I selected a cosy dining room in a hotel nearby the funeral home/ chapel to host the receptions thus the tables and chairs and buffet table and décor were already in place and comfortable for many of the seniors; the dining room was one Dad and Mum liked as the retired chef was an old buddy who had trained the present staff; some of the items on the buffet table were specifically requested as they were favourite foods of my parents (e.g. Mum's love of chicken strips and chips or grilled cheese sandwiches for lunch), as well, a dessert buffet was presented (everyone knew they loved sweets and fruit). I worked with the restaurant catering manager to organize special ideas (e.g. boxes of Dad's favourite Purdy's chocolates around the room, the type and colour of center flower arrangements on the tables…). We included personal details whenever possible to create warmth and cause further reminiscing among friends and family.

- ☑ Have all details regarding the reception been arranged – room space, table/chairs arrangements, food/beverages, servers, space for disabled (e.g. walkers, wheelchairs)?

- ☑ Is there a special location during the reception for immediate family to sit, so each member is able to greet all the guests and visit easily with everyone in attendance?

✓ What if more food or beverages are required, will all be forthcoming upon request, who is keeping an eye on what?

✓ What of the reception room ambiance?

✓ What of mementos? *(For example, many very close friends and relatives attended the services as one might expect and many had traveled a great distance to be there, leaving soon at the end of the day again to travel. Thus, the night before Mum's service, my husband and I spent the time at Mum's home and wrapped a small memento for each close relative and special friend. We had the packages close by at the reception and quietly gave the appropriate ones to the people there. It was a small token and certainly appreciated. For the most part, it was either a miniature clock or a miniature ornamental shoe or a small carving as Mum had collections of these over the years. My mother had also mentioned throughout the years what articles she would like to leave to special nephews and nieces, so I had those items securely wrapped as well and delivered the items to the cars of those persons involved. For each of us a reception is to reflect on the person being remembered and celebrated—I feel all aspects at these receptions were as Mum/Dad would have enjoyed and appreciated.)*

Section Five: At home later – Plan for the unexpected.

For example, in the evening after Mum's service, my husband and I invited my out-of-town relatives who were staying over as well as in-town close relatives to a dinner. We hosted the dinner in a winery on a hill over looking the valley where Mum lived in the Okanagan—a winery that she loved as it was close to her house, looked oveer the lake, and she and I used to go there for lunches. For this dinner, we had arranged taxis to take everyone to the location and pick us all up which was appreciated as the out of town guests did not want to be driving at night in a country-side they didn't know well. We also had preprandial drinks in our room – we stayed in a hotel for these days – and everyone attended this casual event. My husband and I wanted to thank all our family for their efforts and love—the evening was a success as family members who had not been together in decades sat and wandered memory-lane.

☑ Who will be going back to the main house later and what is expected during this personal time? What must we have on hand at home?

☑ Will all the out-of-town relatives want to come to the house in the evening, what of a late dinner, what is needed, what of the next morning before departures?

☑ Will my other parent and I be able to capture a few private minutes together on this day? Who is tired?

☑ If a family dinner is planned, location and transportation are extremely important.

Section Six: Later – What are the basics requiring attention:

☑ When can the certificates, copies, other items be picked up from the funeral director?

☑ Have all the persons who sent condolence cards been sent a service folder or prayer card (within one month)? Have donations been acknowledged?

☑ Has my other parent had an opportunity to talk about the service a few times, what type of closure does she/he require?

☑ Do we want to set up any type of memorial within the community, if so what (this decision may be made later)?

Section Seven: The first weeks after – We must attend to:

☑ Category 1 – Legal affairs.

☑ Category 2 – Financial affairs.

☑ Category 3 – Government-related matters.

☑ Category 4 – Business affairs impacting our surviving parent (if immediate changes are to be made).

To begin, we should:

☑ Make a list of the basics in each category.

☑ Telephone the appropriate group/body/agency regarding each item on the list as to the documents required.

☑ Complete any required forms.

☑ Set up appointments for follow-ups, now or as required.

☑ Complete the paper work involved.

For example:

- *Reading of Will – family legal firm. (Note: Probate may be required – a procedure to obtain approval that the Will is officially recognized as the last Will and Testament and that the Executor named is the legal representative of the estate.)*

- *Surviving parent Will – redo, family legal firm.*

- *Surviving parent property transfer – original death certificate required, fee to be paid, title certificate search, forms from Land Titles Office to be completed and returned to family lawyer.*

- *Financial affairs – death certificate or photocopy notarised required by each financial institution – contact financial institutions, managers – change joint bank accounts to the surviving spouse; Safety Deposit Boxes open; contact financial planner for investments. (Note: The Canadian Bank Act permits a bank to release $5,000 from the deceased spouse's account for funeral expenses.)*

- *Vehicle transfers for registration/insurances – original death certificate (and copy of the will in some cases) fees, forms to be completed and handed in.*

- *Driver's License – send to Department of Motor Vehicles.*

- *Destroy credit cards – inform the companies, send a note.*

- *Medical plans – contact former employer/Health Card/Government plan (B.C. Medical if spouse was a dependent of the deceased, the identity number is needed).*

- *Old Age Security (a final cheque will be received at the end of that month, deposit, write on it "To the Estate of…") and other Pension Plans – death certificates required, application spousal transfer forms to be completed, copy of funeral payment/receipt if reimbursement applies. To obtain CPP benefits (lump-sum and/or monthly survivor's pension, a death certificate is required).*

- *Insurance companies – contact, death certificate and maybe marriage certificate necessary for claims.*

- *Club – contact for death benefits, notarised copies of the death certificate are required.*

Notes:

_____

_____

_____

_____

_____

_____

_____

_____

_____

_____

_____

_____

"I am ready to meet my Maker. Whether my Maker is prepared for the great ordeal of meeting me is another matter."
– Sir Winston Churchill, 1874-1965

Suggestion 53: *Be there for our other parent – a priority now*

Our surviving parent is going to feel somewhat alone, even though we will be close by (e.g. my parents had been married for over six decades when Dad passed away and his passing signalled another large-scale adjustment for Mum).

If we live out-of-town, we need to put aside time, a couple of weeks minimum, to stay and be with our other parent during this transition period.

No matter where we live, within the first month, we can:

☑ Stay with our parent for a period of time (move into the house – just be around).

☑ Be sensitive to our parent's need to talk. *(For example: Mum took a long time to get over the shock that Dad had a heart attack when he had no previous heart problems, she couldn't grasp the severity of his heart congestion; since she was the one with a poor heart history she told me that she had prepared herself "to go before him" and "never thought it would be the other way around". Mum also took a long time to adjust when a few years later she lost her younger brother whom she was extremely close to; then a couple of years later once again, she lost her good friend, her sister-in-law....now, she was alone, the last of both her and Dad's family. She never said too much about them even when asked, just "I really miss them" and I guess that said it all.)*

☑ Be available for meals, especially breakfast (to start the day) and evening supper (to chat).

☑ Mention our deceased parent, not all the time, but in passing when appropriate (e.g. "I'll be in Dad's room if you want me, I am just putting some things away.")

☑ Laugh and cry together at times, let our parent reflect back, assure our parent that tears are very acceptable.

☑ Do some spontaneous activities together in the near future in order that our parent doesn't stay within the house only (go for a drive, visit a close friend, have a relative plan a quiet dinner one night...).

☑ Discuss personal effects, in a timely fashion *(e.g. it took Mum and me many months before we sorted Dad's closets and drawers, but when on my own I re-did all of Mum's home within one month of her passing)*.

☑ Begin to discuss the future and what it may look like .

Genes The Key: Researchers are probing why some people live longer, but while a health lifestyle and a little luck are involved there's no getting around genetics.

Scientist will soon embark on a first-of-its kind, globetrotting mission to four locales around the world—including Nova Scotia — where there are clusters of healthy seniors still living past their 100th year. The goal of the three-year Life-Quest Expedition, as it is called, is to find out what makes some people "successful agers".

The U.S. government-sponsored and National Geographic-documented mission will go to Yarmouth, N.S.; Sardinia, Italy: Hainan, China; and Okinawa, Japan. ...There are about 3,800 centenarians in Canada and while the national rate is 1.1 per 10,000 population, in Nova Scotia, it is two per 10,000 people, believed to be the highest rate in North America.

People over 100 in Nova Scotia have previously attributed their longevity to frequent consumption of fish and fresh Atlantic lobster, but experts in aging believe the high rate of centenarians there may be due to the gene pool.

(continued...)

...It is believed people need two traits to live long, healthy lives – a longevity-enabling gene (or genes) plus the absence of genetic mutations associated with diseases such as Alzheimer's, says Dr. Thomas Perls, a LifeQuest investigator and centenarian researcher at Boston Medical Centre. His research indicates that behaviours like exercise, social engagement and avoiding smoking are key ingredients for longevity, but he also makes a strong case for a genetic component.

University of Illinois professor, Jay Olshansky, another LifeQuest project adviser and one of the world's leading aging demographic experts, said the DNA testing will yield important information about whether it is factual to say that there exist people "who win the genetic lottery."

Perls says that once the biochemical pathways involved in longevity genes are understood, it may be possible to develop drugs that could alter the human lifespan by slowing or even preventing the onset of various diseases.

"But you have to be careful what you hope for because you might see something you don't like," says Olshansky, who believes the purpose of efforts to delay aging should not be about immortality or dramatic extensions of life, but rather, improvements in the health and vigour of seniors and reductions in their frailty and disabilities, which would also cut health-care costs.

...Gloria Gutman, director of the Gerontology Research Centre at Simon Fraser University, said there is no doubt there is a genetic component to longevity, ever since studies on identical twins showed they often had longevity in common. But she says when she asks the best experts in the world how much of a factor heredity is in longevity, they tell her it's about 25 per cent.

While the LifeQuest expedition will highlight the search for longevity genes, most gerontologists and aging researchers agree that the span of life is also attributable to several factors, including biological processes, lifestyle (behaviours) and environmental effects.

(Excerpts from "Aging Gracefully", January 20, 2005, The Vancouver Sun...Note: Much of the material for the article was gathered at the International Longevity Centre in New York, an affiliate of the Mount Sinai School of Medicine.)

Suggestion 54: *Enjoy and appreciate memories –*
And go 'forward' when your
caregiving ends.

A memory of a deceased parent can cause a laugh, a twinge, a smile, a tear, a frown, a question, a prayer, or a knowing nod – when least expected.

Memories surround us – some of those memories are set in motion deliberately in that we choose to remember certain events and dates; some are fleeting in that we hear a piece of music and reflect on a past event; some are imposed, especially at certain times of the year; some are constant as with pictures around our home; some are surprising in that a friend tells an old story….We must be prepared and accept that fact that memories are almost tangible in that they are so vivid once our parents pass.

When our caregiving ends — 're-entry' – establishing a 'renewed normal'…not only do we find that we are missing our parent(s) and grieving, but simultaneously, we are attempting to adjust, without our loved one (and the love they have always given us) and without the demands of time that caregiving required. At this point, we find we can no longer define ourselves in a manner that has become second nature to us over the years….we are no longer a 'loving daughter/son caregiver', we are once again, a 'loving daughter/son'. The words are hard enough to whisper for most past-caregivers due to the loss, but the actual renewing of our own lives takes an equal effort and some thought and lots of time.

After my 10-year caregiving journey with my parents ended and upon discussing this immense change with my cousins and with other caregivers across Canada, who had been on a similar journey, I started to recognize a completely new phenomenon occurring in our country and that is 'the adjustment-year following a caregiving role'. Just as others have had to adjust to a new reality following a change in a long-term role or job, we are finding now, due to the length of time we are spending as caregivers that healthy adjustment is key to our well-being in the months and year plus following the death of a parent who has been in long-term care.

This adjustment involves a re-entry into our lifestyle, a reclaiming of our independence, an acknowledgement of time, an immersion into our immediate family and friends and a reawakening of our interests.

We have to be prepared for this 'new time in our lives'. What can we expect — going back to our old 'normal' it seems is not an option, as too much time has passed and too much learning has taken place. So, just as we were faced with creating a 'new normal' during our care-years journey for our parents and ourselves, now we are faced with establishing a 'renewed normal' for ourselves.

We must make contact with friends; we must look to new or lapsed interests; we must find a part-time or full-time job (if we left such during caregiving); we must volunteer; we must ....do many things. But most of all, we need to recognize that we have to go slowly and have patience and not expect the re-entry process to be overnight.

We must give ourselves time to become familiar once again with our independence. We have changed, we have improved due to our caregiving experiences, and we see our selves differently now. (I realize that some of the same messages have been repeated in other parts of this guidebook, and for good reason, as I have found them important.)

We have to remember that our journey and commitment and love for our parents has enhanced our life...now it is up to us to go forward...and the sun will shine.

How can I keep memories vivid?

It may seem strange to write a suggestion around this easy-to-answer question, but some ideas. that we all might do, warrant mention, we can:

☑ Cluster photographs in one frame: in youth, growing older, at a special event…

☑ Display mementos – put out some keepsakes such as a piece of jewellery or a favourite tie or book or ornament. *(For example: I have Dad's favourite old cap hanging – I can still see him in that cap, it is special and*

I love Mum's purse hanging in my closet as well – I can reach out and touch it whenever I am passing.)

☑ Revisit a favourite activity or place – once in a while do an activity or visit a place that our parent loved or we shared.

☑ Maintain friendships – take time to telephone or visit our parent's old friends on different occasions or invite them for coffee – it is fun and we will probably learn something new about our parent at the same time. *(For example, Dad never visited Italy and knew little of the village that both his parents came from, so, when an old friend visited, it was interesting to hear stories of the location and to discuss the possibility of distance relatives still there.)*

☑ Complete albums – make time (finally!) to get the family albums up-to date, ask questions of relatives so that names and dates are not lost.

☑ Send extra pictures of family members to next level cousins (relatives) as they will enjoy receiving these.

☑ Play some music that evokes a nice memory *(e.g. Blue Spanish Eyes make me think of Mum and Fats Domino's "Blueberry Hill" and Louis 'Satchmo' Armstrong's music make me think of Dad – but be prepared for tears to flow).*

☑ Continue to celebrate Father's/Mother's Day/Birthdays – create a small ceremony or event which can be done each year. *(For example: I decided to plant a little tree in my garden on the 1st birthday year of each of my parents' passing – Dad's is a beautiful Maple and Mum's is a Pink Dogwood. I also buy a flowering plant to celebrate certain parent-related special days.)*

☑ As well, some memories will be created because of the many close caregiving times we spent with our parent. *For example, I kept this card on my computer desk for years from Mum – her way of saying 'thank you' during one care-year – it reads:*

> *I've always had this feeling, even before you were born, that there was some special reason that you, and not some other baby girl, came into my life... I still don't know what that reason is – What I do know is that in my heart of hearts, you were meant to be my daughter. You've been all that a mother could ever hope for, and I just wanted to let you know how very much I love you.*
> (Hallmark Card, 1999)

☑ Add to the family photo gallery in a hallway or bedroom with all the combined photos you have from your parents' albums. I found it was nice to spend a moment when passing these pictures and remember. Have shadow boxes made to house special items *(e.g. For a grandfather's watch)*. Also hang the paintings you have inherited in special locations in your home.

☑ Use special event decorations/home accessories at appropriate times (e.g. my husband and I both enjoy putting out items and revisiting memories of the parents we have lost).

A special idea: My parents are interred on a family grave site – we have had bronze plaques placed for each (now with their parents). There are now six loved ones together. It is a wonderful place to sit and visit.

How do I go forward when my caregiving role ends?

There is no one answer to this!

Everyone a past-caregiver will speak to will have a different answer. But, past-caregivers have told me that they started slowly and found themselves doing some of the following once again or more often:

☑ Chatting with a spouse/loved one by setting aside a special 'hour' each day *(for example, my husband and I, when I am not traveling obviously, have our 'glass of wine chat time' at the end of each work-day now—and it a wonderful oasis in our day and fills a need that we have to connect and laugh and take time to reenter the world of regular events)*.

☑ Browsing book stores and reading more often *(for example, for the first six-months after my caregiving journey ended, I found I was reading 'self-help' books, then I moved onto 'books recommended' and now, I grab several books of any type at a time and keep one on the go. I have discovered that I truly enjoy 'biographies'...as my husband is a voracious reader, I am learning to reclaim my 'time' by once again making quiet time to read).*

☑ Enjoying 'short 3-4day mini-vacations' with a spouse/friend or on one's own *(for example, several months after my mother died, I took a week vacation in Mexico on my own when my husband couldn't get away and yes, it felt strange not to have 'to worry', but I sat at the beach, took long walks, and got to know me once again...I forced myself to make time. As someone who always traveled in the past, either on her own, or on the job and considers travel a passion, I now can 'plan' mini vacations and have reclaimed this past aspect of my life).*

☑ Entertaining small dinner parties; having family brunches (intimate time with close persons 'fills one's cup').

☑ Looking to start a new hobby or interest or finding out more about something one may have had an interest in a long-while ago *(for example, a girlfriend of mine right at the beginning of her caregiving journey decided that she had to do something for herself -- so she started to train once again to run marathons... she recognizes the changes that are going to take place both now and later in her life...a wise woman to be thinking ahead).*

☑ Reconnecting with working friends, by having once-a-month luncheons at favourite restaurants *(for example, reconnecting with other working women has proven rewarding for me...we meet for long luncheons and we do not rush...I have tried to do a luncheon-thing on a semi-regular basis over my adjustment year and a half. I also attend speaking engagement luncheons being held in my city now as I can plan that far in advance.)*

☑ Getting the family 'archives' up to date –how often do we hear ourselves say that we need time to do the family album, to put the pictures on disks, to organize documents....(a great feel of accomplishment goes with this job well-done).

☑ Volunteering on a regular basis or for a cause once-a-year...new acquaintances with new perspectives are to be valued always but especially during this transition period.

☑ Taking a course, try a new hobby or new sport — doing something to enrich our everyday life takes acknowledgement that we have 'time'; it doesn't have to be all-consuming, but it does have to be enjoyable.

☑ And do nothing once and a while...go for a walk with the dogs, stop for a cup of coffee when running errands, go to a documentary or Imax movie during the week, visit a gallery, plant a garden or a series of flower pots...just relearn to appreciate your independence and your time...you don't have to fill your days, you do have to reclaim them.

☑ Now, you decide....go forward because you are a much more interesting and alive individual for having been on a care-years journey!

After Caregiving: Picking up The Pieces
By Brenda Race –FROM "CAREGIVER MAGAZINE", OCTOBER 2006
For further information or to subscribe to "Caregiver Magazine" go to www.caregiver.com

As a caregiver, we totally commit ourselves to caring for another person who no longer functions as they once did in the normal scheme of life. We move in with them or move them to us. We give up our jobs, our own independence, and very often our family and friends. We become so involved with the care of that person out of love that we ourselves are removed from normal day to day living. Our entire life revolves around comforting and making our loved one feel loved. We protect them at all costs. In a very real sense we have given our life for another.... not out of obligation but out of LOVE! The ultimate test of LOVE for another! Then one day we wake up and our commitment has been released to a far greater LOVE in a place of no more pain or suffering! We grieve and then the process of finding our way back into the world begins anew. How do we pick up the pieces and start to live again? I guess there is no so-called normal pattern that each of us has to follow. It seems to come down to taking one step at a time...some walk slower than others and some speed their way back out into the world! Often we take one step forward and two backwards ... it is not an easy process but there is a life after caregiving! We just have to look forward and find opportunities that are once again there for us.Renew old friendships, find a job that you feel good doing, do volunteer work (we already know you are a caring concerned person!), find a new or renew an old hobby.... but begin to take a few small steps towards living again! One of the best therapies is finding a friend you can talk to... one who will listen and support you as you ease back into the world! Soon you will find that life does still exist and you are a part of it! Butterflies are still flying and the birds are still singing. The light of another day is showing through the clouds, and all that you gave up was well worth it in the end! We are better than ever for our commitment. We are forever changed in a good way.... no one can ever take that total love away from us as we again join the world!

Brenda Race, R.N. was caregiver to her mother.

"Neither fire nor wind, birth nor death can erase our good deeds."
– *Buddha*

"Ever has it been that love knows not its own depth until the hour of separation."
– *Kahlil Gibran, from The Prophet*

A poem selected by the Queen to celebrate the life of her mother—the poem and article were printed in the Globe and Mail April 12, 2002.

Mom

You can shed tears that she is gone

Or you can smile because she has lived.

You can close your eyes and pray she'll come back

Or you can open your eyes and see all she's left.

Your heart can be empty because you can't see her

Or you can be full of the love you shared.

You can turn your back on tomorrow and live yesterday

Or you can be happy for tomorrow because of yesterday.

You can remember her and only that she's gone

Or you can cherish her memory and let it live on.

You can cry and close your mind, be empty and turn your back

Or you can do what she'd want: smile, open your eyes, love and go on.

-Anonymous

TOPIC 11

Let's Talk: Recognizing that life doesn't stop, it just keeps rolling on when we become caregivers – learning about ourselves as time goes on

---

What might I have to balance when I become a caregiver?

Personal Anecdote: "Why is there no education readiness program for the care-years, when the emergencies and impacts are so significant?"

Personal Anecdote: "Be prepared for everything and anything during a care-years journey with parents!"

Personal Anecdote: "Do I laugh or what? Okay, I'm laughing."

Suggestion:

55: Remember, being caregivers can't help but affect our lives on many levels – so we must take one day at a time, expect enormous changes and learn as we go

What changes will I notice when I become a caregiver?

Personal Anecdote:
"Why is there no education readiness program for the care-years, when the emergencies and impacts are so significant?"

"Why can't life's events stop for just a brief moment during care-years and give us a chance to catch our breath and adjust? Why is it that life just seems to keep rolling along at its own pace, forcing us to accommodate potential new surprising realities?"

2001 - How did I think life was going to unfold for my parents as they grew older - did I think that they would remain healthy and that the status quo of their retirement regime would continue indefinitely and then one day, they would die? (What about my spouse or partner as we grow older...?) What an 'ostrich' I was.

Where did I form my ideas about how we age - not from books since it not a glamorous topic; not at work as companies only address retirement years from a 'get your ducks in order' savings point of view; not from our peers as they are just now experiencing this chapter of their lives too; not from our governments as they ony speak in general terms about the billions in health care costs which we don't seem to identify with personally. The impact of 'old age' doesn't really hit home, it seems, until it is happening to us and our family.

Perhaps I was a victim of the mass media and I absorbed all those cheerful retirement promises and advertisements. Ah, but those messages are very misleading since they never quite go far enough - they never show what happens later in the lives of those wonderful grey-haired spry seniors who go on cruises, garden daily, take classes, laugh with their grandchildren - the messages never seem to touch on possible the last phase of lifestyle/retirement, the care-years. And the ads certainly never show what happens in the lives of the children of those aged seniors - it seems the care-years is one more taboo topic in our modern society.

So, as daughter/son-caregivers, we learn about the impacts of taking care of our parents first-hand, on-the-job training, with little awareness and sadly even less preparation.

My parents' need for care and their dependency on me, over an extended period of time, combined with my own desire to make sure that their days were as safe, worry-free and as peaceful as possible had a significant impact on my life - and I know that I am no different from all the other daughter/son caregivers, across our country.

What are those big changes that take place when we become care-givers? Some of them are very obvious within the first week but all continue throughout the journey - first of all, there is a huge spike in one's everyday stress level; second, there is a massive learning curve around the issue of caregiving and what is involved; third, 24-hour days don't seem long enough as there is much to organize, re-slotting one's personal, family and work needs to later (ie. clubhouse gerneration); and fourth, there is an anxiousness each month about dollars as care needs are costly.

While in the middle of chaos and health emergencies in the first few years, I didn't have time for reflection, but what a difference a few years 'in the role' makes. Now, I 'see' how our community, our systems and our culture handle 'old age' and I recognize and 'feel' the changes that affected my life starting when my parents entered their care-years.

Less I mislead any reader, I want to mention that there are very important positive impacts as well - I've learned much about my parents and who they are/were, as I spent lengthy *periods time with them over those care-years, listening to their stories and facing serious health problems with them.*

Becoming a caregiver helped me develop into a much more considerate person and definitely a much better daughter. Even though this statement sounds very girlguideish, it remains true; those care-years with my parents strengthened me as an individual (a tug-o-war some days), as your days with your parents will strengthen you.

Yes, I definitely think that there should be a readiness program for this phase of our lives (at the very least, a media campaign), and yes, there certainly must be an easier way for some of us to learn some of life's lessons, but maybe our scripts are written - we are to learn by experiencing the care-years up close.

Personal Anecdote:
"Be prepared for everything and anything during a care-years journey with parents!"

2003 - A raging, out-of control forest-fire firestorm becomes part of our care-journey's experiences and learning.

In the last years of my mother's care-journey, the area she lived in, Kelowna, British Columbia, was faced with mass evacuations due to a fierce forest fire-firestorm. It had been a hot summer and in August a lightning storm hit, splitting a tree in Mum's backyard ,and more significantly starting a fire on a mountainside park in the valley, 30 miles plus from her home city. At first, no one had really thought the fire would get any where near the actual homes in the suburbs and in the city itself, even though the fire was raging uncontrollably close by on the surrounding mountains. As the weeks passed, people still felt that "the firefighters would have it under control any day now". But it continued to burn viciously mile upon mile and then often sporadic winds seemed to encourage it to pick up speed. It filled the province's news headlines as fire fighters were recruited from across the country.

During this time, I flew into the city one afternoon in order to take my mother to a special social event and give the caregiver a respite time. Almost instantly the severity of the circumstance was staring me in the face, as I had to use my window-wipers in order to keep the falling ash off the car. People in Mum's neighborhood were put on 'evacuation alert'; they had been told by the police and emergency fire fighting units to have bags packed for evacuations, just in case, therefore the caregiver had packed some articles of Mum's clothing into a suitcase earlier that week.

That evening, after helping Mum into bed, I decided that I would pack up what she told me was important—her photo albums, some paintings and some of the family memorabilia. I placed all into the car along with her wheelchair, walker and medication bag...as we were told to do, just in case. Just before nine o'clock that same night, as I closed the curtains in the kitchen, a huge red glare was visible—I was shocked— the actual flames now could be seen as it had reached the bluff above Mum's home. I decided that the time had come, we had to evacuate within the hour. I gently woke Mum and explained that we weren't rushed but we should leave the house, as the fire was getting closer. (There were regular bulletins on the radio and television by now in the area.)

Everything and everyone, it seemed, was 'on the move'. As I was buckling Mum into the passenger seat of the car, with darkness all around except for the frightening bright red glow all across the night-sky, I noticed a large black bear a few feet away by at the plum trees just off the carport—all the animals and bird life were fleeing the fire and moving into urban centers—it seemed as if that bear and I formed a silent agreement at that precise moment, we would leave each alone as we both had bigger worries to contend with right then. Mum, at the same time, kept her head bowed, she said she did not want to look up at the fire as she had seen the damage fire had done before in her lifetime to her family. (When she was growing up, her family lost their home on the prairie, Manitoba, to a fire; her oldest brother had lost his home to a fire and Mum and Dad lost much of their home, in Trail, B.C. pre-retirement, to a massive flood.) I felt so sorry for her having to relive these memories at 91 years old.

As we left the cul-de-sac, we witnessed an alarming sight, a traffic line of hundreds and hundreds of cars snaking their way slowly along this quiet road, all fleeing. The horse-trailers carrying prized animals; valued antique rocking chairs and dressers strapped on roof tops of cars, seniors and children sitting quietly in back-seats, flash-lights and police directing everyone in an orderly manner was the stuff of television shows not our real-life. Mum kept her head bowed. The sky glowed all around us from the smoke and ash in the air.

My cousin lived a few miles away, closer to the city and so we went to her home; we settled Mum in bed and brought in some of the bags, by now it was close to ten-thirty. As we watched the local news bulletins, we were told that many neighborhoods now were being evacuated, and that the one we now were in was now being put 'on alert' for pending evacuation. It seemed impossible - the fire had reached many residences and suburbs. I immediately started to telephone motels in what I assumed might be safe areas and eventually found a motel on the other side of Lake Okanagan where the fire was not threatening at all. My cousin and I packed up and once again, woke Mum and for the second time that night, evacuated. The three of us now moved into a motel to wait out this emergency. The next morning, we registered with the local municipal government authorities (especially as all seniors needed to be accounted for), lining up for the paper-work with thousands of others who now found themselves living in gymnasiums, in schools, in friend's homes and in hotels. I had kept in contact with our then live-in caregiver during this period and with relatives.

My cousin stayed with Mum, and under the watchful eye of the police, I went back to Mum's house for a few hours or so to do tasks that were deemed necessary. With large pieces of smoldering bark and ciders landing on my mother's house, a sprinkler system was quickly mounted on the roof-top to keep it cool. As I grabbed a chain saw along with my cousin-in-law who was helping me cut down the surrounding shrubs that were right against the house to prevent them from catching on fire if hit by burning ashes, I began to wonder what I would do if we were to loose Mum's home. What were my options then for her care—I had not, during our journey to date, thought of that option, as I assumed Mum would live in her home as long as her health allowed her to—now this choice may not be ours to make—it was out of our control.

Weeks passed, and Mum and I found ourselves back in a line-up finally, but, this time heading home as her neighborhood was declared safe...the fire continued to rage but had changed direction and preventive measures were in place so it would not threaten this area again. Mum always shook her head when she thought of that threatening fire in her beloved Kelowna; and every time for the next two years when she saw her yard, she would blink away small tears remembering the many beautiful 20-year old shrubs she and Dad had planted, those that had been cut down around her home. My mother never complained once during that unbelievable summer event that threatened her lifestyle. As a matter of fact, one day we actually ended up laughing about it, as while we were in the motel she joked, "Well, I wanted a vacation away for a few days this summer, I guess this is it!"

I learned a lot about myself and my mother and the treatment and care of seniors during this emergency. I am proud of how she handled this unpredictable time and proud of how the leaders and volunteers in her city and our province also responded.

Again I must reiterate the lesson - we must be ready to acknowledge the fact that life's events will just keep on coming...even when we are busy trying to balance a care-years journey!

By the year 2020 there will be more than one billion people 60 years or older in the world, nearly double the current number, WHO (World Health Organization). *(Source: The Vancouver Sun, October 2, 1998.)*

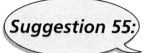 **Suggestion 55:** *Remember, being caregivers can't help but affect our lives on many levels – so we must take one day at a time, expect enormous changes and learn as we go*

Taking care of our parents is more than assisting, working with and looking out for our parents so that they can have quality days throughout their care-years. Caregiving also includes coping well with challenging changes taking place in our personal lives during this period and learning about ourselves and our communities as we travel this journey with our parents.

How will being involved in the care-years affect my life?

The following lists some of the impacts of caregiving – if already on the journey, these will be familiar – if preparing for the care-years, these can be expected.

☑ **When a caregiver, there is reduced personal time.**

We can expect to have to condense our time on a daily, weekly, and monthly basis to include the numerous tasks and details involved in caregiving.

We will try to squeeze all that we are presently doing at our own home (work, leisure, sleep, house chores, family time, children's functions) into a shorter time frame; in other words, at first, rather than eliminating or delegating, we will attempt to fit everything in and then will be surprised to find we are not producing the same results.

We will feel exhausted, as we will have 'less personal time to fill our (empty) well'. We can expect to hear ourselves whisper from time to time, "My life just isn't my own anymore".

> "If you are all wrapped up in yourself, you are overdressed."
> – *Kate Halverson*

☑ When a caregiver, there are organizational matters to attend to, always.

We can expect to have numerous medical, legal, financial and household matters to attend to on behalf of our parents. We can expect that some of these matters will require attention on a regular basis in response to on-going health situations. We know that some tasks can't be left until later, that we have to organize on-going methods that will work for us.

We realize that it is urgent that we get a handle on what is going on in our parents' affairs right from the start and that if we don't make the effort now, we may be in a real mess tomorrow.

We may tend to procrastinate initially especially if there are forms and documents to attend to; we will learn over time to handle each matter as it arises. We might find ourselves thinking, "I don't really want to do that right now".

> "The conscience of well-doing is an ample reward."
>
> – *Seneca*

☑ When a caregiver, there is less spontaneity.

We can expect that some of our usual spontaneity ("let's do this, let's try that") with our family and close friends will be reduced and replaced with careful planning.

We recognize that vacation times have become shorter than before care of our parents was required.

We admit that we probably could stray off from our normal schedule, but we remain constantly aware of the fact that we can't change our plans too greatly as others have to know where to contact us in case of emergencies. We feel guilty thinking, "I just don't seem to be having much fun these days".

> "The most wasted of all days is one without laughter."
> – *E. E. Cummings 1894-1962*

✓ **When a caregiver, there are increased monthly expenses to consider, always.**

It doesn't take long to find out that caregiving costs tend to be significant each month and can deplete nominal savings rapidly.

We realize that it is important to pay attention to expenses as soon as possible, to reduce everyone's worry.

If our parents are financially secure, with good savings and investments, and have planned for their care-years, then the topic of monthly expenses will not consume time and will not be an anxious item in our personal life.

If our parents are comfortable but do not necessarily have a large savings, then an increase in our personal monthly expenses may be felt when caregiving needs extend beyond a few years.

If our parents live comfortably but have few savings, then the need for care dollars will be immediately felt.

We realize that our parents did not plan/were not able to plan for their own long-term care needs, yet we know that there is no way around these care costs as services and special equipment are required – it is up to us to guarantee that they get them.

We understand fully that good planning could have helped reduce care-related financial concerns and we chastise ourselves for not paying attention to our parents' finances earlier.

From time to time, we may hear ourselves wonder, "Where am I going to get the money from".

> "Necessity is a hard nurse, but she raises strong children."
> – *Unknown*

☑ **When a caregiver, there is a feeling of being on a roller-coaster ride, day after day.**

We know that on our caregiving journey there will be tears – and laughter – and frustration – and relief – and quiet time…After the first care-year, we will feel like we have been on a roller-coaster ride for a long period of time.

We realize that it is never 'one thing at a time', as our days include many mini-problems, and these are time-consuming and emotional regardless of size. After a troubling phone call, we may think sadly, "There always seems to be something".

As our parents' health and safety are constantly on our minds, we can expect to get less quality sleep time.

We understand that exercise and nutrition are very important in maintaining our health right now and we know we sometimes neglect these, but it seems we are on a non-stop treadmill.

We carry an unspoken awareness and fear of a parent dying unexpectedly.

> "What lies behind us and what lies before us are tiny matters compared to what lies within us.
> – *Ralph Waldo Emerson, 1803-1882*

☑ **When a caregiver, there is a realization that family members and a few close friends are needed now more than ever for support.**

We can expect to need the support of family members and very close friends perhaps more so than in the past – we need them to lend an ear.

We know that we will need to talk to our partners/spouses about our caregiving responsibilities and hope that they will continue to be supportive helpers, available sounding boards, great companions as our care-years journey continues.

We begin appreciating all the people around us in a different way. At the end of a telephone call, we will hear ourselves saying, "Bye and oh, thanks for being there for me".

"Friendships multiply joys and divide griefs."

– Unknown

☑ **When a caregiver, there is a reassessment of job/career demands in light of caregiving demands.**

We acknowledge that tending to our caregiving responsibilities is like having a second or third job. We can expect that balancing these multiple 'jobs' is going to be challenging. (*That's why care-giving is at times described as "the career we never planned for ourselves".*)

We will come to the conclusion quickly that a demanding career is very difficult to sustain with a level of high energy and commitment along side demanding care-years commitments. (*SuperWoman/Man is a myth.*)

Whether we have children at home or not, whether we are working full-time or part-time, whether we have our own business or work for a large corporation, whether we have to travel on the job or not, it will be clear that our job/career is just one more responsibility that is going to have to be adjusted so we can 'fit everything in'.

"When I look at the world I'm pessimistic, but when I look at epople I am optimistic."

– Carl Rogers

☑ **When a caregiver, there is a need to focus on the moment.**

We should expect to over-react at crisis times during the first year and to become calmer as care-years continue.

We will learn to take a deep breath when the telephone rings and we are told of a health or care problem with one of our parents, even when our stomachs are flipping into knots during emergency times.

We realize that what we have to do is think, that is, think before reacting, to 'take a minute' to gather our thoughts and focus on what is important at that precise time.

"I never think of the future – it comes soon enough."
– Albert Einstein, 1879-1955

☑ **When a caregiver, there is an awakening regarding personal care plans.**

We can expect that our 'care-years wake-up call' with our parents will turn up some thought-provoking questions which we will want to address (sooner versus later) regarding our own future care needs – questions such as: why have I got insurance policies for when I die – and not for how I want to live down the line? "Where do I want to live? Who is going to take care of me? Have I told my family of my plan? Do I have a plan?"

Author's Note: (Oh yes, I have become very aware of the need for a living-benefits insurance package! I approach these policies like I do house and car or earthquake insurance – I don't like paying for them monthly and hope that I may not ever have to use them soon – but I wouldn't be without them. It really boils down to the fact that I want peace of mind knowing that I have covered my bases where LTCI is concerned plus I am free to enjoy all my retirement in the future without worrying over the eventual high costs for my own future care-years.)

A new wine for seniors – A smile for the day for all of us as we age.

Vintners in several grape growing areas of Canada, especially those which primarily produces Pinot Blanc, Pinot Noir, and Pinot Grigio, have developed a new hybrid grape that acts as an anti-diuretic. It is expected to reduce the number of trips older people have to make to the bathroom during the night.

The new wine will be marketed as Pino More.

"To look backward for a while is to refresh the eye, to restore it, and to render it more fit for is prime function of looking forward.
– *Margaret Fairless Barber*

☑ **When a care-giver, there is a need to alter one's own personal semi-retirement and long-term retirement plans to some extent.**

We can expect to have to adjust our semi-retirement plans – both the timing of and savings for – to some extent due to the impact of our parents' care needs.

We may feel that 'we have to work a bit longer than we originally planned'. We realize that taking care of our parents may require that we also re-think any relocation plans, especially if an only child.

We know that we will find it necessary to dip into our personal retirement savings to help meet care-years costs if over time the costs exceed what our parents have saved on their own – without planning, this is a very likely scenario.

> "Do not take life too seriously. You will never get out of it alive."
> – *Elbert Hubbard*

This smile is for women readers—It is my only gender-biased chuckle in the book (I hope). A woman who had attended one of my LTC seminars sent it to me.

Susan was driving home from one of her business trips in Northern Arizona, when she saw an elderly Navajo woman walking on the side of the road. As the trip home was a long and quiet one, she stopped the car and asked the woman if she would like a ride. With a silent nod of thanks, the woman got into the car. Resuming the journey, Susan tried in vain to make a bit of small talk with the woman. The old woman just sat silently, looking intently at everything she saw, studying every little detail, until she noticed a brown paper bag on the seat next to Susan. "What's in the bag?" asked the old woman. Susan looked down at the brown bag and said, "It's a bottle of wine. I got it for my husband". The Navajo woman was silent for another moment or two. Then speaking with the quiet wisdom of an elder, she said, "Good trade."

☑ **When a care-giver, there is a growing awareness of the larger societal issues involving the elderly and their care.**

As a result of our caregiving role, we can expect to become a great deal more interested in our health care system, government programs, seniors' issues, use and abuse of medications, support groups, services available, financial planning options, safety concerns within the home, income tax regulations...

We will realize that the all-encompassing issue of 'the elderly' touches on many areas and that the care-years is a big business within our society.

We may catch ourselves, while reading a newspaper story or watching a television program, saying, "I don't know why our government doesn't do something about that" or " I don't know why I haven't thought of that."

> "Problems cannot be solved at the same level of awareness that created them."
>
> *– Albert Einstein, 1879-1955*

☑ **When a daughter/son care-giver and/or care-guide, we live with an unsettling feeling that someday our caregiving will come to an end.**

We know all too well that some day our caregiving will no longer be required and we silently acknowledge why.

We can expect that there will be days when we will really struggle with this knowledge and other days when we will be able to accept the future somewhat.

We can expect to feel uncomfortable at unexpected times – and alone when we catch hold of parent memories.

We may hear ourselves saying to a close friend or family member, "I just don't know what I'll do when…" or "I just don't want to think about that". We know that we carry unspoken fears.

We can expect that our thoughts and prayers late at night will include not only many "thank you's" for the day, but also our constant wish for our parents' good health and happiness tomorrow and tomorrow…

> "Worry never robs tomorrow of its sorrow, it only saps today of its joy."
>
> *– Leo Buscaglia*

☑ **When a care-giver, there are many opportunities to laugh at oneself.**

We can expect that there will be many days when we will look at a something taking place between our parents and ourselves and the humour of the moment will be hit us. *(For example: Mum's telephone calls were often 'interesting' to say the least and did give me cause to laugh at my own reactions. One day, when I asked what she was doing, she replied, "I'm watching the Gay Rights Parade, and what do you think of it, I think it is okay and fine." So, we talked on a topic I certainly hadn't thought would be raised by my mother, at this point in our lives, but then again, why not? Another time she called and said she had just watched a program on AIDS and what a dreadful disease it was; she then went on to express the opinion that if she had a choice this day and age, she wouldn't have sex, "too much risk" (smile, smile) – now the humour of this story you ask is where. Well, it was evident when I mentioned, during this AIDS conversation, the need for one and all to use condoms, and she responded, "Yes, well that's precisely what I want to talk to you about." Yikes, my 90-year old mother was cautioning her newly-divorced daughter – she had phoned me to have a 'mother-daughter talk'. What to do but laugh, I was speechless!)*

We can expect that some of our parents' habits/routines/timing will strike us as quite humorous, even when we are in the midst of a care-problem.

We may retell a specific story often and laugh at ourselves over and over again. At the end of a story describing a crazy care-related incident, we will hear ourselves saying to our patient listener, "It really is too, too much you know."

A smile sent to me by a caregiver – Have you ever been guilty of looking at others your own age and thinking, surely I can't look that old? I was sitting in the waiting room for my first appointment with a new dentist and I noticed his DDS diploma, which bore his full name. Suddenly, I remembered a tall, handsome dark haired boy with the same name had been in my high school class some 40-odd years ago. Could he be the same guy that I had a secret crush on, way back then? Upon seeing him, however, I quickly discarded any such thought – this balding gray-haired man with the deeply lined face was way too old to have been my classmate. HMMMM or could he? After he examined my teeth, I asked him if he had attended Morgan Park High School. "Yes, Yes, I did. I'm a Mustang," he gleamed with pride." "When did you graduate?" I asked. He answered, "In 1961, why do you ask?" "You were in my class" I exclaimed. He looked at me closely, then that wrinkled old son of a bitch asked, "What did you teach?"

"Laughter is the shortest distance between two people."
– *Victor Borge*

Personal Anecdote:
"Do I laugh or what? Okay, I'm laughing."

One afternoon, my cousin and I, quite by accident, met at a pancake house for lunch. She had her 81 year old mother, my aunt with her, who had at that time been placed, for a short period, in a mental assessment residence due to medication problems and accompanying complex personal behaviours; I had Dad (86) with me from the caremanor, as it was our time together during one of my visits.

Our luncheon proved chaotic from the get-go. At the beginning, my aunt wasn't hungry ("I just want coffee, nothing more") but later reached over to nibble from everyone else's plate causing each of us to complain a little. Soon, my aunt decided to order her own meal long after our meals were served - while all this was taking place, Dad concentrated quietly on eating his favourite of pancakes, bacon, eggs, toast and coffee.

As my aunt was experiencing free time waiting for her lunch, she turned and asked a woman at a neighbouring table for a nail file - upon being given one, she started filing her fingernails at the table. Before my cousin could object, a couple who knew both our parents stopped to say hello, my aunt quit filing, my Dad paused and everyone chatted happily for a few minutes.

Within seconds, our luncheon atmosphere unexpectedly changed once again - my cousin casually made a little comment about her mother's dramatic weight loss, whereupon my aunt, ignoring her daughter's remark, slyly looked up and catching Dad's eye quipped, "Everything gets smaller with age, right Chuck!" and winked at Dad.

Needless to say, my cousin and I smiled across the table at each other due to the quickness of this comment, but Dad, taking offence, promptly pushed himself up, grabbed his walker and headed rapidly for the door of the restaurant. My aunt thinking that Dad's movement signalled lunch was over, speedily got up, grabbed her walker and immediately followed Dad out the door. Like in a freeze-frame picture, my cousin and I stared at each other, coffee cups still in hand.

Action! Realizing that we now had two disabled and confused senior parents wending their way between moving cars crossing the busy mall parking lot, we scrambled to get the waitress' attention, pay the bill, grab our coats and get outside.

After Dad and I were settled safely in the car, he commented that he was annoyed with my aunt - when I asked him why, he said he couldn't quite remember the exact words, but he felt that my aunt "was being her usual self" and had "made a joke at (his) expense".

My cousin and I still share a laugh regarding that day - not at our parents' behaviours - but at our own frenzied actions as daughters. It really was too, too much.

"When a person can no longer laugh at himself, it is time for others to laugh at him."
– *Thomas Szasz, "The Second Sin", 1973*

Seniors jailed for bank heists... Rudolf Richte, 74, and Wilfried Ackermann, 73 of the so-called Grandpa Gang, were convicted of robbing 14 German banks and getting away with more than $1.23 million over 16 years.

Hagen, Germany—Three men dubbed the Grandpa Gang because of their ages were convicted of robbing 14 banks of more than $1.23 million, sometimes using guns dating back to the Second World War.

..."It's unbelievable how easy it is to rob a bank once you've done it a couple of times" Wilfried Ackermann said during his trial, adding that fear of having no money and spending the rest of his years in a nursing home drove him to commit the crimes.

Richter said he was motivated by the fact that he had already served time in prison for a bank robbery he did not commit. "Many years were already gone from my life," he said. "When I got out of prison I said to myself, "Now I'm going to get even."

The three men also were convicted of violating weapons laws, and they were accused of using handguns dating from the war, as well as automatic weapons and sometimes even fake hand grenades.

...They were arrested last year in a parking lot in the town of Wimbern, where they allegedly were preparing another heist. *(Source: Associated Press, June 11, 2005)*

☑ There is huge personal growth.

As our care-journey progresses, we can expect to seek a greater understanding of the impact of this time on our lives. We can expect significant personal growth because of this caregiving time with our parents.

We may make conscious decisions that we want to become more caring individuals or better listeners; we may begin to take a moment and talk a bit longer to seniors in our neighbourhood because we are now more aware of that type of need...

We may find that we have gained an interest in different types of books (from self-growth, spiritual to financial planning…) simply because the time seems right; we may begin to listen more closely to radio talk shows or watch television documentaries on issues pertaining to seniors.

We will also find ourselves wanting to ask probing questions of our politicians regarding issues impacting the health and quality of life of seniors.

We will reflect, from time to time, saying to whomever will listen, "I can't begin to tell you what I've learned during this period of my life."

"We must become the change we want to see."
– Mahatma Gandhi

☑ And finally – when no longer a caregiver

When our care-years journey with our parents is over, we can expect large-scale adjustments will have to be made 'within', especially if the journeys have been long and/or challenging.

Re-entry into a non-caregiver world, a lifestyle we previously had, takes time – give yourself that gift of time.

"There is no joy for birth and death save to enjoy the interval."
– George Santayana, 1863-1952

TOPIC 12

Let's Talk: Settling in – Finally

Can our family expect to settle into a normal lifestyle during our LTC years?

Personal Anecdote: "A mother-daughter vacation – We had a great time!"

Suggestion:

56: Accept a 'new normal' lifestyle – stay positive

57: Hug your parent(s) – at every opportunity – seniors need physical contact just like everyone else

Can our family expect to settle into a "new normal" lifestyle during our LTC years?

Personal Anecdote:
"A mother-daughter vacation – We had a great time!"

Mum's 'normal' lifestyle all her life was to take a summer holiday, so when she telephoned me early in 2000 and asked, "Where are we going on our summer vacation?" (we hadn't vacationed together much since I was a very young teenager), I was surprised yet pleased. I now knew that Mum had accepted our 'new normal' lifestyle. Yes, Mum knew if she was to go on a vacation during her care-years, it would have to be with me - our "new normal" way of doing holidays was established.

So, Mum and I went on a three-week vacation in August 2000 - driving from British Columbia south through Washington State, through Oregon, to the northern tip of California and return. It was an amazing time for both of us.

When asked, Mum said the highlights of her holiday were seeing the power of Mount St. Helen's, the physical beauty of the Oregon coast, and the massive California Redwoods - I might add that she also enjoyed discovering factory outlets!

My highlight was spending an extended holiday period with my mother. We enjoyed the daily adventures, the hotels and resorts, the views along the ocean, the afternoon sundaes, the souvenirs and the continuous chatter with each other....

The key to our successful holiday together was two-fold, first, very careful organization months in advance (thank gosh for the Internet), second, Mum's easy-going manner and appreciation of adventure.

One could say that Mum and I had settled into a regular care-years lifestyle. Mum was positive, secure, had established *enjoyable routines and knew that she had a good caring team of people to support her daily. As for me, I - finally - had become a little more relaxed knowing that all was in order and we were doing the best we could do. We both continued to miss Dad and Mum, without saying, missed her independence.*

We learned to take one day at a time, one month at a time and so it went year after year - we settled into our care-years lifestyles - trying to make them a rewarding experience, accepting 'a new normal' way of living as part of the care-years.

Notes:

_____

_____

_____

_____

_____

_____

_____

_____

_____

_____

_____

_____

_____

_____

_____

_____

_____

"I promise to keep on living as though I expected to live forever. Nobody grows old by merely living a number of years. People grow old only by deserting their ideals. Years may wrinkle the skin, but to give up interest wrinkles the soul."

– Douglas MacArthur

Suggestion 56: Accept a 'new normal' lifestyle – stay positive

I ask in this section if we can eventually expect to settle into a "new normal" lifestyle during our family's care-years? In all honesty, after ten years and a great deal of reflection, I remain unsure.

So in response to my own question, I have to say that 'change' must be incorporated as part of one's 'norm' and an aspect of one's overall lifestyle when on a care-journey. We can learn to live with that factor on an everyday basis and plan for it in our activities. So if 'success' means 'accepting change', that is, accepting a new way of doing an everyday activity, and as well being as prepared emotionally and organizationally and financially as possible, then, yes, it is possible to settle into a 'new normal' way of living during the care-years.

I want to emphasize (again) what now seems obvious in hindsight, but really does come as a surprise at the time one is absorbed in caregiving, and that is, that life's relationships/children/careers do not go on hold because one is absorbed with caregiving. *(For example, during the span of my decade-long care-journey with both my parents, I changed jobs; went through a divorce; repurchased my own house; and remarried.)* Life's regular activities do continue rolling along, with everyone involved being absorbed into a 'new normal' lifestyle.

Looking back, I think that my parents settled into a regular care-years lifestyle better than I did in some way, as they lived in the moment and looked forward to the next day's events; whereas, it seemed I was constantly looking to tomorrow and trying to be prepared for the next step – would we need new sets of caregivers; would Dad be fine in the nursing home in the long-run; would Mum have an unexpected heart-emergency; were the costs of care going to increase; would new equipment be needed; would the government subsidized program continue; would my parents' house itself need attention (e.g. over the years, the house required a new living quarter for the caregivers, a new roof, new microwave, new toilet, a new garage and then there was the forest fire…) would I be close by when needed. Yes, this way of living sounds very unsettling, but as each day unfolded over the years, we seemed to adapt to our 'new normal' way of living as a family. In this way then, our care-journey proved rewarding for all of us.

...And I shall eat dessert every single day!

"What's it like to be old?" I was asked. The other day a young person asked me how I felt about being old. I was taken aback, for I do not think of myself as old. Upon seeing my reaction, she was immediately embarrassed – but I explained that it was an interesting question, and I would ponder it, and let her know.

Old age, I decided, is a gift. I am now, probably for the first time in my life, the person I have wanted to be.

Oh, not my body! I sometime despair over my body – the cellulite, the wrinkles, the baggy eyes, the jiggly thighs, and the sagging butt – and often I am taken aback by the old lady who lives in my mirror, but I don't agonize over those things for long.

I would never trade my amazing friends, my wonderful life, my loving family for less gray hair or a flatter belly.

As I've aged, I've become kinder to myself, and less critical of myself. I've become my own friend. I don't chide myself for eating that extra cookie, or for not making my bed, or for buying that cement ornament that I didn't need, but looks so avante garde on my patio.

I am entitle to overeat, to be messy, to be extravagant. I have seen too many dear friends leave this world too soon; before they understood the great freedom that comes with aging. Whose business is it if I choose to read until 4 AM and sleep until noon? I will dance with myself to those wonderful tunes of the 50s and 60s and if I at the same time wish to weep over a lost love, I will.

I will walk the beach in a swim suit that is stretched over a bulging midriff, and will dive into the waves with abandon if I choose to, despite the pitying glances from the bikini set. They, too, will get old.

I know I am sometimes forgetful. But here again, some of life is just as well forgotten and I eventually remember the important things. (continued...)

Sure over the years my heart has been broken. How can your heart not break when you lose a loved one, or when a child suffers, or even when a beloved pet gets hit by a car? But broken hearts are what give us strength and understanding and compassion. A heart never broken is pristine and sterile and will never know the joy of being imperfect.

I am so blessed to have lived long enough to have my hair turn gray, and to have my youthful laughs be forever etched into deep grooves on my face. So many have never laughed, and so many have died before their hair could turn silver. I can say "no" and mean it. I can say "yes" and mean it. As you get older, it is easier to be positive. You care less about what other people think. I don't question myself anymore. I've even earned the right to be wrong.

So, to answer your question, I like being old. It has set me free. I like the person I have become. I am not going to live forever, but while I am still here, I will not waste time lamenting what could have been, or worrying about what will be. For the first time in my life, I don't have to have a reason to do the things I want to do.

And I shall east dessert every single day!

(This e-mail story was sent March 19, 2005 from a friend)

Notes:

_____

_____

_____

_____

_____

_____

_____

_____

_____

"Remember that happiness is a way of travel, not a destination."
– Roy Goodman

 **_Suggestion 57:_** _Hug your parent(s) – at every opportunity – seniors need physical contact just like everyone else._

Who reaches out to touch your arm? Who hugs you? Who pats your shoulder or your hand? Think of all the ways we have daily physical contact and think, who provides that. Then ask yourself, "Could I go through a day, a week, or more without any of that contact?" Then ask a logically answered question, "Do elderly people need physical contact too – will I later?" So where does it come from – from whom?

As… a daughter/son-caregiver, we have to keep in mind our priority during this period of our lives, as it never waivers – to care for our parents each day, to remain positive and to give them attention.

All of us will define 'attention' differently when it comes to our parents, but it is important to remind ourselves that 'hugs' (yes, that touchy-feely word) are an important component of 'attention' for seniors. We all need human contact and that need obviously continues when we are 'old-old'; but where do we receive such contact from as a senior (a spouse may have died or be residing in a different location, friends are probably in-care too at about this time, there may be little interaction with all the outside public and family members…). So, a hug from a daughter/son, as often as possible, is important to each of our parents' well-being and joy.

We should not take for granted that because we start off as daughters or sons who love our parents, that we will automatically be able to be good caregivers for them too – we have to work at that new role – caregiving truly does involve effort, dedication, time, involvement and a great deal of commitment.

Hugs, I have come to understand, are part of good caregiving—and make for great care-receiving!

 "We make a living by what we get. We make a life by what we give."

– *Sir Winston Churchill, 1874-1965*

TOPIC 13

Let's Talk: Gaining a greater understanding of your own future care-years

Should I be thinking about and planning for my own care-years now?

Suggestions/Information/Exercises:

 **Test yourself – are you ready for your care-years?**

The colour 'grey' – possesses the ability to stimulate reflection and imagination, therefore suggesting an aura of intelligence and wisdom *(Pavey, 1988.)*

How well are you prepared for your care-years?

1. I know that my retirement years consist of 2 parts—the well-deserved, relaxing, independent years *and* the changing health, increased dependency care-years...and I have an understanding of the needs of 'both' stages.................. *(yes/no)*

2. I have a good grasp of my financial, legal, and insurance affairs—I feel confident that all my necessary documents are up-to-date and in order.................. *(yes/no)*

3. I have made my end-of-life wishes known (e.g. written a will and discussed services with a family member)............... *(yes/no)*

4. I feel confident that I have a good retirement plan in place—because it takes into consideration the financial impact from my changing health needs............... *(yes/no)*

5. I know at least one government agency in my community with the responsibility for seniors' health needs and I am aware of one of the programs offered through that department............ *(yes/no)*

6. I know what to look for and how to elder-safe my home (inside and out) in order to reduce potential accidents............... *(yes/no)*

7. I understand the medications I am taking and I have asked about many of the possible side effects related to those medications and the signs to watch for..................... *(yes/no)*

8. I know what to do during health emergencies and I am familiar with some of our local health unit's resources for seniors......... *(yes/no)*

9. I am aware of some of the subtle signs of dementia to watch for in my family members (e.g. the need for routines)............ *(yes/no)*

10. I am aware of the various care-programs in my community (e.g. at-home services, live-in caregivers, rehabilitation services, adult daycare options, care home living, assisted living complexes) and know how to request assistance to obtain these............ *(yes/no)*

11. I understand many of the costs associated with the care-years (e.g. carehome fees, live-in caregiver salaries, therapy costs, medications, cleaning services, special equipment...) and realize that there is now a special insurance policy available to help me cover certain care-related costs when needed..................... *(yes/no)*

12. I am confident that there will be 'few surprises' for my family to contend with during my senior years because my care plans are in place.................. *(yes/no)*

Results: If you have 2 or more 'no' circles, you need to put forth some effort to get your planning in order...no surprises later!

Start at **www.longtermcarecanada.com**

"Though no one can go back and make a brand new start, anyone can start from now and make a brand new ending."

(Anonymous)

Food For Thought As The Century Ended: On October 12, 1999, person number 6 billion was born. If you look at your life you may list hundreds of thousands of people you know, but 6 Billion makes any number look small. Our world is getting smaller. The Web allows us communication around the globe. Yet, do we really know each other? If you were to shrink the exact proportion of the world population to create a village of 100 people, here's what the village would look like: 57 Asians, 21 Europeans, 14 North and South Americans, 8 Africans, 51% female, 49% male, 70 non-white, 66 non-Christian, 70 would not be able to read, 50 would suffer from malnutrition, 75 would have never made a telephone call, less than 1 would be on the internet, 1 would have a college education, half of the entire villager's wealth would be in the hands of 6 people, all 6 would be citizens of the USA. *(Source: Fax received January 20, 2000.)*

Notes:

Suggestion59: *Know what is available – how well do you understand Canada's retirement income system?*

If you think that you're too young to start planning your retirement, consider these facts:

✓ Your retirement years could last a very long time—almost as long as your working years

✓ Fewer than half of workers in Canada are covered by employer pension plans

✓ People are starting to save earlier for retirement

Rule of Thumb! Many financial planners say that you will need about 70 percent of your current (pre-tax) earnings to maintain your standard of living in retirement. ...However this is only a general rule. But the real question is: How much are you going to need for your LTC years?

Do you know what you will receive/should be receiving during your retirement?

Canada's Retirement Income System
Simply Stated...Our retirement income system consists of three levels:
#1: OAS, Old Age Security
#2: CPP, Canada Pension Plan/QPP Quebec Pension Plan
#3: Private Savings/Employee Pensions

1ˢᵗ Level:

OAS: Old Age Security provides the first level, or foundation. If you meet certain residence requirements, you'll be entitled to a modest monthly pension once you reach the age of 65

✓ You must be 65 and a resident of Canada for at least 10 years after your 18ᵗʰ birthday to receive OAS in Canada.

☑ If you wish to receive the basic OAS pension outside Canada, you must have lived here for at least 20 years after your 18th birthday. The (GIS) Guaranteed Income Supplement, an income tested benefit paid in addition to the OAS, and the Allowance (an income tested benefit paid to a spouse or common-law partner of a GIS recipient) are only for seniors who live in Canada. They stop if you leave Canada for more than six months. If you return to Canada you must reapply.

☑ Have you lived or worked outside Canada? Canada has international social security agreements with many countries that could help you meet the OAS residence requirements or get other social security benefits from either country.

☑ Apply for it 6 months before you turn 65.

☑ OAS is taxable.

☑ If your net individual income before adjustments (line 234 on the tax return) is above a set threshold, your OAS pension will be reduced. This threshold ($59,790 in 2004) is adjusted each year for inflation. Only about 5 percent of seniors receive reduced OAS pensions, and only 2 percent lose the entire amount.

☑ For example:

The threshold for 2004 is $59,790. If your income in 2004 was $75,000, then your repayment would be 15% of the 'difference' between $75,000 and $59,790. $75,000 − $59,790 = $15,210. $15,210 × 0.15 = $2,282. You would have had to repay $2,282 in 2004.

GIS: Guaranteed Income Supplement is an additional monthly benefit for low-income OAS pensioners. GIS is not taxable and the application must be renewed each year. This is usually done by filing an income tax return before April 30. You must apply in writing for GIS.

The Allowance provides a monthly benefit to low-income people between the ages of 60 and 64. It is available to the spouses or common-law partners of OAS pensioners and survivors to help bridge the gap until they become entitled to receive OAS at 65. It is not taxable. You must apply for the allowance. There is also an "Allowance for the Survivor" one can apply for.

2nd Level:

CPP: Canada Pension Plan is the second level of the system. It provides you with a monthly retirement pension as early as 60, if you have paid into it. The maximum, in 2006, is $844.58.

- ☑ The CPP (which began in 1966) also acts as an insurance plan, providing disability, survivor and death benefits for those who qualify.

- ☑ Quebec has a similar plan, called the Quebec Pension Plan.

- ☑ Your CPP contributions are based on earnings between a minimum and maximum amount.

- ☑ CPP contributions are tax-deductible.

- ☑ Generally all workers over the age of 18 pay into the CPP (or QPP) and qualify for benefits.

- ☑ Over the course of your career and if you raise a family, there may be years when you have low or even no earnings. This would normally reduce your CPP benefits because of the lower contributions you make during those years.

- ☑ Credit splitting – separated or divorced spouses or common-law partners equally divide CPP credits for the years they have lived together; an applicant's ex is notified of the request in writing.

- ☑ CPP excludes 15 per cent of your lowest earning years when calculation your retirement pension. Time spent away from work while you raise children under the age of seven can also be 'dropped out' of the calculation. These provisions ensure that your future pension is not reduced because of a few low-earning years.

☑ CPP pensions are adjusted for inflation every January to keep up with the cost of living.

☑ You can receive your CPP retirement pension regardless of where, if outside of Canada.

☑ It is not automatic, you must apply for CPP benefits (at least six months before you want it to start).

☑ You can request an official statement on-line at:
www.sdc.gc.ca/en/isp/common/proceed/socinfo.shtml

These first and second levels of Canada's retirement income system make up Canada's public pension system. Today, these pension form a significant part of the income of Canada's seniors. But public pensions are not intended to meet all your financial needs in retirement. Rather, they provide a modest base for you to build upon with additional, private savings.

3rd Level:

Private Pensions and Savings—it is important to know where your other income for retirement will come other than from OAS and CPP.

☑ **Employer pension plans**. About 40 per cent of workers in Canada are covered by an employer pension plan. Formally called, Registered Pension Plans (RPPs).

There are two main types: In a 'Defined benefit plan" you are promised a monthly pension income that is determined (or 'defined') by a formula. It is generally the employer's responsibility to ensure that sufficient funds are available to pay your pension when you retire. The employer assumes the risk of investing all contributions wisely to guarantee the future value of your pension. The second type is a "Defined contribution plan' whereby the amount of the pension you receive is not set in advance. Instead, you and your employer contribute a set (or 'defined') amount to the plan, usually determined as a percentage of earnings. An account is set up in your name and the contributions are invested by your employer. Your pension will be based on the funds that have accumulated in your account when you retire.

☑ **Savings: RRSPs Registered Retirement Savings Plans** are the most popular method of personal savings for retirement.

- They are individual, personally managed savings plans.

- Contributions are tax deductible and investment income is not taxed as it is earned.

- The tax is paid when funds are withdrawn from these plans.

- You must have earned income from employment, professional or business activity in order to contribute to an RRSP.

- You are allowed to contribute as much as 18 percent of your previous year's earned income to an RRSP, up to 'a maximum set dollar amount' each year.

- Two programs allow you to make withdrawals of RRSP funds without paying tax immediately: the Lifelong Learning Plan and the Home Buyers' Plan.

- You may contribute to an RRSP up until the end of the year in which you turn 69.

(Source: Human Resources Development Canada, renamed Social Development Canada as of 2006, call 1-800-277-9914 (English) or 1-800-277-9915 (French) or 1-800-255-4786 (TDD/TTY) or browse www.sdc.gc.ca)

Hint: Know what you may receive.

Rates for Canada pension Plan (CPP) and Old Age Security (OAS) and Guaranteed Income Supplement (GIS) – Allowance
These rates are for 2006 –
Check each year for updates–1-800-277-9914 English or 1-800-277-9915 French
(Source: Social Development Canada www.sdc.gc.ca)

Canada Pension Plan 2006 Maximum Rates			
Retirement (Age 65)	$ 844.58	**Flat Rates**	
Disability	$1,031.05	Disability Pension's Flat Rate	$ 397.58
Death Benefit (Lump Sum)	$2,500.00	Survivors under age 65 Flat rate	$ 155.13
Survivors (Under age 65)	$ 471.85	**Combined Pensions**	
Survivors (Over age 65)	$ 506.75	Survivor/Retirement (Over age 65)	$ 844.58
Child's Benefit	$ 200.47	Survivor/Disability	$1,031.05

Old Age Security $484.63 and Guaranteed Income Supplement – Allowance				
(Rates in effect April - June 2006)				
Table	Recipients who are:	Yearly Income Limit (Excluding OAS)	Maximum Monthly Supplement	Maximum combined Monthly Pension + Supp.
1	single, widowed, or divorced pensioners	$14,256.00	$593.97	$1,078.60
2	married/common-law partners, both pensioners	$18,720.00	$389.67	$ 874.30
3	pensioners whose spouses/ common-law partners are not pensioners	$34,368.00	$593.97	$1,078.60
4	pensioners whose spouses/ common-law partners (between ages 60 & 64) are in receipt of the Allowance	$26,496.00	$389.67	$ 874.30 **Maximum Allowance**
5	Allowance payable to widowed spouse or common-law partner	$19,368.00	$967.24	N/A

2006 OAS pension repayment level $62,144 to $100,914

Thinking Of Retiring?

Do you know what you will receive in Canada Pension Plan (CPP)?

2006 data only, please call to update this information each year

Canada Pension Plan **Retirement benefits** can be paid as early as age 60. The benefit is reduced by half of one percent (.5%) for each month you are under age 65. The advantages of taking early **Retirement benefits** may outweigh the disadvantages.

2006 Early Flexible Retirement Table
Maximum retirement pension payable in 2006 is $844.58

AGE	60	61	62	63	64
Monthly CPP taken early	-60 months	-48 months	-36 months	-24 months	-12 months
Present decrease @ 1/2% per month	70%	76%	82%	88%	94%
Monthly payments	$591.21	$641.88	$692.56	$743.23	$793.90
Monthly decrease	$253.37	$202.70	$152.02	$ 101.35	$ 50.68
Payments prior to 65	$35,472.60	$30,810.24	$24,932.16	$17,837.52	$9526.80
Make-up time in months	140	152	164	176	188
Make-up time in years	11.66	12.67	13.67	14.67	15.67
Breakeven point at age	77	78	79	80	81

* In order to take advantage of an early retirement pension you must have completely or substantially stopped working. Amounts shown are based on an individual making maximum contributions.

For additional information concerning the Canada Pension Plan and Old Age Security or to schedule an appointment to see a counsellor, please call:

English 1 800 277-9914 **French 1 800 277-9915** **TTY 1 800 255-4786**
or visit our website at **www.sdc.gc.ca**

Hint: Use this tool for a glimpse of your retirement future – found at: https://srv260.hrdc-drhc.gc.ca

CANADIAN RETIREMENT INCOME CALCULATOR
Plan Your Retirement Today!

An excellent tool for glimpsing one's retirement future – this tool allows all of us as Canadians to figure out what will be there from government sources and how much more we might need for our retirement

The Government of Canada has developed this calculator to help you plan for retirement. The calculator takes you step by step through an estimate of the ongoing income you may receive throughout your retirement from:

- Old Age Security (OAS);
- Canada Pension Plan (CPP) or Quebec Pension Plan (QPP);
- Employer pension(s);
- Registered Retirement Savings Plans (RRSPs); and
- Other sources of ongoing income.

The Old Age Security program and the Canada Pension Plan (or Quebec Pension Plan) provide a modest secure base on which to build your private savings. The calculator helps you assess your personal financial situation and helps you decide which steps to take to reach your retirement goals.

Go to https://srv260.hrdc-drhc.gc.ca to glimpse your retirement future.

Hint: Calculate your RRSP Contributions: Are you contibuting the maximum possible?

RRSP Contributions Too Often Overlooked

At middle age, it becomes all the more important to put something away for the non-working years that lie ahead, say experts

Statistics Canada reported in October that Canadians invested $28.8 billion in their RRSPs in 2004—which sounds like a lot but is only about eight per cent of what they could invest. Moreover, during 2004, only 30 per cent of eligible taxpayers made any contribution at all.

"I don't think people take responsibility for their financial security. It's an epidemic in this country," says Warren Baldwin, regional vice-president of T.E. Financial Consultants, a national firm based in Toronto.

"People don't understand the issue. They think there is a free lunch. They figure 'I've got Canada Pension. I've got a pension from my employer. I'll be fine." Rubbish! Do they want to live in the poor house? Do they want the government running their finances for them in the future?"

Baldwin acknowledges that some couples might be able to cobble together a reasonable retirement income from a combination of CPP, OAS, and pension money if they have saved diligently, their mortgage is paid off, and they live modestly. But he adds, that in all likelihood even they would have to accept a much lower income and lower their standard of living.

Moreover, warns Robert Snowdon, a chartered accountant in Ottawa, people who live off a fixed amount of CPP and OAS are going to be facing added costs for such basics as gas, hydro, property taxes, and house insurance. "People might be able to make ends meet now, but tow year later find they don't have the money they need," he says. It is essential to have some independent means of retirement income, advisers say.

(Source: RRSP Extra, The Vancouver Sun, February 15, 2006, article by Jeff Buckstein, CanWest News Service)

Do you know what you'll need – and for how long?

RRSP: Saving for future: Retirement, Financial planners say people underestimate how long they will live. A person 65 should be planning for another 30 years.

"Government benefits will not be enough for most of us to live on in retirement, Floyd Murphy, a financial planner and president of the Nakamun Group in Vancouver. "They'll prevent us from starving, but a single person with maximum CPP and OAS benefits will collect about $1,300 a month. Can we live on that?"

(Source: RRSP: Saving for future, legitimate tax shelter, The Vancouver Sun, CanWest, February 15, 2006)

Average annual savings of Canadians is $5,947

(Statistics Canada and CIBC)

 **Long-term care insurance, an option for Canadians – LTCI is as much about caregiving as it is care-receiving.**

Cross reference to Topic 9

Long-Term Care and LTC Insurance in Canada – I believe that:

☑ Long-term care is not a sexy, glamorous or trendy issue – it is a complex problem with the ability to devastate families emotionally and financially.

☑ Care-years planning is not considered a major component of lifestyle or retirement planning – it is an urgent one that cannot be overlooked by adult Canadians in our turbulent, ever-changing environment.

☑ Long-term care insurance is not a frill, accessory or supplementary product – it is a 'must-have' necessity element of any adult Canadian's overall financial plan.

☑ Long-term care insurance does not replace family love and care, it 'completes it'.

☑ Long-term care insurance is for caregivers AND care-receivers.

☑ Having long-term-care insurance can aid in the long-term health of your whole family, contact your financial advisor or insurance company—educate, educate, educate yourself…be informed.

Author's Note: As I am not in the financial services field, when questioned on the details of a long-term care policy, I always refer the person to his/her financial planner or an insurance expert for quotes, as each person is different in terms of her/his needs and health history and age.

But one point I do want to emphasize, when asked "What will it cost?", is the following as I believe it to be true, "There is no one answer to that, just keep in mind that the amount paid in premiums will always end up being a fraction of the cost of long-term care itself when needed."

LTC (whether in one's own home or in a health facility) is the single largest out-of –pocket cost for adults over 60 – *therefore it is a significant form of risk!*

I receive many requests for information on long-term care insurance. As I am not a planner, an insurance representative or a broker, I am only expressing "my personal opinion as a consumer" of this product.

Long-term care planning is an important part of retirement planning and should be done with a person qualified and experienced in both areas, retirement and long-term care planning. (Note: It is a very wise person who purchases LTCI when younger and with good health.)

I believe LTC insurance truly is a product for the 21st century.

Patty Randall,
Advocis Conference,
Banff School, 2004

The following are a few hints to use if/when you are 'considering' the purchase of LTC insurance – keeping in mind, this is from a 'consumer's perspective':

1. **What companies offer the product?** There are only a few companies in Canada that have this product. Always consider the company's history and reputation before purchasing. You likely won't be using the benefits for many years in the future so 'company experience and stability' are important considerations.

   Review these major players in Canada's LTCI market – alphabetically they are:

   ☑ AXA Financial Services www.axa.ca

   ☑ Clarica/Sun Life www.clarica.com

   ☑ Desjardin Financial www.dfs.ca

   ☑ Knights Of Columbus (www.kofc.org) for members only.

   ☑ Manulife Insurance www.manulife.com

   ☑ RBC Insurance www.rbc.com

   ☑ 10-Star www.tenstar.com

2. **How to purchase?** You can purchase LTCI from your trusted financial planner or insurance agent. If you don't have an advisor to discuss this type of policy with, you might:

☑ Telephone the Advocis Association (Canada's professional association for insurance and planning) 1-800-563-5822 or visit the Association's web site at www.advocis.ca, under the tab "Consumer Information... Find an Advisor" and search for a list of insurance agents in your area then call around to find out who has 'expertise' in LTCI. (Look for someone who is actively selling LTCI.)

☑ Go to the websites of the companies listed above and ask them for a representative in your area or you may also want to ask your Bank or Credit Union for guidance (Of course you must then realize that each are going to refer you to an agent who sells their particular product).

In short, do call around, compare features and benefits and costs – <u>and</u> – understand the terminology (is it limiting or freeing).

3. **When to buy?** Buy LTCI 'sooner rather than later' as health is always unpredictable, in other words, don't wait, this policy is 'health sensitive' and 'years sensitive'. (Hint: Better to buy 5 years too early than 5 minutes too late!)

   Try to buy <u>well</u> before age 65 as costs are based on age; look for a 'spousal discount'; one must be 'health eligible' to qualify. (Note: Even if you have a certain health problem now, it doesn't mean you won't qualify – so always ask.)

4. **Coverage?** Very important: If possible, buy a policy that allows you to have for BOTH 'home care' and 'facility care'. (As we can't read the future, try to have your bases covered!)

5. **Benefits?** Look at your present lifestyle and ask carefully about all of the 'benefits'--many are common in different companies' policies. Always try to buy a policy that will best meet your future needs and your personal situation. Always buy inflation coverage if possible.

6. **Some questions to ask re: the features of the policy**—What are you buying and what are you wanting to receive? (Note: Always take notes when in a discussion on this type of policy.)

   • What are the exact services I will get from this policy, if/when I need to use it (claim)?

   • What are the daily/monthly benefit amount ranges, such as: how much a day will I get, how many services per year?

   • What method of payment does the company use? Are the $$$ paid going to be paid monthly as a lump sum directly to my family or me eventually for my care? Or are the care-bills paid only when incurred? Which is best--consider all aspects (e.g. the use of the dollars if paid directly; family disputes over money; the elimination of financial abuse if the bills are paid; the management of the care payments and so forth.) Again think about policy payment methods in the context of your family situation and who will care for you, then decide which type of policy is best for you.

- Do you want a policy where some of your premiums are 'refunded' to your estate; are you willing to pay extra for that feature? (Opinion: This is not a good savings plan method, but you should ask about this feature.)

- Can you renew?

- Is there a special coverage for Alzheimer's?

7. **Your Personal Care-Guide?** Have you considered who will be your 'care-years guide', a child, a relative, a younger sibling, a best friend— whom do you value to help you out and make decisions with you? Notify the person if/when you buy a policy so they can access it at the time needed (maybe communicate via a letter or note so no one forgets later). (*Note: No use buying LTCI if no one knows or remembers you have such a policy when the time comes and you need it.*)

8. **Claiming?** What is the language you need to understand? Activities of Daily Living (ADLs)? Ask your long-term care specialist/agent/advisor to give you a sample policy from the company he/she is recommending to you. Then, ask that agent/planner/specialist to explain carefully how the policy works: understand the definition of 'activities of daily living'; understand the ADLs of the policy you are considering; understand how the ADLs trigger a claim, you don't want any surprises later! Understand if your policy allows you/your family to hire 'licensed certified caregivers' on your own or if you will have to go through a 'licensed care agency'—important question as it relates to expenses later.

9. **Think about it?** Look carefully at fixed-amount policies (pay only to a maximum amount) and also be careful when 'switching/substituting one policy for another'. Any amount of long-term care insurance is better than nothing at all in place when planning for care-years stage of life, but fixed amount policies, for say, e.g. $100,000, may run out of money before you run out of 'need'! In addition, some companies do not offer pure LTCI but do offer you the opportunity to transfer your disability/ critical illness insurance for LTC needs. Because new products and new hybrids of the LTCI product are being announced often, always check!

10. **Cost of the insurance?** Very important: Try to put the risk of needing care as you age in perspective…what are you already paying for and what is it costing? What are the trade-offs? What are your priorities right now—is your future care one of your priorities? Should it be one of your priorities?

What is the break-even point when you come to claim?

For example, as mentioned in Topic 9, in the last personal anecdote, *"I felt I have/had no choice, I incorporated long-term care insurance into my care plan…"* one of my LTCI policies cost me $84.65 a month when I purchased it. It provides me with a $70 a day benefit (for either nursing home or at-home care). It was a 'capped rate' so I know the monthly cost can only go up by 50% ever and I also knew at purchase that I would have to pay on it for the next 20 years (unless I started to claim on it prior to the 20 years, then no further payments would be required during the claim period).

So how did I quickly calculate the approximate break-even point when I purchased this policy? Let's say, I pay $84.65 a month for the next 20 years (I didn't factor the increase into it for this exercise as I just wanted to get 'a feel'), I will have paid $20,316 into this LTCI policy over the 20 years. Then let's say I require care after that and begin claiming my $70 a day or $2170/month benefit. ($20,316 divided by $2,170/month = 9.36 months). So, I will have spent all of the $20,316 I paid into this policy in 9.36 months (my break-even point) and then for the rest of my care-years (which could last 5 - 8 or so years!), after that first 9.36 month, I would be living on the insurance company's dollars, from which I purchased the policy. So, my break-even point for what I will have paid into this policy is 9.36 months.

*Special note from a financial planner who sells LTCI--Most of us will only purchase long-term care insurance once in our lives. Therefore, choosing the 'right' company and product is important. As a consumer, sometimes I'm attracted to products because of lower prices. When it came to my long-term care insurance decision, however, I choose to focus on product 'guarantees' not just current rates. Most companies have five-year price guarantees but after that the price can increase without any limits (currently in Canada there is only one company that guarantees the ultimate cost of its plan but more companies will probably follow soon perhaps). The financial

consequences of long-term care can be catastrophic for families. I didn't want my family or my retirement plan to be at risk by choosing a long-term care insurance plan that didn't have some future cost guarantees built into the plan.

When talking with my girlfriend, who is an insurance agent and loves her job of helping people, she put it this way, "You put insurance in place to pay for care-year expenses, this way you don't have to spend valuable retirement income on these expenses. In other words, using insurance proceeds frees up cash for your retirement FUN".

So, be sure that you ask the following important question regarding the cost of your premium over time: How is my premium going to go up in cost over the 5-10-20 years that I will be paying. The cost of any premium may be increased 'about' every 5 years by the insurance companies—but what you are trying to gauge is 'what is the maximum cost you may have to pay for this coverage' (let's say, when you are in your 70's or 80's and you are now watching your budget a little more carefully). Do you prefer an insurance policy from an insurance company that can guarantee you the cost 'when' you buy, as you don't want to have to let your policy go just about when you might need it. But again, the benefits and claiming processes may be more important to you, and so these considerations will take on a significance when talking to an advisor.

CONCLUSION:

- LTCI is a complex product. And yes, the cost maybe one big obstacle to buying—but personally, I would rather make do without some other type of item in my life than this particular insurance plan given our demographic, economic environment combined with our health system circumstances and long life expectancy. (This is not a 'fear' tactic – as mentioned, I do not sell insurance – it is just my conclusion after years with this issue.)

- What it comes down to is your peace of mind and need for independence and quality care—it is simply, the costs of care per month or per year later versus the cost of my policy per month or per year now—you do the math and think about your needs. (On my care-years journey, I lived 'the math' and thus have purchased two LTCI policies over the past few years for myself and my husband has one for himself. – I want to enjoy myself now and later – peace of mind!)

- **Finally, compare an LTCI policy to other insurance policies you hold—as LTCI should just be considered like all other policies you have to reduce your risks**

What about your house insurance? How much a year do you pay for it? Yet the chances of your house burning down are 1 in 1,200… but none of us would go without this type of insurance would we, we wouldn't risk a catastrophe to such a major asset—and even if we never get to use our house insurance, we won't even think that we have 'wasted all that insurance money' over the past decades…having this type of insurance policy in place gives us peace of mind to know we and our loved ones are covered in event of a rare happening to our homes. (Think about it from an insurance perspective: Once you reach age 65, the chance that you will need long-term care is 10 times greater than the chance your house will burn down.)

What about car insurance? How much a year do we pay for it (are you a one or two car family)? Yet the chances of a catastrophic crash are 1 in 240…but we wouldn't be without this type of insurance either would we, we wouldn't risk the accident—and even if we never get to use our car insurance, we won't question that we've 'wasted all of that insurance money', as a matter of fact we are usually proud of our driving record….having this type of insurance policy in place gives us peace of mind to know we and our loved ones are covered in the rare event of a major accident that we might have to spend a long period recovering from.

So, what about long-term care insurance? How much a year might this be worth to you? AND the chances of using our long-term care insurance were estimated at 1 in 2 in 2005 and 70% in 2006…so are you weighing the value of this type of insurance…are you risking that you could reach old-old and need some services…are you risking your loved ones health and lifestyle in that they, who love you, will then be faced with the financial costs of your care….and growing older is not even considered a rare event! So, you decide, compare your risks and decide if your care is another risk, just like your house and car that you should think about insuring!

Author's note: I did compare my risks and I am not going to self-ensure my LTC just as I would not self-ensure a risk to my home; I am not going to be in denial either that I will probably need some LTC in my later years as I just might reach an advanced old age (or need help before that); and I certainly don't want to be dependent on government programs for my care as I am unsure what they might be or how often I may be able to get help and of course, I don't want to be dependent on my family either because I want to spend quality time with them, not be sitting watching them doing all the care activities for me (someone else can do that while I sit and have a cup of coffee with my children), so, for the same reasons I purchase house and care insurance, peace of mind, I considered LTCI right for me. I don't want to worry over my future, especially if there is a product in place right now in Canada that can help me insure my quality of life when I am unable to do my normal everyday activities each day due to my advancing age (when my 'biological warranty period' may be running out) and/or problems with my health.

Just think about it...and put **a plan** in place for your long-term care years, whether it means purchasing LTCI (that is, transferring the risk to an insurance company) or doing something else—but, please, do anticipate needing care sometime during your retirements years and do some financial planning for that stage of life.

Female Baby Boomers?

US based Study – Re: Female Baby Boomers – Are we thinking correctly or what? A groundbreaking study commissioned by the Center for Financial Learning, the leading online resource for objective financial education, finds that 63% of female Baby Boomers believe that when the time comes, their spouse will provide them with long-term care. However, research indicates 59% of women over the age of 65 won't have a spouse to take care of them due to divorce, widowhood and increased longevity. *(Conducted by the Center for Aging Research & Education, CARE, and entitled, "Secure Tomorrow's Autonomy Today" the study is the first in a series of GE-sponsored studies designed to underscore the myths and realities of the retirement experience, July 23, 2001, Business Wire)*

Only children?

US based Study – Re: Only Children – Food-for-thought for Canadians? The study shows the issue (of long-term care) is particularly important for only children, who often carry the familial burden. Respondents with only one child are four times more likely to believe that they can rely on their child for long term care needs than those with two or more children. As a result this group (those with only one child) is more likely to forego planning for long-term care needs. "Surprisingly, this study supports the notion that individuals with only one child may be placing unique familial expectations on them," said Dr. Hayes. "Conversely, those without any children have the most knowledge of long term care planning and insurance and are more positive about growing older." To avoid facing a long-term care crisis, women need to educate themselves about long-term care options and be aware of the risks associated with being unprepared. *(Conducted by the Center for Aging Research & Education, CARE, and entitled, "Secure Tomorrow's Autonomy Today" the study is the first in a series of GE-sponsored studies designed to underscore the myths and realities of the retirement experience, July 23, 2001, Business Wire)*

For all of us—do the math

USA -based article (excerpts): Food for thought for Canadians Even with The Differences in Our Health Care Systems….

(*Author's note: This article has been edited in order to have each reader complete it in the context of his/her province or territory. The USA has offered Long-term care insurance for many years, for Canadians this is still a relatively new product being offered by Canadian insurance companies.)

I *(Ron Caballer, vice president of Academy Mortgage LLC)* have spent much of my career in estate and tax planning, and until last year, I never considered the costs of long-term care an issue. Perhaps you were there, too. For you, this is a reminder. For others, it is a refresher to reinforce the significance of long term care planning and LTCI in your clients' lives. This applies to those in the financial service industry as well as to those working with seniors in other professional capacities.

There are many reasons for doing estate planning at as early an age as possible, particularly when considering the purchase of LTCI (lower premiums – both annually and over a lifetime – and the absence of disqualifying health problems).

LTC is either custodial or supervisory:

• Custodial care helps people perform the six "activities of daily living:" bathing, dressing, toileting, continence, eating and transferring, which is the ability to get into and out of chairs and beds.

• Supervisory care is required in cases of cognitive impairment, which is caused dementia. Causes include Alzheimer's, Parkinson's, stroke and head injures. Cognitive impairment does not include purely psychiatric conditions, such as depression or schizophrenia.   (continued...)

LTC is common and expensive. Nationally, good nursing homes charge an average of (fill in blank $ for your province) per year, though some regions and facilities are slightly less. Other regions or facilities are considerably more expensive – fill in for your city. And good assisted living facilities charge (fill in blank $ for your area) per year.

Remember, those are the room-and-board charges. Both nursing homes and assisted living facilities charge extra for other services and supplies, which typically range from (fill in approximate blank costs for your area per year).

LTC is frequently provided at home. The need for and cost of home care varies enormously. For someone needing three to four hours of (extra) assistance (over an above what the government programs provide per week in your area) to take a bath and dress, home care costs approximately (fill in blanks per hour and then per month and per year for your area). 24-hour-a-day care costs (fill in blanks per month, per year for this service). (*Author's Note:* In Canada, *less than one in four (23%) family caregivers are currently receiving any formal home care services to assist in caring for their family member, in the form of a personal care worker, nursing or homemaking assistance*).

More than 50 percent of those over 85 need some form of long-term care service. Eleven percent of Americans (one in nine) who reach age 65 will need more than five years of nursing home care, in addition to any care at home or in assisted living facilities, and it is not unusual for someone to need 10 to 20 years of care. (*Author's Note: In Canada, one is most likely to be receiving care because of physical disabilities (61%), but close to one in five have both physical and mental difficulties requiring longer than 6 months of care – six in ten (62%) of the caregivers have already been providing such care to their family member for at least three years, and one in five (20%) have been doing so for more than 10 years.*)

Long-term care is one of the worst risks to self-insure because of the high incidence of need and the high expense. Consider: Only one in 1,200 people use his fire insurance, and the average loss is $3,428. Only one in 240 uses his automobile insurance, and the average loss is $3,000 US.

(continued)...

Nearly one in two people over age 65 will spend some time in a nursing home* (average stay, 2.3 years**) *(Author's Note: In Canada, the average stay is closer to 3.5 for men and 4⁺ years for women)*. More than 70 percent of those over 65 are expected to use home health care.* The catastrophic risk is for the one in nine (11 percent) who requires nursing home care for longer than five years at an average cost of $50,000 to $60,000 each year. *(Author's note: This varies in Canada greatly especially as we have subsidized care.)* This expense is expected to triple in the next 20 years (in the USA).

Even the wealthy do not 'self-insure' homes and cars. Shouldn't we advise our clients not to self-insure for LTC – a potentially greater cost? While many high-net-worth clients could certainly afford to self-insure, the peace of mind of a long term care policy allows them to more freely consider lifetime gifting options that will benefit worthy causes, future heirs and reduce estate taxes.

*Source: HIAA, "Long Term Care: Knowing the Risk, Paying the Price"

**Source: U.S. Census Bureau

(Source: Article, 'LTCI expands options in estate planning', from ProducersWEB.com, by Ron Caballer, vice president of Academy Mortgage LLC)

(Canadian Data Source: National Profile Of Family Caregivers in Canada, 2002, Statistics Canada, Health Canada)

No extended warranties available—As LTC Insurance is relatively new in Canada, we can perhaps learn from the USA experience, even though our health systems are different.

Boomers and The Urgency to Buy LTC Insurance Now

From the USA National Underwriter, letter to the Editor from Jack Stayer President Northern States Brokerage, In Menomonee Falls, Wisc.

Jack Stayer writes: Here are some questions to raise with boomer (clients or yourself), to help them understand why they need to buy LTC insurance now.

"How long do you keep a car? Two years? Three years? Six years? How many miles will you tolerate on your car before you start to worry about possible mechanical problems? When you purchase a new car, the possibility of mechanical problems or failure are probably the furthest from your mind, right? But as the car gets more and more miles (years) on it, that little nagging doubt starts to creep into your mind about the possibility of 'something going,' right?"

Then, point out how we all believe we are invincible, up to some point, even though we are not.

You might say: "Haven't you been hearing more these days about baby boomers who are no longer in the picture of health? They are having heart attacks, bypass, and angioplasty. Others are suffering from cancer or diabetes. They're outside the 'warranty years.'"

The point is, boomer clients can't "afford," health-wise, to wait any longer to buy long-term care insurance. As I tell my own clients, "health buys LTC insurance, not premium." It doesn't hurt to point out that there's no "extended warranty" on this, either.

Notes:

"Kind words can be short and easy to speak but their echoes are truly endless."

– Mother Theresa

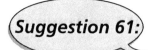 **Suggestion 61:** *Looking to the future – are you planning accordingly?*

These clips offer you food-for-thought in six areas:

- **Debt and Your Future**
- **Investments and Your Future**
- **Technology and your Future**
- **Medical Procedures and Your Future**
- **Staying on the Job Longer and Your Future**
- **Retirement and Your Future**

☑ Debt and Your Future—Where do you stand now? In the future?

Canadians Retiring With Debts…. Canadians are retiring during prime earning years with a more lackadaisical attitude toward debt, a new survey suggests, but economists warn the trend can't continue. The average retirement age is now 58, according to an Ipsos-Reid survey conducted for RBC Financial Group. And while 85 per cent of working Canadians polled believe it's important to pay their debts before retiring, 48 per cent don't believe it's necessary to retire debt-free. Currently, about one-third of retired Canadians have debt, with the average load weighing in at about $35,000. *(Source: Canadian Press, December 2005)*

Debt vs. Income for Canadians

A survey from the Vanier Institute of the Family shows average household debt at $70,920, up 40 percent from 1990, while the average household income is $55,000, up only $500 from 1990.

(Source: Smart Money, Vancouver Sun, February 17, 2006)

☑ Investments and Your Future—Will your money be able to last as long as you do?

Ensuring that your money lasts as long as you do.

Managing our investments is something we'll be doing for a long time now that life expectancies have increase. The good news is that we are living longer. But that means developing investment strategies that may have to deliver 30 years of income, after retirement, said mutual fund analyst Ranga Chand…. "You certainly need to have a plan. You need to know where you are going, "he said. "In other words, will your money last as long as you do?" Chand urges us to put money into registered retirement savings plans. They will help plan for a future that is handing us both short and long-term challenges. *(Source: Ensuring that your money lasts as long as you do, Smart Money, The Vancouver Sun, excerpt from article by Carla Wilson, February 17, 2006)*

Aging by the numbers

- The number of Canadians aged 80 and over rose 41 per cent to 932,000 in 2001. That is expected to jump by 43 per cent between 2001 and 2011, when it will top 1.3 million.

- Just over eight million tax-filing citizens, aged 25 to 64, put money into RRSPs and RPPs (registered pension plans) in 2001.

- Average percentage of those savings into RRSPs was 52.3 per cent.

- Average share of income going into RRSPs and PRRs was 11 per cent.

- Average annual savings of Canadians is $5,947

- The personal savings rate of Canadians was negative, at -0.2 per cent in the third quarter of 2005. That is -1.6 per cent change from the previous year.

(Source: Statistics Canada and CIBC, February 17, 2006)

☑ Technology and Your Future—What might be available and what might you want 20 years from now or more in the future?

Use of Robots

Robot can recognize 10,000 words…. Japanese-built device can recognize and talk to 10 people…. A child-shaped humanoid robot that can recognize about 10,000 words….The Wakamaru robot can recognize the faces of up to 10 people and talk to them. When linked to mobile phones, it can also work as a monitor to check situations at home, such as a burglary or someone falling ill, Mitsubishi-Heavy Industries Ltd said. It would be the first time a robot with communication ability for home use has been sold. "This is the opening of an era in which human beings and robots can coexist," it said.

(Source: Associated Press, August 2005)

☑ Medical Procedures and Your Future—What are the trends? And why are they coming about?

Travelling for hard-to-get medical procedures

"Medical tourism' not all sutures and sunshine…Timely Medical Alternatives' clients are seniors 'simply bypassing the lengthy waiting lists here' They're a new breed of traveling patient who combine surgery with a stay in an exotic locale. Some call it "medical tourism", an industry predicted to hit the $1-billion mark in India alone by 2012, as rising health costs and long waiting lists at home send North Americas and Europeans packing. As well as hard-to-get medical procedures, cosmetic surgery also primes the market for surgical tripping.

But it isn't all sutures, sunshine and Singapore slings for those ducking Canada's take-a-number-and wait-your-turn health-care system. *(Source: The Vancouver Sun, June 14, 2005, an excerpt)*

☑ **Staying on the Job Longer and Your Future—Early retirement? Regular retirement? Who will define it for us?**

Stay on the job longer: Caisse head

Early retirement incentives adding funding pressure to pension system

The growing funding crises at many of Canada's largest pension plans cannot be resolved until incentives for early retirement are removed, warns Henri-Paul Rousseau, head of the Caisse de depot et placement du Quebec, the country's largest institutional investor.

"We do not have a pension plan problem, we have a retirement crisis," said Mr. Rousseau, chief executive officer of the Caisse, which manages assets worth \$122-billion for 20 pension and insurance funds in the province.

Over the past five year, poor returns and low interest rates have created a growing deficit at more than half of the country's traditional pension funds, Mr. Rousseau said. These funds do not have the assets they need to cover future pension promises. The first response, he said, has been to try to increase investment returns or change the structure of the plan so that employees are no longer guaranteed a pension based on wages and years of service–a move from a traditional defined benefit plan to a defined contribution plan.

But changes in plan design or investment strategies, Mr. Rousseau said, cannot be expected to solve a growing and fundamental problem with the pension system–people are entering the job market later, living longer and are spending an increasingly smaller percentage of their life in the work force.

Indeed, under many generous traditional pension plans with early retirement options, workers are spending more years collecting a pension than they are punching the clock, he said. "This is the major problem in my books concerning pensions. This is just not sustainable….Something has got to give." continued...

….Since it is unlikely that Canadians will be willing to shorten their lifespan to solve the country's pension problems, Mr. Rousseau sad the obvious solution is to reform the system so that it no longer rewards workers for leaving the job market before they turn 65.

"We have to stop the tend to subsidize early retirement. That has to be stopped. That's nonsense,"" said Mr. Rousseau, who at 58, said he is not planning to retire any time soon.

….pension plans should be providing incentives to workers to remain on the job. If no action is taken, he predicted that by 2030 the retirement age would have to move to 72 to keep pension plans funded.

For that reason, Mr. Rousseau told his Bay Street crowd, brought together by the association of Canadian Pension Management, that the government and the industry need to seriously study Canada's whole retirement system as it was designed more than 40 years ago.

(Source: Globe And Mail, March 30, 2006; article by Elizabeth Church, Toronto)

☑ Retirement and Your Future—The Big Unknown?

Not Shy About Planning: Baby-boomer seniors-to-be are thinking about life after work in ways their parents never did. Get ready for the next wave of Third Agers

(Note: The First Age is the development phase, the Second Age is the productive phase and the Third Age is retirement years).

"Previously you retired and that was it. You sat around and read, played golf, sailed, whatever. Now people are looking for a more active, more fulfilling retirement."

Such preparations were foreign to his parents' generation. "There was never much thought given to retirement. I never heard it discussed in my household, Crawford recalled (John Crawford is a retired gerontologist/professor of Simon Fraser University, and founder of Canadian Academy of Senior Advisors which offers training across Canada for people who want to become certified senior advisors). continued...

Baby boomers do not want their parents' retirement. ... "They want a totally different lifestyle." The baby boomers who are retiring now are better educated than their parents, they're healthier, they're more urban, they want more excitement in their lives. They have ahead of them an expected 30 years of retirement life whereas their parents often worked right through to 65, retired and didn't have that long a life after that.

"This new retirement is really a whole new life stage for the baby boomers," (Barbara) Walker, a retirement counselor said. "That's the challenge for them—to make it personal, to make it fun, to make it exciting." Financial planning is only a small part of retirement preparations. For the most part, baby boomers have heeded the advice on that front, although they still worry about their income. That's why many seek new forms of employment, set up small consulting firms, return to their former employer on a contract basis, work part-time or train for a new career.

But they also need to think about their attitudes towards aging, their health and their relationships with spouses and friends, she said. "All of these factors are going to change as soon as they retire." *(Aging Gracefully, second in a four part series, by Janet Steffenhagen, WestCoast News, The Vancouver Sun, January 19, 2005)*

What is the retirement 'red zone'?

The Retirement "Red Zone" Years

Stakes get higher and mistakes are more costly

Most investors know they are supposed to save. But far too many do not know what to do immediately before or after they retire.

"The retirement 'red zone' – the crucial five years before and five years after retirement – creates a new framework for thinking about retirement security," says Jac Herschler, senior vice-president and head of marketing for Prudential Annuities.

For investors, the stakes get much higher and the mistakes much more costly during this period. While a young investor, over time, could recover from two years of 15% losses, it is almost impossible to make up for such a loss in a year or two before retirement.

"The impact can be depletion of assets years later when a person can't work, "Mr. Herschler says. Some older investors hedge their bets during these 10 years by investing more conservatively. The drawback to that approach is, even at this stage, people should keep much of their assets in equities or their investments won't grow enough to keep up with inflation, Mr. Herschler says.

"The pre-retirement period is the most important stage because a lot of people don't evaluate whether they should retire," says Dallas Salisbury, president and chief executive of Employee benefit Research Institute. "Before they sign that paper to retire, they should know where they spend money."

..."Individuals dramatically underestimate the cost of living," Mr. Salisbury says. They often don't take into account the cost of inflation.

"People also think they will not live a long time," Mr. Salisbury says. As a result, they frequently overspend in the early years of retirement by annually withdrawing 12% to 20% of their assets even though financial advisors recommend using only 3% to 4%. (continued...)

….Investors need to focus on the red zone before retirement and determine before the exit interview whether they can afford to leave work.

"Think of these five years as an opportunity to examine your situation and fine tune your plan," recommends Christine Fahlund, a senior financial planner at T. Rowe Price Group Inc

"Even one year delayed could have a huge impact on what you draw in retirement."

Assuming 8% growth in assets, delaying retirement by one year could increase income by 12% because it means one less year of spending and one more year of saving. A three-year delay would be a 41% increase in pre-tax income.

(Source: Dow Jones; National Post, January 23, 2006; article by Jillian Mincer)

Fifty dollars a month really can make a difference

That's especially true if it is invested at a young age, Brown, senior vice-president of sales, marketing and support services of Envsion Credit Union (3rd largest credit union in B.C.)

With compounding, a person investing $50 a month starting at the age of 20 would have more than $230,000 at retirement, which would yield an annual income of $24,000 for 20 years, she said. But someone who starts investing the same amount at age 40, would end up with only $4,400 a year.

(Source: The Vancouver Sun, February 15, 2005; article by Fiona Anderson)

Are you prepared or not for retirement?

Boomers Unprepared For Retirement

(Survey: BMO finds the 'me' generation worried about the next stage of their lives)

They've been disparagingly labeled the "me" generation and they say they're happy, but many baby boomers are so busy taking care of their kids and their aged parents that they haven't yet got around to feathering their own nests, a report (July 12, 2006) reveals.

And now many worry that they're not prepared for the next stage in their lives–retirement.

"The generation known for its 'me-first' mentality is juggling the needs of their parents and children with their own future retirement needs," says the report "State of the Baby Boomer" by BMO Financial Group.

The survey on which the report is based found that three in five boomers with children aged 18 and over are still providing some kind of financial support to their kids. "Adding to the pressure, one-quarter of those boomers whose parents are still alive have one or more elderly parents that need their assistance on a regular basis," it added.

….Only 28 per cant of boomers are very confident that they will be financially secure in their old age, well below the 41 per cent of adults who are under age 40, and the 47 per cent of those over age 60, the survey fund.

A third of boomers also are concerned that their standard of living is likely to drop in retirement, double the 16 per cent of younger Canadians who expressed such concerns.

Many baby boomers are also having challenges balancing the books, as nearly three-quarters are still burdened with debt. Only 28 per cent say they have savings and investments of $100,000 or more, the report noted. Further one in five of the boomers not yet retired say they have no savings at all.

Unlike current retirees, many will not have access to relatively generous defined benefit pension plans which are being phased out by many employers, Ms. Tina Di Vito, BMO retirement planner noted. continued...

"This is uncharted territory, so it's all the more important for boomers to start considering a variety of contingencies and lifestyle choices today," she said, adding that the average Canadian should plan to fund at least 20 years of retirement.

Despite the tenuous financial picture of many boomers, 91 per cent say they are satisfied with their lives, with almost half very satisfied. And many do have financial options to help support themselves during retirement, according to the survey, which found that 80 per cent own, rather than rent, their homes, and 20 per cent have a second house. While two-thirds are at least somewhat willing to sell their assets to fund retirement, only a third intend to do so.

(Source: CanWest News Service, article by Eric Beauchesne, July 13, 2006)

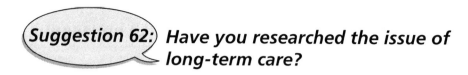

Suggestion 62: *Have you researched the issue of long-term care?*

For information on long-term care, visit the 'one-stop shopping website' created by the author for your use:

www.longtermcarecanada.com

It is the first national educational resource of its kind in Canada on the LTC issue.

- ☑ It was developed to create easy access to information for those already immersed in a care-years journey and those interested in planning for their loved ones and their own the care-years.

- ☑ This website links to all the Government Of Canada research sites and offers a list of free materials available for use by you and your family.

- ☑ It also links to the programs and services offered by each of the Provincial and Territorial Governments for their citizens.

- ☑ It offers information on the long-term care issue and the key age-related trends in Canada.

Although each of the following are accessible through the above-mentioned website, these are worth highlighting:

- ☑ An excellent source of information on seniors and care-related topics; can search by subject or by alphabet:

  Seniors Canada On-Line (Canada's Trusted Information Source for Seniors, Caregivers, Families and Service Providers): http://www. seniors.gc.ca

- ☑ A very good source of information on seniors' health topics:

  Public Health Agency of Canada: http://www.phac-aspc.gc.ca

☑ A great source of information on housing needs; explains loan and grant programs available to assist seniors living in their own homes:

Canada Mortgage and Housing Corporation: http://www.cmhc-schl.gc.ca

☑ A web site to serve all the needs of the over 50 age group:

Wired Seniors http://www.wiredseniors.com

☑ Other websites of interest and value to Canadian families and seniors:

Canadian Prevention Of Elder Abuse: http://www.cnpea.ca

Alzheimer's Association of Canada: http://www.alzheimer.ca

Arthritis Canada: http://www.arthritis.ca

"Success is just a matter of attitude."

– *Darcy E. Gibbons*

 **Suggestion 63:** *Think about becoming a 'senior' yourself*

Old Age

By Edgar A Guest

I used to think that growing old was reckoned just in years,
But who can name the very date when weariness appears?
I find no stated time when man, obedient to a law,
Must settle in an easy chair and from the world withdraw.
Old Age is rather curious, or so it seems to me.
I know old men at forty and young men at seventy-three.

I'm done with counting life by years or temples turning gray.
No man is old who wakes with joy to greet another day.
What if the body cannot dance with youth's elastic spring?
There's many a vibrant interest to which the mind can cling.
'Tis in the spirit Age must dwell, or this would never be:
I know old men at forty and young men at seventy-three.

Some men keep all their friendships warm,
and welcome friendships new,
They have no time to sit and mourn the things they used to do.
This changing world they greet with joy and never bow to late;
On every fresh adventure they set out with hearts elate
From chilling fear and bitter dread they keep their spirits free
While some seem old at forty they stay young at seventy-three.

So much to do, so much to learn, so much in which to share!
With twinkling eyes and minds alert some brave both time and care.
And this I've learned from other men, that only they are old
Who think with something that has passed the tale of life is told.
For Age is not alone of time, or we should never see
Men old and bent at forty and men young at seventy-three.

Two quick titles to kick-start our thinking on 'becoming a senior'
(and then I am sure the discussion will flow rapidly)

Your thoughts on 'ageing'?

☑ What is your image of 'old'? of 'senior'?

If we look up 'ageing', we find these synonyms: growing old; maturing; becoming old.

If we look up 'seniors', we find these synonyms: older; further up the ladder; higher-ranking; elder.

☑ If asked, what one synonym would you mention for "ageing or becoming old or senior"?

☑ Do you view women as 'old' before you do men (i.e. are women 65 years subject to more negative stereotypes than men of the same age)?

☑ Do you talk about seniors as a group, as being wise and experienced, and so forth; yet also think of them as forgetful, frail, lonely and dependent? Is some of your thinking based on myths? Do you have some mixed images of seniors? Should some of your thinking be discarded?

When are we 'old"? Redefining aging!
'Old at 65' is passé!

1900..........Age 50

1950..........Age 65

2000..........Age 75

2040..........Age 85?

Do you have a stereo typical view of ageing?

☑ Do you have any stereotypes about seniors based solely on the fact that they are persons past the age of 65?

☑ How are you going to overcome your stereotypical thinking if it does exist?

☑ Do you want this type of thinking to continue when you are a senior?

"Ageism" is defined as the prejudices and stereotypes that are applied to seniors based solely on their age.

Have you ever been guilty of looking at others your own age and thinking, surely I can't look that old?

I was sitting in the waiting room for my first appointment with a new dentist and I noticed his DDS diploma, which bore his full name. Suddenly, I remembered a tall, handsome dark haired boy with the same name had been in my high school class some 40-odd years ago.

Could he be the same guy that I had a secret crush on, way back then? Upon seeing him, however, I very quickly discarded any such thought – this balding gray-haired man with the deeply lined face was way too old to have been my classmate. HMMMM or could he?

After he examined my teeth, I asked him if he had attended Morgan Park High School. "Yes, Yes, I did. I'm a Mustang," he gleamed with pride. "When did you graduate?" I asked. He answered, "In 1961, why do you ask?" "You were in my class," I exclaimed. He looked at me closely, then that wrinkled old son of a bitch asked, "What did you teach?"

(An email story sent—my apologies if the language offends anyone.)

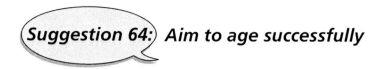

Suggestion 64: *Aim to age successfully*

My mother used to say that 'we have to age with dignity'. She was able to do that most of her life and I have to admit that I try to remember her message–but–at times, I struggle with and laugh at the whole process.

I am, at times, confronted by my aging casually, usually when doing everyday little things, such as trying to open a jar (it seems the manufacturers have started putting the lids on tighter over the past few years); or zipping up a short flight of stairs at an airport pulling a suitcase and carrying a laptop computer. Does my attitude, as I am aging, include the question of 'exercise'? What I should be questioning is if more exercise is needed at any age (knowing the obvious answer)?

At times, I struggle (and grumble) when I feel 'getting older' is affecting a much-loved lifestyle activity–travel–since I sometimes now judge destinations in terms of the strenuous efforts I may have to put forth while there having the adventure (asking myself questions such as, why didn't I make time to climb Mount Kilimanjaro when I worked in East Africa years ago). We all have an activity, or hobby that we have enjoyed much of our life and when it appears to be affected by what we conveniently like to call our 'aging', then 'growing older' seems a tad negative.

As a result of my journey with my parents, I have come to the conclusion that growing older should not be limiting and what I really have to do, from time to time, is examine my attitude. Our family's care-years journey gave me an opportunity to see seniors through a new lens and subsequently now when researching the topic, I tend to come across the most amazing stories of the most amazing seniors (refer to Suggestion 65 for some of these stories.)

Is it our society's focus on youth that alters our view of growing older, becoming a senior…? Is it the marketing and media messages that surround us? What is normal, happy ageing today? What is normal, happy ageing going to be for you?

Should we define ageing by chronology alone or by our health and wellness, our social interactions, our independence...?

We must dispel that myth that seniors can be categorized and all described in the same manner. Each senior is unique. How do you want to be thought of when a senior or 'older person'....do you want the younger worker, the clerk, the doctor, whomever to put you instantly into a category simply because you are 71 or 88? We have all met a 76 year old who seems 'younger' than a 59 year old we may know – is she/he healthier, still working/volunteering, doing a sport....?

We are not all alike as we age—'young-old' seniors (65-74), 'old' seniors (75-84) and 'old-old' seniors (85+) (as categorized by gerontologists) are not all the same. My care-journey with my parents prompted me to see clearly that all seniors are definitely different—no real surprises here, but none-the-less, an eye-opener for the future. Every age group is different (is every 'teenager' the same); therefore, why should 'seniors' be treated or thought of in a group, as the same. Seniors are different depending on each of their experiences—just as we are now and will continue to be in the future.

The question then becomes:

☑ **Do we want to be viewed as we always have been, as vital 'individuals'** *regardless of our chronological age!*

It is revolution time—let's decide that our goal will be 'to age successfully', to be seen as unique individuals at any period of time in our lives.

And let's walk the talk, as the saying goes, and change our attitudes towards our senior parents, our senior neighbours, seniors in the mall having a cup of coffee, senior drivers, senior travelers, senior customers... and see them, not as seniors only, but as unique individuals first. Because we are seeing our destiny.

Long-wed couple credits the magic of a kiss

Percy and Florence Arrowsmith (London, England), who celebrated their 80th wedding anniversary June 1, 2005, say the secrets of the world's longest marriage are don't sleep on an argument, always share a kiss and hold hands before going to bed. Percy Arrowsmith, 105, and his 100-year old wife were married June 1, 1925. Guinness World Records said the pair held records for the longest marriage for a living couple and the oldest aggregate age of a married couple. *(Associated Press, June 2, 2005)*

Notes:

The Age of Reason: a Liberal interpretation

(Source: Gary Graves, CBC News Online September 23, 2003)

In August 2002, the president of Turkmenistan, Saparmurat Niyazov, who's generally referred to by your average Turkman as "Turkmenbashi the Great," decreed that the country would change its perspective on how its citizens view aging. It's interesting to compare this worldview with our Euro-American take on time.

Turkmenbashi the Great, whom I will refer to as Niyazov for short, has defined and divided the Ages of Man into nine segments, each of which is a dozen or so years long. This lifetime calendar has stretched the potential life span to an optimistic 109 years, although statistics show a peculiar tendency of the average Turkman to come up about 49 years short of that goal.

The president declares that "childhood" shall last for 13 years from birth. That's pretty much what we in the West say, too.

Then come the years 14-25, which Niyazov categorizes as "adolescence." Here we begin to diverge in perspective. While there's not much disagreement about the initial teen year, thanks to such enlightened and progressive industrial world advancements as food laced with growth hormones and a popular media which uses sex to sell everything from soup to – er – nuts, our adolescence tends to end at, say, age 15. Then you're an adult, if not legally then certainly physically and attitudinally.

After adolescence comes a dozen years of "youth," terminating at 37. I can't think of anyone I know in that age bracket who would care to disagree with that definition, although some of their cardiologists might.

Until age 49, one enjoys the "Age of Maturity." Again, it's hard to disagree with the definition, although there is the bizarre Western tendency toward immaturity in the later stages of this phase. We call it "mid-life crisis," but obviously we may have to adjust that as acceptance of the Niyazov Numbers becomes more widespread. (continued...)

An amusing pun comes forth in the next phase, the "Age of the Prophet," which lasts until one's 62nd year. Again, this closely follows our Western outlook, with only a spelling change to make it "Profit" instead.

Then the "Age of Inspiration" kicks in. This also is encouraging, especially for Turkmen, since this is greater than their actual expected life span. Nothing like a little inspiration to keep you going.

Starting at 73 comes the age of the "White Bearded Elder." Providing one still has hair, this time of one's life could be quite ego flattering.

And here's good news for the federal pension plan: under the Turkmen calendar "Old Age" doesn't kick in until age 85. This, of course, conflicts by two decades with our own definition. But you don't need to be an actuary to see how our country could benefit financially by delaying old-age benefit payments until people reached this new, imaginative chronological benchmark.

Next, at 97, Turkmenbashi the Great pays homage to Oguz Khan, an ancient figure who led his country presumably up until age 109. This will be, Niyazov declares, a person's "Age of Oguz Khan". Perhaps Oguz could, but not many others can, lead a nation at that age. Not many of us would disagree if Canadian political figures who reached triple digits were criticized for hanging on to the job too long. Definitely, that's too old to run… or even walk alone in the snow. You could fall and break a hip.

Niyazov, who himself has just turned 62 and looks like he has a tenacious grip on his leadership, is just a few years less inspired than our own – outgoing – Jean Chrétien. Perhaps his insight should be taken as encouragement, not senile doddery, by Ottawa's pundits and powerbrokers. After all, one of his first inspired acts in addition to this inspired new calendar was to rename the month of January… after himself.

"I intend to live forever, or die trying"
– *Groucho Marx 1890 – 1977*

Suggestion 65: *Be an amazing senior*

We have all read of amazing senior citizens. Are they anomalies? No, I would like to think that they are the 'norm'.

Is it possible that we can reach a critical mass and strive to become amazing seniors when the time comes—locally, provincially, nationally, or internationally?

Let's give it a try when we become seniors—we have much to contribute and we have much to gain both personally and as a county with an aging demographic.

There are many inspiring stories – these are a few:

TRULY AMAZING SENIORS:

☑ **Record-Breaking Pilot is Senior Citizen With Slew of Records – Steve Fossett has records in many endeavors in air, on land and on sea**
March 5, 2005 – The world knows about the record-breaking endurance flight by the GlobalFlyer that landed Thursday after the pilot became the first person to fly around the world alone without stopping or re-fueling. What many may not know is the pilot Steve Fossett, 60, is a senior citizen who has set a number of records in the air, on water and on land. He says, too, he has more on the way.

☑ **Dodo Cheney, 88, Wins International Tennis Tournament to Add to Legacy**
Sept. 27, 2004 – Dodo Cheney, 88 years young, won the championship match of the women's 85 and over bracket at the 24th International Tennis Federation World Seniors Tennis Championships. It was just another notch on the racket for the senior star that was greeted into the International Tennis Hall of Fame in July.

☑ **91-Year-Young Lucille Borgen Wins National Water Ski Title**
Aug. 9, 2004 – Lucille Borgen of Babson Park, Florida, amazed the crowd at the 62 Annual Water Ski National Championships by winning the Women 10 slalom and tricks event on her 91st birthday. She is the oldest competitor to ever ski at the Nationals.

The cancer and polio survivor was the lone competitor in the age group event. Borgen scored 4-1/2 buoys at long line to win slalom and tallied 390 points to win tricks.

Nearly 1,000 water ski athletes – ages 5 through 91 – from across the United States competed for national titles in slalom, tricks, jumping and overall in 26 age divisions and two Open divisions during the five-day tournament that ended on Aug. 7.

☑ 63-Year Old Becomes First Private Astronaut

June 22, 2004 – Mike Melvill, 63, was greeted by his four grandchildren as he landed SpaceShipOne after becoming the first private pilot to earn astronaut wings. It was the high mark so far for seniors in a month that has seen a 101-year old Frank Moody of Australia and 80-year old former President George H.W. Bush parachute from airplanes.

Under the command of test pilot Melvill, SpaceShipOne reached a record breaking altitude of 328,491 feet (approximately 62 miles or 100 km}.

Melvill, who has set world records for altitude and speed and logged more than 6,400 hours of flight time in fixed-wing aircraft and seven helicopters, said the experience "blew me away."

☑ Dr. Solomon Margolin, 82, Still Contributing Great Discoveries to Mankind

Oct. 25, 2004 – Most careers span about 45 years, and if you're lucky, there are significant accomplishments to reflect on when you retire. Then there are the uncommon examples of people who continue to work past age 65, even though they have achieved what most people consider incredible accomplishments. Dr. Solomon Margolin is one of those people. While most of his peers retired at the usual age, Dr. Margolin continues to arrive at his Dallas office every day to continue his life's work – discovering new drugs – so that others can benefit. At 82, he still has a passion for science and finding drugs that benefit those in need. "Why do I keep working? There's still more to do and we're making breakthroughs that will help people long after my career is over. Besides, I'd be bored if I didn't come to work every day," says Margolin.

☑ **Bill Anderson, 78, Starts Quest to Bicycle Across Nation Both Directions**

Sept. 15, 2004 – W.J. "Bill" Anderson, 78 years young, will jump on his bicycle and leave San Diego, California, on September 25 and head for Jacksonville Beach, Florida. His goal is to become the oldest person to ride a bike across the U.S. from north to south and west to east – and to raise money for Crossroads Mission in his hometown, Yuma, Arizona. He may actually be the only one to ever accomplish this fete at any age. In June the World War II paratrooper became the oldest bicyclist to ride from Canada to Mexico – a trip that took him only 10 days and 15 hours. In this effort he raised $6,000 for the homeless people served by Crossroads. The funds are raised through people donating per mile traveled by Anderson and matching funds given by corporations and businesses.

TRULY AMAZING CAREGIVER, FATHER AND SENIOR DICK HOYT
From Sports Illustrated, By Rick Reilly

I try to be a good father. Give my kids mulligans. Work nights to pay for their text messaging. Take them to swimsuit shoots. But compared with Dick Hoyt, I suck.

Eighty-five times he's pushed his disabled son, Rick, 26.2 miles in marathons. Eight times he's not only pushed him 26.2 miles in a wheelchair but also towed him 2.4 miles in a dinghy while swimming and pedaled him 112 miles in a seat on the handlebars--all in the same day.

Dick's also pulled him cross-country skiing, taken him on his back mountain climbing and once hauled him across the U.S. On a bike. Makes taking your son bowling look a little lame, right?

And what has Rick done for his father? Not much--except save his life.

This love story began in Winchester, Mass., 43 years ago, when Rick was strangled by the umbilical cord during birth, leaving him brain-damaged and unable to control his limbs. "He'll be a vegetable the rest of his life;"

Dick says doctors told him and his wife, Judy, when Rick was nine months old. "Put him in an Institution."

But the Hoyts weren't buying it. They noticed the way Rick's eyes followed them around the room. When Rick was 11 they took him to the Engineering department at Tufts University and asked if there was anything to help the boy communicate. ``No way," Dick says he was told. ``There's nothing going on in his brain."

"Tell him a joke," Dick countered. They did. Rick laughed. Turns out a lot was going on in his brain. Rigged up with a computer that allowed him to control the cursor by touching a switch with the side of his head, Rick was finally able to communicate. First words? "Go Bruins!" And after a high school classmate was paralyzed in an accident and the school organized a charity run for him, Rick pecked out, "Dad, I want to do that."

Yeah, right. How was Dick, a self-described 'porker' who never ran more than a mile at a time, going to push his son five miles? Still, he tried. "Then it was me who was handicapped," Dick says. "I was sore for two weeks."

That day changed Rick's life. "Dad," he typed, "when we were running, It felt like I wasn't disabled anymore!"

And that sentence changed Dick's life. He became obsessed with giving Rick that feeling as often as he could. He got into such hard-belly Shape that he and Rick were ready to try the 1979 Boston Marathon.

"No way," Dick was told by a race official. The Hoyts weren't quite a Single runner, and they weren't quite a wheelchair competitor. For a few Years Dick and Rick just joined the massive field and ran anyway, then they found a way to get into the race officially: In 1983 they ran another marathon so fast they made the qualifying time for Boston the following year.

Then somebody said, ``Hey, Dick, why not a triathlon?" How's a guy who never learned to swim and hadn't ridden a bike since he was six going to haul his 110-pound kid through a triathlon? Still, Dick Tried.

Now they've done 212 triathlons, including four grueling 15-hour Ironmans in Hawaii. It must be a buzzkill to be a 25-year-old stud Getting passed by an old guy towing a grown man in a dinghy, don't you think?

Hey, Dick, why not see how you'd do on your own? "No way," he says. Dick does it purely for "the awesome feeling" he gets seeing Rick with a cantaloupe smile as they run, swim and ride together.

This year, at ages 65 and 43, Dick and Rick finished their 24th Boston Marathon, in 5,083rd place out of more than 20,000 starters. Their best time? Two hours, 40 minutes in 1992--only 35 minutes off the world Record, which, in case you don't keep track of these things, happens to be held by a guy who was not pushing another man in a wheelchair at the time.

"No question about it," Rick types. "My dad is the Father of the Century."

And Dick got something else out of all this too. Two years ago he had a mild heart attack during a race. Doctors found that one of his arteries Was 95% clogged. ``If you hadn't been in such great shape," One doctor told him, ``you probably would've died 15 years ago." So, in a way, Dick and Rick saved each other's life.

Rick, who has his own apartment (he gets home care) and works in Boston, and Dick, retired from the military and living in Holland, Mass., always find ways to be together. They give speeches around the country and compete in some backbreaking race every weekend, including this Father's Day.

That night, Rick will buy his dad dinner, but the thing he really wants to give him is a gift he can never buy. "The thing I'd most like," Rick types, "is that my dad sit in the chair and I push him once."

To watch a video of Dick and Rick doing a triathlon, visit www. longtermcarecanada.com, click on 'information & articles' tab and go to the drop-down menu of 'LTC issue in Canada'. In the right margin, in a box titled "A truly amazing story" you will be able to see the video.

NATIONALLY RECOGNIZED AS AMAZING CANADIAN SENIORS:

ALBERTA

2006 Minister's Seniors Service Award recipients

☑ **Nellie Befus of Calgary** – Nellie Befus is a dedicated volunteer who has been making a difference in the lives of seniors in Calgary for more than 32 years. She began sharing her love of reading through the Homebound Reader Program at the Calgary Public Library in 1974. Nellie continues to provide companionship to seniors through this program today, and still uses public transit to travel to seniors' homes to provide this service. She has also delivered for Meals on Wheels for 14 years and she remains a volunteer at Bethany Care Centre, where she is a librarian, brings books to residents and accompanies residents on trips to the doctor and dentist. Nellie's concern for seniors is also evident in her volunteer work with the Salvation Army and the Sarcee Nursing Home, where she assists residents in going to and from the chapel on Sundays.

☑ **Reta Elder of Innisfail** – Reta Elder's commitment to seniors in Wetaskiwin and area began nearly 30 years ago when she joined a seniors society and began volunteering. A few years later, she started the community's first handibus service for seniors by using her own vehicle. Then in 1983, she began helping seniors complete benefit applications and has assisted with as many as 400 tax forms a year. Reta continues to be well-known for helping seniors complete forms. She still makes regular trips to help seniors in Wetaskiwin, even though she now lives in Innisfail where she also assists seniors. In addition to volunteering with other organizations, Reta recently contacted Revenue Canada to organize a training session for 18 new volunteers to help with tax forms. She also assisted in arranging a training session for volunteers to help seniors with benefit applications.

☑ **Douglas Heine of Medicine Hat** – Douglas Heine has been supporting his community for more than 50 years and has focused his past 10 years of volunteer service on assisting seniors. One of the programs he helped introduce to Medicine Hat is the Wise Owl program, which educates seniors on how to protect themselves from fraud and financial abuse. He also assisted in bringing the Community Response to Abuse and Neglect of the Elderly (CRANE) program to the city. The program provides local seniors with a 24-hour a day, seven-day a week phone number that connects residents with the support services they need. Douglas has been involved with many other services, including the Bus Buddy program that teaches seniors how to use Medicine Hat's public transit system and a service that provides an emergency response system for seniors with health concerns. He also volunteers two mornings each month to assist seniors with completing benefit application forms.

☑ **Edna Jolly of Edmonton** – Edna Jolly is a retired nurse who has shared thousands of hours of her time promoting the health and well-being of seniors. She began volunteering with the Westend Seniors Activity Centre 15 years ago, and remains very involved. Along with serving as the centre's president, she currently assists with planning, fundraising and club activities. Edna has also started many clubs for seniors, such as a travel club whose members have travelled over most of Alberta. In addition, she established a Toastmasters club and an international dinner club for diners to experience cuisine and entertainment from around the world. As well, she helped start the Seniors Outreach Network Society to assist lonely and isolated seniors. She was the society's first president and helped to write its bylaws, draft policies, fundraise and hire staff. Edna remains involved in the community with several organizations and makes educational presentations for a seniors studies institute and seniors association.

☑ **Esther McIntosh of Calgary** – Esther McIntosh has improved the lives of many seniors by volunteering with the Bowness Senior Citizens' Club for nearly 20 years. When she joined the club in 1987, she immediately began to volunteer in its office and served as secretary before being elected president. As president, Esther volunteered thousands of hours for eight years. She started several social programs, organized fitness and other classes, attracted new members and inspired members to volunteer. She also coordinated an expansion to the club's building by serving as the project manager, submitting grant applications and fundraising. Esther currently donates 1,800 hours each year to the club and enjoys instructing quilting classes, planting flowers at the centre and helping fundraise to benefit her fellow seniors. She also volunteers with the Society of Bowness Residents and a church auxiliary group.

BRITISH COLUMBIA

The Province of British Columbia annually proclaims the second week of June as "Seniors' Week", to increase public awareness of the important role of seniors in the province. The Province also engages in various activities every year to promote the celebration of October 1st, the International Day of Older Persons.

October is Women's History Month and this year Canada's theme was Aboriginal Women. As part of British Columbia's celebration of exceptional women, the Government recognized 10 Aboriginal women for their contributions. Of the women who were honoured, over half were senior women. Honourees were recognized in each of five categories: Language, Culture and the Arts; Family and Community; Health, Sports and Science; Education; and Public Service, Business and Entrepreneurship.

In addition, there are a number of annual awards in BC for seniors…the Lighthouse Leisure Care Awards. The Awards recognize adults ages 62 and over living in the Lower Mainland and coastal British Columbia who have contributed to their communities.

2006 Leisure Care Lighthouse Awards

The Lighthouse Awards recognize adults ages 62 and over living in the Lower Mainland and coastal B.C. who have made a difference in their communities through volunteer service or by serving as an inspiration and role model for others.

☑ **Roz Davidson:** The "Wisdom of Age Mentorship Award", which recognizes an individual who has demonstrated a commitment to making a difference in the lives of children, was won by Roz Davidson who has been nicknamed "The Granny Rapper" for her anti-bullying songs. The 71-year-old visits schools, libraries, and special events performing her original work.

☑ **Phil Horton:** The "Picture of Health Award", which recognizes exemplary commitment to good health and fitness as an older adult, was won by 70-year-old Phil Horton, an avid runner and biker. In his most recent major runs, he placed first and second in his age group. Phil also volunteers with a number of fitness groups.

☑ **Marg Oakes:** "The Shining Light Award", which recognizes an individual or group for outstanding volunteer service to the community and/or advocacy on behalf of seniors, was won by 89-year-old Marg Oakes. Mrs. Oakes has been caring for others ever since she lost her young son in a traffic accident. She continues to volunteer and encourage other seniors to be involved.

☑ **Vera Rutledge:** "The Philanthropy Award", which recognizes an individual or group who has/have demonstrated a concern for humanity by providing significant financial resources and personal time, was won by Vera Rutledge. At 83, Mrs. Rutledge volunteers with the Crossroads Hospice Society and the Eagle Ridge Hospital Foundation. She is also a major donor, helping out whenever she can, to improve the lives of others.

The Centre on Aging based at the University of Victoria presents the Valued Elder Recognition Award annually to mark the International Day of Older Persons. The Award honours individuals who have made an exemplary volunteer contribution within the Capital Regional District (CRD) for a minimum of ten years.

The Simon Fraser Gerontology Research Centre presents the Seniors Leadership Award that recognizes the contribution British Columbia seniors make to education and aging. The Award recognizes British Columbia residents over the age of 65 who have contributed time and experience to a post-secondary institution in British Columbia and/or provided exemplary service to or on behalf of their peers.

MANITOBA

☑ **Jaring Timmerman**
Winnipeg, Manitoba

"Who knows how long I'll live. Right now, I feel like a million dollars."
If you want a few pointers on how to live a healthy, active life in your later years, Jaring Timmerman has some advice. Jaring is 95 and very active, so who better to trust than somebody who is putting many half his age to shame with his seemingly inexhaustible energy.

Jaring suggests starting each day with stretching and deep breathing, as he says it 'gets the blood flowing.' G.E.D.S. is an acronym Jaring formulated that he follows. G stands for GENES, E stands for EXERCISE, D for DIET and S for SPIRIT—maintaining a good relationship with your Creator.

Understanding that we inherit genes, Jaring believes that they can be improved on. Both of his parents lived to be in their mid-eighties. He already has 10 years on them and with his healthy lifestyle and optimistic outlook, he's sure to have many more. Disciplined healthy eating habits, avoiding heavy fats, is essential. Each day, Jaring and his wife, Gladys, have breakfast with protein-rich nuts, cereal and a slice of whole wheat toast without butter or margarine. Lots of fruits and vegetables are a major part of their daily diet, as well.

Exercise is a must. Swimming has always been a part of Jaring's life since early childhood. When competing, Jaring would swim every day, but now only swims three days a week giving his muscles time to rejuvenate.

In 1987, at the age of 78, thirteen years after retiring at the age of 65, Jaring began swimming competitively. He first entered the Arizona Senior Olympics in Phoenix, more for fun and curiosity, and was surprised when he came home with the Gold for the 200 metre race in his age category. This was a qualifying event for the U.S. National Senior Olympics held in St. Louis, Missouri, the same year, where Jaring went on to win a Silver in the 400 metre race along with several other medals.

Jaring competed in Denmark for the World Masters Games in 1989 where he won Gold in the 400 metre freestyle meets and 2 Silvers in the 100 and 200 metre freestyle meets in his age category. He has been to Montreal in 1994 for the World Masters Championships, in Munich, Germany, in 2000 for the VIII FINA World Master Championships, and many others in Canada and the U.S.

The World Masters Games will be held in Edmonton in July of 2005 and Jaring is already planning to be there. But, before that, in April, he will compete in the Manitoba Masters. He would participate in many more but it gets very costly as there is no funding or sponsorship for sport for seniors. His Munich trip alone cost $8,500.00 Cdn, for both

Jaring and Gladys, who goes to all of the competitions.

Today, Jaring proudly stands behind 160 medals in the course of 17 years. Online, we came across a CNN transcript of an interview with Jaring and Gladys by CTV Correspondent Jonathan Gravener in Winnipeg after the 2000 World Masters in Germany. He spoke comedically how Jaring had 'been awake enough to win more medals than he can count.' Gladys had referred to Jaring, then, as 'a 91-year-old teenager.' Jaring was quoted as saying that he was concerned about the young bucks coming in at 90 for the 2005 Games in Edmonton and walking all over him at his senior age of 96.

Jaring recently broke the world record for the men's 50 metre backstroke in his age category and currently holds the national record for the men's 100 metre freestyle swim. Let's hope he can maintain that status in the upcoming competitions.

Much recognition has been given to Jaring for his efforts. The City of Winnipeg presented Jaring with the 1995 Outstanding Achievement Award for his swimming, the province presented the Order of Sport Excellence Achievement Award in 1995 for the 1994 World Masters Championships, and in 1996, he received a Canadian NIKE Masters Swimming Championship plaque, plus various others.

Jaring has received more than just swimming medals. Most recently, he was a recipient of the Manitoba Council on Aging Recognition Awards for 2004 for outstanding contributions to seniors.

He received the Governor General's 2002 Caring Canadian Award for 'unpaid, voluntary contributions providing extraordinary help or care in the community.'

He was presented with the Queen's Golden Jubilee medal in 2002 for significant contributions to fellow citizens, their communities or to Canada.

Jaring truly is a humanitarian who advocates healthy living to people of all ages. He has been volunteering for 30+ years serving his church, being a Sunday school teacher, a friendly visitor, and sitting on a variety of boards. He served on the Salvation Army advisory board and now is a life member. He sat on the Grace Hospital board for 13 years, two and a half of which he served as chair.

Jaring served for three years in WWII, trained as a navigator for the Lancaster bombers. He had a lengthy career with the Grain Insurance & Guarantee Co. and was President and General Manager of this company when he retired.

Jaring advocates the benefits of sports participation of older adults. He would like our government to realize that many more would participate in major competitions if there was some financial assistance. He learned that the Australian government recognizes that such program subsidies are beneficial in reducing national health care costs with fewer older people occupying beds in nursing homes, hospitals, etc. Jaring states that it is practical and sound economics.

Keeping busy is important to both Jaring and Gladys and they have six grown children, 14 grandchildren and 10 great-grandchildren between the two of them to help them do that.

☑ Anna Kibsey
Winnipeg, Manitoba

"I'm just a simple woman who takes care of myself."
This is no simple woman by any means. Anna Kibsey sees herself as a simple woman, but others surely see her as a simply wonderful woman.

Always ready to help others, Anna definitely is a friend in need. She wouldn't think twice about hopping on a bus in sub-zero temperatures to travel to her church to help make perogies for fundraising. Before Christmas, Anna and several others spent up to nine hours a day, three times a week, on a hard cement floor making perogies to fill volume orders from companies and organizations. The rest of the year, they make perogies less often, but still twice-weekly at the St. Ivan Suchavsky Church on Main Street in Winnipeg.

Now, you may think, 'Big Deal!' But, Anna is 88 years old and had undergone surgery for two knee replacements—one five, and one six years ago. So, as you see, it's not such an easy task.

But, Anna makes it look easy. Since her surgery, she walks more than ever. Her legs are stronger, now, making her pace hard to keep up with. Her doctor once told her that there was no point in putting new tires on the car if she wasn't going to drive it. Before the surgery, Anna often concocted a home remedy of a garlic and whiskey mixture that she put on her knees wrapped in plastic to help ease the pain. Those days are long gone.

One downfall of having knee replacements is if Anna falls, it is difficult getting up without using her knees as she doesn't want to damage them. So she has to be extremely careful wherever she is. Still, that doesn't slow her down. She was even dancing the Butterfly at a family wedding in December, last month.

Anna is fortunate to be able to do the things she does. She is enjoying her life and friends immensely. She goes out often and participates in bingo, cards, dinners or other functions at senior centres or churches close by. Centres she attends regularly are the Gwen Secter Creative Living Centre and the Age & Opportunity Norwin 55+ Centre, both on Main Street near her home in Winnipeg. Anna has her routine of outings for almost every day of the week. If she doesn't want to venture far, she can go next door to the St. Joseph Church and play bingo. Last year she won twice in one evening taking home a total of $1,318.00. Anna shared it generously with her grandchildren.

Before moving to Winnipeg in 1964, Anna lived in Chatfield with her husband, Nick, where they had farmed dairy for 22 years. They raised one daughter, Marie, and two sons, Gregory and John. Life was so different then. Luxuries were few and far between. All clothing was hand-sewn or knitted. Even the wool was hand-spun for clothing or carted for quilting.

The farmwork was done by hand. There were no milking machines like there are today. Horses were used for making hay and planting crops. Children had to walk two to four miles to school in all kinds of weather. There were no snow plows, or even roads. Looking back now, they were difficult times for Anna. But, she survived like others, and you have to wonder if it was all that hard work that made Anna the healthy, strong, resilient woman she is today.

Like most, Anna has had her share of hardships and heartaches. Her husband passed away 19 years ago, the day before their son's wedding while picking up the wedding cake. The wedding was to take place in their home. It was devastating for Anna and her family.

Anna is extremely independent and that could be credited partly to her knack for creative thinking. After her knee surgery, she took care of herself in her home without the help of a nurse's aid. Thinking ahead, she had meals prepared and frozen.

Like everyone else, Anna has her aches and pains, but she insists that by keeping active and moving around, she doesn't notice them as much. With her creative mind, she sewed her own tension bandage for her sore wrist for when she needs to use her hands for a length of time, as when she's making perogies. It is complete with snap buttons and velcro fasteners. She used to have cataracts but underwent eye laser surgery to correct them and now she sees more clearly. And, last year she had her badly abscessed gallbladder removed. She was in hospital for 19 days and doesn't even remember several of them.

Healthy living, healthy attitude and having fun all seem to contribute to Anna's longevity. Angels must also have been a contributing factor as Anna has had so many close calls. At three months of age, her mother thought Anna had actually died. A time later, her mother noticed Anna's lips moving. It was her strong will to survive that pulled Anna out of her high fever. Many farming mishaps could have easily claimed her life too, but there always seemed to be a force on her side.

Eating healthy is important to Anna. She bakes all her own bread and cookies. They are never store bought. Her bread is made with whole wheat flour plus seven grains including flax seed, and she bakes it long enough to ensure her allergy to yeast isn't triggered. She enjoys buckwheat recipes because she learned that buckwheat is cholesterol-free and can help reduce the bad cholesterol.

Anna has a vivid and keen mind as you probably already observed. She is up-to-date on current events as she has always followed the news throughout her life. Her clever thinking and observant nature keep her wise to cunning deception, too.

Many might seem intimidated by Anna's determination. When she sets her mind to something, she forges ahead until mission is accomplished. She didn't get her driver's license until she was 65 and she proudly passed the first time.

Anna goes about her business and takes advantage of her ability to be active while she can… like anybody would. She has no expectations of anyone and is just grateful for the friends she still has, as so many have passed on. Coming from a large family of 14 children, Anna was the second oldest. She has one brother who is 85 and five younger sisters still living.

Anna will undoubtedly continue with her bustling life. When she isn't out and about, she likes to sew and claims she can knit in the dark. We won't dispute that at all.

✓ Rudi Busch
Beausejour, Manitoba

We are going to introduce you to a fellow who has been pegged as an 'Unsung Hero' by members of his community. We are talking about Rudi Busch and he certainly lives up to this accolade.

Rudi, his wife Ida, and their three young children came to Canada in 1962. They came by ship from Germany and travelled by train from Montreal to Winnipeg, ending up in Beausejour where Ida already had relatives settled.

Life for the first while here was not comfortable by any means. The buildings on their property were old. They were not used to living without indoor plumbing and other comforts, but they managed to make do for a few years here.

Rudi had been trained in masonry in Germany and brought his skills to Canada. Here, he furthered his training and in 1975 he started his own business called Busch Masonry in Beausejour. He specialized in fireplaces and house fronts. In the beginning, Ida helped with the business, including mixing cement. Both worked extremely hard.

A regular day started with loading up his truck, and then heading off to a job which often was an hour away. After a day's work here, he'd go home for a bite to eat and then off again to quote on a job. After that he'd return home and calculate an estimate. By then, it was time for bed only to start all over again early the next day. There also were regular trips to the supplier in Winnipeg.

Their son helped out eventually freeing Ida to tend to her other obligations. He studied masonry at Red River Community College and apprenticed with his father. Rudi had another long-term helper as well. Rudi retired from his business in 1990. Today, at 77, he takes time to do more of the things he enjoys. Things he never had the time for while in business. He took up cross country skiing again in 1980, ten years before retiring. When the Chryplywy Nature Park opened up in Beausejour, thanks to the generous donation of property by a local resident, Rudi decided to take advantage of the ski trails there. Depending on the weather, he would ski either 2 or 4 kms. He started out bringing some seeds to scatter all over for the birds.

Later, he built self-standing wood feeders that he could easily fill on his daily ski trips. Fifteen years later, he has bird feeders (squirrels are welcome too) all along the trails and even rabbit feeders that he fills with hay. Rudi's sense of humour was revealed when he painted, "ALL YOU CAN EAT" on the roof of the rabbit feeder for passersby to have a chuckle.

Local wildlife know and trust Rudi. Chickadees will often perch on his hand taking his offering of seeds. The squirrels in his yard will take nuts from his hand as well.

The most impressive thing about Rudi feeding the wildlife here is that he does it all at his own expense. He goes through about six bags of seeds each season at the cost of about $15 each and purchases hay locally for the rabbit feeders, plus much more. Rudi is not looking for any big publicity for what he does. He's just showing his gratitude and appreciation for what nature gives to him.

This park has a special place in Rudi's heart. He has contributed so much to it. He even planted trees here from seedlings from his own yard. One in particular is 10 years old and now stands roughly 7-8 ft tall.

Rudi has become quite the naturalist and spends a lot of time outdoors enjoying all that nature has to offer. He enjoys walking in the summer and up until two years ago, Rudi would bike 20 miles every other day which he did for five consecutive years. He likes to stay in motion as much as possible to alleviate stiffness, in his spine especially, because he has fused discs as a result of a form of arthritis. Rudi is unable to raise his right arm, too, but manages to keep active.

Other hobbies occupy Rudi's time since retiring. He built a remote controlled hobby plane—with a wing span of over four feet—that actually flies. He and a local friend mow a runway in a nearby field for takeoff and find suitable places for soft landings. Rudi also built a glider that is smaller.

Woodworking keeps Rudi busy in summer, as well. He builds bird feeders and one windmill each year that stands 5 feet tall for family only. Another enjoyable pasttime for Rudi is going out in the community or in nature with his camcorder. He records scenes and finds appropriate music for the background.

Birds are often the topic of his videos but he has filmed other wildlife including local bears, turtles, squirrels and more. It appears he came dangerously close to a skunk in one scene. Of the birds, he captured images of chickadees, nuthatches, jays, grosbeaks, goldfinches, orioles, hummingbirds, loons, and most impressive, bald eagles which nest each year on his son's property along the Brokenhead River not far away from Beausejour. On a rare occasion, Rudi captured what he thinks was a Red-capped Woodpecker not common to this area.

Rudi's creative talent has passed on to his children. One son, Rolf, is a talented artist and many of his paintings adorn the walls of his parents' home. You may recognize his name as the Art Director for the local 'Style Manitoba' magazine several years ago. Rolf and a few others were instrumental in starting this 'stylish' glossy magazine. He has since pursued his career in Ontario.

NEW BRUNSWICK

Since 2001, presentation of the Family and Community Volunteer Awards aims at recognizing and celebrating volunteer contributions to the well being of families and communities all over New Brunswick.

☑ **Alfreda Bérubé,** has made a remarkable difference in the daily lives of many communities, families and persons with special needs. She has influenced change and made a difference at the parish, regional, provincial, national and even international level. A cause close to Madame Bérubé's heart has been the establishment of L'éclosion, a sheltered workshop for people with special challenges. From humble beginnings this shelter has become the local training and support centre. She has also prepared a manual for individuals with special needs, their families and caregivers.

NEWFOUNDLAND/LABRADOR

The province of Newfoundland/Labrador is in the midst of developing a Healthy Aging Plan and is very active in developing responsive policy to address its aging population.

Current demographics indicate that Newfoundland/Labrador will have the highest median age in Canada within ten years (Statistics Canada reports October 2006 — NL has highest median age in Canada at 41.3); and in 2006, NL was the first Canadian province to experience more deaths than births. As a province, it has acknowledged the importance of seniors through creation of a Provincial Advisory Council on Aging and Seniors.

NOVA SCOTIA

The province of Nova Scotia recognizes seniors every year at the 50+ expo. There are three categories: volunteerism, leadership and community service—these are called "Remarkable Seniors". There are usually 2 seniors selected in each category and they are presented with a plaque and a dozen red roses.

ONTARIO

Ontario senior achievement award recipients announced for 2005 (From Ontario Senior Secretariat, March 7, 2006)

22 Recipients Honoured For Making Important Contributions To Their Communities

✓ **Tom Atkins of King City** – As the founding president of Oak Ridges Moraine Land Trust, Mr. Atkins turned a volunteer grassroots environmental group into one of Canada's leading environmental organizations.

✓ **Hugh Boggs of Kingsville** – With an outstanding 34-year-history of providing volunteer service to his community, at age 90 Mr. Boggs is known as "Mr. Service to Others" and was given the highest award possible by Branch 188 of The Royal Canadian Legion of Kingsville.

✓ **Shirley Broostad of Acton** – Ms. Broostad exemplifies the helpful spirit of small town living through her advocacy on behalf of seniors. She actively participates in the Halton Hills Injury Prevention Committee, the Isolated Seniors Committee, the Acton Seniors Centre and the local All Star Reading school program.

✓ **Marjorie Colbourne of Alliston** – Ms. Colbourne is a lifeline for housebound seniors. She single-handedly operates a shut-in service on behalf of the New Tecumseth Public Library, delivering books and helping individuals maintain a positive link with their community.

✓ **Dr. Donald Curtis of Peterborough** – Dr. Curtis put Peterborough on the map as the home of a museum of national importance. Through his efforts, he helped establish the Canadian Canoe Museum and preserved, for future generations, an important part of our history.

✓ **Melba England of London** – For the past sixteen years, Ms. England has served as a choir master at McCormick Home, a residence for seniors. At age 90, Ms. England is an inspiration lifting spirits and turning anxiety into comfort and praise.

✓ **Margaret Ferguson of St. Catharines** – Ms. Ferguson has spent a lifetime volunteering her time on behalf of the Children's Discovery Centre of

Niagara, the St. Catharines Museum, and the St. Catharines Hospital Auxiliary. In 2004, Ms. Ferguson and her husband Bob were presented with the T. Roy Adams Humanitarian Award.

☑ **Gwynneth Foster of Barry's Bay** – Ms. Foster created the innovative "Wheels to Meals" program and helped bring lonely and isolated seniors together for a luncheon on the first Wednesday of each month. Ms. Foster's leadership is recognized in the Renfrew-Nipissing-Pembroke area for the volunteer service she provides at the Opeongo Seniors Centre and the programs she initiated in support of literacy among seniors. She is a recipient of the Frances Lever Memorial Award by the Ontario Literacy Coalition.

☑ **Mendel Good of Toronto** – A survivor of Nazi labour and death camps, Mr. Good has dedicated himself to preserving the history and memory of the Holocaust. For more than 30 years, he has spoken to thousands of individuals, mostly students, of the need to protect human rights wherever they are threatened.

☑ **Lois Gun-Munro of Toronto** – An outstanding volunteer for ten years at the west-end Toronto office of the Canadian National Institute for the Blind (CNIB), Ms. Gun-Munro personally understands the challenges that a visually-impaired person faces. It is her own triumph over adversity that allows her to run two support groups and inspire others in similar situations.

☑ **Boyd Hipfner of Toronto** – Mr. Hipfner is responsible for the Designated Waiting Areas we now see on subway platforms. His contributions have made an enormous impact upon the lives of the blind, visually impaired, and deaf blind people in Toronto and across Canada. He is also an active member of the Toronto Transit Commission's Advisory Board for Accessible Transportation.

☑ **Shirley Martin of Grimsby** – Ms. Martin is a former Member of Parliament who served Grimsby, Lincoln and the Niagara Peninsula. Her contribution to education, culture, health and economic development have been invaluable to the growth and prosperity of her community and Niagara Region.

☑ **Edwin Matthews of Peterborough** – Epitomizing the Rotary Club's golden rule – Service Above Self – Mr. Matthews is a well-known artist who has devoted his time and art to establish one of the finest art galleries in Canada and assist many local charities to raise funds.

☑ **Lloyd Morgan of Windsor** – For the past 25 years, Lloyd has been the driving force behind the Rotary Club in Windsor region. He has been a tireless promoter of the ethics stressed by Rotary Clubs in secondary and elementary school boards in Windsor and Essex County.

☑ **Prue Morton of Thunder Bay (posthumous)** – Ms. Morton was a champion of seniors and an advocate for patients. As a valuable resource regarding community social services, Ms. Morton made significant contributions to the quality of life for citizens living in Thunder Bay.

☑ **Wei-Ling Qiu of Toronto** – As vice-president of the Chinese Medicine and Acupuncture Association of Canada, Professor Qui has played a significant role in having Oriental healing practices accepted and regulated in Ontario. She has also contributed as a volunteer to the social and economic needs of the Chinese community.

☑ **Odino Soligo of Thornhill** – He broke more records and is the current world record holder for the 50k and 100k runs in his age group. Mr. Soligo is an 84-year-old marathon runner who sees his mission as motivating people of all ages to play an active role in helping others.

☑ **Edna Staebler of Waterloo** – Even though she only started writing at an age when most people consider retirement, Ms. Staebler has authored over 20 books including Canada's bestselling hardcover cookbook Food That Really Schmecks. Few people have motivated so many to write, shared their craft with others and promoted Canadian pride through literature. Ms. Staebler is a member of the Order of Canada.

☑ **Ernie Weeks of Hamilton** – At the youthful age of 94, Mr. Weeks is a hometown hero. He served his country as an airman in the Second World World, operated a successful hardware store for 32 years, and volunteers his time to those in need. As an active member of the Rotary Club, his energy and positive outlook on life make him an outstanding role model and champion.

☑ **Frank Welsh of Tillsonburg** – Named Citizen of the Year in 2002 by Tillsonburg District Chamber of Commerce, Mr. Welsh is a founding board member of the Tillsonburg & District Multi-Service Centre.

☑ **Dr. Robert Williamsof Bolton** – This retired veterinarian is providing outstanding leadership to the Caledon community. Through his leadership, the community built Rotary Place, a 6,000 square foot civic club for seniors.

☑ **Gordon Wright of Becton** – As an active and long-serving volunteer and fundraiser for Junior Diabetes and Diabetes charities, Mr. Wright founded the Banting Memorial High School Run/Walk for Diabetes, which raised almost $40,000 in 2002. Mr. Gordon was awarded the Queen's Jubilee Medal for community service in 2003.

PRINCE EDWARD ISLAND

Six seniors honoured for exceptional community involvement

☑ **Sisters Aline and Doreen Reid:** The Reid sisters have been serving their community through their involvement with their church, driving elderly people to appointments and to church, providing financial help to the needy, baking for family or acquaintances, supporting individuals who are grieving, visiting nursing homes, helping refugee families, and a variety of other activities for various groups.

☑ **Al and Belle LeBlanc** have worked together for twenty three years with Meals on Wheels, ten years with the Let Older Volunteers Educate Program, and ten years with the Heart and Stroke Foundation. They have worked as volunteers for both Wedgewood and Summerset Manors, with their local community school, at the Parkside Seniors Club in Summerside, transporting patients requiring medical treatments back and forth between Summerside to Charlottetown, and in the Seniors' Organization for the Blind and Handicapped. This dynamic team also arranged the Guinness World Records Kissing Contest in Summerside a few years ago.

☑ **John H. Fitzgerald:** Fitzgerald is a founding member of the Helping Hands Band, which has raised more than $500,000 for charity since its beginning seven years ago. He has been on the board of the Angel Network – an Eastlink program that raises money for people who need to travel off-Island for medical services – for six years, and is a past member of the West Prince Caring Cupboard food bank. Fitzgerald's music is his way of reaching out to those in need. In addition to his work in the Helping Hands Band, he is a member of the choir of Grace Christian Church, which appears regularly on Eastlink, and a regular performer on that channel's Community Showcase. John performs regularly at manors, seniors' residences, birthday parties for seniors, at the chronic care wing of the O'Leary Community Hospital, and at the Tyne Valley Hospital.

☑ **Clarisse Gallant:** Gallant has been a volunteer for most of her life. Since moving to Souris some 50 years ago, she has worked tirelessly for the betterment of the community, particularly on behalf of senior citizens. She has been a member of the Silver Threads Seniors Club for 30 years and president for two terms. During this time, the building underwent major renovations, and the Foot Care Clinic and Vials for Life Program were established. She was instrumental in securing two garden suites for the area. Other involvements include the Parent-Teacher Association, Co-op Housing, Catholic Women's League, fifty years in the church choir, volunteer driving for seniors, the Eastern Kings Tourism Association, and the St. Thomas Aquinas and Acadian Societies.

QUEBEC

L'activité "Hommage" est un événement visant à souligner l'apport d'une personne engagée dans son milieu, qui a contribué au développement social, économique et culturel, démontrant ainsi l'importance de la place des aînés dans la société. Chaque année, les dix-sept tables regionales de concertation des aînés sont invitées à soumettre une candidature pour leur région. Le comité de sélection du Conseil des aînés détermine le ou la récipiendaire et une activité est organisée afin de lui rendre hommage dans le cadre des événements entourant le 1er octobre, « Journée internationale des personnes aînées ». Ce thème a été choisi pour sensibiliser la population à la place, à la contribution et au role essentiel des aînés dans la société d'aujourd'hui. Il souligne également l'importance de la solidarité et du partage entre les générations.

Madame Pierrette Lehoux Chaudière-Appalaches

Native de Saint-Méthode, dans la région de Chaudière-Appalaches, madame Lehoux est une pionnière en ce qui concerne le maintien et l'amélioration de la qualité de vie des aînés. Elle possède une détermination et un leadership indéniables pour mobiliser les gens et assurer la mise en œuvre des idées et des projets qui l'animent. Femme d'action et de décision, madame Lehoux a su aller de l'avant, avec des idées créatives, pour rapprocher jeunes et moins jeunes, créant et consolidant ainsi les liens entre les générations. Elle a mis sur pied des activités entre jeunes et aînés visant la transmission de valeurs et de connaissances : les programmes Point-Rouge, Vigilance de quartier et Moisson- Beauce qui permettent d'assurer une sécurité aux aînés ainsi que de favoriser l'insertion sociale de jeunes en difficulté. Attentive au désir des aînés de vieillir en santé à domicile, elle a contribué à la réalisation d'activités communautaires d'entraide, de soutien et de loisir, entre autres par son implication:

- dans le mieux-être physique des aînés depuis dix-huit ans en animant le programme VIACTIVE;

- depuis vingt-sept ans, dont seize à la tête de l'Association bénévole des cantons, qui a aussi créé sept popotes roulantes.

Madame Lehoux, par son dévouement, a contribué à l'avancement de la cause des aînés et à l'amélioration de leur bien-être. Elle demeure toujours impliquée quotidiennement à titre de bénévole au sein d'organismes régionaux. Un hommage lui a d'ailleurs été rendu par la Table de concertation des aînés de Chaudière-Appalaches en 2006.

Outre ces réalisations, madame Lehoux se distingue par:

- sa *Détermination*

- sa *Disponibilité*

- son *Dynamisme*

- ses multiples *Habiletés relationnelles et sa Ténacité.*

Par ses actions et son engagement dans sa communauté et auprès de ses pairs, madame Lehoux a contribué à l'amélioration de la qualité de vie des aînés, de leur participation et de leur intégration sociale de même qu'au maintien et au développement de liens intergénérationnels. L'impact et les retombées de ses réalisations sont inestimables et se font toujours ressentir dans le quotidien des aînés de sa région.

SASKATCHEWAN

The Government of Saskatchewan declares a Seniors' Week each year in recognition of the valuable contributions that Saskatchewan seniors make to our province. This year Seniors' Week was September 25-October 1st. In addition, the Seniors' Gold Plan was recently introduced as another way of recognizing the contributions of seniors. The following benefits are available to all Saskatchewan residents 65 years of age and older:

- Free entry to provincial parks
- Free fishing licenses
- 30% discount on fares from Saskatchewan transportation Company
- Free non-driver photo ID from Saskatchewan Government Insurance

Saskatchewan doesn't recognize individual seniors but the province collectively recognize this segment of the population in various ways.

cᴂℭᴂ⅁

*   **AND TWO OTHER AMAZING SENIORS I WANT TO ADD TO THIS LIST ARE MY PARENTS:**
     CHUCK CAPUTO AND ALETA (IVENS) CAPUTO

They traveled the 'LTC road' with dignity, setting an example and hopefully helping many Canadian families in the future.

> *"Let's strive to be amazing caregivers...*
> *And amazing seniors"*
>
> *– Patty Randall*
> *2006*

JUNE IS "SENIORS MONTH" NATIONALLY IN OUR COUNTRY

In addition, several provinces have established their own seniors' recognition months

WHEREVER YOU LIVE IN CANADA,
DO SOMETHING TO ACKNOWLEDGE
SENIORS MONTH
WITHIN YOUR OWN FAMILY
AND CIRCLE OF FRIENDS
AND CLOSE NEIGHBOURS

CELEBRATE SENIORS' CONTRIBUTIONS,
THEIR COMMUNITY SERVICE,
THEIR WISDOM
AND
THEIR LONG-LIVES

And remember always this senior message:
"Remember me, for I am you"

LETTER TO ELECTED REPRESENTATIVES

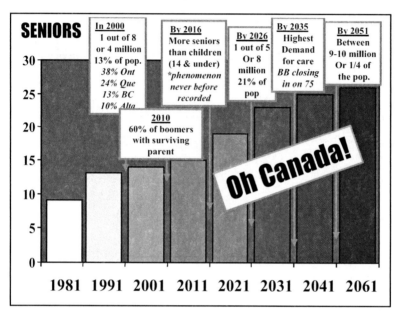

"Though no one can go back and make a brand new start,
Anyone can start now and make a brand new ending"

*From "Let's Talk—The Care-Years...Taking Care of Our Parents/Planning For
Ourselves" by Patty Randall*

Dear _____

There is a care-years education gap in our country and I want you
to provide a long-term care education program for those of us who are
boomers with aging parents, soon-to-be retirees or young seniors. Long-
term care (whether in my own home or in a nursing home) is the single
largest out-of-pocket cost my loved ones and I face over 60 and therefore
it is a significant risk to my family and me! We need information on this
issue as well as guidance and incentives on planning for this stage of our
lives. We want to do the right thing!

Yours truly, a concerned voter,

_____

Patty

If you think the issue has the potential to impact you
and your family, take a moment, clip this page out,
sign it and send it to your elected representative...for
more copies, refer to www.longtermcarecanada.com

"When it comes to long-term care, we must define what 'taking care of our parents' and 'planning for ourselves' mean—what is needed, what each of us can do, what will we do.

Family care-years can be a rewarding period for all involved—you decide...

My very best wishes to you and your family on your care-years journeys."

– Patty

good wishes,
Patty

ISBN 0-9782215-0-8

9 780978 221508